PLACING MEMORY
AND REMEMBERING PLACE
IN CANADA

Edited by James Opp and John C. Walsh

PLACING MEMORY
AND REMEMBERING PLACE
IN CANADA

UBCPress · Vancouver · Toronto

20 19 18 17 16 15 14 13 12 11 10   5 4 3 2 1

Printed in Canada on acid-free paper.

Library and Archives Canada Cataloguing in Publication

Placing memory and remembering place in Canada / edited by James Opp and John C. Walsh.

Includes bibliographical references and index.
ISBN 978-0-7748-1840-7 (bound); ISBN 978-0-7748-1841-4 (pbk.)

  1. Collective memory – Canada. 2. Human geography – Canada. 3. Geography – Social aspects – Canada. 4. Canada – Civilization.

GF511.P53 2010   304.2'30971   C2010-903467-8

e-book ISBNs: 978-0-7748-1842-1 (PDF); 978-0-7748-5962-2 (epub)

Canadä

UBC Press gratefully acknowledges the financial support for our publishing program of the Government of Canada (through the Canada Book Fund), the Canada Council for the Arts, and the British Columbia Arts Council.

This book has been published with the help of a grant from the Canadian Federation for the Humanities and Social Sciences, through the Aid to Scholarly Publications Programme, using funds provided by the Social Sciences and Humanities Research Council of Canada.

Publication of this book was supported by an Aid to Workshops and Conferences Grant provided by the Social Sciences and Humanities Research Council of Canada.

UBC Press
The University of British Columbia
2029 West Mall
Vancouver, BC V6T 1Z2
www.ubcpress.ca

Contents

Introduction: Local Acts of Placing and Remembering / 3
James Opp and John C. Walsh

PART 1: COMMEMORATIONS: MARKING MEMORIES OF PLACE

PART 2: INSCRIPTIONS: RECOVERING PLACES OF MEMORY

List of Illustrations

PLACING MEMORY
AND REMEMBERING PLACE
IN CANADA

Figure I.1 Marlene Creates, *where my grandmother was born* from the series *Places of Presence: Newfoundland kin and ancestral land, Newfoundland 1989-1991* © CARCC 2010.

Assemblage of 13 black and white photographs, 1 colour photograph, 6 memory map drawings, pencil on paper, 6 story panels and 1 title panel, screen print on plexi, aspen leaves and one beach stone from the site, and a wooden shelf.

Installed dimensions: 63½ inches high × 21½ feet long × 7¼ inches deep (161cm high × 6.5m long × 18cm deep), plus floor space.

Introduction
Local Acts of Placing and Remembering

JAMES OPP AND JOHN C. WALSH

When we describe the land – or, more frequently, remember events that occurred at particular points on it – the natural landscape becomes a centre of meaning, and its geographical features are constituted in relation to our experiences on it. The land is not an abstract physical location but a *place*, charged with personal significance, shaping the images we have of ourselves.

> – Marlene Creates, *Places of Presence: Newfoundland kin and ancestral land, Newfoundland 1989-1991* (1991)

For her 1991 series, *Places of Presence: Newfoundland kin and ancestral land, Newfoundland 1989-1991*, artist Marlene Creates arranged a set of hand-drawn memory maps and stories from her Newfoundland relatives. The maps and texts were aligned with contemporary photographs of the locations narrated, namely, the birth places of her grandmother, her grandfather, and her great-grandmother. The framed words and pictures were then assembled with "souvenirs" of these places, such as rocks and leaves. In her discussion of *Places of Presence,* Joan M. Schwartz notes that "past links to present, place to space, identity to landscape. In the slippages between past material reality and remembered lived experience are the imagined communities, invented traditions, performative memories, and cartographic illusions of the geographical imagination."[1]

Placing Memory and Remembering Place in Canada is a collection of essays and an assemblage of a different sort, although it shares many things in common with Creates's project. The scholars here have their own stories to tell, narratives constructed with found objects and other souvenirs: texts, postcards, maps, photographs, and oral histories. These essays are also concerned with "imagined communities," "performative memories," and "cartographic illusions of the geographical imagination." Most of all, however, the contributors to this volume assert the significance of *place* as a site made meaningful by memory and commemorative practices. In return, they, like Creates, are also cognizant of how *placing* is critical to memory's making and to its social, cultural, and political power.

So why would we return to themes outlined so elegantly by a visual artist two decades ago? After all, both "place" and "memory" are broad concepts with shelves of books, essays, and dissertations devoted to their elucidation.[2] Indeed, the global explosion of interest in memory studies over the past two decades has led some to ask whether we are facing a "memory crisis" or at least suffering from "memory fatigue."[3] Inspired by Pierre Nora's understanding of "*lieux de mémoire*" and Benedict Anderson's concept of the nation as an "imagined community,"[4] Canadian scholars have followed international trends, producing a wide-ranging body of literature that explores monuments, memorials, commemorations, and a variety of other civic rituals and performances.[5] However, Nora's extensive multi-volume collection on "sites of memory" in France, particularly the condensed form translated into English as *Realms of Memory* (1996-98), tended to reinscribe the nation rather than problematize it.[6] Similarly, in Canada much of the work sidesteps the actual "place" of memory making in order to frame the analysis in relation to more abstracted notions of nation and empire. In these studies, the key questions centre on how historical representations consolidated and legitimized political authority and the nation-state. And yet, as Andreas Huyssen suggests, "the form in which we think of the past is increasingly memory without borders rather than national history within borders."[7]

Nora's work attracted attention in part because his "sites of memory" were spatial expressions as much as they were temporal. This was hardly surprising since Nora was heavily influenced by the pioneering work of French sociologist Maurice Halbwachs, who argued that "every collective memory unfolds within a spatial framework" and devoted a whole chapter to the topic.[8] However, for Nora, the very externalization of memory in the form of monuments, memorials, or commemorative performances signifies a sense of loss. *Lieux de mémoire* carry only the residue of once-meaningful attachments; the spaces and places in which they are located appear inert and static, unable to resist the assault of "history" in the modern era.[9] In contrast, the growing cross-disciplinary literature on the significance of "place" as a "geographical space that is defined by meanings, sentiments and stories rather than by a set of co-ordinates" has recast the role of memory.[10] Memory not only enacts on but is itself embedded, inscribed, and shaped by landscapes, topographies, and environment. This dynamic understanding allows for a more fluid series of interactions between memory and place, as seen in Gaston Gordillo's *Landscapes of Devils* (2004), a rich ethnographic account of the Toba of the Argentinean Chaco. For Gordillo, place does not simply carry a collective memory, but rather the tensions of place are themselves manifested in the spatialization of memory, and ultimately "every memory is, in a fundamental way, the memory of a place."[11]

Closer to home, Brian Osborne's deep reflections on identity and place have been particularly important in bringing a geographical dimension to the study of memory in Canada. Osborne calls attention to the significance of landscapes in shaping identity through the "emotive power of imagined place." His wide-ranging studies of monuments and historic sites demonstrate how such seemingly place-less socio-political processes as nation-making, heritage tourism, and democratic citizenship are made meaningful to people through their anchoring and locating in place and their invocation of shared public memory. Although Osborne recognizes that "people are affected by their engagement with the palpable immediacy of local places, and with the nested abstractions of the regional, the national, and the global," his main interests ultimately lie in the articulation, formation, and contestation of national identities.[12]

This book charts a different course not by ignoring national identities but by shifting the focus more directly onto the "palpable immediacy of local places." Just as Marlene Creates's assemblages of mental maps and individual stories infuse the landscape with profoundly personal and localized meanings that resist nationalizing narratives, this volume reasserts the significance of the local as the "centre of meaning." Even though all of our case studies are from Canada, our goal has not been to identify and explain something uniquely "Canadian." Rather, our chapters tell stories about people living in place, exploring how they influence and are influenced by the commemorative inscriptions that mark place. Conversely, we also interrogate the personalities and institutions that remember the past by questioning how the conditions of place have shaped acts of memory. In approaching these intersections of memory and geographical imagining, we have deliberately situated these processes within a deeply localized context.[13]

Turning to the "local" invariably raises questions surrounding the vast and growing literature on globalization. Local knowledges, cultures, customs, and economies are often framed as points of resistance to the homogenizing forces of global capitalism. Although the pairing of global/local has become standard fare, many scholars note that the emphasis on globalization has tended to overshadow the local and, in the process, has marginalized place.[14] Arturo Escobar reasserts the importance of place-based strategies, arguing that "it might be possible to approach the production of place and culture not only from the side of the global, but of the local; not from the perspective of its abandonment but of its critical affirmation; not only according to the flight from places, whether voluntary or forced, but of the attachment to them."[15] We share Escobar's sensibilities, but we also resist essentializing local places as organic, whole, or ahistorical. The "local" is a fluid and uncertain category, reminding us that, despite the claims of planners, architects, and other spatial engineers, the production of place is always unfinished and uneven.[16]

Within Canada, two recent works have sought to deepen the relationship between memory and the local.[17] William Turkel's *The Archive of Place: Unearthing the Pasts of the Chilcotin Plateau* repositions the land itself as an "archive," an entity to be studied, surveyed, and "mined" for information.

Although commemorations and memorial acts take place, Turkel maintains a strict division between the actual physical "place" defined by the geographical features of the plateau and the memory making that plays out within it. Drawing on a vast array of material clues, Turkel insists that a place carries on its surface all sorts of markers of its past, things big and small that convey very deep, and often long-term, historical understandings. The material evidence and the scales of time multiply as more and more voices lay claim to these embedded traces, contesting the memories and meanings attached to the plateau.[18]

From a different perspective, Julie Cruikshank's *Do Glaciers Listen?: Local Knowledge, Colonial Encounters, and Social Imagination* situates glacial landforms and topography as active participants in making memory, positioning both Aboriginal "local" knowledge and the colonial archive against a dynamic landscape. Cruikshank complicates our understanding of memory and place not only by centring Native voices in her narrative (and effectively decentring official archives) but also in pointedly asking, "Do glaciers listen?" As this question would suggest, Cruikshank is interested in understanding how place is complicit in its own representation and knowing. Glaciers, she explains at the outset of her book, are historical actors that "make moral judgments" and "punish infractions."[19] Rather than extracting clues from these glaciers, and from the larger ecology to which they belong, Cruikshank is more interested in showing how glaciers helped author Tlingit oral tradition, compelled surveyors to re-draw maps, and both facilitated and limited what all travellers, explorers, and even later recreational canoeists could see and know. Public memory is not only made on or about the glaciers but was also historically made *with* them.

While appreciating both perspectives, our approach to the study of place generally follows Henri Lefebvre's admonitions for a dynamic, diverse, and bold spatial history: "[A history of social space] must account for both representational spaces and representations of space, but above all for their interrelationships and their links with social practice."[20] Place is made and remade in these interactions. Like Lefebvre, we consistently cast our analytical gaze on what people did (and do) in affecting place making, particularly as it involves or affects memory. As Edward Casey argues, "place is not entitative ... but eventmental, something in process, something unconfinable to a thing. Or a simple location. Place is all over the place."[21] The very title of this collection emphasizes *placing* and *remembering,* active verbs that signal the dynamic nature of the social acts and processes analyzed by the contributors.

Each essay in this volume deals with one specific geographic location, but the scalar dimensions that intersect place and memory vary widely. In "The Highland Heart in Nova Scotia: Place and Memory at the Highland Village Museum," Alan Gordon traces the currents of global Scottishness that were incorporated into Cape Breton's Highland Village. Here, place is both the physical environment that surrounds the museum and an imagined land-scape that links the local to an international identity. Gordon's chapter reframes Anderson's "imagined communities" and challenges us to think about com-munity formation in ways that leap across and beyond the nation. In contrast, Frances Swyripa's "Edmonton's Jasper Avenue: Public Ritual, Heritage, and Memory on Main Street" focuses on a more geographically narrow subject. Through a close examination of the commemorations, parades, and perform-ances of memory that transpire over more than a century, Swyripa points to the frictions of competing communities that vie for official recognition in staging public acts of memory. Whereas Gordon notes that local investments in place increased over time as donations of artefacts flowed into the Highland Village Museum, Swyripa points to the decline of Jasper Avenue as a site of public memory. Class, ethnicity, gender, and politics are set against larger structural changes in the urban centre that reshape the rituals of civic identity. As these chapters and many others in the volume indicate, remembering and commemorating are acts that can define the "local," declaring who is "of" this particular place (and, conversely, who is not).[22]

Such local considerations of place are also significant even when na-tional and imperial histories are at stake, as Cecilia Morgan argues in "History and the Six Nations: The Dynamics of Commemoration, Colonial Space, and Colonial Knowledge." Morgan connects the investments of the Six Nations in local acts of memory with long-standing concerns over land claims, territor-ialization, and the remapping of new political spaces. Using a gendered an-alysis of inter-community divisions, Morgan exposes the complexity of power relationships that surround the inscription of public memory on and within local places. Although the colonizing state remains a hegemonic force, it is one that the Six Nations countered through their own histories and narratives, local conditions, places, and memories. Furthermore, in locating her analysis *in* and not merely *about* the Six Nations, Morgan also reveals how the politics of memory and commemoration can disturb the neat binary between colonizers and colonized that is perhaps too easily mapped onto Aboriginal reserves and their borders. As the examples of Morgan, Swyripa, and Gordon demonstrate, this volume reasserts the local as a meaningful centre for our narratives, not to avoid but rather to clarify the overlapping regional, national, and imperial concerns embedded within the acts of placing memory and remembering place.

As a whole, *Placing Memory and Remembering Place in Canada* engages with "public memory" – memories that are made, experienced, and circulated in public spaces and that are intended to be communicated and shared.[23] However, in "'That Big Statue of Whoever': Material Commemoration and Narrative in the Niagara Region," Russell Johnston and Michael Ripmeester note that scholars too often overlook the question of how audiences interact with, utilize, or simply ignore memorial spaces and the stories they convey. Through a set of comparative surveys, this chapter maps the mnemonic landscape of the Niagara region, tracing some of the tensions and gaps between the histories recalled by local citizens and the actual monuments that mark the region, often clustered near tourist attractions. By calling attention to competing modes and scales of communication that shape our understandings of history and place, their work cautions that sites of commemoration may not be as powerful as we assume. Whereas Gordon and Morgan emphasize the anchoring of memory and community identities to local material sites, Johnston and Ripmeester point to the uncertainties that exist between memorials and history. As with Swyripa's analysis of the decline of memory and attachment to Edmonton's Jasper Avenue, we need to be aware of acts of forgetting and disenchantments of place. And yet, as Johnston and Ripmeester conclude, local sites of memory continue to carry within them potential reactivations as new narratives recast the histories of these sites in new ways.

Placing Memory and Remembering Place in Canada is structured around two central concerns. The first half, "Commemorations: Marking Memories of Place," focuses on "official" celebrations, museums, and memorial acts. In the second half, "Inscriptions: Recovering Places of Memory," the subject matter shifts toward "vernacular" expressions of memory situated in oral stories, photographs, and the landscape itself. And yet, in both parts of the volume, the mobility of memory emerges as an important theme. John C.

Walsh's opening chapter of the first part, "Performing Public Memory and Re-Placing Home in the Ottawa Valley, 1900-58," traces the return of former residents to Eastern Ontario in order to celebrate Old Home Weeks and Old Boys' Reunions. James Opp's chapter, "Finding the View: Landscape, Place, and Colour Slide Photography in Southern Alberta," follows his parents on photographic outings to the foothills. For both Walsh and Opp, as with many others here, it is the acts of inhabiting, returning, or moving through specific locations that produce or confirm memories of place. Rather than dismiss the longing to return or represent "home" as little more than romantic nostalgia for a lost age, Walsh and Opp call attention to the social and economic contexts that have shaped contemporary geographic imaginings. Indeed, although their chapters offer very different perspectives on how memory and place intersect, they share a common desire to explore, in Walsh's words, the "location of culture in places we seem to have forgotten."

And yet it is not just the mobility of people but also photographs, souvenirs, and other representations of place that carry memories within and beyond the local. Collective remembering occurs within a "world of things," and a great deal of scholarship has focused on the relationship between materiality and memory.[24] This has been especially important to heritage studies and archaeologies of memory, which share a common interest in how monumental and everyday objects are invested with mnemonic significance.[25] As Katharine Hodgkin and Susannah Radstone suggest, memory "does not operate only as an abstract (mental) system; it is generated by and channelled through an endless variety of media and artefacts."[26] Like Johnston and Ripmeester, both Walsh and Opp consider how memory is communicated through a variety of media: newspapers, souvenirs, postcards, calendars, and photographs. Such analyses compel us to reconsider not only the materiality of the traces left behind but also the contexts and performances of their production in and through place, from pageantry and parading to collecting and designing. It is the connections between practice, object, and space that draw our collective attention, compel our theorization, and form the spines of our narratives. And it is here that the afterword by Joan M. Schwartz, "Complicating the Picture: Place and Memory between Representation and Reflection," pushes us to think through the implications of a world without material sites of memory, where virtual fragments in digital archives reshape our consciousness of space, time, and self. Might such changes, Schwartz asks, herald a "sea change in the nature and locus of memory and its relationship to place"?

In his influential book *Time Maps: Collective Memory and the Social Shape of the Past* (2003), Eviatar Zerubavel argues that societies emphasize the unchanging materiality of place as an anchor between the past and the present. Souvenirs and relics serve as bridges that allow us, regardless of our current location, to take a cognitive journey back in time and across space to the point where we acquired the object.[27] Although these interconnections are important, Zerubavel's work strictly divides materiality from the mental work of memory, forged against the "constancy of place."[28] However, as Matthew Evenden demonstrates in his chapter, "Immersed: Landscaping the Past at Lake Minnewanka," local places and landscapes are hardly constant entities. The flooding of a small settlement within the boundaries of a national park in order to generate power erased the place and reassembled it as a landscape to be viewed through the windshields of automobiles. For Evenden, competing memories do not simply play out on a static stage, but rather the lake itself is constantly evolving as a place and site of memory. Here, some narratives are commemorated and others ignored; parks officials struggle to present a "compromise with nature" while trying to control the souvenirs left behind by those who now frequent the settlement submerged under water. The remaking of place seen in the contributions of Evenden, Opp, Swyripa, Walsh, and many other chapters supports the argument of Tim Cresswel' ___ ___ Hoskins that "places are a complicated mixture of fixity and flow, ___ change."[29]

In order to explore how people have historically made thei___
with, in, and through the material culture of place, scholars need ___
the institutions where these resources have been "re-placed." For n___
authors in this collection, the archive in particular emerges as b___
and subject for analysis, whether referring to established "official" i___
or seen as more "vernacular" collections of souvenirs and photog___
archive stands as an intentional site for preserving and organizing th___
of memory and embodies its own spatial logic.[30] In "Archive and Myth: The Changing Memoryscape of Japanese Canadian Internment Camps," Kirsten Emiko McAllister situates herself within the space of the archive, reconnecting representations of place with narratives of community. Unlike the colour slides

[handwritten margin note: Japanese internment camps]

that Opp traces in his parents' basement, these visual representations document traumatic spaces of forced removal. And yet they simultaneously serve as representations of distinctive places and markers of identity for the postwar Japanese community. For McAllister, as for several of the authors here, the archive is not merely an accumulation of material but also a theatre of performance and practice. To "dwell in the archive" as a researcher is to be both an observer and a participant in these experiences.

For scholars interested in the history of memory and in the history of power-knowledge relations, the archive is perhaps modernity's purest architectural expression, or at the very least an architecture that rightly takes its place alongside the museum.[31] Both of these institutions, and their related practices, belong to an episteme that, following Pierre Nora, we might call "the will to archive":

> Modern memory is, above all, archival. It relies entirely on the materiality of the trace, the immediacy of the recording, the visibility of the image. What began as writing ends as high fidelity and tape recording. The less memory is experienced from the inside the more it exists only through its exterior scaffolding and outward signs – hence the obsession with the archive that marks our age, attempting at once the complete conservation of the present as well as the total preservation of the past.[32]

Nora romanticizes an "authentic" collective memory, contrasting what is "experienced from the inside" with the "exterior scaffolding" of sites of memory, and critics have rightly called attention to the problems with such essentialist constructions.[33] Nevertheless, Nora's wider comment on the significance of the archive for "modern memory" and his emphasis on the materiality of traces (i.e., memory inscribed on and through objects) raise important themes that connect to many of the chapters in this volume.

Steven High's "Placing the Displaced Worker: Narrating Place in Deindustrializing Sturgeon Falls, Ontario" documents the "will to archive," but his chapter disrupts the usual framework of state authorities using the archive and administrative standardization to structure populations and economic activity. In the course of conducting oral interviews of former mill workers, High encountered the "mill history binder," the unfinished product of years of collecting and archiving. Circulated among workers and safeguarded from managers, the binder served, High argues, as a "surrogate for the mill itself" even as the mill was being erased from the local landscape. The determination of workers to secret out materials and the instructions of the company to destroy the buildings even with many valuable historical documents still inside are stark reminders of how authority and resistance operate in both memory making and place making.

Exploring archives, archiving, and other forms of memory work provides insight into how the local knows itself.[34] In other words, we examine public memory as part of a more complex epistemology of self, community, space, and place that inhabits the local. The narratives we tell about this process do not therefore simply make room for local voices; we want to know how the local speaks as well as why and how people give voice to the past that dwells within and among them as individuals and as communities.[35] Like High, Patrizia Gentile turns to oral interviews in her chapter, "Capital Queers: Social Memory and Queer Place(s) in Cold War Ottawa." And as with McAllister, the queer spaces she analyses are both traumatic sites of surveillance and places of community formation. Gentile's work, however, provides an even more extensive consideration of the cartographies of memory that intersect and disrupt the Royal Canadian Mounted Police's own intensive mapping of a perceived security threat. Memory is especially significant for Gentile in light of the particular nature of Ottawa's queer spaces, which were entwined within the city's elite sites of political power and were therefore largely invisible to outsiders. Retrieving this hidden past requires a reconsideration of the "geographies of vulnerability," a recovery of local places and the networks that sustained the gay and lesbian communities during the Cold War and beyond. In these chapters, and indeed throughout this book, we are reminded that history does not exist in the past; it makes the past, as public memory, useful for current needs and desires.

From official commemorations to vernacular expressions, *Placing Memory and Remembering Place in Canada* confronts the politics of public memory by insisting on the significance of the politics of place. In this vein, we are building on a much wider literature, particularly among geographers, that emerged in the mid-1990s. In a series of articles, Doreen Massey emphasizes that every public memory of and in place is always in competition with other memories and suggests that "the past of a place is as open to a multiplicity of readings as is the present." Place is thus both a site and a subject of struggle, a "conjunction of many histories and many spaces."[36] For Massey, studies that de-naturalize place memories offer history a politically useful role, one that can reassert the primacy of "place" in any serious consideration of power. For David Harvey, in contrast, place normalizes a history of entitlement and exclusion through the arrangement, regulation, and policing of space, including memorial space. In particular, Harvey worries that the "quest for authenticity" leads only to artificial "invented traditions and a commercialized heritage culture."[37] The fetishization of an a-historical, phenomenological spirit that defines place as it really was, is, and ought to be operates as a mechanism of social exclusion and alienation.[38]

In Canada, Ian McKay's important work on the invention of "the folk" in twentieth-century Nova Scotia follows a similar path. Like Harvey, McKay emphasizes the totalizing and exclusionary power that can accompany place memories. The cultural production of tradition constructs a dominant and relentless place memory of Nova Scotia as distinctively Scottish, overwhelming other ethnic and local memories of place.[39] The pessimism of Harvey and McKay stems partly from the classic formulations of Eric Hobsbawm and Terence Ranger in which "tradition" is the by-product of the elite and the powerful using cultural production to normalize and consolidate their sociopolitical authority.[40] In contrast, Massey understands "tradition" as being in a constant state of renewal, not just reproduction, and thus as potentially capable of being changed. Massey does not deny the power relationships affected by "tradition" and by other dominant discourses of place memories; instead, she refuses to see such things as iron cages from which there can be no escape.[41]

The chapters in this book confront many of the same issues that haunt Harvey and excite Massey. We share both an awareness of and a concern for the politics of place as they involve public memory and tradition, and our interventions suggest that there remains great possibility for politically progressive place memories and memory places. However, in focusing closely on local practices and local understandings, we resist the tendency to frame the productions of place and public memory as simply overarching tools of exclusionary power. Certainly, the authors here recognize that acts of memory and the structuring of place serve particular interests, from Ottawa Valley towns writing out Aboriginal presences to the reworking of the view from Lake Minnewanka. However, the strategies and tools of "placing memory" and "remembering place" also serve as active points of resistance, from mill workers archiving documents from their former workplace to the oral narratives that re-situate places of danger and community for gays and lesbians in Ottawa to the collection of photographs in Japanese Canadian archives. In each of these instances, the will to archive and the will to be archived are part of a politics of refusal, whether a refusal to accept job loss, to accept being labelled criminals and threats to national security, or to accept dislocation and dissolution as an ethnic community.

The fluidity and uncertainty that characterize the remakings of place and memory offer spaces of disruption that are often visible only when set within a deeply localized context. Landscape photographs of the foothills offer very different meanings when situated within local spaces and local memories. Monuments built with much care and purpose by political authorities and tourist promoters can seemingly disappear or be forgotten when they are encountered and experienced as elements of a lived-in, everyday local landscape. As a resident of St. Catharines, Ontario, told Johnston and Ripmeester about the city and Niagara Region's commemorative landscape, "I know where the big things are, but really know them? I notice more when I am travelling." Within this volume, "the local" is not simply a convenient scale for our case studies but rather a fundamental aspect of addressing the nuances and slippages between the politics of place and the politics of memory.

At the same time, we argue that in order to take "the local" seriously as an important category of analysis, we need to engage with the empirical richness that we face in the narratives, memories, and material traces of place. *Placing Memory and Remembering Place in Canada* delves into layers of context and detail, not to avoid theorizing but to make the study of "local" memory and place meaningful in acknowledging the lived experiences of those who inhabit or traverse or remember these places. The contributors to this volume have not shied away from telling these stories with a strong narrative voice; in coming to terms with their own "place" in this process, several authors insist on being a part of the history being recovered, analyzed, and narrated. In the afterword, Schwartz also follows this strategy by locating herself within the narrative, but in drawing on her personal recollections of place, she complicates the very division of public and private memory.

These stories show the high costs involved if our place memories and memory places do not accommodate difference, acknowledge injustice, and demonstrate a willingness to share authority over "the past." To this end, we must accept that places and memories are always in a state of becoming, of being worked on, struggled over, celebrated, mourned, and even, it bears repeating, ignored. Such a future can emerge, however, only from an increased understanding of our collective pasts, one that might inspire us to look again and anew at our own placing of memory and remembering of place. To return to the epigraph from Marlene Creates at the beginning of this introduction, "The land is not an abstract physical location but a *place*, charged with personal significance, shaping the images we have of ourselves." If we are to reflect on and remake ourselves, it is vital that we reconsider our own memories of place and the emplacement of memory.

ACKNOWLEDGMENTS

We wish to acknowledge the support of an Aid to Workshops and Conferences Grant from the Social Sciences and Humanities Research Council of Canada, which made it possible for us to host the workshop for this book at the Carleton Centre for Public History. Additional funding was provided by Carleton University, notably the Faculty of Arts and Social Sciences, the Office of the Vice-President for Research and International, the Department of History, and the Shannon Endowment Fund. Special thanks to A.B. McKillop, Bruce Elliott, and Ruth Phillips for their support, Jennie Wilhelm for her administrative assistance, and Susan L. Joudrey for her editorial skills. At short notice, Madelaine Morrison gave the completed manuscript a careful and helpful read. UBC Press has supported this project from the beginning. Thanks to Melissa Pitts for guiding us and championing our cause and to Megan Brand for keeping us on track. Joan M. Schwartz, Wayne McCready, and especially Matt Dyce all provided valuable comments on early drafts of this introduction. Our anonymous readers were constructive in their criticism and pushed us to think through the local with more clarity. Finally, we wish to thank Marlene Creates for allowing us to use her work.

NOTES

1   Joan M. Schwartz, "Constituting *Places of Presence:* Landscape, Identity and the Geographical Imagination," in Marlene Creates, *Places of Presence: Newfoundland kin and ancestral land, Newfoundland 1989-1991* (St. John's, NL: Killick's Press, 1997), 11.

2   See the syntheses in Tim Creswell, *Place: A Short Introduction* (Oxford: Blackwell, 2004); and Geoffrey Cubitt, *History and Memory* (Manchester, UK: Manchester University Press, 2007).

3   On "memory fatigue," see Andreas Huyssen, *Present Pasts: Urban Palimpsests and the Politics of Memory* (Palo Alto, CA: Stanford University Press, 2003), 3. The popularization of the notion of a "memory crisis" comes from Richard Terdiman, *Present Past: Modernity and the Memory Crisis* (Ithaca, NY: Cornell University Press, 1993).

4   Pierre Nora, *Les Lieux de Mémoire*, 3 vols., rev. ed. (Paris: Gallimard, 1997); Benedict Anderson, *Imagined Communities: Reflections on the Origin and Spread of Nationalism*, rev. ed. (London and New York: Verso, 2006).

5   Notable examples include H.V. Nelles, *The Art of Nation Building: Pageantry and Spectacle at Quebec's Tercentenary* (Toronto: University of Toronto Press, 1999); Jonathan Vance, *Death So Noble: Memory and Meaning in the First World War* (Vancouver: UBC Press, 1997); Ronald Rudin, *Founding Fathers: The Celebration of Champlain and Laval in the Streets of Quebec, 1878-1908* (Toronto: University of Toronto Press, 2003); Alan Gordon, *Making Public Pasts: The Contested Terrain of Montreal's Public Memories, 1891-1930* (Montreal and Kingston: McGill-Queen's University Press, 2001); Cecilia Morgan and Colin Coates, *Heroines and History: Representations of Madeleine de Verchères and Laura Secord* (Toronto: University of Toronto Press, 2001).

6   Hue-Tam Ho Tai points out that "the French nation of *Realms of Memory* is a given rather than a problem or project. The contests and conflicts that are so amply documented in the collection are not about France per se but about the nature of its national identity." See her "Remembered Realms: Pierre Nora and French National Memory," *American Historical Review* 106, 3 (June 2001): 910.

7   Huyssen, *Present Pasts*, 4.

8   Maurice Halbwachs, *The Collective Memory*, trans. Francis J. Ditter Jr. and Vida Yazdi Ditter, originally published in 1950 as *La Mémoire collective* (New York: Harper and Row, 1980), 140. A four-volume translation of *Les Lieux de Mémoire*, divided thematically, is currently being published by the University of Chicago Press, and not surprisingly, the second volume is dedicated to "space." See Pierre Nora, *Rethinking France: Les Lieux de Mémoire*, vol. 2, *Space*, trans. David P. Jordan (Chicago: University of Chicago Press, 2006).

9   A useful critique of Nora along these lines is offered by Steven Legg, "Contesting and Surviving Memory: Space, Nation, and Nostalgia in *Les Lieux de Mémoire*," *Environment and Planning D: Society and Space* 23 (2005): 481-504.

10   This understanding of place is provided by Cliff Hague, "Planning and Place Identity," in *Place Identity, Participation and Planning*, ed. Cliff Hague and Paul Jenkins (New York: Routledge, 2005), 4. Also cited in Brian Osborne, "From Patriotic Pines to Diasporic Geese: Emplacing Culture, Setting Our Sights, Locating Identity in a Transnational Canada," *Canadian Journal of Communications* 31, 1 (2006): 154.

11   Gaston R. Gordillo, *Landscapes of Devils: Tension of Place and Memory in the Argentinean Chaco* (Durham, NC: Duke University Press, 2004), 4.

12   Osborne, "From Patriotic Pines," 154. Also see by Brian Osborne, "Figuring Space, Marking Time: Contested Identities in Canada," *International Journal of Heritage Studies* 2, 1-2 (1996): 23-40; "Constructing Landscapes of Power: The George Etienne Cartier Monument, Montreal, 1910-1996," *Journal of Historical Geography* 24, 4 (1998): 431-58; "Landscapes, Memory, Monuments, and Commemoration: Putting Identity in Its Place," *Canadian Ethnic Studies* 33, 3 (2001): 39-77; "Moose Jaw's 'Great Escape': Constructing Tunnels, Deconstructing Heritage, Marketing Places," *Material History Review* 54 (2002):

16-28; and with David L.A. Gordon, "Constructing National Identity in Canada's Capital, 1900-2000: Confederation Square and the National Monument," *Journal of Historical Geography* 30 (2004): 618-41.

13 In this respect, we share interests with Steven High and David W. Lewis, *Corporate Wasteland: The Landscape and Memory of Deindustrialization* (Toronto: Between the Lines, 2007); Martha Norkunas, *Monuments and Memory: History and Representation in Lowell, Massachusetts* (Washington, DC: Smithsonian Institution Press, 2002); David Glassberg, *Sense of History: The Place of the Past in American Life* (Amherst: University of Massachusetts Press, 2001); Dolores Hayden, *The Power of Place: Urban Landscapes as Public History* (Cambridge, MA: MIT Press, 1995); and Gerald Pocius, *A Place to Belong: Community Order and Everyday Space in Calvert, Newfoundland* (Montreal and Kingston: McGill-Queen's University Press, 1991).

14 Arturo Escobar, "Culture Sits in Places: Reflections on Globalism and Subaltern Strategies of Localization," *Political Geography* 20 (2001): 139-74. See also Roxann Prazniak and Arif Dirlik, eds., *Places and Politics in an Age of Globalization* (Lanham, MD: Rowman and Littlefield, 2001); Geert De Neve and Henrike Donner, eds., *The Meaning of the Local: Politics of Place in Urban India* (London: Routledge, 2006); Doreen Massey, "A Global Sense of Place," in *Space, Place and Gender* (Minneapolis: University of Minnesota Press, 1994), 146-56; and Steven Hoelscher and Derek H. Alderman, "Memory and Place: Geographies of a Critical Relationship," *Social and Cultural Geography* 5, 3 (2004): 347-55.

15 Escobar, "Culture Sits in Places," 147-48.

16 Lucy Lippard, *The Lure of the Local: Senses of Place in a Multicentered Society* (New York: New Press, 1998). For a rather different perspective, see Andrew Herod and Melissa W. Wright, eds., *Geographies of Power: Placing Scale* (Oxford: Blackwell, 2002).

17 We have focused our discussion on major monographs in the field but are aware of the wider, growing interest in exploring the historical depths of place and memory from a local perspective in Canada. See, for example, recent articles by Robert Summerby-Murray, "Interpreting Personalized Industrial Heritage in the Mining Towns of Cumberland County, Nova Scotia: Landscape Examples from Springhill and River Hebert," *Urban History Review* 35, 2 (2007): 51-59; and Paul B. Williams, "A Local Sense of Place: Halifax's Little Dutch Church," *Canadian Journal of Communication* 31 (2006): 59-83. Less focused on commemoration, Joy Parr and her colleagues are producing some innovative work in their examinations of place memories and high-modern technological megaprojects; see http://megaprojects.uwo.ca and Joy Parr, *Sensing Changes: Technologies, Environments, and the Everyday, 1953-2003* (Vancouver: UBC Press, 2010). Tina Loo develops important arguments about high-modern technological megaprojects, place memories, and environmental justice in her "People in the Way: Modernity, Environment, and Society on the Arrow Lakes," *BC Studies* 142-43 (2004-5): 161-91; and "Disturbing the Peace: Environmental Change and the Scales of Justice on a Northern River," *Environmental History* 12 (October 2007): 895-919.

18   William J. Turkel, *The Archive of Place: Unearthing the Pasts of the Chilcotin Plateau* (Vancouver: UBC Press, 2007).

19   Julie Cruikshank, *Do Glaciers Listen?: Local Knowledge, Colonial Encounters, and Social Imagination* (Vancouver: UBC Press, 2005), 3.

20   Henri Lefebvre, *The Production of Space,* trans. Donald Nicholson-Smith (1974, 1984; reprint, London: Blackwell, 1991), 116.

21   Edward S. Casey, *The Fate of Place: A Philosophical History* (Berkeley: University of California Press, 1997), 337.

22   For a case study of the exclusionary power of some "local" historical representations, see Elizabeth Furniss, *The Burden of History: Colonialism and the Frontier Myth in a Rural Canadian Community* (Vancouver: UBC Press, 1999). Tim Cresswell offers some important insight into peoples and practices being identified as "out-of-place" in his *In Place/Out of Place: Geography, Ideology and Transgression* (Minneapolis: University of Minnesota Press, 1996).

23   John Bodnar defines public memory as "a body of beliefs and ideas about the past that help a public or society understand both its past, present, and by implication its future. It is fashioned ideally in a public sphere in which various parts of the social structure exchange views. The major focus of this communicative and cognitive process is not the past, however, but serious matters in the present such as the nature of power." See his *Remaking America: Public Memory, Commemoration, and Patriotism in the Twentieth Century* (Princeton, NJ: Princeton University Press, 1992), 15.

24   Alan Radley, "Artefacts, Memory and a Sense of the Past," in *Collective Remembering,* ed. David Middleton and Derek Edwards (London: Sage, 1990), 57. See also Marius Kwint et al., eds., *Material Memories* (Oxford: Berg, 1999); and Annette Kuhn and Kirsten Emiko McAllister, eds., *Locating Memory: Photographic Acts* (New York: Bergahn Books, 2006).

25   See, among others, Ruth M. Van Dyke and Susan E. Alcock, eds., *Archaeologies of Memory* (Oxford: Blackwell, 2003); Pamela J. Stewart and Andrew Strathern, eds., *Landscape, Memory and History: Anthropological Perspectives* (London: Pluto Press, 2003); G.J. Ashworth, Brian Graham, and J.E. Tunbridge, *Pluralising Pasts: Heritage, Identity and Place in Multicultural Societies* (London: Pluto Press, 2007); "Special Issue: Sense of Place: New Media, Cultural Heritage and Place Making," *International Journal of Heritage Studies* 14, 3 (2008).

26   Katharine Hodgkin and Susannah Radstone, "Introduction: Contested Pasts," in *Contested Pasts: The Politics of Memory,* ed. Susannah Radstone and Katharine Hodgkin (London: Routledge, 2003), 11.

27   Eviatar Zerubavel, *Time Maps: Collective Memory and the Social Shape of the Past* (Chicago: University of Chicago Press, 2003), 40-46.

28   Ibid., 46.

29   Tim Creswell and Gareth Hoskins, "Place, Persistence, and Practice: Evaluating Historical Significance at Angel Island, San Francisco, and Maxwell Street, Chicago," *Annals*

of the Association of American Geographers 98, 2 (2008): 395. Bob Jessop, Neil Brenner, and Martin Jones develop a complex model for researching and writing about space and social relationships in their "Theorizing Sociospatial Relations," *Environment and Planning D: Society and Space* 26 (2008): 389-401. Although their article emerged after this book's first draft was written, there is a shared theoretical sensibility about the need for multidimensional paths of analysis. Their "TPSN" model-building, however, seems to be inconsistent with their strong emphasis on the overlapping and intersecting elements (e.g., territory, place, scale, networks) of telling place stories.

30 Here, we are inspired by some rich thinking from postcolonial studies, including Antoinette Burton, *Dwelling in the Archive: Women Writing House, Home, and History in Late Colonial India* (Oxford: Oxford University Press, 2003); Antoinette Burton, ed., *Archive Stories: Facts, Fictions, and the Writing of History* (Durham, NC: Duke University Press, 2005); Ann Laura Stoler, *Along the Archival Grain: Epistemic Anxieties and Colonial Common Sense* (Princeton, NJ: Princeton University Press, 2009); and Anu Pamarao, "Affect, Memory, and Materiality: A Review Essay on Archival Mediation," *Comparative Studies in Society and History* 50, 2 (2008): 559-67. The literature on archives is voluminous, but on the question of archives and memory, a good starting point is Francis X. Blouin Jr. and William G. Rosenberg, eds., *Archives, Documentation, and Institutions of Social Memory: Essays from the Sawyer Seminar* (Ann Arbor: University of Michigan Press, 2006). Joan M. Schwartz cautions that despite the proliferation of scholarly work on "the archive," much of it ignores the social practices and theoretical foundations of actual archives; see her "'Having New Eyes': Spaces of Archives, Landscapes of Power," *Archivaria* 61 (Spring 2006): 1-25.

31 Tony Bennett, *The Birth of the Museum: History, Theory, Politics* (New York: Routledge, 1995); Tony Bennett, *Pasts Beyond Memory: Evolution, Museums, Colonialism* (New York: Routledge, 2005).

32 Pierre Nora, "Between Memory and History: Les Lieux de Mémoire," *Representations* 26 (1989): 13.

33 Kerwin Lee Klein provides the most sustained critique of both Nora and the wider field of memory studies on this point, lamenting that "memory" is often imbued with essentialist notions, "re-enchanted" by Freudian or mystical language. Klein is also critical of the "materialization" of memory, whereby "any cultural practice or artifact that Hegel might have excluded from History seems to qualify as Memory." See his "On the Emergence of Memory in Historical Discourse," *Representations* 69 (Winter 2000): 135-36.

34 Anthropologists have provided some invaluable understanding of this process by emphasizing the roles played by storytellers and oral tradition among different Aboriginal cultures. Two important examples, dealing with two different cultures and places, are Julie Cruikshank, *The Social Life of Stories: Narrative and Knowledge in the Yukon Territory* (Vancouver: UBC Press, 1998); and Keith H. Basso, *Wisdom Sits in Places: Landscape and Language among the Western Apache* (Albuquerque: University of New Mexico Press, 1996). For more of an approach one might call "historical epistemology"

or "historical ontology," see Joy Parr, "Local Water Diversely Known: Walkerton, Ontario, 2000 and After," *Environment and Planning D: Society and Space* 23, 2 (2005): 251-71.

35 For a similar claim about how scholars ought to understand life stories as "evidence," see Mary Jo Maynes, Jennifer L. Pierce, and Barbara Laslett, *Telling Stories: The Use of Personal Narratives in the Social Sciences and History* (Ithaca, NY, and London: Cornell University Press, 2008).

36 Doreen Massey, "Places and Their Pasts," *History Workshop Journal* 39 (1995): 184-85, 191. Many of the ideas in this article are developed more fully in Doreen Massey, *Space, Place and Gender* (Minneapolis: University of Minnesota Press, 1994). More recent directions in Massey's work can be seen in her *For Space* (Thousand Oaks, CA: Sage, 2005); and her *World City* (Cambridge, UK: Polity Press, 2007).

37 David Harvey, "From Space to Place and Back Again," in *Justice, Nature, and the Geography of Difference* (Oxford: Blackwell, 1996), 302.

38 As he explains in "From Space to Place and Back Again," Harvey is especially concerned about literatures that, at least in purpose, follow Martin Heidegger's emphasis on the pressing need for the authenticity of "dwelling" in a modern world. See Martin Heidegger, "Building, Dwelling, Thinking," in *Poetry, Language, Thought,* trans. Albert Hofstadter (New York: Harper and Row, 1971). See also Stuart Elden, *Mapping the Present: Heidegger, Foucault and the Project of a Spatial History* (London and New York: Continuum, 2001), 8-28; and Jeff Malpas, "New Media, Cultural Heritage and the Sense of Place: Mapping the Conceptual Ground," *International Journal of Heritage Studies* 14, 3 (May 2008): 197-209.

39 Ian McKay, *Quest of the Folk: Antimodernism and Cultural Selection in Twentieth-Century Nova Scotia* (Montreal and Kingston: McGill-Queen's University Press, 1994), 275. Alan Gordon's contribution to this book builds on but also moves away from McKay's pioneering work.

40 Eric Hobsbawm and Terence Ranger, eds., *Invention of Tradition* (Cambridge, UK: Cambridge University Press, 1983). For an updated reflection on tradition, see Mark Salber Phillips and Gordon Schochet, eds., *Questions of Tradition* (Toronto: University of Toronto Press, 2004).

41 Writing in the mid-1990s, Massey was especially influenced by postcolonial studies of "tradition" and cultural practices in Paul Gilroy, *The Black Atlantic: Modernity and Black Consciousness* (Cambridge, MA: Harvard University Press, 1993); and in Homi Bhabha, *The Location of Culture* (New York: Routledge, 1994). Although Harvey also speaks of place and memory as potential sites of struggle, it is difficult to escape the despair that haunts his understanding of these issues and the inevitably of their historical trajectories.

Part 1

COMMEMORATIONS: MARKING MEMORIES OF PLACE

Performing Public Memory and Re-Placing Home in the Ottawa Valley, 1900-58

JOHN C. WALSH

On an otherwise unremarkable Tuesday afternoon in late March 1879, a steam train pulled out of the main station in Ottawa burdened with "its load of living freight, farm implements and household effects." The "living freight" was 250 persons, some travelling alone but most as families. They had gathered at the train station at the first light of morning, their lives packed into crates, stuffed into bags, and crammed into trunks. They did not come to the station alone. Each person holding a ticket seemed to be accompanied by two more others who were there to help them make their train and to see them depart. Together they listened to musicians hired by the train company while they waited, but we can imagine that the music was overlaid with a buzz of excited conversations, of last words and tears and laughter before the 3:30 p.m. departure. As the train groaned and its massive wheels began turning, those left on the platform broke out into *Auld Lang Syne* and, waving handkerchiefs, "gave a final adieu" to the passengers, who were headed to Manitoba and the promise of new beginnings.[1]

Scenes like this became regular in the Ottawa Valley in the late 1870s and through the 1880s, so much so that one newspaper described the cumulative effect as "an exodus."[2] For many in the late nineteenth century, this exodus to the Canadian and American Wests resembled a reversal of fortune for the Ottawa Valley. Since the decades right after the War of 1812, the valley had been a site of arrival for white migrants, many of them from Ireland but also from England, Scotland, the United States, and Quebec. A significant number of the first white settlers were in fact former military men who had their service rewarded with land grants of sizes concomitant with their rank and family networks. Starting in the mid-1850s, this Anglo-Celtic and French Canadian white population became even more diversified with significant arrivals of Prussians, Germans, and Poles, who were eager to take advantage of a colonization scheme that provided free land grants of 100 acres to all males at least eighteen years old. This scheme also attracted many from older settled areas in Canada as well as people from upstate New York and New England, where the availability of affordable, good agricultural land was increasingly in short supply. By the late 1870s, however, the fantasies of that colonization scheme were replaced by the frontier-settler fantasies attached to the Prairies and the American West. The Ottawa Valley was no longer a geography defined by the arrival of white settlers but instead had become a geography of departure.[3]

After the trains left, people drifted away from the platforms, returning to their homes and their everyday lives. Although no doubt saddened by the loss of "some of their best residents – the bone and sinew of the community," they certainly did not forget those family members, friends, and neighbours who had left.[4] As early as 1905, calls for the departed to come back home began to emerge from towns scattered all over the Ontario side of the Ottawa Valley: "No town that I know, in this fair domain / Should be prouder to see her sons again / Than the town on the Tay, dear, good, old Perth / Whose sons are scattered o'er the earth."[5] As this short poem indicated, those "scattered o'er the earth" were invited to come "home" and wander again over the streets, fair grounds, schoolyards, and church lots that had once been the locus of their lives. In doing so, they would see both the familiar and the new, traces of what the town had been when they left but also evidence of what the town had become since their departure. As "sons," and daughters for that matter, expatriates were also provided with the opportunity to affirm their identification with the local community just as this community affirmed its identification with them.

Perth's expatriates and residents were hardly alone. As in other areas of Ontario and the north-eastern United States, formal and elaborate home-coming festivals were an important public celebration in the Ottawa Valley over the first half of the twentieth century. The best attended of these were the Old Home Weeks and Old Boys' Reunions held in Perth (1905, 1923, 1948), Arnprior (1909), Lanark (1913), Almonte (1920), Renfrew (1923), Carleton Place (1924), Smiths Falls (1925, 1950), Pembroke (1928, 1958), and Eganville (1948).[6] These celebrations ran anywhere from three to twelve days and involved countless speeches, sermons, parades, historical pageantry, temporary museum displays, sporting competitions, and a great deal of music, dancing, eating, and drinking. In preparation, each host town constructed a series of arches across its main street, hung flags, strung bunting, swept streets, painted build-ings, trimmed lawns and hedges, planted flowers, and polished all of its monu-ments. All of this hard work strove to produce an event that would be spectacular and meaningful, historical and memorable.

In the weeks leading up to and through the celebrations, the host town's newspapers swelled with details about the impending events. Not incidentally or accidentally, this included a wide range of writings from both resident and expatriate "old boys" recalling stories from their own personal pasts as well as the more public history of the town.[7] The *Pembroke Standard-Observer* went so far as to create a special sixty-page souvenir edition devoted to telling stories of the town's becoming, careful to highlight of course the accomplish-ments of local merchants who, not coincidentally, filled the edges of the newspaper with advertisements welcoming the visitors and offering all sorts of tantalizing specials on goods and services.[8] Local newspaper presses also published the commemorative programs that accompanied these events, ones that ranged from sixty-five to two hundred pages in length. Like the news-papers, these programs explained what events were occurring, and they also featured lengthy, detailed histories of the town, heavily illustrated with photo-graphs that ran right up to the then present.

The histories and other narratives provided in newspapers and programs were intended as manuals for the celebrations, explaining the significance of all the traces of the past (even the most recent past) that could be seen in the landscape. This is how one of these newspapers described its role: "Hand in hand with a reunion walks the history of the place holding it and the *Courier* this week endeavours to give Perth's reunion its companion."[9] In many ways,

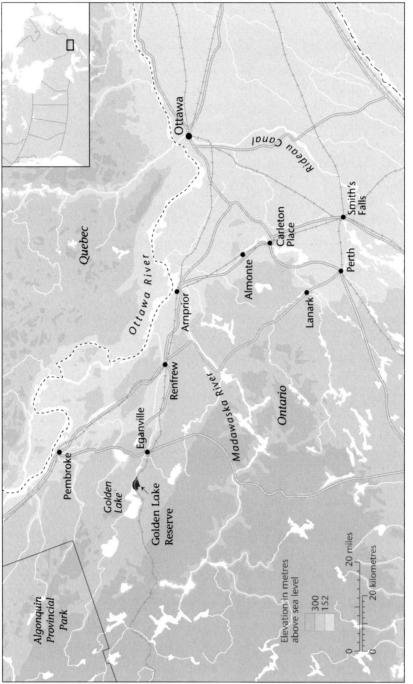

Figure 1.1   Old Home Weeks and Old Boys' Reunions in the Ottawa Valley, 1900–58.

the newspapers and programs worked much like captions on a photograph or a travel guidebook; they sought to educate the eye and also frame the meaning of what people saw and experienced in the landscape even before they saw (or in some cases re-encountered) it. The 1948 program for Perth's Old Home Week underlined its intended utility by also including blank pages of two columns that, it explained, were for collecting signatures from other visitors and for recording impressions.[10] The returning old boys and old girls were expected to explore the town on a journey of rediscovery, encountering both the familiar and the unfamiliar. Like good ethnographers, they could record both on these blank pages. For them and for residents, these blank pages allowed them to document this experience and to produce a souvenir whose value as a preserved "document" would grow as the events of Old Home Week grew farther away in time and space.[11]

Much of what was published before, during, and after the homecoming festivals was intended to be a part of and also an archive for the experience of being there. This provides us with both an interpretive challenge and an opportunity: Do we flatten or even neutralize this archive's historical effect if we leave its writing and images, its narratives, on the page? How might our own historical imaginations and critical thinking be affected if we put this archive back into history, as material and knowledge making rather than material and knowledge made? What might become possible if we think of the archive's storytelling as performance, as an active verb rather than a static noun?[12]

By focusing on the archiving of homecoming, my history of these festivals complements but also departs from the current scholarly literature. Françoise Noël convincingly argues that such performances were geared toward generating much-needed tourist dollars. Michael Woods reminds us that local elites used local historical pageantry to affirm their class status and power. Examining the United States in the nineteenth and twentieth centuries, Susan Matt identifies a broader historical pattern of homecoming in which the act of going "home" again affirmed the historical experience of relocation involved with both voluntary and forced migrations.[13]

However, I want to suggest something different. Like Matt, I want to take seriously the efforts of Ottawa Valley residents to know and to experience their "home" towns. But rather than focusing on the psychologies of the returned, I share Noël's and Woods's interests in the hosts, in those who still lived in town.[14] Still, there is an opportunity to think anew about these homecoming festivals and about local historical pageantry if we read their archival traces as narratives of inscription, as the making of representations and the making of knowledge, rather than as mirrors or epiphenomena of some other historical reality.[15] We shall see that, at the same time as historical stories of becoming and belonging were celebrated and enjoyed by so many, storytelling performances also drew and re-drew the boundaries of place and community. This boundary-work was hardly incidental; it reflected conscious efforts not merely to cope with the dislocation of the exodus but also to affirm the nobility and significance of those who stayed behind. The homecoming celebrated returning expatriates, but these celebrations were in honour of the town and those who made it, developed it, and, perhaps most important, preserved it. Expatriates were involved in some, but not all, of that history. The result, I suggest, was that the small-town "folk" of the Ottawa Valley were able to insist on their own modernity, a claim anchored by their efforts to place these hometowns in the landscape of white, settler North America and within the historical time of Western civilization.

COMING HOME

People were summoned home through newspaper advertisements and through letters from family and friends who had stayed behind. In Arnprior, a lumber town established at the junction of the Ottawa and Madawaska Rivers, these invitations also took the form of postcards such as that shown in Figure 1.2.

Lisa Wilford of 20 Delaware Avenue in Ottawa received this postcard with one sentence written rather beautifully across the back: "You'll be sure to come, won't you?"[16] The sentiment was hardly unique. As the *Lanark Era* told its readers in 1913, "This is the week of the Reunion. The old boys are with us. Many have come thousands of miles for the sole purpose of attending this home-coming ... As we clasp your hand and look into your face, and fond recollections bring up out of the dim recesses of the past memories that are sweet of old associations, we say that no happier moment of our lives have ever been."[17]

Expressing this joy and celebrating the return of expatriates involved both formal and less formal encounters with local residents. It was in these moments, as the remarks of the *Lanark Era* editor suggest, when the old boys and old girls seemed to function as living monuments, mnemonic devices who would

Figure 1.2   Souvenir invitational postcard, Arnprior 1909. *Source:* Arnprior and McNab/ Braeside Archives.

offer representations of the local past while also spurring the memory of others. At a large dinner in Carleton Place in 1924, for example, the old boys were feted with speeches and toasts. In return, the guests entertained for hours with their "reminiscent stories, songs and old time stories."[18] In 1905 Perth resident J.M. Walker said this is what he expected to learn from the returning expatriates: "Doubtless when the 'Old Boys' get together they can supply one to another much that has been unrecorded and forgotten by the majority, and so history can be made to live again when their fond recollections of a dim past and a 'tale that was told' long ago pass again from one old neighbour to another."[19] Dinners and picnics were especially important for this kind of encounter, something the Walter J. Robertson General Store sought to capitalize on in an advertisement it ran during the lead-up to Lanark's 1913 Old Boys' Reunion: "It is good to hear a visitor at the table comment on the excellence of the food. Old Boys will say it reminds them of the good old times, and they will pass over their plate for another helping."[20] As the advertisement also explained, it was up to husbands to buy ingredients of the best quality, which thankfully the store could provide, in order for their wives to prepare the kind of meal that would make it a meaningful encounter for them and their old boy guests.

Like meals, parades produced both formal and less formal encounters. The most common featured the old boys in a formal procession along with the town's militia units and other formal civic organizations. Weaving their way through the town's commercial district, the routes usually ended with a pass underneath a great "Welcome" arch erected in the town core. In some cases, such as Almonte's Old Home Week in 1929, the parading old boys were part of a larger performance of historical pageantry where floats representing key moments in the town's history offered a moving tableaux of the past. Here men, women, and children from the town joined the old boys, further blurring the boundaries between performer and audience.

Although the formality of those processions sought to emphasize the monumental elements of the old boys' return, these were not the only parades. In Carleton Place in 1924 and again in Smiths Falls in 1950, local residents of all ages joined the old boys and old girls in putting on their pyjamas and taking to the downtown streets for a Nightshirt Parade and an evening of festivities.[21] Here the encounters were supposed to be festive and informal so that participants could simply enjoy the absurdity of the moment. Even in this carnivalesque context, however, the old boys and old girls were in public and on display, albeit different from the more formal processions.[22]

The ways that formal and informal encounters were narrated in local newspapers underscored their perceived significance. In Lanark in 1913, "it was a beautiful sight when all these people gathered together, either on the Government Grounds, on the streets, or on the picnic field ... There came the spontaneous word of fraternal sympathy that enquired for friends of the long ago and recalled scenes and associations that live green on the bosom of memory."[23] In Carleton Place in 1924, "a pleasant incident occurred on the street one day. Mr. Fred H. Mears, who is somewhat of an expert on photography had been 'snapping' groups of the old boys, and presently all the old boys wanted copies ... Jim Anable, on behalf of the group presented Mr. Mears with a silver cigarette case as a souvenir, a gift that Fred ... says he will treasure as a souvenir of the best week he ever had in his life."[24] In 1928, the *Pembroke Standard-Observer* wrote, "All the old boys and old girls are essentially human. They have not forgotten the old associates and it is the joy of a lifetime to be renewing acquaintances."[25]

In the early twentieth century, at the same time as the Ottawa Valley's local newspapers sought to capture the meaning of the personal encounters between expatriates and those who stayed behind, the very definition of "nostalgia" was undergoing a revealing etymological transition. From the mid-eighteenth century until the late nineteenth century, nostalgia was a pathologized illness for which the prescribed cure was "going home." That definition of nostalgia was replaced by a new term, "homesickness," in the early twentieth century.[26] "Nostalgia" instead began its association with its now more familiar meaning: an often pejorative sentimentalism that attaches itself to the ephemeral and the prosaic and that, as a result, produces unimportant, false, and inauthentic memories.

Indeed, it is rather easy to read excerpts like those above (and countless others in the archive) and shake our heads at the sugary romanticism oozing on the newspapers' pages. But this would be a rather limited, and limiting, reading. Instead, we ought to follow scholars like Mieke Bal, Svetlana Boym, and Annie Coombes and ask how nostalgia enables various practices and experiences as it involves people's understandings of themselves and the past.[27] Here we set aside the concern for "accuracy" or "veracity" in such writing and instead track nostalgia's influences over practice and representation. In doing so, we must take seriously the pages of names of returning expatriates that were published in local newspapers in the days that followed the celebrations. Why did the papers do this? It certainly was not to affirm that lots of people attended; residents simply looked outside their front windows and saw that for themselves. Instead, I suggest that in publishing the surnames of those who had come "home," the newspapers added some much-needed specificity to the boundary-work going on in these festivals, a social ordering that seemed to carry deep emotional resonance. Nostalgia was crucial in representing the returning old boys and old girls within the bonds of local community. They may have moved away, but in coming home, in being in the town's public space and engaged with the public, their relocation away was reconciled within a town's "us." In this case, the boundaries of the imagined local community were stretched over great distances even though the encounters and representations were very much rooted in the local.[28] In its structuring role, therefore, nostalgia collapsed time and the distance of separation by returning many to a local world that once was, a time and place before expatriates boarded the trains and the exodus began.

This effect was perhaps strongest when childhood memories written both by local residents and by expatriate old boys were published in newspapers or, as we saw earlier, passed around orally in song and storytelling. Few childhood memories seemed stronger than those of going to school, a point not lost on Chris Forbes as early as 1906: "Men and women revisiting the scenes of childhood always love to look on the dear old school where many happy days were passed. Happenings almost forgotten rush back into memory's seat with gladness like the meeting of long separated friends."[29] When Forbes wrote this a year after Perth's 1905 Old Boys' Reunion, he might have had in mind the locally well-known John W. Douglas, an officer with the 42nd Regiment. In the spring of 1905, Major Douglas was asked to share some personal memories of growing up in Perth. He began his story with education, he said, on the premise that "a good beginning may portend a happy end." He then talked of going to school "over Malcolm McPherson's carpenter shop," of the walk to school past "Ellis' corner ... in deadly fear of Brooke's dog Brisco," and of his early teachers "Mr. Scott" and "Rev. Duncan Morrison." Of the latter, Douglas said, "He was no joke, and leather rose in price for those who did their duty [to misbehave] relentlessly." The use of place names that only a certain audience would know and of personal names that only a certain audience would care to know underlines the localness of this discourse as well as the memories it represents. But it was offered to the public because, Douglas said, "My school days ... were full of episodes of entrancing interest to 'Old Boys' old enough to remember them."[30] In other words, Douglas made public his personal memories of going to school because of the connectedness they offered.[31] They made visible the "home" that the old boys had known. But they also had an effect on a much larger audience. In circulating these personal memories of childhood, narratives such as that of Major Douglas made the imagining of this now-gone local world a public experience of recollection and nostalgia.

If nostalgia and public encounters at meals, parades, and chance meetings on the street seemed to broaden or extend the boundaries of local community, the production of formal, historical narratives about the making of place often made these boundaries more exclusive. Consider the example of Pembroke's 1928 historical pageant. Produced by the well-known, Ohio-based John B. Rogers Producing Company and declared to be a "mammoth spectacle" with

Commemorations

"hundreds in the cast," the Pembroke Historical Pageant ran much of the Old Home Week, beginning at 8:30 p.m. in the newly named Centenary Park.[32] Unlike the historical pageant held twenty years earlier in Quebec City, which was entirely about national and imperial histories, the one in Pembroke offered a narrative of local history that, for the most part, incorporated the national and the imperial into its localized chronology and story of becoming.[33] This was signalled from the very beginning of the pageant when, in a prologue, Miss Pembroke made a speech of welcome to Miss Canada and her "daughters, [the] Fair Provinces."[34] Young women from the town performed all of these characters in the pageant, and over 200 other residents joined them in the cast. Although mostly women, the cast seemed to reflect the ethnic diversity of the town; if the names in the program can be trusted as a rough guide, the majority of the performers appear to have been Anglo-Celtic, but there were also strong representations of those with French and German names.

Perhaps this is one of the reasons why the pageant ended with "The Masque of Nations," although this scene was the least "local" in its narrative orientation. The program told the audience that the actors "symboliz[ed] the unity of Canada and showed the merging together of the different people who came here to settle and later confederated into one great Dominion."[35] This language owed much to the diamond jubilee celebrations held only one year earlier, in 1927, where audiences witnessed a very grand historical pageant on Parliament Hill in Ottawa.[36] "The Masque of Nations" involved over 120 actors (all women), who adopted the "costume" and what the program called the "character dances" of a wide range of ethnic and racial groups: Japanese, Chinese, French, Italian, English, Belgian, Dutch, Irish, and Scottish. Rather than emphasizing the hierarchy and differences among these groups, the pageant depicted their fusion into a whole in the form of the largest group within "The Masque of Nations": the "Canadian Girls."[37] Ethnic and racial differences were recognized, but they were narrated as history in the flattening of these differences as "Canadian."

The use of local young women as performers and thus as representations minimized the moral and political danger then associated with groups like the Japanese, Chinese, and Italians, which could be ignored in the scene's narrative of assimilation. Furthermore, local white women performing Japanese and Chinese "character dances" also likely fulfilled, for some, an Orientalist fantasy about the sexuality of these performed "others."[38] The liminal space of the pageant allowed these women to pretend to be something they were not, a convention that both audience and performer understood completely. It is thus likely that much of the audience would have seen these performers in such a state of obvious transgression as being humorous, again defusing and ignoring the racialized politics involved with such a representation. All the same, the pageant's performance and historical narrative of "race" would have likely pleased those in the Ontario Publicity Bureau who took out a very large advertisement in the local newspaper that spoke to these very themes. "The Centenary of Pembroke recalls much of the heroic story of exploration in Ontario," the advertisement began, "a Country for men of virile races." It then concluded, "Realize all your Province holds and aspires to and give your Canadian and British Patriotism new life."[39]

Local Aboriginal people were conspicuous by their presence/absence in the pageant's narratives of "race." The cover of the program featured a stock image of the "savage Indian" in which a muscular, bare-chested Aboriginal man, in a long, feathered head-dress and holding a spear in his raised right hand, rides a horse bareback and appears to be letting out a war-whoop.[40] As the pageant moved from its first scene, "The Dawn of Creation," to its second, "Indian Camp Life and Primitive Occupations," a slightly different and more locally specific set of representations emerged. The program explained, "At the time of the advent of the first white man to this country, this territory was occupied mostly by the Hurons, Iroquois, and Algonquin Indians," who "were very much alike in appearance, character, manners and customs."[41] The scene presented to the audience was a domestic one, in which some "braves" went hunting while young women set up teepees and began cooking food. "As evening comes, we see the picturesque courtship of an Indian maiden and a brave." Just as this courtship begins, however, it is interrupted by the arrival of Samuel de Champlain. In the scene, Champlain joins these local Aboriginal peoples in various pow-wows, conducts some trade, shows off his "new and strange firearms," and then forms a partnership with his Native hosts by hiring guides to take him and his party farther inland.[42] Although no doubt a lengthy scene, it was effective as a cultural production. It combined the anthropological desire of non-Aboriginal peoples to see the domestic space and social lives of "the Indian" with the larger imperative to tell a local historical narrative.[43]

At this point in the pageant, aboriginality then disappeared from the narrative for several scenes before it reappeared in "The Lone Pioneer." This reappearance, however, was radically different. The program describes the scene as devoted to the experience of a white pioneer family who are moving into the forest but have stopped on their journey to make camp. Father goes off to hunt for dinner while Mother goes to a nearby creek to wash some clothes. Here is what the program told the audience happens next:

> The children, a girl of six and boy of five, are happy in their play around the campfire, little realizing the danger of a nearby tribe of savage Indians who are sneaking, crawling, upon the camp. With one blood curdling yell, the Indians kidnap the girl and scalp the boy, leaving his limp body as mute evidence of their visit.[44]

The violence and horror of this scene played on the captivity narratives that had been a popular genre since the late nineteenth century in the context of the armed conflicts between Aboriginal peoples and national troops in both Canada and the United States.[45] However, situated within a local historical narrative, it added a very disturbing and discomforting picture of otherness for the Algonquin and Nippissing peoples who lived on and off reserve in the Ottawa Valley. Furthermore, unlike Wild West Shows, exhibitions, and national historical pageants, the performers in the Pembroke pageant were all white, engaged in the same liminality that allowed young white women to "play" Chinese and Japanese.[46] There was no opportunity, in other words, for Aboriginal performers (local or otherwise) to find ways to subvert this representation or to at least use the pageant for some economic or even political gain. In their absence/presence, local Aboriginal peoples were represented as being outside the boundaries of the imagined community of the nation and also that of Pembroke.

As shown in Figure 1.3, the cover of Pembroke's souvenir program, despite offering a more benign representation of aboriginality, achieved the same effect of situating Aboriginal peoples firmly outside the boundaries of local community. Looking back over her shoulder at the urban topography of Pembroke, this Aboriginal woman in her canoe is not headed to the town, nor does she seem likely to do so. The currents of the Ottawa River seem to be taking her to a different destination.[47]

Figure 1.3 Front cover of Pembroke souvenir program, 1928. *Source: Official Program and Pictorial Souvenir of Pembroke Centennial* (Pembroke, 1928).

Local historical pageants such as those in Pembroke (1928), Almonte (1929), and Smiths Falls (1950) were effective inscriptions of local community and place because of the relationship between audience and performer. Even though the producers of these pageants were not local and likely had little or no grasp of local history, the narrative of the pageant was localized in large measure because of who was performing it, the location it was being performed at, and the context in which it occurred. More so than any other element of Old Home Weeks and Old Boys' Reunions, these pageants speak to the conditions that Greg Dening says are fundamental to any effective representation of a meaningful past: "The 'theatricality of history-making' involves the notion of viewing in a space so closed around with conventions that the audience and actors enter into the conspiracy of their own illusions. The paradox is that self-awareness, performance consciousness, does not disturb the realisms of their understanding."[48]

To be excluded from the "theatricality of history-making" in Old Home Weeks and Old Boys' Reunions was to be excluded from the experiences and identifications of belonging that such a process made possible. This happened explicitly to the Ottawa Valley's Aboriginal population, not only at Pembroke in 1928 but also at Smiths Falls in 1950 when a local dance teacher and her white students performed an "Indian Dance" in costume as part of its historical pageant.[49] This pattern stands in marked contrast to the involvement of Aboriginal peoples from the Six Nations reserve in the Brantford Historical Society and its activities (including historical pageantry) in this same period. As Cecilia Morgan demonstrates in the next chapter of this book, although this involvement was hardly a marker of equality or unquestioned inclusion, it did allow for Aboriginal men and women of the Six Nations to exercise some power over their self-representation as historical actors. This was not, however, the case for those Native peoples living on the Golden Lake reserve or off reserve throughout the valley, including areas in and around Pembroke.[50] It was also not the case for the region's Métis population, who almost never appeared in any representation (in pageants or elsewhere) despite having a history of place in the valley that extended back to the seventeenth century when Champlain put his "first white foot" on the banks of the Ottawa River.[51] Indeed, the Métis are the anti-represented, completely imagined out of the memories of place and community as they emerged in Old Home Weeks and Old Boys' Reunions.

SPATIAL HISTORIES OF HOME

The 1928 cover image of the program for the Pembroke Centennial and Old Home Week reproduced in Figure 1.3 is also instructive for how it represents the town's landscape. As the unidentified Aboriginal woman drifts away from the town, she looks back and sees its moral and industrial topography in the form of the church spire and the waterfront timber mill. This social and cultural scene is set against the dominant presence of the pine-rich forest and the Ottawa River. This representation of place, however, was rather different from those that dominated in the nineteenth century. In the Ottawa Valley, and elsewhere, the forest's nineteenth-century "other" was the farm. Clearances that led to farms were understood to bring light to darkness, order to disorder, and productivity to waste and neglect. Even as the demands of the region's timber industry established mills and towns, in the nineteenth century this urbanism was set into a represented pastoral rural landscape emerging from the cleared trees.[52] In the twentieth-century narratives of Old Home Weeks and Old Boys' Reunions, however, the forest's "other" was less the farm and more so the built town.

This focus on the built town placed a great deal of emphasis on a more recent history of spatial change, one that occurred after the exodus that marked the last quarter of the nineteenth century. Although this was especially visible in the celebrations after the First World War, it was also important in Perth in 1905: "When the 'Old Boys,' their sisters or wives are revisiting the old town ... they will contrast the beauty of the residences, the masses of tree foliage along the streets, the excellent roadways and clean cement sidewalks with what they left behind them ten, twenty or forty years ago."[53] In making these kinds of representations within the context of homecoming, local residents were engaged in more than boosterism (although this was clearly the goal for those seeking to attract new commercial and corporate investment in town).[54] They were also making some powerful inscriptions on the town's space as historically meaningful.

The program from Carleton Place's 1924 Old Home Week celebration provides a useful example. As can be seen in Figures 1.4 and 1.5, these pages of the program were made to look like family photographic albums, as the pictures carefully taken are given the appearance of being glued to the album page by some excited or clumsy fingers. It reflects, in part, more of nostalgia's structuring effect as well as conventions of photographic display.

Commemorations

1. ST. ANDREW'S PRESBYTERIAN CHURCH 2. ST. JAMES ANGLICAN CHURCH
3. BAPTIST CHURCH 4. METHODIST CHURCH
5. ZION PRESBYTERIAN CHURCH 6. ST. MARY'S R. C. CHURCH

Figure 1.4 Images of churches in Carleton Place, 1924. *Source: Souvenir Program, Carleton Place Centenary Celebration and Old Home Week* (Carleton Place, 1924).

1. CENTRAL SCHOOL   2. VICTORIA PUBLIC SCHOOL *(Old Town Hall)*
3. PRINCE OF WALES PUBLIC SCHOOL *(Old High School)*

Figure 1.5   Images of schools in Carleton Place, 1924. *Source: Souvenir Program, Carleton Place Centenary Celebration and Old Home Week* (Carleton Place, 1924).

Commemorations

Although programs overflowed with photographs of churches and schools, and often included a brief history of each building in the text, the 1948 program produced for Eganville's Old Home Week also offered an explanation for what was missing from their town's built landscape: "It's a village where churches are foremost, / Where peace and contentment prevail; / And since law and order are cherished / They find little Need for the jail."[55]

The socio-political implications of this emphasis on civic architecture are perhaps best explained by a self-described Perth old boy: "We honour the memory of the pioneer heroes who invaded the forests. Amid privations and labors, such as later generations know little of, they founded an empire more magnificent than the storied nations of Greece and Rome. The latter ravaged peoples and countries and made serfs. The former built school houses and made men and women."[56] The "making" of "men and women" underscores how the narratives of Old Home Weeks and Old Boys' Reunions concerned themselves primarily with defining the genealogy of place: architecture did not simply replace forests (although we shall see how important that was) but also produced the next generation of a town's population. The church and the school were black boxes of both local community and citizen making: into them went the sinful and the young and out came the improved, the reformed, and the strong. Those who did not pass through these black boxes were deprived of "improvement" and lacked some of the necessary social capital to be of the local community. Although many personal memories were no doubt attached to this architecture, the guides and newspapers emphasized the public memories that they wished to situate in them by attaching the brick and stone to a very ambitious historical narrative of civilization and modernity.

Indeed, civic architecture also represented a distinct "other" to what local historian Andrew Haydon described in 1925 as "the ancient forest home of Algonquin tribes whose wigwams once dotted those picturesque tributaries of the Ottawa."[57] Wigwams dotted the landscape, but great stone and brick buildings consumed it, colonizing not simply the ground but also vertical space. Wigwams came and went: they were intended to be portable, to follow migrating cultures like the Algonquin and Nippissing of the Ottawa Valley. Stone and brick buildings, such as those seen above in 1924 Carleton Place or in 1928 Pembroke, were permanent, foundational spaces on which to build a place, to build those citizen men and women, boys and girls. Imagine the satisfaction that many local readers had when one old boy visitor to Carleton Place's 1924 Old Home Week wrote to the local newspaper, "To those of us who have been absent for years, it sure was a pleasure to see the beautiful buildings on old main street, but the magnificent homes that have been erected by the boys who stayed at home was a revelation indeed."[58]

The built town was also one of energy and busyness, filled with the sounds of commerce, children going to school, farmers bringing goods to market, train whistles, church bells, and so forth. "For centuries before," the *Lanark Era* told its readers in 1913, "no sound save the drip of a passing Indian's paddle had disturbed the silence which hung upon its [the valley's] sinuous bosom."[59] The making of a town, of a home-place, filled up this silence, providing an entire soundscape of urban everyday life, one distinctly different from the "vast silent forest of virgin pine"[60] that was punctuated only by that "drip of a passing Indian's paddle." Such comments remind us that the Aboriginal woman in the canoe in Figure 1.3 was also a historical figure who was clearly out of place against the urban modernity of churches, schools, mills, markets, and brick residences where the comings and goings of everyday life filled the silence she and her canoe signified.[61]

The "forest of the virgin pine" was understood, however, as more than a stage on which the town was made. It was also represented as an obstacle to be overcome, as a landscape of danger and immorality. As we explored earlier, in Pembroke's historical pageant of 1928 it was in the forest where a five-year-old boy was murdered and his six-year-old sister kidnapped. Not surprisingly, overcoming the obstacle of the forest was important to local historical narratives, especially when extolling the heroic masculinities of the "first" white settlers.[62] These stories of firsts are very common and always linear – a white, pioneering man, sometimes with family but just as likely without, entered the forest and overcame it by building a farm, a mill, a store, a church, and a house (first out of wood and later brick or stone). If not married, he then married and raised his children in or nearby the town. Like all narratives, however, this one had different variants, and one of the more interesting emerged in the context of the 1948 Perth Old Home Week:

> Many of the single men, however, got sick of the backwoods life, the work being too hard for them, and they either turned trappers or hunters, or else sought employment in the more settled parts of Canada, and the United

States. The married men having the responsibility of wives and families to provide for, stuck manfully to the task before them and were not long in laying the foundation of a career of prosperity.[63]

Here the forest as "backwoods" was the testing ground for establishing the authenticity of the true town builders, where their rugged and moral masculinities distinguished them from other men who lacked the same physical (those who went to the "more settled parts") and moral (those who "turned trappers or hunters") strength. In either case, however, the "wives and families" were disconnected from narrative's explanation of how a manful masculinity built the town.

The gendering of landscape and memory in these narratives was also prominent in the unmistakable presence of technologies of mechanical power. Water, steam, electric, and later atomic power were an enduring constant in the Old Home Week and Old Boys' Reunion narratives even though the move through these different ages involved new and evolving technologies. Two sets of images of industrial landscapes from the program for the 1928 Pembroke Old Home Week provide some useful examples. Let us consider each in turn.

As shown in Figure 1.6, the first set of images involves the "old wooden bridge" and the "new stone bridge" over Pembroke's Muskrat River and immediately conjures up the gendered narratives associated with town architecture. But several things about these images are somewhat different. First, the use of the "before" and "after" contrast is an effort to visually narrate historical change, a use of photographs that is different from but also complements the family album mode seen earlier. The contrast narrative includes at least three revealing elements: (1) the tidiness of the after image versus the before; (2) the authority of the stone versus the ramshackle wood; and (3) the inclusion in the first image of a group of fishermen using the river either for leisure or subsistence and the complete absence of any bodies in the after photograph. The first image, a nineteenth-century photograph, demonstrates the pioneering efforts to harness and conquer the Muskrat River, but the latter is an image of unfettered, technological modernity that has thoroughly domesticated it and incorporated the river into the urban landscape of Pembroke.

In Figure 1.7 the pairing of the "Old Sawmill," which offers a glimpse of the "First Plant of the Pembroke Electric Light Company," and the "Present Modern Power Plant" also sees the landscape both emptied and incorporated.

Figure 1.6 "Old" and "new" bridges over the Muskrat River. *Source:* Illustrations from *Official Program and Pictorial Souvenir of Pembroke Centennial* (Pembroke, 1928).

Figure 1.7 "Old Saw Mill" and "Present Modern Power Plant." *Source:* Illustrations from *Official Program and Pictorial Souvenir of Pembroke Centennial* (Pembroke, 1928).

Here, however, it is the bodies of workers that are essential to this narrative shift. The rough-and-tumble nature of work done in the lumbering industry is in marked contrast to the unseen labour being performed in the modern power plant below. Hiding labour, consciously or not, allows the technology and built environment to speak more clearly to the viewer. It also sanitizes the landscape, maintaining the emphasis on masculine power but now displaying it more prominently in the power architecture of the plant rather than in the bodies of the workers. Even though nature is still prominent in the "Present Modern Power Plant," it has been landscaped as part of the city rather than depicted as something requiring back-breaking labour. In some ways, this image reflects what we might identify as a garden masculinity of domesticated, ordered nature in contrast to a frontier masculinity embodied by the workers and stacked timber in the "Old Sawmill" image.

The incorporation of nature into place that appears in the above two examples belongs to the genre of what David Nye calls "second creation" narratives.[64] Second creation narratives promote the march of progress that emerges from the use of technologies working in harmony with God's first creation, nature. Second creation is thus about spatial change, but it is also about creating the ideal landscape within which an ideal, Christian social and moral geography, could flourish. The above representations of civic architecture and industrial architecture should therefore be considered as related narrative inscriptions of both place and local community. Together, these built environments signified a colonization of nature whose architectural traces were monuments to the civilizing process and state formation, to the effective "improvement" of both space and the social body. The documenting of this history in the pages of a souvenir program reinforced this narrative of change and of the meanings that these monuments held for all those who looked on them, whether in person or, as here, on the page.

CONCLUSIONS

I began this chapter on homecoming with a story of departure. Instead of boarding the train and heading to the West, and then getting back on the trains to return to the East, this chapter stayed in the Ottawa Valley.[65] This was perhaps an unusual choice; after all, the longing to "go home" happens only after one leaves. Yet as we saw in much of the evidence presented in the first half of this chapter, it was a desire for "homecoming" that gave Old Home Weeks and

Commemorations

Old Boys' Reunions much of their meaning. For local residents, these events were an opportunity to tell their story of becoming to themselves through things like written histories, historical pageants, and oral storytelling. The imperative for this was explained in 1905 by one of those residents trying to do just this: "The modern historian ... seeks to give us insight into the social life of the common people, and to make us acquainted with their struggles to better their social, moral, and material condition."[66] Old boys and old girls who came back to town were perceived as making it possible for residents to recover that history and to make it a public memory that would meet the needs of the present. Indeed, the last section of this chapter showed that narratives emphasizing the built environment that occurred after the exodus of the late nineteenth century insisted on the heroism of those who pioneered but especially those who persevered.

This category of "those who persevered" was not, however, applied to everyone who made their home in the Ottawa Valley before and after the exodus. Returning old boys and old girls were reintegrated into the imagined community even though they had moved away. In contrast, Aboriginal and Métis peoples who had stayed, who had persevered in the valley, suffered a very different fate. They were imagined outside the boundaries of local community and place, sometimes in ways that vilified them as "savages" but more often in ways that simply saw them as belonging to the past and to a local world that was no longer there or had gone, like that unnamed Aboriginal woman in the canoe, somewhere else. A similar narrative of disappearance affected working-class men, who were literally removed from the picture of industrial work, hidden behind the modern architectures that cleaned the landscape of its clutter. And despite being so visible within the events of the celebrations, women were far less visible in these representations, consistently framed as helpers to the men who pioneered, who persevered, and who built the modern town. Whether inclusive or exclusive, all of this cultural and historical work was invested in very contemporary politics of place and community. In each of these instances, the effect was to frame the misrepresented and under-represented as peoples without history, as markers rather than makers of place and community.

In their form, in their representations, and in their ambitions, Old Home Weeks and Old Boys' Reunions are therefore perhaps best understood as efforts to come to cultural terms with the structures of modernity as they affected the Ottawa Valley in the late nineteenth and first half of the twentieth centuries. This understanding is in keeping with Homi Bhabha's insistence that a postcolonial approach to "culture" ought to render the concept "as much an uncomfortable, disturbing practice of survival and supplementarity – between art and politics, past and present, the public and the private – as its resplendent being is a moment of pleasure, enlightenment or liberation."[67] Culture-as-practice included all those performances in pageants and parades, whether "on stage" or in the audience, and it also included all the narratives (textual and photographic) that sought to "capture" these events as meaningful encounters between past and present, public and private, pleasure and enlightenment, art and politics. When we take this culture seriously, when we dare to immerse ourselves in "the local," we are able to understand place as a site of mediation in which the "here and now" is produced against and with the "there and then."

There was little in these local cultural productions that could (or can) be reconciled with how rural and small-town Canada was being represented by heritage tourism elsewhere in the country in the first half of the twentieth century. In that context, historians argue, "the folk" who lived in rural and small-town settings were being imagined in a context of antimodernism then emanating from larger industrial and capital cities. In the cultural work of folklorists and tourist promoters, the everyday life of "the folk" was simple and a-historical, a represented source of authenticity in a world of modern artifice.[68] In this view, "the folk" lived, at best, on the margins of modernity's geography. The landscape and location of heritage tourism appears somewhat different, however, from the perspective offered by small towns in the Ottawa Valley. As we saw in this chapter, the memory-work of Old Home Weeks and Old Boys' Reunions represented an everyday life in small towns that was thoroughly historical and as "modern" in purpose and form as that lived in larger cities. This stands, perhaps, as a reminder that we ought to explore the location of culture in places we seem to have forgotten.

All of these conclusions rest not merely on the facts recovered from an archive but also on a willingness to explore how the facts were made and archived, or what, following Greg Dening, we might think of historical facts performed. Such an exploration seeks greater understanding of how the facts were (and are) involved in the making of experiences and identities. Here, I have sought to do this around the practices of ceremonial homecoming that thrived in the Ottawa Valley in the first half of the twentieth century, but I am not alone in doing so. One of the important threads that stretches across the following chapters, but is also picked up and explained in unique and compelling ways, is a focus on how the entanglement of place and memory both draws on and (re)makes the facts of their historical relationship. Rather than a simple reproduction and re-circulation of those facts, something else emerges in these chapters, a perspective that is both critical and respectful of this history. And this is how it should be. In our own encounters with these facts, in our own storytelling performances about place and memory, we cannot sacrifice our critical relationship to the archive; nor should we, however, sever the archive's relationships to those peoples and places who inhabit it.

ACKNOWLEDGMENTS

My thanks to those who suffered through various takes on this material (but also sharpened its focus) at the 2007 Underhill Graduate Student Colloquium, the 2007 Annual Meeting of the Canadian Historical Association, and most directly the 2008 Placing Memory and Remembering Place Workshop. Steven High started all of this more than a decade ago (!) and he continues to set an example. Karen Reyburn, Matt Dyce, Jean Manore, Jess Dunkin, Peter Anderson, and Christine McGuire were among those who read drafts and explained to me what I was saying. In person, on the phone, or via e-mail, I talk with Jim Opp every day, and I regret those days when I do not because I know I have missed a chance to learn something new.

I dedicate this chapter to Greg Dening, the former Jesuit priest then historical ethnographer whose death in March 2008 left not only a legacy of brilliant writing but also a lament for the books we will no longer receive from him.

NOTES

1   This reconstructed scene is based on the coverage provided in the *Ottawa Citizen*, 25 March 1879, and in the *Ottawa Daily Free Press*, 25 March 1879.

2   *Ottawa Daily Free Press*, 17 May 1879.

3   On migration patterns to the Ottawa Valley, see Bruce Elliott, *Irish Migrants in the Canadas: A New Approach* (Montreal and Kingston: McGill-Queen's University Press, 1987); and Chad Gaffield, *Language, Schooling, and Cultural Conflict: The Origins of the French-Language Controversy in Ontario* (Montreal and Kingston: McGill-Queen's University Press, 1987). I examine this colonization project in my "Landscapes of Longing: Colonization and State Formation in Canada West" (PhD diss., Department of History, University of Guelph, 2002).

4 *Ottawa Daily Free Press,* 25 March 1879.

5 *Perth Courier,* 30 June 1905. The language of diaspora, such as "scattered" or "dispersed," was common in this discourse, and it speaks back to the use of "exodus" in the late 1800s.

6 One of these names was always used, sometimes with "Centennial," but the celebrations were identical in structure and purpose. So it was, for example, that the language of "old boys" and "old girls" was used in the context of Old Home Weeks. There was never, however, a mention of an "Old Girls' Reunion" before 1958. (I have also not seen a mention of one in the recent revival of these festivals in the Ottawa Valley.) I found no explicit definition of "old boy" or "old girl," except that it denoted someone who had been born or spent childhood in town. The term was certainly new, as prior to the 1920s it was commonly placed in quotation marks.

7 The most extensive examples of this appeared in the *Perth Courier,* 30 June 1905.

8 It appeared on 2 August 1928. The commercial elements of these celebrations are developed more fully in Françoise Noël, "Old Home Week Celebrations as Tourism Promotion and Commemoration: North Bay, Ontario, 1925 and 1935," *Urban History Review* 37, 1 (2008): 36-47.

9 *Perth Courier,* 30 June 1905.

10 *Souvenir Program Perth Old Home Week* (Perth, 1948).

11 Special editions of newspapers and many of the programs even included "Souvenir" in their titles. Of course, they vied with the wide range of souvenir postcards, flags, plates, and even rugs, which local merchants aggressively advertised for sale. These souvenir newspapers and the programs were the least expensive, however, and likely the most common collectable purchased. Derek Gregory explores a similar process in nineteenth-century tourist travel to Egypt in his "Emperors of the Gaze: Photographic Practices and Productions of Space in Egypt, 1839-1914," in *Picturing Place: Photography and the Geographical Imagination,* ed. Joan M. Schwartz and James Ryan, (London: I.B. Tauris, 2003), 195-225.

12 This insistence on the archive-as-history comes from an admittedly eclectic reading of anthropologies, histories, historical geographies, and social studies of science and technology. See, among others, Ann Laura Stoler, *Along the Archival Grain: Epistemic Anxieties and Colonial Common Sense* (Princeton, NJ: Princeton University Press, 2008); Joan M. Schwartz, "More than 'competent description of an intractably empty landscape': A Strategy for Critical Engagement with Historical Photographs," *Historical Geography* 31 (2003): 105-31; Diane Taylor, *The Archive, The Repertoire: Performing Cultural Memory in the Americas* (Durham, NC, and London: Duke University Press, 2003); Julie Cruikshank, *The Social Life of Stories: Narrative and Knowledge in the Yukon Territory* (Vancouver: UBC Press, 1998); John Law, *Organizing Modernity: Social Order and Social Theory* (Oxford: Blackwell, 1993). See, too, the chapters in this book by Kirsten Emiko McAllister, Steven High, and James Opp.

13 Noël, "Old Home Week"; Michael Woods, "Performing Power: Local Politics and the Taunton Pageant of 1928," *Journal of Historical Geography* 25, 1 (1999): 57-74; Susan J.

Matt, "You Can't Go Home Again: Homesickness and Nostalgia in U.S. History," *Journal of American History* 94, 2 (2007): 469-97.

14 In this regard, see also Christina Burr, *Canada's Victoria Oil Town: The Transformation of Petrolia into a Victorian Community* (Montreal and Kingston: McGill-Queen's University Press, 2006), 189-236.

15 Timothy Mitchell, "The Stage of Modernity," in *Questions of Modernity*, ed. Timothy Mitchell (Minneapolis: University of Minnesota Press, 2000), esp. 16-20. I am also inspired by Michel Foucault, especially his "Truth and Power," in *The Foucault Reader*, ed. Paul Rabinow (New York: Pantheon, 1984), 51-75.

16 The example discussed here was found in "Old Boys' Reunion" folder, Arnprior and District Museum Collection, Arnprior General History, Arnprior and Braeside Archives. The postcard's depiction of an industrial waterfront scene was consistent with the importance accorded lumberman Daniel McLachlin and his descendants in the local history provided in *Official Programme of the Old Boys' Reunion at Arnprior* (Arnprior, 1909).

17 *Lanark Era*, 2 July 1913.

18 *Carleton Place Herald*, 13 August 1924.

19 *Perth Courier*, 30 June 1905.

20 *Lanark Era*, 2 July 1913.

21 *Carleton Place Herald*, 13 August 1924; *The Day by Day Programme: Smiths Falls Old Home Week* (Smiths Falls, 1950).

22 My thinking about these festival spaces has been deeply influenced by Keith Walden, *Becoming Modern in Toronto: The Industrial Exhibition and the Shaping of a Late Victorian Culture* (Toronto: University of Toronto Press, 1997).

23 *Lanark Era*, 9 July 1913.

24 *Carleton Place Herald*, 13 August 1924.

25 *Pembroke Standard-Observer*, 9 August 1928.

26 *Oxford English Dictionary*, s.v. "nostalgia." Matt, "You Can't Go Home Again," 491, offers a brief discussion of the sense of dislocation that returning New Englanders felt in the context of Old Home Weeks held in the early 1900s.

27 Here, I follow an interpretive direction suggested in Mieke Bal, "Introduction," in *Acts of Memory: Cultural Recall in the Present*, ed. Mieke Bal, Jonathan Crewe, and Leo Spitzer (Hanover, NH, and London: University Press of New England, 1999), vii-xvii; Svetlana Boym, *The Future of Nostalgia* (New York: Basic Books, 2001); Annie E. Coombes, *History after Apartheid: Visual Culture and Public Memory in a Democratic South Africa* (Durham, NC: Duke University Press, 2003), esp. 116-48; and Janelle L. Wilson, *Nostalgia: Sanctuary of Meaning* (Lewisburg, PA: Bucknell University Press, 2005).

28 John C. Walsh and Steven High, "Re-thinking the Concept of Community," *Histoire Sociale/Social History* 32, 64 (1999): 255-73.

29 *Perth Courier*, 9 February 1906.

30 *Perth Courier*, 30 June 1905.

31 Schools were a very popular element of these celebrations right through the 1950s. In Smiths Falls in 1950, for example, the program's list of events included "OLD TIME SCHOOL. This will be a highlight of the Old Home Week and you mustn't play hookey. There will be no homework but you should come dressed as you did during your school days." See *Day by Day Programme*.

32 On the Rogers company, see David Glassberg, *American Historical Pageantry: The Uses of Tradition in the Early Twentieth Century* (Chapel Hill: University of North Carolina Press, 1990), 237. All of the details of the Pembroke pageant are from *An Historical Pageant of Pembroke* (Pembroke, 1928). The program was given to audience members and included explanations of each of the scenes in the pageant as well as a list of all of the cast and crew.

33 This incorporation of the translocal into the local is also evident in the French imperial theme so prominent in the image of the float from Almonte's 1929 parade, discussed earlier.

34 *Historical Pageant of Pembroke*, 4.

35 Ibid., 10.

36 Robert Cupido, "Appropriating the Past: Pageants, Politics, and the Diamond Jubilee of Confederation," *Journal of the Canadian Historical Association* 9 (1998): 155-86.

37 In this respect, the Pembroke pageant was even more ambitious than the fusion of two "races" that Earl Grey sought to accomplish through the pageant and celebrations of the 1908 Quebec Tercentenary. See H.V. Nelles, "Historical Pageantry and the 'Fusion of the Races' at the Tercentenary of Quebec, 1908," *Histoire Sociale/Social History* 29 (November 1996): 391-415.

38 The classic statement on this remains Edward Said, *Orientalism* (New York: Vintage Books, 1978), but see also Anne McClintock, *Imperial Leather: Race, Gender, and Sexuality in the Colonial Contest* (New York: Routledge, 1995).

39 *Pembroke Standard-Observer*, 2 August 1928, 22. The quotation "a Country for men of virile races" is attributed to then British prime minister Stanley Baldwin, and although it would imply he was speaking of Ontario specifically (Canada is not mentioned in this advertisement, but there is no explanation provided), I have been unable to locate this quotation anywhere else.

40 This was an archetype that emerged in the American and Canadian Wests but became universalized as a result of Wild West Shows. The woodland peoples who lived in the Ottawa Valley neither appeared in that dress nor adopted those poses (in 1928 or ever), but it was an image incredibly popular and expected by non-Aboriginal audiences by the end of the 1800s.

41 *Historical Pageant of Pembroke*, 5.

42 Ibid., 6.

43 The late-Victorian origins of this desire are brilliantly illuminated in Paige Raibmon, *Authentic Indians: Episodes of Encounter from the Late-Nineteenth-Century Northwest Coast* (Durham, NC: Duke University Press, 2005).

44 *Historical Pageant of Pembroke*, 8.

45 Sarah Carter, *Capturing Women: The Manipulation of Cultural Imagery in Canada's Prairie West* (Montreal and Kingston: McGill-Queen's University Press, 1997).

46 Philip J. Deloria, *Playing Indian* (New Haven: Yale University Press, 1998).

47 Neither the pageant nor this image offers much of the cultural work of "incorporation" that Alan Trachtenberg sees emerging in elite and popular culture in the United States in this period. See his *Shades of Hiawatha: Staging Indians, Making Americans, 1880-1930* (New York: Hill and Wang, 2004). This image does speak, however, to the anachronistic space of indigenous peoples in imperial representations as analyzed in McClintock, *Imperial Leather*, 40-42.

48 Greg Dening, *Performances* (Chicago: University of Chicago Press, 1996), 105.

49 *Day by Day Programme.*

50 See the position of Golden Lake reserve in Figure 1.1. The complex histories of both status and non-status First Nations in the Ottawa Valley cannot be adequately discussed here. An overview is provided in Peter Hessel, *The Algonkin Tribe: The Algonkins of the Ottawa Valley: An Historical Outline* (Arnprior, ON: Kichesippi Books, 1987); and in several chapters in Edward S. Rogers and Donald B. Smith, eds., *Aboriginal Ontario: Historical Perspectives on the First Nations* (Toronto: Dundurn Press, 1994).

51 This quotation is from a headline in the *Pembroke Standard-Observer,* 2 August 1928, 11. Champlain's arrival was endemic to all Ottawa Valley histories of place produced during Old Home Weeks and Old Boys' Reunions.

52 For the Ottawa Valley, this landscaping is especially vivid in H. Belden and Company, *Illustrated Atlas of Lanark County, 1880, Illustrated Atlas of Renfrew County, 1881* (1881; reprint, Owen Sound, ON: Richardson, Bond and Wright, 1972).

53 *Perth Courier,* 30 June 1905.

54 On boosterism in small-town Canada in this period, see Donald G. Wetherell, "Making New Identities: Alberta Small Towns Confront the City, 1900-1950," *Journal of Canadian Studies* 39 (2005): 175-97.

55 *Eganville and District Old Home Week Historical Souvenir* (Eganville, 1948), 2.

56 *Perth Courier,* 30 June 1905.

57 Andrew Haydon, *Pioneer Sketches in the District of Bathurst,* vol. 1 (Toronto: Ryerson Press, 1925), 4. This was the only volume ever completed. Haydon's personal papers include dozens of scrapbooks of nineteenth-century Ottawa Valley newspapers that he culled for his own history. Although I cannot explore the point further in this chapter, his scrapbooks and published history are examples of how these historical narratives circulated and were reproduced. See "Report on Old Boys Reunion, July 2-9 1913," Andrew Haydon Fonds, vol. 4, Library and Archives Canada, MG27-IIIC28.

58 Jim Anable, Philadelphia, "Letter to the Editor," *Carleton Place Herald,* 20 August 1924.

59 *Lanark Era,* 2 July 1913.

60 Ibid.

61 Tim Cresswell, *In Place/Out of Place: Geography, Ideology, and Transgression* (Minneapolis: University of Minnesota Press, 1996), esp. 3-27, 149-62.

62 See, for example, the historical narrative in the *Pembroke Standard-Observer*, 2 August 1928, 10, which provides a number of different heroic men overcoming the forest: a lumberman, a farmer, and a Catholic priest.

63 *Souvenir Program Perth Old Home Week*, 8.

64 David E. Nye, *America as Second Creation: Technology and Narratives of New Beginnings* (Cambridge, MA: MIT Press, 2003).

65 Some important historical work in the United States has in fact followed the white settlers who went west: David M. Wrobel, *Promised Lands: Promotion, Memory, and the Creation of the American West* (Lawrence: University Press of Kansas, 2002); and David Glassberg, "Making Places in California," in *Sense of History: The Place of the Past in American Life* (Amherst: University of Massachusetts Press, 2001), 166-202. See also the discussion in Forrest D. Pass, "'The Wondrous Story and Traditions of the Country': The Native Sons of British Columbia and the Role of Myth in the Formation of an Urban Middle Class," *BC Studies* 151 (2006): 3-38.

66 *Perth Courier*, 30 June 1905.

67 Homi Bhabha, *The Location of Culture* (1994; reprint, New York: Routledge, 2005), 251.

68 See Ian McKay, *The Quest of the Folk: Antimodernism and Cultural Selection in Twentieth-Century Nova Scotia* (Montreal and Kingston: McGill-Queen's University Press, 1994); and Stuart Henderson, "'While There Is Still Time ... ': J. Murray Gibbon and the Spectacle of Difference in Three CPR Folk Festivals, 1928-1931," *Journal of Canadian Studies* 39, 1 (2005): 139-74. My conclusion has strong resonance with that made in Alan Gordon's contribution to this volume.

History and the Six Nations
The Dynamics of Commemoration, Colonial Space, and Colonial Knowledge

CECILIA MORGAN

> I, as Speaker of the Council, have the honor of welcoming you to our Council fires. In the name of the chiefs and warriors of the Six Nations, I bid you welcome ... We welcome you not as strangers, but as brothers whose forefathers fought side by side with ours in the past, in defence of our country – as brothers whose fathers were devoted and loyal through many dangers and difficulties, privations and sorrows to this land and country, and to the throne of Great Britain, our great ally over the water ... We hope to benefit much by the deliberations of your council-meeting today, and we hope that you, in turn, will carry with you to your own homes and people a better knowledge of your red brother, that you will know now that he has benefited by the years of settlement, civilization and educational advantages, and is not behind in the progress of all things good in this country.
>
> – Chief Dehhehnagaraneh, to the Ontario Historical Society's Annual Meeting, Oshweken, June 1898

A pleasing feature of the evening was the presence of three representatives of the Six Nations Indians who proffered their assistance in advancing the interests of the Society ... Chief Hill supported the vote of thanks to Provincial Archivist Alex Fraser, who delivered the talk.

> – Brant Historical Society minutes, 14 April 1910

We are tired of being presented as anthropological studies. We are human beings. We have been the object of years of research and investigation. We have long felt it was more than time to turn the light on the other side.

> – Ethel Brant Monture, Indian Folk School, Petrolia,
> Ontario, 22 March 1964

These three quotations come from different periods: the end of the nineteenth century, the years prior to the outbreak of the First World War, and forty-three years ago. They also were issued in different locations: the Oshweken longhouse, the parlour of a member of Brantford's non-Native middle class, and the Fairbanks historic home in the south-western Ontario town of Petrolia, host to a two-day, all-Native school. And they were issued by different individuals: a hereditary Mohawk chief, the Euro-Canadian secretary of the Historical Society, and Ethel Brant Monture, a Mohawk woman who spent much of her adult life lecturing and writing about the history and contemporary state of affairs of the Six Nations. They bear witness to Euro-Canadians' fascination with Aboriginal peoples, particularly members of the Six Nations, a long-standing social and cultural phenomenon that a number of scholars have documented.[1] They also suggest that, far from being passive recipients of imperial gazes, members of the Six Nations also desired, in Monture's words, to "turn the light on the other side." Through their work in historical societies and their writings and speeches over the course of the twentieth century, various members of the Six Nations presented narratives of Canadian history that claimed it as their own. In doing so, they sought to establish their presence as national subjects in these narratives and to contest the forms of colonial knowledge that placed them outside of the historical time of the nation. However, their commemorative activities were complex, being shaped by a range of social and political attachments, desires, and locations. In particular, the politics of both gender and place complicates our understanding of these narratives.

Scholars of memory and commemoration in North America have acknowledged the centrality of Aboriginal peoples to many of these processes: the ubiquity of symbols and images of Native men, women, and children in various genres and their physical participation in events such as pageants and exhibitions.[2] Although historians have pointed out how little control Native people exercised in such national spectacles of the nation, their research has demonstrated that, no less than their non-Native counterparts, Aboriginal peoples often had their own political and strategic reasons and motivations for being involved in these projects.[3] These discussions have done much to expand our understanding of the racial and imperial dimensions of historical commemoration and have demonstrated the positions from which Native peoples might speak and act. As well as the important work that has been done on large-scale events, such as Samuel de Champlain's tercentenary or the erection of monuments to Ontario's Loyalists, local and individual writings and performances of history also have much to offer us. Shifting our focus from the creation of national narratives on national stages to examine their reception and contestation at the local level helps us to understand the complexity of history as a form of social knowledge: it has been intertwined with colonial projects and used to buttress relationships of power while simultaneously being used to negotiate with and, at times, counteract colonialism. The Six Nations, although forced to engage with the nation-state, produced historical ways of knowing that simultaneously challenged its borders, not least because of the particular place from which this work emanated.[4]

The specificities of the Six Nations' history and its context facilitated the creation of such narratives and made them available to non-Native historians.[5] Founded in 1784 on the banks of the Grand River on land purchased by the Crown from the Ojibwa Mississauga, the community was created out of the dispersal of Iroquois people by the American Revolution; it became home to members of the Six Nations Confederacy (Mohawk, Cayuga, Onondaga, Seneca, Oneida, and Tuscarora) and a number of Delawares, Nanticokes, Tutelos, Creeks, and Cherokees. In 1847 the Mississaugas, their tenure to their lands on the Credit River threatened by the colonial government, were invited by the Six Nations to move to the Grand River, where they formed the New Credit reserve.[6] While the reserve was not without tensions and problems brought about by the Dominion government's colonial policies, its members exercised a considerable amount of control over their affairs and enjoyed a much higher level of economic prosperity than did many other Aboriginal communities in late nineteenth- and twentieth-century Canada.[7] By the 1890s the Six Nations was a community with prolonged contact with Europeans; many from both sides of the reserve boundaries were well aware of this history. Nineteenth- and twentieth-century transportation networks – first trains, then cars – linked the Grand River reserve to nearby Brantford but also to Toronto, Buffalo, and other parts of New York State. Ethnographers and archaeologists, both from Canada and the United States, were drawn to the reserve for their research; when the Ontario Historical Society's secretary and provincial archaeologist, David Boyle, became interested in conducting fieldwork on Native societies, he turned to the Six Nations.[8] Such conditions facilitated contact with Euro-Canadians in the Ontario Historical Society (OHS) and the Brant Historical Society (BHS).

Between 1897 and 1911 the Six Nations and the OHS maintained an ongoing relationship, one marked by the confederacy's desire to see its history with Britain and Canada honoured and recognized and by the society's fascination with the community's artefacts and archaeological sites. Members of the Six Nations attended OHS meetings as delegates, and the community became an official affiliate of the society, hosting part of its 1898 meeting at Oshweken and adopting the OHS president, David Williams, in a ceremony at Oshweken in 1911.[9] OHS members consistently expressed their admiration for the Six Nations' courtesy, oratory, and dignity; they also praised the "evidence of prosperity and progress" attested to by the Six Nations' homes, farms, churches, and schools, spaces that "manifested a determination to keep pace with modern times." The Six Nations could be justly proud of their history, for which they had "the sincere and heartfelt appreciation of their brother Canadians from end to end of this fair country."[10] For their part, Six Nations delegates not only agreed with such assessments but took them one step further to call for more dramatic political change. Chief Nelles Montour (Delaware), an OHS executive committee member, told the society in 1898 that his people's history, record of loyalty to the Crown, and well-ordered affairs warranted the appointment of an Iroquois superintendent of the reserve: "Among ourselves and of our own blood, there are men capable of filling the position with credit and dignity."[11]

Matters went further in 1911, when Chief W.M. Elliott asked the OHS to support the confederacy's fight for legal equality, citing the long-standing history of "systematic government" that had produced an "Indian empire" before Christopher Columbus's arrival, followed by a history of support for Britain during the latter's time of need. That support in 1776 had led to the loss of their territories, a loyal service that Britain had recognized with treaties that the Dominion government was now infringing upon, robbing them of their rights, treating Six Nations men as children, and lumping the Six Nations in with all other Canadian Indians, an insult that took no notice of their distinct and unique history with the Crown and British Empire: "If the Six Nations chiefs and warriors were men enough to fight for Canada and the supremacy of the British crown upon this North American continent ... why should the legislation of this country now place them in the category of minors?" Elliott concluded by asking the OHS to "use its influence in advocating [the Six Nations'] cause," appealing to them as fellow descendants of the United Empire Loyalists, men who were "comrades in arms in the fighting time." He entreated, "let us today fraternize as common brothers in peace and endeavour to accord to all the freedom which the British constitution grants us all under the British flag."[12]

Elliott's request for the OHS's support cannot have come as a complete surprise to its members. Over the course of the past two decades, the previous president, James Coyne, and his colleagues had opened up the possibility of such discussions, with statements such as "to the Red, as well as the white, loyalists is due the credit which belongs to those who preserved Canada as an integral portion of the great empire."[13] Other members of the Six Nations, such as the Mohawk lecturer, historian, and performer John Ojijatekha Brant-Sero, had stated that their people's historical record legitimated a distinct national status within the British Empire, a position of alliance with, not subjection to, imperial power.[14] However, the delegates voted to steer clear of this potentially contentious issue, arguing that their constitution prevented them from discussing political matters. After 1911 the Six Nations allowed their membership in the OHS to lapse.[15]

Yet even though they might have renounced formal affiliation with the society, the OHS's caution did not prevent certain individuals from continuing such contact. In 1922 Asa Hill, the secretary of the Six Nations Council, presented a paper to the OHS entitled "The Historical Position of the Six

— apart of official history

Nations," in which he repeated the points made by his predecessors: the history of the Five Nations Confederacy, the specific position of the Iroquois in colonial conflicts, the Six Nations' ability to preserve their traditions, and the Crown's recognition of the confederacy's "rights and sovereignty." Hill cited treaties of the late seventeenth and eighteenth centuries to prove his point and to establish that the confederacy and Crown's relationship existed well into the nineteenth and twentieth centuries and was underscored by the War of 1812 alliance and by the Six Nations' presence "in the awful scenes on Flanders fields."[16]

Thus Hill's paper must be seen as part of an ongoing argument in which "history" was critical in legitimating certain forms of government and the Six Nations' contemporary control over their affairs. To be sure, like his predecessors involved with the OHS, Hill saw the history of Six Nations-British relations not simply as a narrative of the former being brought to Euro-Canadian civilization and nationhood by the latter, with the accoutrements and signs of progress such as schools, churches, and those "neat farms" so beloved by the OHS. Such was the "history" produced by Euro-Canadians about Native peoples, whom they saw as being on the path to enfranchisement, the final act of incorporation into the Canadian nation.[17] Rather, Hill's narrative reversed the customary tropes of progress and enlightenment often favoured by non-Natives in English Canada.[18] "History" was not something that had merely occurred to the Six Nations, nor was the latter's past a burden of superstition and ignorance. Instead, it was a liberating and protective force, one in which they had been historical actors in the various theatres of war in which the modern Canadian nation had been staged: the War of 1812 and, in particular, the First World War. Moreover, these performances had been critically important sites in which Iroquois masculinity had been proven and reaffirmed, in forms both "traditional" and "modern," to be one of dedication to both the Six Nations' community and the Canadian nation.

However, the events of the war that Hill celebrated and the context in which he wrote his narrative suggest, as James Opp and John Walsh point out in the introduction to this volume, that "conditions of place have shaped acts of memory." The Six Nations' service in the First World War became a matter of contestation on the reserve, to no small extent as a result of conflicting interpretations of past practices and local political positions. During the war a number of men had served under the Dominion government's command.

Their volunteering sparked much acrimony between different groups on the reserve, as the hereditary council did not believe the men should have answered any recruitment call not issued by the Six Nations. At the time Hill delivered his paper, the tensions that had been brewing before the war over the hereditary system of government versus an elected council were about to erupt openly. In 1923 the Cayuga chief Deskeheh (Levi General) travelled to Europe to argue the Six Nations' sovereignty case before the League of Nations; the following year, the Royal Canadian Mounted Police arrived at the Oshweken council-house to seize the Six Nations' wampum and council records and to announce the first band election.[19]

Nevertheless – and somewhat ironically – continuous and long-standing attempts to include the history of the Six Nations as part of the "national" narrative were more successful at the local, not the provincial or national, level. Founded in 1908, the Brant Historical Society (BHS) specialized both in the history of Euro-Canadian "settlement" of the area and in the history of Native-white contact at the Grand River. Indeed, from its inception, the society did more than just demonstrate an interest in the Six Nations' history, for it built much of its identity on the premise of its "authority" on such issues.[20] At times, the society's pronouncements and actions were tinged with imperial paternalism: in 1913, for example, it expressed concern for the safety of the artefacts housed in the Mohawk chapel, and in 1918 it formed a committee to investigate the education of Native children in their own history, a suggestion that did not consider that they might have been learning their history from their parents and elders through oral histories and ceremonies.[21] However, on a number of occasions, the society supported the Six Nations in their opposition to federal initiatives and lobbied the federal government to take better care of important commemorative sites of the Six Nations' history.[22] Moreover, members of the Six Nations themselves claimed the BHS as a place in which their versions of history could be presented and discussed. Over the course of the 1930s, a number of individuals from the reserve had begun to attend BHS meetings, presenting papers, performing musical solos, and participating in historical pageants.[23] By 1937 Six Nations members also sat on the executive, and by 1941 Elliott Moses, a Delaware, was the society's vice-president; two years later he became its president, a post he held for the next decade.[24]

Although the records of the BHS show evidence of this increased participation by members of the Six Nations, they say little – at least explicitly – about the racial dynamics and consequences of these encounters between Natives and Euro-Canadians. I wonder, however, whether the latter were prodded to rethink what might have been understandings of colonial relations, Native inferiority, and the "natural" decline of Native cultures and society. For one, non-Native audiences were frequently reminded of the Six Nations' history, the fact that they could lay claim to an organized system of government, one in which women had participated and one that had only recently ended on the reserve.[25] Moreover, members of the Six Nations appeared both as constituents of the society and as representatives of their own nation/s. The number of times that they claimed both territories simultaneously may have helped to dislodge whites' notions that Native peoples, literally and metaphorically, occupied only their reserves. Instead, they came to sit in their Brantford neighbours' parlours and the library meeting rooms, wearing suits and dresses, discussing historical issues and participating in administrative matters. At other times, they assumed Native "traditional" clothing for recitations of Pauline Johnson's poetry or performances of historical pageants staged on the reserve.[26] Thus, despite the efforts of the federal government to delineate spaces neatly as "Indian" and "white," such boundaries were permeable under particular conditions, even though both parties might well have approached and negotiated them with degrees of hesitation and apprehension. Might it have been more difficult in such circumstances to see these members of the Six Nations as belonging to a "dying race" or as inhabiting, in Anne McClintock's phrase, "anachronistic space," removed from the temporality of modernity?[27]

Of course, it would also have been easy to see the Six Nations as "exceptional Indians" or assimilated, bearing a few vestiges of their history, but having been so changed by their exposure to Western cultural norms they no longer resembled "authentic" or "traditional" Indians. Certainly, some of the BHS's reports hinted at this attitude. A 1931 talk given by Reverend Snell on the Mohawk Institute, for example, told members how 2,000 Indians "had profited by its training." Snell also praised the institute for its foresight in investing over $1 million in education and missionary work that had raised the "local Indians" well above "the average of Indian mentality."[28] However, the Six Nations' BHS members and speakers countered this discourse and, like their predecessors in the OHS, asked the society for support for their separate status. At their January meeting in 1951, Arnold Moses (Delaware) spoke about the "effect of modern culture on Indian life and outlined the attitude of the

Indian people to the proposed new Indian act." The Canadian government, Moses argued, was trying to abolish reserves, meaning that "Indians" were faced with either "living as a separate social structure or going out into the world and competing with the white man and being absorbed and losing their identities. This they had no wish to do." Moses acknowledged the government's provision of social welfare, medical, and legal services, but his message concerning assimilation was clear. The society thanked him for his "thought-provoking address" and passed a resolution to write to the minister of citizenship and immigration, demanding that "Indians must be consulted" before any changes were made to their treaties.[29]

The BHS, then, represented a space where Natives and non-Natives claimed an overlapping and at times shared history, one tied to the reserve, to the nation, and to imperial and transnational settings. For non-Native historians, the nearby Six Nations reserve could be claimed as an intrinsically interesting space, an exotic attraction that brought educated outsiders to the area. It also served to remind themselves and others of Brantford's lengthy history, both national and imperial: it could not be dismissed as merely another small Ontario city with a history and landscape fundamentally interchangeable with that of other, similar communities. For the Six Nations, however, local history was a narrative that was intimately and inextricably tied to that of multiple nations and empires, one that intermingled with the narratives of their non-Native neighbours but that also spoke to other territories and other conceptions of nationhood. These were not the abstract constructs of nation and empire that have marked much of the scholarship on commemoration, nor were they invoked in ways that simply reinscribed power and reinforced political boundaries.[30] Instead, as we shall see, Six Nations historians argued that national and imperial histories had been marked by the nation-state's failure to uphold treaties and by its imposition of the Indian Act, both of which affected the contemporary lived experiences of the Grand River residents on an ongoing, daily basis.

As well as the more collective and collaborative work in commemoration of the BHS, individual members of the community also argued throughout the twentieth century for the importance of historical knowledge, albeit from a range of perspectives. This group included historians and performers Ethel Brant Monture and Bernice Loft, who, as I have argued elsewhere, strove to establish Native peoples' central place within narratives of the modern

Canadian nation while simultaneously insisting on the significance of Native cultural practices and traditions.[31] As well as Monture and Loft, Native men such as Elliott Moses pondered the need for historical knowledge and produced work that engaged with such narratives.[32]

Whereas Monture believed that her community's history was one of progress, in which the Iroquois (and especially the Mohawk) had taken up various aspects of Euro-Canadian society to be incorporated within Mohawk identity, Moses' perspectives on these matters were more fractured and shifting.[33] Born at the Six Nations reserve in 1888, the second-oldest son in a family of eight boys and two daughters, Moses' father, Nelson, was a Delaware, his mother an Irish-Canadian housemaid at the reserve's Anglican rectory. Moses followed his father in becoming a farmer, although prior to taking up farming in 1917 he attended Guelph's Ontario College of Agriculture. Director of the Ontario Plowman's Association for thirty-nine years, Moses travelled to Britain in 1949 with the Ontario Champion Plowmen and held a number of positions in the Six Nations' agricultural associations. As well as his work in agriculture, Moses was the inspector of soldier-settlers and the estate clerk in Brantford's Indian Office and chairman of the Ontario Provincial Indian Advisory Committee. Throughout his life, then, Moses occupied and claimed a number of places: on the reserve, within the nearby institutions of the Canadian nation-state, and on an international stage.

But in doing so, Moses also crafted positions on Native history and Native identity – particularly the relationship of the Six Nations to the Canadian nation-state – that were, to say the least, complex and in many ways contradictory. Like Monture, Moses argued that the Six Nations were a "progressive" people and had a history of which they should be proud. Their past both affirmed their contributions to the Canadian nation-state and demonstrated that they had advanced by learning from Europeans: they could not be denigrated as "primitive savages."[34] To be sure, Moses also attacked the Indian Act and its provisions as "perfectly racist," as it placed Indians in an inferior category and freed them from the obligations and responsibilities of first-class citizens: they were not held responsible for debts owed to non-Natives, reserve land was exempt from taxes and could not be used as collateral, and they could not have liquor stores or warehouses on reserves. Moreover, the Act was frequently administered improperly to Native peoples' detriment, as when illegal timber cutting on the Six Nations reserve had led to the "decimation" of the reserve's stands. "The whole Indian Act with more than one hundred clauses causes Indians to feel they are nothing more than tenants of the department of Indian affairs," Moses declared, rather than national subjects with a clear stake in their homes and country.[35]

In this and in many other speeches and articles, Moses insisted that the Act mapped out Aboriginal peoples' lives from "cradle to grave," a form of racial discrimination that "separated them from all other citizens giving them an inferior rating compared to all other ethnic groups of Canada." To be sure, Moses was not alone in his disdain for the Act; for many Aboriginal peoples, it symbolized the Canadian state's domination over them, right down to its definition of "Indian" status. But for Moses, the problem with the Act was that it denied Aboriginal peoples the advantages and benefits of "white" society, not their Native history and communities. The Act created distinct and distinctly inferior spaces for Native people, ones in which they were denied access to other spaces, such as educational institutions, businesses, or new types of families, that might have improved their lives. Little or no consideration, he charged, was given "to the future advancement that might be made in copying and successfully mastering the white man's way of life."[36]

As this passage suggests, Moses' public critiques of Native-white relations in Canada were based on a liberalism that believed in equal treatment to produce equal results. He had little sympathy, particularly by the 1950s and 1960s, for other Native writers and activists who called for a different and special status for Aboriginal peoples, calling their work a "waste of time and energy," for they were based on notions of a way of life impossible to restore. Moses had particularly harsh words for those "non-Indian organizations" – the media, church and service groups, and women's clubs – whose members were "gullible and seemingly willing to believe ridiculous reports of the filth and poverty across Canada" on reserves; in many of his speeches, Moses went to great lengths to deny that all Native people were living in such conditions. Rather, the key to "Indian" success was education and integration, including intermarriage: "We find Indians working side by side, with non-Indians, many having come from the old land and possessing a very different national background by working together [and] sharing each other's tasks day by day." Such a state of affairs, Moses claimed, "causes them to accept each other on a human basis as fellow men and citizens, thereby helping to destroy one of the world's greatest curses, that of racial discrimination[,] and replaces it with a quality of true pride and loyalty, to their country which grants them equal rights and privileges and a standard of living second to none in the whole world."[37]

Moses may well have been influenced by the growing civil rights discourse of the post–Second World War decades. But his thoughts on equality for Native peoples may also have been affected by an earlier eugenic discourse and knowledge of recent history, when eugenics in both Europe and Canada had been used to define who was and who was not a first-class citizen. Repeatedly, Moses stated that any problems that "Indians" might face were cultural, not the result of biological inferiority. Here, Native history (sometimes understood as that of the Six Nations, sometimes meant to include a variety of First Nations) was deployed in a number of ways to counter any suspicion of biological determination. "History" demonstrated that the Six Nations had had their own system of government prior to European contact and their own beliefs, languages, and values. However, Native societies (at least the more "advanced" ones) had not stood still but had evolved, a state of affairs that all must emulate since "for Indian people, to stand still means stagnation whereas progress and enlightenment means [sic] cultural development." Although government and non-Natives must shoulder their fair share of the blame for the problems that did exist, it was up to Native peoples to exercise their agency and move forward.[38]

Time and again, Moses stressed that there was no reason why this happy state of affairs could not come to pass, particularly with education. He suggested that those "Indians" who believed that "Indians think differently to non-Indians and should not be disturbed in their natural thinking and ... advocate that due to this fact Indian children should be taught differently in school" were mistaken.[39] But Moses also denounced non-Natives and the government for their opposition to Native teachers. In a 1968 address delivered to the Waterloo Historical Society, Moses told his audience that it was crucial that Natives take charge of their children's education: "In spite of the fact that missionaries on the reserve and other interested non-Indians claimed the system of Indians teaching Indians would be a failure, the very opposite is true and the system has proven to be a complete success." Out of thirty-five teachers, only three or four were non-Indian. "This underrating and lack of confidence by non-Indian people in the capabilities of Indians has always been and still is [the] thinking of seemingly intelligent non-Indian people who view Indians racially."[40]

Moses did not go unchallenged by other First Nations. In December 1960 a writer named Big White Owl criticized him for his depiction of reserves as backwaters that should be eradicated. Moses, Big White Owl charged, was born and raised on a reserve "and owes everything that he is and ever will be, to his Indian ancestry." Furthermore, Moses probably did not know that "he and his family had been living under a borrowed name for the last century," as his proper ancestral name is Stonefish. Rather than sniping at reserves and their residents, Big White Owl contended, he should have proposed the creation of an all-Indian province, with its own government, premier, and federal representatives in Ottawa: "He would have been introducing a real ultramodern idea that makes sense and his people probably would have agreed with him."[41]

"Not Quite White," a piece published in the *Brantford Expositor*, also disagreed with Moses' attitude toward Native tradition and culture. "His arguments have always indicated an attitude of compromise, on any subjects pertaining to people of our race," wrote this author, who, despite having been brought up to respect elders, reluctantly broke with tradition on this point. "Indian tradition and culture are beautiful and wholesome, with the power to teach whites much about humility, gratitude, and reverence. I am amazed that a person of Mr. Moses' ripe years should be so naive as to think we can solve the Indian problem by integration when integration means, 'no Indians, no problem.'"[42] There are suggestions in these rebuttals of Moses that he was simply behind the times, that his position represented an older, more accommodating stance that did not speak to 1960s Native nationalism.[43] Talk of integration may have seemed incongruous during a decade when Aboriginal people were increasingly publicly celebrating Native identities and histories.

To be sure, Moses' defence of Native peoples on the grounds of their capacities and intelligence challenged the Canadian state's paternalism toward them, a point that his critics did not point out. Moreover, by crafting these narratives of the Six Nations' history and placing men such as himself at their centre, Moses was participating in a form of discourse with its own particular history. His deployment of history, both to counter and to participate in colonial knowledge of Native people, had its antecedents in the work of Native historians and activists such as Peter Jones or George Copway, men who, like Moses, moved across a number of boundaries and inhabited multiple places in nineteenth-century colonial society.[44] Even his activities within the BHS suggest the degree to which Moses fashioned himself as a link between

Native and non-Native histories and spaces, as he spoke on and introduced topics that covered both the Six Nations' history and their contemporary experiences at the Grand River and across Canada.[45] Moses' perception of his role was, perhaps, best symbolized by the part he played in the Grand River pageant held to mark the bicentennial of William Johnson's arrival in America, when he translated the various languages used by Native actors in their re-enactment of an eighteenth-century council meeting for the large – and, according to the press, international – non-Native audience.[46] Two years later, Moses was credited with organizing a display of "Indian handicrafts" at Toronto's Canadian National Exhibition, one meant to demonstrate the range of skills Native Canadians had displayed in order to "work their way" off relief and out of dependency during the Depression (see Figure 2.1). And, like Jones, Moses' mixed-race background – albeit in his case a Native father and white mother – may also have shaped his choices of political tools and strategies.

But there was more to these debates than the issue of Native acquiescence to dominant definitions of "Canadian" national identity versus distinct and separate "Indian nation(s)." Moses' repudiation of the "traditional" form of the Six Nations' governance and his recognition of the Canadian nation-state's sovereignty also were shaped by the politics of gender and an acceptance of Euro-Canadian gendered norms, particularly as they related to Native women's role in shaping both time and place, lineage and land, in choosing hereditary chiefs. To be sure, Moses was careful not to denigrate the role of Iroquois women as clan matrons and believed that they had selected morally upright, honest, and temperate men. As well, the matrons could unseat a chief if he did not live up to the position's requirements. However, Moses did not believe that the clan matrons had any "special qualifications ... other than that I assume they would be selected from well known families." Moreover, although the hereditary system had worked well "so long as the Six Nations were a nomadic people" (particularly important because "no educational standards were required"), a more "progressive" system of government was needed once they settled at the Grand River and became farmers and wage earners.[47]

Moses did not state explicitly that a government ran by women and answerable to them – which is how he understood the hereditary system – was a "retarding" factor in the Iroquois' progress. However, it does not take much of a logical leap to note that his understandings of progressivism and modernity

ONTARIO INDIANS COME TO EXHIBITION TO DEMONSTRATE THEIR NEW INDEPENDENCE

Figure 2.1 "Ontario Indians come to exhibition to demonstrate their new independence." Elliott Moses' photo is in the top-right corner; he's described as one of the organizers of this demonstration. The other figures are Abby Schuyler (with loom), Arnold Moses (with violin), and Chief Little Bear George Green, from the Six Nations. *Source: Toronto Daily Star,* 23 August 1939. Courtesy of Toronto Reference Library, Toronto Public Library.

were gendered. Elected governments would be composed of educated Native men who, in the context of the 1924 election, had attained their offices with the direct intervention of the Dominion government, itself implicated in stripping Aboriginal women of their political status and history, thus insisting on their dependency on men, both Aboriginal and non-Native. Furthermore,

Moses' account of the "push" for elected government made much of the role of those Six Nations men who had volunteered during the First World War (albeit with the support of their mothers and sisters "at home"). As loyal soldiers, they had had a "right" to proper, progressive political representation, for it was these men who saw that the more enlightened and contemporary solution was a "democratic" government, in which there was no hidden, feminine influence.[48]

And Moses seems to have made no secret of his father's public condemnation of the hereditary council on precisely that point. In 1908 Nelson Moses was summoned before the council concerning the publication of "verses of a libelous manner entitled 'To the Chiefs,'" which had appeared in the *Haldimand Banner*. In this poem, Moses made frequent references to the "rusty chiefs, all born that way, your grannies say, you must obey," who, "like the ancient Sanhedrin," had no judgment, "for granny's choice, and granny's pride, rules a nation." The poem ended with advice and expressed the author's hopes:

> We long to see their places filled
> With men of judgment and self-willed
> Men who love a civilization
> Progressive things for the nation.
> The time is come, the change is near
> Warriors brave – you must not fear
> Strike for your rights and rest you not;
> Strike sir! While the iron is hot
> Go back ye chiefs to your grandmas
> For your advice and for your cause;
> Can you not see the toscin knell
> Pealing forth the chief's farewell.[49]

Thus, for Six Nations men, abnegating the past meant embracing a newly independent and "civilized" form of masculinity, a militant and progressive gender role in which elderly women did not make decisions of both local and national importance. As well as Elliott Moses' understanding of modern political governance on the Six Nations reserve, his conceptions of Six Nations society prior to the Iroquois' arrival at the Grand River were also shaped by conceptions of gender relations and roles. As a farmer who was active in various agricultural associations, and who often spoke proudly of the Six Nations' agricultural achievements, Moses frequently described the latter as a fairly recent phenomenon. Raising bountiful crops and tending healthy livestock was, he often argued, a feature of Six Nations society learned from Euro-Canadians. Here again, however, was a new meaning of Iroquois masculinity, as Moses insisted that "his people" were "naturally" inclined to the hunt. However, Six Nations men had often superseded their instructors, becoming hard-working, successful men who had disciplined themselves to the land and, despite the racist limits imposed on them by the Indian Act, had also become successful men of property, owners of implements, seeds, and livestock.[50] In Moses' discourse on Native "advancement," then, these men were indistinguishable from their white, male counterparts whose farms lay just beyond the reserve's borders.

Such a vision of progress through changing gender relations was, of course, not confined to Moses; it had been precisely the policy of the Dominion government and the vast majority of missionaries who worked among Aboriginal peoples, particularly in residential schools.[51] But what is also surprising in reading Moses' version of narratives of socio-economic (and, of course, political) change among the Iroquois peoples is his complete omission of women's role in agriculture and their influence in shaping the local landscape. In his particular "national narrative," the confederacy's members survived on hunting and trapping, not because of Iroquois women's work in planting, cultivating, harvesting, and distributing squash, beans, and corn (as well as other fruits and vegetables). Their work is completely absent in his narratives of his peoples' history. Thus the motor of progressive change, in Moses' view, was masculine: Native men gave up their hunting, fishing, and trapping and instead adapted to an entirely new means of subsistence, that of the farmer – with the happy result that subsistence became surplus, a surplus that, although he rarely made the point explicitly, was also controlled by men. The "grannies" who drew Nelson Moses' scorn could not be historical actors in this narrative of the "modern" Iroquois nation.

To be sure, there were times when Moses expressed an admiration for existing patterns of "traditional" Iroquois culture. He frequently lectured on the longhouse peoples, believing that non-Native Canadians should receive the correct view of their religious beliefs and practices. Six to seven hundred people on the Six Nations reserve belonged to this group; the Great Spirit was their supreme being, who taught them to live upright and honest lives, to perform religious dances, and to mark the year's agricultural changes with festivals. Elliott Moses described these events with great respect, adding that "through their religion, the Long House people have kept our traditional Indian dances alive and authentic. Now many of us Christian Indians are concerned about the Long House religion dying out, for, should this be the case, our Indian dances would soon be gone forever." He argued that most of the longhouse members had been integrated into the rest of the reserve's industry, recreation, and social life. Over time, they would embrace Christianity, a process that would not pose many problems, given their existing worship of a power believed to control the universe. But Moses ended this speech on a note more wistful, more ambiguous, and possibly more defiant than in many of his other talks to non-Native audiences:

> In many respects it seems unfortunate that the Indian has to sacrifice most of his culture in accepting the non-Indian way of life. In closing I recall a story which has a bearing on such conditions. An old Indian said, "When white man come to our country we had great forests, lots of wild game and fish. White man, he kill all game, take all fish out of the river and lake; then he go away. Soon he come back. He cut down big trees – big trees all gone. He start to cut small trees. Trees, game, furs, fish now all gone; he go away for a long time. Now, 'by gosh,' he come back for rock." How true this is from an Indian point of view.[52]

Despite Moses' eagerness to point to the ways that historical changes had produced new types of spaces within the Grand River Territory – churches, productive farms worked by male heads of households, and European-style homes presided over by wives and mothers – he could not entirely detach himself from the space of the longhouse, one in which gender relations were configured differently from his mapping of political space.

Moreover, Moses would discover that his rejection of Iroquois gender relations, particularly the concept of matrilineal descent, would directly affect his own family's residency on the Six Nations reserve. The elected council refused Moses' daughter, Ethel Rose, and her two children permission to remain in her parents' home on the reserve, as she had married a non-Native man and had been struck off the band's list. Although public speculation attributed the council's decision to Moses' lack of popularity within certain sectors of the community, the Indian Act's excision of Native women married to non-Native husbands from official treaty status also underpinned and, in the eyes of the state, legitimated the council's decision.[53]

Asa Hill claimed that the Six Nations did not operate under the "uncertainty and doubt" suffered by their North American Indian counterparts. And certainly, the narratives presented by members of the community reiterated that the Six Nations' participation in the forging of "Canada" and the maintenance of the imperial tie had been marked by confidence, honour, and dignity, qualities with, as I have suggested, a distinctly gendered dimension. But Elliott Moses' just-cited description of the relationship between place and time – the changes in a landscape brought about by Europeans' depredations – also warrants consideration as part of this narrative, particularly since many of the Six Nations' historians who engaged with non-Native audiences left such depredations unsaid, creating gaps and absences that haunted the telling of more celebratory narratives and performances of history. The historic places claimed and honoured by members of the Six Nations were both intensely local – the chapel of the Mohawks, the Oshweken Council House, the Grand River Territory itself – but they also were intimately tied to and produced by more remote geographies shaped by histories of imperial expansion and conflict, marked by loss and suffering: the Mohawk Valley, Upper Canadian battlefields of 1812, or the overseas theatres of the First World War. And national, transcontinental, and transatlantic conflicts also had left their mark on the Grand River Territory, whether through the actions of poachers and squatters who had encroached on the community's resources, the damages suffered at the hands of the Grand River Navigation Company, the conflicts between community members over forms of government (elected vs. hereditary), or tensions over the participation of Six Nations men in the Canadian forces.

Moreover, the absence of the Mississaugas' narratives from the BHS files – a subject that warrants its own treatment – suggests that their presence at the New Credit reserve attracted very little attention in comparison to that accorded the Six Nations. Such an absence underscores the need, as Arif Dirlik has pointed out, for us to consider that places are more than "locations of inherited inequalities and oppressions," as "the struggle over history" may also take place between colonized peoples themselves, not just colonizer and colonized.[54]

The Six Nations' remembrances of place thus suggest the need for a more nuanced perspective, one that bridges those commemorative processes pre-occupied with narratives of nation-states and, in turn, indigenous forms of memory focused primarily on local spaces and their temporalities.[55] Although both approaches have been extremely significant in demonstrating the power of nation-states and the ability of colonized peoples to resist them, they do not entirely capture how complicated identifications with both colonial powers and indigenous agency, ones in which were mingled strength and loss, pride and mourning, might structure these narratives. As we have seen, members of the confederacy insisted on their inclusion in official commemorations of Canadian nationalism while simultaneously arguing that their participation necessitated that "nation" be understood in more intricate ways, ones that emanated from and incorporated places beyond the boundaries of the nation. To be sure, I do not want to suggest that they wished to completely dissolve the political boundaries of mid-twentieth-century Canada. Rather, as Dirlik argues more generally about colonized peoples' conceptions of time and place, they may well have believed that a return to the Mohawk Valley or "to a past that was constructed" in that place was no longer possible but that neverthe-less the past could be mobilized for future projects "in place-based ways."[56] Moreover, as we have seen, the political specificities of a history lived "in place" could make these claims with very different valences and visions of those future projects. Certainly, Elliott Moses believed that certain aspects of his peoples' past could serve to shape future places for them in the so-called "mainstream" of Canadian society. Others, however, used conceptions of time and place, past and present, to call for a vision of Canada that would create new places and new futures for the Six Nations.

NOTES

Epigraphs: "Epitome of Chief Deh-ka-nen-ra-neh's Speech," *Ontario Historical Society (OHS) Report* (1899), 41; Minute Book 1, 4 April 1910, Brant Historical Society Records (BHSR), Brant County Historical Museum; "Indian Folk School 'Unqualified Success,'" *London Free Press,* 22 March 1964, n.p.

1 See Robert F. Berkhofer Jr., *The White Man's Indian* (New York: Random House, 1979); Daniel Francis, *The Imaginary Indian: The Image of the Indian in Canadian Culture*

(Vancouver: Arsenal Pulp Press, 1992); Philip J. Deloria, *Playing Indian* (New Haven, CT: Yale University Press, 1998); Paige Raibmon, *Authentic Indians: Episodes of Encounter from the Late-Nineteenth-Century Northwest Coast* (Durham, NC: Duke University Press, 2005).

2   H.V. Nelles, *The Art of Nation-Building: Pageantry and Spectacle at Quebec's Tercentenary* (Toronto: University of Toronto Press, 1999); Norman Knowles, *Inventing the Loyalists: The Ontario Loyalist Tradition and the Creation of Usable Pasts* (Toronto: University of Toronto Press, 1997); Peter Geller, "'Hudson's Bay Company Indians': Images of Native People and the Red River Pageant, 1920," in *Dressing in Feathers: The Construction of the Indian in American Popular Culture,* ed. S. Elizabeth Bird (Boulder, CO: Westview Press, 1996), 65-78; Kathryn McPherson, "Carving Out a Past: The Canadian Nurses' Association War Memorial," *Histoire sociale/Social History* 29, 58 (November 1996): 418-29.

3   Nelles, *Art of Nation-Building,* 172-81; Geller, "'Hudson's Bay Company Indians,'" 68-73; Knowles, *Inventing the Loyalists,* 123-25; Raibmon, *Authentic Indians,* ch. 3.

4   The Six Nations' situation can be contrasted and compared with that of the Toba of Argentina, of whom Gastón Gordillo has written that "the spatial product of their immersion within a capitalist political economy, the bush, is also the place where they carved out relative shelter from it"; see his *Landscape of Devils: Tensions of Place and Memory in the Argentinean Chaco* (Durham, NC, and London: Duke University Press, 2004), 2. For the use of historical knowledge within colonial projects, see Dipesh Chakrabarty, *Provincializing Europe: Postcolonial Thought and Historical Difference* (Princeton, NJ: Princeton University Press, 2000); and Cheryl Walker, *Indian Nation: Native American Literature and Nineteenth-Century Nationalisms* (Durham, NC: Duke University Press, 1997), 13-23.

5   Sally M. Weaver, "The Iroquois: The Consolidation of the Grand River Reserve in the Mid-Nineteenth Century, 1847-1875," and "The Iroquois: The Grand River Reserve in the Late Nineteenth and Early Twentieth Centuries, 1875-1945," both in *Aboriginal Ontario: Historical Perspectives on the First Nations,* ed. Edward S. Rogers and Donald B. Smith (Toronto: Dundurn Press, 1994), 182-212 and 213-57.

6   Weaver, "Iroquois: The Consolidation"; Carl Benn, *The Iroquois in the War of 1812* (Toronto: University of Toronto Press, 1998), 19.

7   Weaver, "Iroquois: The Consolidation," 182.

8   Gerald Killan, *Preserving Ontario's Heritage: A History of the Ontario Historical Society* (Toronto: Love Press, 1976); Gerald Killan, *David Boyle: From Artisan to Archaeologist* (Toronto: University of Toronto Press, 1985), 180-86.

9   Killan, *Preserving Ontario's Heritage,* 43, 48-49; *OHS Report* (Toronto: Ontario Historical Society, 1898), 28-29. This was not the first time that the Six Nations had pointed to their historical legacy. Seth Newhouse's (Onondaga) history was prepared in the 1870s. See Weaver, "Iroquois: The Consolidation," 207.

10   *OHS Report* (1911), 47-48.

11 *OHS Report* (1898), 42.

12 *OHS Report* (1911), 44-47.

13 Ibid., 43.

14 On John Ojijatekha Brant-Sero, see Penny Petrone, *Dictionary of Canadian Biography,* vol. 14 (Toronto: University of Toronto Press, 1998), 137-39; and Cecilia Morgan, "'A Wigwam to Westminster': Performing Mohawk Identity in Imperial Britain, 1890s-1900s," *Gender and History* 25, 2 (August 2003): 319-41.

15 Killan, *Preserving Ontario's Past,* 44.

16 Asa R. Hill, "The Historical Position of the Six Nations," *OHS Papers* 19 (1922): 108-9.

17 See Colin M. Coates and Cecilia Morgan, *Heroines and History: Representations of Madeleine de Verchères and Laura Secord* (Toronto: University of Toronto Press, 2002), 146-49.

18 For a very insightful discussion of this perspective as it pertained to commemoration and historical preservation, see Andrew Nurse, "'But Now Things Have Changed': Marius Barbeau and the Politics of Amerindian Identity," *Ethnohistory* 48, 3 (Summer 2001): 433-72.

19 Weaver, "Iroquois: The Grand River Reserve," 245-48.

20 Minute Book 1, 9 February 1911, BHSR.

21 Ibid., 14 March 1918. In 1917 the BHS struck a committee to get more pictures of Pauline Johnson into Native schools and to set up a prize for the best essay on "Indian life and history on the reserve"; see ibid., 10 May 1917.

22 Ibid., 18 January 1934, 11 December 1913, 13 March 1914, 3 February 1917, 18 September 1929, 20 May and 10 June 1931, 4 July and 5 October 1933, 20 April 1937.

23 Minute Book 2, 20 March 1935, 21 November 1939, 18 March 1941, 19 November 1947, BHSR.

24 Minute Book 2, 26 January 1937, 18 March 1941, 22 January 1943, BHSR.

25 See, for example, Hilton Hill, "Ancient Customs of the Six Nations Indians," in Minute Book 2, 1 May 1944, BHSR.

26 "Pageant Presented in Connection with the Celebration, by the Six Nations, of the Sir William Johnson Bi-Centennial, May 24, 1938," Elliott Moses Files, vol. 1, file 9, "Memoranda 1928-70," Library and Archives Canada (LAC), MG30, C169; "Seventh Annual Pageant at Ohnedagowah (Great Pine) Forest Theatre, Six Nations," 12-20 August 1955, Kathleen Coburn Papers, file 3, box 7 (Ethel Brant Monture), Victoria University Library.

27 Anne McClintock, *Imperial Leather: Race, Gender and Sexuality in the Colonial Contest* (London: Routledge, 1994), 40-42.

28 Minute Book 1, 12 January 1931, BHSR.

29 Minute Book 2, 21 January 1951, BHSR.

30 See James Opp and John Walsh's introduction to this volume.

31 Cecilia Morgan, "Performing for 'Imperial Eyes': Bernice Loft and Ethel Brant Monture, Ontario, 1930s-1960s," in *Contact Zones: Aboriginal and Settler Women in Canada's Colonial Past,* ed. Myra Rutherdale and Katharine Pickles (Vancouver: UBC Press, 2005), 67-89.

32 Milton Martin (Mohawk) also offered different perspectives on the Six Nations' history. Martin (1893-1957) joined the air force in the First World War and, after the war, became a high school teacher, principal, and outspoken advocate of the abolition of stereotypical depictions of Native people in Canadian history textbooks. See "Oliver Milton Martin Biography," unpublished paper; "Magistrate Martin Dies," *Globe and Mail*, 19 December 1957; and "Magistrate Martin Dies at 64," 19 December 1957, all in Oliver Milton Martin File, Woodland Cultural Centre, Brantford.

33 This biographical sketch of Moses is from Elliott Moses Files finding aid, LAC, MG30, C169. See also Elliott Moses, "Seventy-Five Years of Progress of the Six Nations of the Grand River," address to the Waterloo Historical Society's Annual Meeting, 22 October 1968, Elliott Moses Files, vol. 1, file 1, "Articles by Elliott Moses, 1957-1975," LAC, MG30, C169.

34 "Mayors Entertained at Rotary-Civic Luncheon. Elliott Moses of the Six Nations Gave an Eloquent Address. Indians Present," *Brantford Expositor*, 5 March 1937, Elliott Moses Files, vol. 2, file 4, "Scrapbook, 1936-41," LAC, MG30, C169.

35 Elliot Moses, n.t., n.d., Elliott Moses Files, vol. 1, file 1, "Articles by Elliott Moses, 1957-1975," LAC, MG30, C169.

36 Ibid.

37 Ibid.

38 Ibid.

39 Ibid.

40 Moses, "Seventy-Five Years of Progress."

41 Elliott Moses, "Conflicting Views on Indian Reserves," December 1960, Elliott Moses Files, vol. 2, file 4, "Scrapbook, 1936-41," LAC, MG30, C169.

42 "Not Quite White, 'Against Indian Integration,'" *Brantford Expositor*, n.d. The author was probably reacting to a speech Moses had just delivered to the city's Kiwanis Club, "Indian Act Retards Progress." See also "Reservation as Refuge from Rat Race," *The Cayuga*, n.d.; "Two Indians Clash over Social Views," n.p., n.d.; and E.P. Garlow, "A Band Chief's View," *Brantford Expositor*, n.d.; all *Brantford Expositor* clippings in Elliott Moses Files, vol. 1, file 12, "Speeches, 1966-69," LAC, MG30, C169.

43 See, for example, Penny Petrone, ed., *First People, First Voices* (Toronto: University of Toronto Press, 1991), ch. 5.

44 Thanks to Michael Ripmeester for reminding me of this very important point. See Peter Jones (Kahwewaquonaby), *History of the Ojebway Indians* (London: A.W. Bennett, 1861); and George Copway (Kahgegagahbowh), *The Traditional History and Characteristic Sketches of the Ojibway Nation* (London: Charles Gilpin, 1851).

45 See Minute Book 1, 24 January 1935 and n.d. January 1944, BHSR; and Minute Book 2, 16 March 1948, 20 May 1953, and 19 May 1954, BHSR.

46 "Pageant Presented in Connection with the Celebration."

47 Elliott Moses, "Historical Sketch of the Introduction of the Elective System of Council on the Six Nations Reservation in the Year 1924," Elliott Moses Files, vol. 1, file 1, "Articles by Elliott Moses, 1957-1975," LAC, MG30, C169.

48 Ibid.

49 See Josiah Hill, Secretary, Six Nations Council, "Summons to Witness," 10 March 1908, Elliott Moses Files, vol. 1, file 7, "Legal Papers, 1840-1908," LAC, MG30, C169; also Nelson Moses, "To the Chiefs," n.d., Elliott Moses Files, vol. 1, file 5, "Elected Chiefs, 1894-1917," LAC, MG30, C169.

50 Moses, "Historical Sketch."

51 See J.R. Miller, *Shingwauk's Dream: A History of Native Residential Schools* (Toronto: University of Toronto Press, 1996).

52 Elliott Moses, "The Long House People," Elliott Moses Files, vol. 1, file 12, "Speeches, 1966-69," LAC, MG30, C169.

53 Welby Davis, "A Protest," *Brantford Expositor,* n.d., Elliott Moses Files, vol. 1, file 12, "Speeches, 1966-69," LAC, MG30, C169; "Indian Mother to Resist Banishment Order" and "Historian's Daughter Ejected: Claims Indian Ouster Vote Passed by Majority of One," *Brantford Expositor,* n.d., Elliott Moses Files, vol. 1, file 13, "Clippings, 1888-1930," LAC, MG30, C169.

54 Arif Dirlik, *Postmodernity's Histories: The Past as Legacy and Project* (Lanham, MD: Rowman and Littlefield, 2000), xii, 217.

55 The former is typified by Pierre Nora's work in his three-volume *Realms of Memory: Rethinking the French Past,* English language ed. Lawrence D. Kritzman, trans. Arthur Goldhammer (New York: Columbia University Press, 1996-98); the latter is typified by work such as Gordillo's *Landscape of Devils.*

56 Arif Dirlik, "Place-Based Imaginations: Globalism and the Politics of Place," in *Places and Politics in an Age of Globalization,* ed. Roxanne Prazniak and Arif Dirlik (Lanham, MD: Rowman and Littlefield, 2001), 40.

Edmonton's Jasper Avenue
Public Ritual, Heritage, and Memory on Main Street

FRANCES SWYRIPA

In 1917, according to court documents, a would-be pimp used his most convincing argument to persuade a soldier's wife, coping alone in the Alberta capital of Edmonton while her husband fought overseas, to leave her home on Scona Road and come work for him in premises near his laundry on Jasper Avenue. "Why do you live here where you have so much mud?" Mah Yuen reportedly asked Mary Bothwell. "Why not live in Town in a house where you have water and electric light?" She had "fixed up her shack comfortable," the mother of three retorted, adding, "I don't see why I should go and live in town ... where I [am] a stranger and [don't] know anyone."[1] In the 1950s two sisters who had moved to Edmonton from the Ukrainian farming bloc north and east of the city ran a boarding house near the Northern Alberta Dairy Pool on 105 Avenue and 103 Street. On Saturday afternoons they would cross the railway tracks and walk the few blocks to Jasper Avenue to window shop or see a movie. Going "downtown" was special, so they dressed up and put on their best hats.[2] Albeit four decades apart, two views of Jasper Avenue clearly played in the personal imaginations of Edmontonians. The one envisioned an alien, unappealing, and incomprehensible place that sensible folk avoided; the other saw an irresistible magnet that brought glamour and excitement – the latest clothing fashions, cars, and Hollywood stars – to an isolated but eager population.

Surveyed in 1882 and named after Missouri trapper Jasper Hawes,[3] the ribbon of dirt road that emerged on the top of the North Saskatchewan River bank as the fur trade era ended quickly attracted the businesses of the settlement that replaced the fort below. Jasper Avenue's status was confirmed in 1912 when the eight-year-old city of Edmonton amalgamated with and effectively absorbed the town of Strathcona across the river. Almost a century later, as the major artery through downtown Edmonton, the one-time dirt road stretched over forty blocks, or six kilometres. It passed through residential and commercial areas ranging from skyscrapers and burgeoning condominiums in the central core to vibrant Chinese enterprises in the east and an arts district in the west. Probably few Edmontonians gave much thought to their city's main street on a daily basis, as suburban shopping malls (particularly the giant of giants, West Edmonton Mall) and Whyte Avenue in Old Strathcona offered stiff competition for shopping and entertainment (see Figure 3.1). And probably few Edmontonians ever accessed the street's entire sweep or identified it with the exact same neighbourhoods, boundaries, and landmarks. Yet for much of its existence, Jasper Avenue had lain at the heart of the collective consciousness of city residents, the understood gathering place for expressing grand emotions – celebration and merriment, protest, mourning, and remembrance. As such, it not only fired the personal imaginations of Edmontonians but also figured in their public rituals and memory.

As the site for orchestrated events marking pivotal moments in the joint history of the city and its citizens, Jasper Avenue helped to mould an imagined community constructed around common touchstones and experiences, past and present, that transcended things that otherwise might (and often did) divide them.[4] These rituals and traditions also linked the citizens of Edmonton with, and gave localized meaning to, other imagined communities that were provincial, national, and international in scope. Moreover, although they most often represented an organized and officially sanctioned corporate identity, or hierarchy of identities, they sometimes reflected spontaneous grassroots mobilization around the same ideals. In both cases, the effect was to underscore what the surrounding society valued at specific points in history and to indicate how those values, and thus society, changed over time. In contrast to and contesting this mainstream vision, quite separate orchestrated events, rituals,

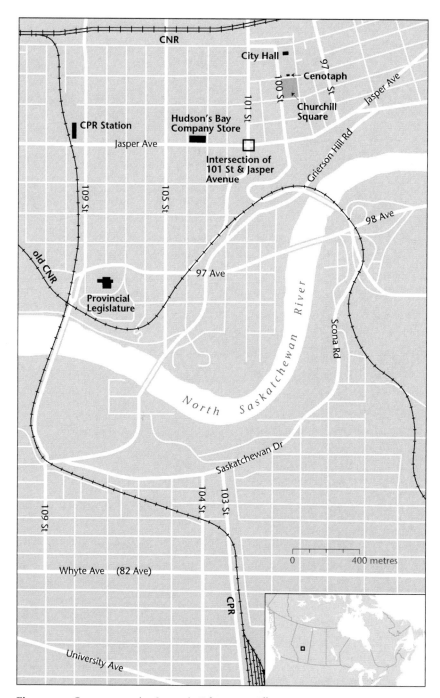

Figure 3.1 Commemorative Spaces in Edmonton, Alberta

and traditions provided a forum for the marginalized by championing alternative beliefs and agendas, showcasing outsiders eager to belong, reinforcing the involuntary and continuing exclusion of others.

Regardless of context or function, Jasper Avenue symbolized public space at its most politically potent.[5] That potency was expressed best in occupation of the open roadway, allowing groups and individuals – milling throngs, formal parades and processions – to appropriate territory normally off limits except at designated controlled crossings. More passively, city-approved banners and arches (as well as the occasional commercial window dressing in adjacent private spaces) simultaneously beautified the streetscape and reinforced community values. Singly and through repetition, by tying past practices and priorities to present ones, such phenomena contributed to a public memory dependent on and inseparable from place, putting Jasper Avenue at the centre of defining the Edmonton community, both as a whole and in its many parts. Equally significant to the street's evolution as a site of public memory and thus identity were its physical landmarks, particularly those with deep historical associations or aesthetic features that resonated widely with residents. Perceived as crucial to the integrity of the streetscape, old and iconic buildings became a visual shorthand for the local heritage – expressed in a few select images and themes – that all Edmontonians shared.

By the end of the twentieth century, however, much of the public life and memory constructed around Jasper Avenue had crumbled, as Edmontonians no longer automatically and inevitably accessed the street to express grand communal emotions or treasured the landmarks connecting them to their past. For many newcomers flocking to the city in the decades after the Second World War, that past was simply not theirs, was too invisible, or was too inconsequential to engage them. Nor could they identify with Jasper Avenue based on generations of participation in its rituals or a lifetime of familiarity with its skyline. But if demographic trends encouraged forgetting, there were also other culprits: oil-fed prosperity that looked forward not backward; changing fashions in public ritual; an evolving transportation structure that sidelined the old downtown core; and a grassroots-powered shift that forced Jasper Avenue to share defining community moments with the rejuvenated heritage district of Old Strathcona, particularly its historical Whyte Avenue.

The fortunes of Jasper Avenue say a great deal about the functioning of place, especially as the centre of an all-important localized memory and meaning. Significantly, as the focus of the community coalescing outside the Hudson's Bay Company fort down on the flats, Jasper Avenue possessed independent meaning, equated with progress and modernity, that reinforced its suitability for grand public gestures yet had no emotional pull on the local memory. Jasper's rise in the rituals of young Edmonton thus reflected in part the predicament of a frontier town lacking traditional sites, embedded in people's consciousness, as predestined venues. The choice of the bustling commercial artery over sentiment for the past (in the still-standing fur trade fort) also reflected changing priorities that privileged place and memory attached to the new settlement order.

Significantly as well, Jasper Avenue highlighted the role of "the local" in shaping a collective identity. The buildings and other structures that evolved into iconic landmarks, their number constantly augmented and redefined by both new construction and successive generations, tied Edmontonians to their surroundings and to the city's unique history within the region as a fur trade post, goods and service centre, provincial capital, and gateway to the North. As a fixture on the street, the Hudson's Bay Company store that replaced the old fort became *the* symbol of place linking past, present, and future. The local context also gave meaning to the parades and processions that tied Edmontonians to the larger worlds of province (region), nation, and empire, suggesting that these and other imagined communities were not so easily imagined or problematized in the abstract and that only the immediate and the concrete made them intelligible. Finally, although developments external to the street were a factor in its decline, local considerations ultimately explained Jasper Avenue's failure to remain at the heart of Edmonton's rituals and to safeguard its material heritage. The tensions generated by a living street whose vitality advertised a successful city contributed both to the avenue's staying power as a site of active memory making and to its relinquishing that role.

The earliest surviving photograph of Jasper Avenue was taken by Charles W. Mathers in 1890 (see Figure 3.2). The ragged row of squat wooden structures, many sporting the false fronts common on the prairie frontier, offered an array of services. Some – such as three hotels, a hardware store, and the *Edmonton Bulletin* newspaper office – were typical of a fledgling urban centre supplying a growing population plus homesteaders in the neighbouring hinterland. Others – a jewellery store, Mathers' own photo studio – were more

Figure 3.2 Jasper Avenue, Edmonton, facing east from 99 Street, 1890. Photograph by Charles W. Mathers. *Source:* Provincial Archives of Alberta, Ernest Brown Collection, B5537.

surprising. Others yet, such as the First Presbyterian Church and the Masonic Hall, forecast British-Protestant supremacy in the new settlement order. Nothing, however, better signalled the end of the fur trade era, and the determination of the Hudson's Bay Company to remain relevant, than the presence of the 200-year-old institution among the business concerns. The core of Jasper Avenue soon shifted westward, no doubt a response to the fact that the original strip snaking along the height of land permitted outward expansion only to the north. As evidence of the permanence of the shift, and of Edmonton's increasing financial importance, the big eastern banks located here, erecting imposing stone and marble buildings with Grecian columns.

In the opening years of the twentieth century, the old focal point of Jasper Avenue around present 97 Street became increasingly multicultural with the arrival of poor and suspect immigrants from Asia and eastern Europe who established the eastern limits of "official" downtown. Their imprint, to many

Edmontonians disturbingly exotic and undesirable, ranged from the shops of Chinese merchants (like the enterprising Mah Yuen) that formed part of a modest Chinatown crystallizing north of Jasper to the onion domes of St. Barbara's Russian Orthodox Church.[6] These years of massive construction also gave Jasper Avenue two of its dominant landmarks. One, the Macdonald Hotel, built by the Grand Trunk Railway, opened in 1915 and immediately became the pre-eminent stopping place for visitors to the city as well as a hub of Edmonton's social life. The second structure marked the western boundary of "official" downtown. With the extension of the railway across the High Level Bridge in 1913, bringing trains to the Canadian Pacific Railway station just north of Jasper, the steel girders of the overpass at 110 Street dramatically sliced the avenue in two. Outside the lengthening downtown core, development was uneven, with portions remaining empty even into the 1940s.

If the early appearance of the Hudson's Bay Company on Jasper Avenue ensured that the memory of the fur trade economy and fort would inform the settlement-era imagination, the store's subsequent history perpetuated the interplay between past and present. Not to be left behind when the commercial core shifted westward, the Hudson's Bay Company in 1892 opened a new store on Jasper at 103 Street, a site that it and later The Bay occupied for the next century. A three-storey brick structure replaced the original wooden building during the prewar boom, the popular observation deck atop the tower on its roof giving a breathtaking view of the city. The old fur trading company's last reincarnation on the spot, a sleek modern behemoth, opened in November 1939, self-consciously engaged in memory making, distilling a proud history into four images carved into the limestone over the entrances. They were, progressively, the Hudson's Bay Company ship the *Nonsuch* (the first to trade in Hudson Bay), a flat York boat used to transport furs along western waterways, a musket-bearing fur trader, and a farmer guiding a hand plough. Engraved texts on the Jasper Avenue corners of the building recounted the establishment of the Hudson's Bay Company in 1670 and heralded its presence in Edmonton "as fur trader and merchant" since 1795.[7] Whether or not Edmontonians scurrying along Jasper raised their heads to notice or reflect on the new department store's facade, the Hudson's Bay Company clearly identified with its local and regional roots and encouraged passersby to do the same. Moreover, it used commercial space to promote a version of the past that both placed the venerable institution at the centre of the unfolding Edmonton story and complemented its location in the physical heart of the city.

Perhaps the best settlement-era example of commemorating the past alongside planning for the present and envisioning the future occurred in conjunction with the creation of the Province of Alberta in 1905 and the naming of Edmonton as its capital. The city pulled out all the stops for inauguration day on 1 September, with tidied-up and decorated storefronts (including illumination at night), ornamental arches across Jasper Avenue, and a parade down the street itself. Exuding civic pride, partners McDougall and Secord, two of the city's oldest merchants, celebrated Edmonton's future with a display in their large window space that featured three dolls fighting over the Capitol: a huge Edmonton looming over both her rivals and the building, a tiny ineffective Red Deer, and a medium-sized Calgary pleading, "Ma, I want it." Madam Alberta, as the adult mannequin was labelled, replied, "Don't be naughty Calgary. Let your sister have it, you're not old enough to handle it safely. Run and play with your CPR."[8] The printed slogans gracing the ornamental arches likewise captured the mood of a city and province confidently looking forward: "Alberta the Fairest and Best," "Industry, Energy, Enterprise," and "Trusted, Tried, True." One striking arch, however, looked backward, reminding celebrants of the debt owed to those whose visions, gambles, struggles, and achievements had secured their bright future. With "The Old Timers" spelled out in hewn branches across the top, the arch featured a miniature log cabin hoisted onto the crosspiece, stretched furs and snowshoes hung on the walls, and antlers attached to the roof (see Figure 3.3).[9] The parade, which ended near the Hudson's Bay Company fort in the river flats where Governor General Earl Grey and Prime Minister Sir Wilfrid Laurier presided over the inauguration ceremonies, also honoured the pioneers. Preceded by a Red River cart, the Edmonton Old-Timers Association marched immediately behind the lead marshal and band.[10]

When Earl Grey returned in the autumn of 1909 to lay the cornerstone of the Legislature Building (an event that drew crowds from across Alberta) Edmonton still basked in provincehood and its own prestige and responsibility as capital. But this time, public memory defiantly began with the present, rendering the old-timers and the foundation they built invisible and irrelevant. It also firmly situated Alberta and Edmonton within the larger national and

Figure 3.3   Jasper Avenue, Edmonton, facing east, 1 September 1905. Photograph by Ernest Brown. *Source:* Provincial Archives of Alberta, Ernest Brown Collection, B6728.

British worlds to which they belonged. Bedecked in Red Ensigns, one of four triumphal arches on Jasper Avenue proclaimed, "Our flag forever." Another boasted, "We Play Our Part as Empire Builders." The remaining two arches gave the abstract concrete meaning through place and the local. The first, a massive four-armed affair at the intersection with McDougall Avenue (now 100 Street) used district products – wheat, coal, cement blocks, pressed and lime bricks – to promote its slogan of "Granary of the Empire." The second, illustrating what the introduction to this volume describes as acts of remembering or commemorating that define the "local" and who is or is not of a certain place, also illustrated how local place shaped claims to membership in the empire. Erected at the intersection with Namayo (now 97 Street) by neighbourhood Chinese, and adorned with lanterns, kites, and "other decorative devices peculiar to the Celestial Kingdom," it instructed the visiting governor general, "Tell King Edward We are His Loyal Subjects."[11]

In the foregoing cases, the mobilization of Jasper Avenue by the state, commercial enterprises, and special-interest groups relied on strategically placed, but static, images and texts to encourage people to think about both past and present in a particular way. Much of the authority of these additions to the streetscape, whether permanent or temporary, derived from their physical location. That is, Jasper Avenue's prominence within the city legitimized and strengthened their message, while the street's drawing power at moments of high ritual and pageantry maximized the number of citizens exposed to its visual propaganda. Along Jasper Avenue itself, one location outshone all others as a site of memory making and thus civic community building around an evolving collective consciousness. That location was the intersection with 101 Street, the physical and psychological centre of downtown. It was here that crowds spontaneously gathered in the summer of 1914, straining to read the declaration of war as it was being handwritten on a large *Edmonton Journal* billboard.[12] And it was here, four years later, that crowds "painted the sky red" with a huge bonfire when news of the armistice arrived by wire and a cacophony of factory whistles, church bells, and fire sirens brought thousands of celebrants into the streets.[13] Finally, during the Second World War the Brewing Industry of Alberta graphically exploited Edmontonians' need to believe in the security of their downtown in order to shock them into purchasing war savings certificates. "Don't Let This Happen!" screamed the headline above a doctored photograph, looking north from Jasper and 100 Street, that showed diving German bombers above gutted and burning buildings.[14]

Unlike the sharply focused wartime emphasis on Jasper Avenue's main intersection and adjacent buildings, the organized state spectacles that over the years tied Edmonton to province, nation, and empire utilized the entire downtown stretch and open space of the street. Parades and processions entered public memory in the guise of rituals and traditions that not only observed an expected and satisfying structure but also decreed what was worthy of patriotic outpouring and how it should be expressed. The act of repeated assembling on Jasper Avenue also entered public memory as a ritual and tradition itself, cementing opinion that the street was unequivocally *the* place within the city for grandiose patriotic gestures. As for their own content and memory making (and like the Chinese arch), official commemorative performances on Jasper exposed the importance of the local, past and present, in Edmontonians' self-image as westerners, Canadians, and British subjects.

The imperial connection deeply informed the public life of young Edmonton, and royal milestones were observed with heartfelt pomp. During the pioneer era, easily the most ambitious and lavish street spectacle was Queen Victoria's diamond jubilee parade in 1897.[15] Its centrepiece, stressing the global nature of a hierarchical family celebration in which local place and memory mattered not at all, featured Britannia surrounded by costumed children symbolizing her colonies: Australia, the West Indies, Africa, India, Newfoundland, and Canada. Other entries expressed a complex and nuanced imperial relationship that, in the words of Brian Osborne, reflected "the palpable immediacy of local places"[16] as Edmontonians forged a vision of empire sensitive to their self-defined heritage and values. A stirring reminder of the prairie past yet equally part of its present, the North-West Mounted Police, who had brought law and order to the West and now headed the parade, not only provided ceremonial colour in the name of the Dominion but also personified the unique prairie experience in both empire and nation building. The St. Jean Baptiste societies from Edmonton and surrounding districts that marched alongside the Scottish St. Andrew's and English St. George's societies acknowledged the role of the French in opening the West as well as their continued, if temporary, high profile in the transition from fur trade to settlement.[17] Significantly, however, the accompanying tableau – Jacques Cartier in the bow of *L'Emerillon* discovering Canada in 1534 – sought imperial legitimacy not in the West but in a remote Quebec-centred past. Queen Victoria's death in 1901 refocused Edmontonians outward as, in gestures replicated across the globe, tolling church bells, flags at half mast, and downtown buildings draped in black and purple proclaimed "the universal sorrow of the community in the empire's loss."[18] The procession down Jasper Avenue that preceded Edward VII's public memorial service nine years later once again cast the empire in local terms, featuring the Alberta Mounted Rifles, Royal North-West Mounted Police, 101st Fusiliers, Royal St. George's Society, Sons of England, Caledonian Society, St. Andrew's Society, Edmonton Irish Association, and Freemasons. They marched, "mournfully and slow," to muffled drums and "the strains of the Dead March" past reverential and respectful crowds.[19]

Commandeering Jasper Avenue to mark distant imperial milestones extended to hosting royalty as well, with the first big test, the September 1919 visit of the Prince of Wales (the future Edward VIII), generating unprecedented excitement. Crucially, despite drawing on locally accumulated experience and tradition as well as on established royal protocol, organizers introduced important innovations. As the royal train bearing the prince crossed the High Level Bridge and railway overpass into the Canadian Pacific station just off Jasper at 110 Street, it was escorted from the air by local First World War flying ace Captain "Wop" May. The conspicuous participation not only of May but also of 1,500 First World War veterans, who marched down Jasper into the station enclosure, incorporated the recent memory of sacrifice on the battlefields of Europe into Edmonton public ritual. Together, they gave the overseas conflict an immediacy that neither Canadians' contribution to the victory, and thus to the empire, nor the visiting soldier-prince could provide. By 1919, however, the ceremonial presence of the Royal North-West Mounted Police, "brilliant in their scarlet tunics, [and] gold striped breeches ... and sitting on their restless horses as though part of the steeds," was de rigueur. In the expansive manner of prewar slogans, the arch spanning Jasper at 109 Street, gateway to the downtown celebrations, greeted the royal visitor with the words "All Edmonton Welcomes the Prince." Elsewhere, the street's festive appearance stood in sharp contrast to the war years, and the decorative arches – acknowledging organizations like the Red Cross, Victorian Order of Nurses, and Imperial Order Daughters of the Empire – introduced a sombre (and gendered) note into the usual patriotic messages.[20] For the two days that the Prince of Wales spent in Edmonton, Jasper Avenue offered the best opportunity to see his party as it moved about from its base at the Macdonald Hotel.

War epitomized the overlapping of national and imperial identities and local place in the collective psyche of Edmontonians. The controlled ceremonial use of Jasper Avenue to showcase servicemen readying or departing for overseas also changed the nature of street spectacles – introducing a new intensity and steely resolve while elevating the parading surface to a sacred space that civilians felt unqualified to enter. The latter ended with the cessation of hostilities, however, especially in 1918 when the unparalleled scale and duration of the conflict, which had dragged in a remote prairie capital, invited (even demanded) improvisation. But although Edmontonians surged onto Jasper following news of the armistice, the spontaneous festivities were soon harnessed by a torchlight procession organized by the First World War veterans, transforming the revellers into spectators who cheered from the sidewalk and joined the Mendelssohn Choir in belting out "Rule Britannia." Yet control

Commemorations

Figure 3.4 Crowds along Jasper Avenue and adjoining streets greeting the trains carrying the 49th Battalion, March 1919. *Source:* City of Edmonton Archives, EA-10-809.

remained tenuous and a clear script elusive. The people resorted to impromptu noisemakers and attached themselves, on foot and in vehicles, to the tail of a parade that circled "round and round" with "no particular destination or stopping place."[21]

The return of Edmonton's own 49th Battalion in March 1919, when thousands massed in the vicinity of 109 Street and the Canadian Pacific station to greet the two trains (see Figure 3.4), had none of the spontaneous frenzy of the armistice. This time, centuries of military ritual and tradition provided the script and guided the public response. The unit's orchestrated march down Jasper Avenue, behind regimental colours retrieved from their temporary home in Canterbury Cathedral, represented the reassertion of control as much as it did a patriotic and moving sight. Furthermore, the parade was purposely opened up to other veterans, the occasion becoming a general tribute to the fighting men of the city and province – including the dead, silent, and invisible among the living, their "cadenced footfalls" inaudible.[22] The unprecedented nature of this particular war, however, simultaneously begged some rewriting of the military script to recognize the service to "king and country" of civilians as well. Twenty war nurses and some members of the Imperial Order Daughters of the Empire, for example, marched in the parade, although the fact that most Daughters reportedly declined the honour suggests that older traditions of female exclusion and propriety prevailed.

Jasper Avenue as a site of public memory, whether stressing contemporary Edmonton's historical roots and connections or cultivating a sense of belonging through repeated shared experience, defined the boundaries of community membership. For at least the first half of the twentieth century, those boundaries confirmed the essential Britishness of the crystallizing settlement order and the marginality of ethnic and racial minorities. During Queen Victoria's diamond jubilee celebrations in 1897, for example, Her Majesty's Indian subjects gathered on Jasper Avenue apart from the official event, on the day after the formal parade. Organizers had also not solicited Aboriginal input. Rather, the request to participate came from Chief Alexander, patronizingly described as an "honest Indian bubbling over with an attack of Jubilee loyalty, who desired to bring in his band to express their sentiments in an appropriate manner," provided they received gifts of "beef, flour, tea, tobacco, etc" to whip up their enthusiasm.[23] Both Ukrainians and Chinese marched in the George V Coronation Day parade in 1911, albeit at the rear in keeping with their subordinate position within society. Unlike Chief Alexander's reception, the Chinese request to participate – presented by the white superintendent of the Chinese school, who emphasized the immigrants' appreciation of the advantages of living "in this part of the great Empire" over which George V ruled – was met with "hearty applause."[24] Although the idea to take part purportedly originated with the Chinese, their spokesman's efforts suggest otherwise. Why Ukrainians participated is unknown, but the marchers were identified as members of the Ruthenian Educational Society, an organization founded by some of Edmonton's most prominent Ukrainian activists, which points to initiative from within the group in pursuit of a group agenda.

Those same interests lay behind Ukrainians' much praised participation in the Dominion Day parade marking the diamond jubilee of Confederation in 1927 and, more importantly, behind their independent use of Jasper Avenue over the Dominion Day weekend in 1928 to celebrate a purely group landmark

– thirty years of Ukrainian life in Alberta and Canada. The historical memory mobilized on these two occasions asserted an identity informed by both a distant old-world past and a local place. In 1927 costumed Cossack outriders provided a colourful escort for the Ukrainian float, while in 1928 they substituted for the Royal Canadian Mounted Police at the head of mainstream parades. These eye-catching figures simultaneously bestowed vicarious prestige on an often maligned immigrant people and identified prairie Ukrainians with the nation-building aspirations of the homeland. At the same time, the organizers of the 1928 parade, sponsored by the newly formed Ukrainian Pioneers (Old-Timers) Association, unapologetically claimed a place for Ukrainians in the city and province. Astutely, they did so by choosing Edmonton for maximum exposure over the countryside, where most Ukrainians lived, and by appropriating Jasper Avenue to confer the legitimacy the group craved. The parade made the message of the celebration explicit: after the Cossacks came the old-timers, followed by a children's float and a banner reading, "We did not come to this country; we were born here."[25] Moreover, Edmontonians heard the message. "It is doubtful if any other class of people in Alberta have better cause to commemorate their arrival here than have the Ukrainians," the *Edmonton Bulletin*'s lead editorial pronounced, offering as proof the pioneers' cultivation of the land, their industry and thrift, and the success of their children.[26]

In taking over Jasper Avenue to showcase their culture and claim a place in the local narrative, Ukrainians let it be known that they realized the importance of ritualistic occupation of the street to mainstream values and identity and thus the validity of their own cause. To them (as well as Chief Alexander and the Chinese), then, Jasper Avenue and its related rituals symbolized boundaries to be breached in the interests of inclusion. But in seeking integration, they contested the official public memory only insofar as it traditionally excluded their specific role and contribution. Other outsiders acknowledged the street's legitimizing potential but rejected its establishment associations. Rather, to them, the space represented boundaries to be emphasized and maintained in espousing goals and a vision of community at odds with the propaganda of mainstream events and the official public memory it promoted. The annual May Day and Labour Day parades that formed part of the ritual and tradition of marginalized left-wing (including ethnic and communist) organizations were a case in point. For example, the 4,000-strong May

Day workers' parade in 1937 during the Depression not only demanded free textbooks for local schoolchildren but also proclaimed unity with workers worldwide and support for "anti-fascist" republican forces in war-torn Spain.[27] Periodically, authorities made uneasy by protesters' subversive use of Jasper Avenue tried to block access. In 1970, for example, the Edmonton Committee to End the War in Vietnam was refused a marching permit on the grounds that a few hundred demonstrators did not justify disrupting thousands of vehicles on their Saturday business. Just as adamantly, and just as appreciative of Jasper's position in the Edmonton imagination, the protesters demanded that the city "provide its most focal area."[28] Yet other demonstrations – notably the estimated 12,000 and 18,000 people who marched down Jasper Avenue on separate occasions in 2003 to oppose the United States-led war in Iraq – enjoyed widespread respectability.[29]

Jasper Avenue's most familiar and seemingly least ideological function was entertainment. But despite lacking the anti-establishment edge of protest demonstrations or the patriotic fervour of imperial commemorations, street festivities were important to a sense of local place and local memory. First, they reinforced the storyline of advancement from the fur-trade-to-settlement and progress storylines through which Edmontonians traditionally related to their surroundings and their past. The Hudson's Bay Company, for instance, publicized its deep roots in the West with a 250th anniversary parade in 1920 and a street barbeque and dance for 10,000 partygoers in 1933.[30] And in 1955, when the annual summer exhibition parade celebrated Alberta's golden jubilee, popular entries juxtaposed "then" and "now" to illustrate the great changes that fifty years had wrought. The province's own entry featured six Alberta pioneers sandwiched between 1905 and 1955 floats, the former drawn by two oxen, the latter pulled by a modern tractor. The organizations and communities participating from outside Edmonton reconfirmed its role as both capital and service centre for the neighbouring hinterland.[31] Second, street festivities as part of the annual summer exhibition reinforced Edmonton's conscious attempt to redefine "the local" with the grafting of Klondike Days onto the agricultural fair in the 1960s. The new summer festival exploited Edmonton's limited contribution as an outfitter for the gold rush in the Yukon in 1898-99 to promote the city's continuing and expanding role as a gateway to the North. In so doing, it cultivated an inauthentic Hollywood-esque mix of can-can girls, prospectors with mules, river boat gamblers, honky-tonk music, bags of gold, and sheriff's posses in which the downtown parade and businesses were complicit.[32] As an exercise in engineering local place and local memory to displace the fur trade and agricultural frontiers, the Klondike theme sat uneasily on Edmontonians, even after forty years, and was thus abandoned early in the new century.

What Edmontonians did wholeheartedly embrace, underscoring that the popular consciousness preferred "the local" defined in the narrowest possible terms, were the successes of city sports teams. Parades and rallies organized by civic leaders to celebrate the Eskimos and Oilers winning, respectively, the coveted Grey and Stanley Cups, emblematic of football and hockey supremacy in Canada, attracted appreciative crowds to Jasper Avenue. The crowds also put themselves centre stage, pouring onto the thoroughfare in the tradition of the spontaneous public response to the armistice in 1918. In 1984, on the night the Oilers won their first Stanley Cup, revellers forced police to stop traffic, trapping motorists and buses. Then, as the *Edmonton Journal* put it, on the night of the official parade and rally, when some 100,000 fans ("the largest crowd ... since V-E Day") jammed downtown, the "party turn[ed] ugly." The youthful, inebriated throng drank openly, threw bottles, and damaged stores and businesses. Police retaliated with nightsticks and attack dogs; firefighters used water hoses. The 30,000 rowdy fans massing along Jasper after the Oilers' third victory in 1987 repeated the scene – openly drinking, pelting police with beer bottles, uprooting trees, smashing glass, climbing onto awnings, falling from hotel windows. Some of the worst violence occurred when police ordered a topless young woman astride her boyfriend's shoulders to cover up.[33] To many Edmontonians, the unauthorized appropriation and misuse of Jasper by high-spirited fans subtly altered the street's image in the collective consciousness. No longer only a place for maintaining or negotiating boundaries, it now also represented an unwanted loss of control and a threat to the social order.

Flying beer bottles, broken windows, and Lady Godiva hockey fans were a world away from the strains of the Dead March mourning the passing of a king or even the bonfires lit to celebrate the peace in 1918. Over the second half of the twentieth century, Jasper Avenue's role as a pivotal site of public ceremony and memory underwent significant change. Part of the explanation lay in the general secularization and democratization of society, increasingly unimpressed by formal ritual and hierarchy. Part also lay in increasingly popular alternate forms of collective celebration and commemoration. But much of the change was due to Edmonton's own peculiarities: oil-fuelled expansion and growth that altered the face of the downtown core, including Jasper Avenue, and technological advances that reconfigured spatial relationships within the city, including the physical convenience of Jasper for hosting parades and processions. But although the street quietly lost most of its ritualistic functions, the demolition or threatened demolition of what a broad segment of Edmontonians saw as its physical landmarks encountered resistance. Despite its sporadic nature and a spotty record fighting indifference to the city's architectural heritage, that resistance implied that Jasper Avenue's material heritage and the streetscape itself exerted a greater pull on residents than did the transitory spectacles staged on it.

By the end of the twentieth century, the area of Jasper around 109 and 110 Streets traditionally marking the western boundary of "official" downtown looked arrestingly different from fifty years before. Not only had the semi-wasteland to the west of the railway overpass been long built up, but re-development now introduced trendy coffeehouses, high-rise apartments and condominiums, and new shops with nostalgic false fronts and awnings. More-over, both the hulking railway overpass and train station were gone, their memory preserved only in the Railtown Park and housing complex erected on the old Canadian Pacific Railway site. The downtown core to the east had been transformed into a shady corridor of concrete-and-glass skyscrapers (see Figure 3.5). It had also lost much of its human bustle. Underground transit reduced bus traffic; a series of commercial towers refocused stores, movie theatres, and patrons north off the avenue; and a labyrinth of tunnels and elevated pedways, Edmonton's answer to winter, meant that no one ever had to venture outside. Stretches of the street's once fashionable central portion had begun to look decidedly seedy and abandoned, leading to repeated calls and proposals for rejuvenation. East of 100 Street, large swathes of buildings disappeared. Many had been equated with inner-city decay and social prob-lems, such as Chinatown, but others were stately old landmarks. Of the hand-ful of iconic pre-1914 structures saved by citizen action, the most prominent was the triangular "Flatiron," or Gibson Block.[34]

The fate of the Hudson's Bay Company store (expanded in 1949 and 1955 in response to Alberta's first oil boom) epitomized Edmontonians' inconsistent attitude toward their material heritage. The company's postwar additions

Figure 3.5 Shift to skyscrapers in the downtown core, looking west along Jasper Avenue from 99 Street, 1982. Photograph by H. Hollingworth. *Source:* City of Edmonton Archives, EA-160-1654.

restated its status as Edmonton's oldest institution, as relevant and as committed to the community as ever – a boast assuredly designed to appeal to potential customers' own civic pride. The engraved texts on the new facade noted how the Hudson's Bay Company had served the people of Edmonton on the site since 1894 and that from the earlier fort, "centre of the fur trade on the western prairies, grew Edmonton, capital of Alberta." Carved above two new entrances were a Red River cart and an Indian on horseback spearing a buffalo. In 1989 Edmonton declared the landmark building a municipal historical resource. One year short of its 100th anniversary on the site, however, The Bay abandoned Jasper Avenue, making a business decision to relocate to the cluster of commercial towers to the north. Shortly thereafter, despite its own historical designation, a developer-sympathetic City Council proved equally unsentimental and approved alterations to the facade. The acquisition of the building by the University of Alberta in 2005 for a satellite campus secured its future but not the company's legacy. Not only was the building renamed Enterprise Square, but the university also applied to have the adjacent underground Bay Station renamed, and, when turned down, appealed. Although some Edmontonians liked the Star Trek-ish sound of Enterprise Station, others resented the attempt to erase the memory of the Hudson's Bay Company, which had been synonymous with the city since its beginnings. Changing the station's name, said one, "makes about as much sense as renaming Jasper Avenue 'Ralph Klein Trail.'"[35]

Changes in the ritualistic role of Jasper Avenue began well before it acquired a different look. The reasons were in part logistical. Official state parades and processions always had to accommodate the Legislature and the Cenotaph, both situated near but off Jasper (the Cenotaph site also focused Remembrance Day ceremonies elsewhere than the avenue itself). Increasingly, however, planners had to accommodate developments in technology and communications as well. In the days of trains, the location of the Canadian Pacific station drew crowds downtown to greet visiting dignitaries or returning troops and facilitated a parade or procession along Jasper. Air travel disrupted that. Not only did arrivals have to be brought to Jasper Avenue, sometimes from great distances and awkward locations and at speeds not suitable for public viewing, but Jasper was also no longer the single focus it had once been. The visit of George VI and Queen Elizabeth in the summer of 1939 during the first tour of Canada by a reigning monarch had required such adjustments – they had to be brought to the city centre from the municipal airport, and a traditional parade was abandoned in favour of an open motorcade.[36] Subsequent royal visits drew complaints about the speed of the motorcades and the inaccessibility of their occupants except at special advertised events across the city. In 1983 the throngs who hoped to see Prince Charles and Princess Diana on the eighteen-kilometre journey to the city centre from Canadian Forces Base Namao north of the city, where they landed, and as they travelled from appointment to appointment also criticized the use of a closed car. Jasper Avenue's only role was to transport the royal couple efficiently, and instead of a parade through downtown streets, well-wishers were invited to a contained walkabout in Sir Winston Churchill Square.[37]

Fashions in celebration and commemoration also had an impact. No arches along Jasper greeted George VI and Queen Elizabeth in 1939, and they would never appear again. Instead of moving spectacles in the open street, differently structured events took place in closed and better-controlled spaces:

when Elizabeth II and the Duke of Edinburgh came to help Albertans celebrate their centennial in 2005, they joined a sparse rain-soaked crowd for a cultural program in Commonwealth Stadium. Then, too, the more frequently Edmontonians hosted royalty, the less novel it became (international "pop star" Diana, Princess of Wales, excepted). They were even less likely to mass in the streets for prime ministers and governors general, who came and went with minimal fanfare. Also, as Edmonton lost its British character, people felt less attached to the empire and monarchy with which the city had long officially identified. For example, no public mourning in downtown streets attended the deaths of George VI and, most recently, the Queen Mother.[38] Nor did Elizabeth II's golden jubilee in 2003 see Jasper Avenue mobilized for a public outpouring of patriotism; in fact, it had not figured in the program marking her coronation.[39]

In addition to the abandonment of parades and the downtown core in favour of alternate events and sites, the focal point within the city centre for communal gathering moved off Jasper to Churchill Square and City Hall. An enclosed and compact space, unlike the six-kilometre thoroughfare, it was ideal for something like a royal walkabout. Following the relocation of the Cenotaph in the 1990s, it also suited Remembrance Day observances, although concern for aging veterans soon saw them moved to the Butterdome at the University of Alberta, negating decades of tradition at the monument (if not the site). When Edmonton welcomed home the 3rd Battalion, Princess Patricia's Canadian Light Infantry, from its tour in Afghanistan in 2002, the fragility of place and public memory and ritual centred on Jasper became obvious. First, and in sharp contrast to the return of the 49th Battalion after the First World War, the soldiers deplaned at Edmonton International Airport thirty kilometres south of downtown and were immediately whisked by bus to their base at Edmonton Garrison far to the north. Yellow ribbons, an American touch, lined the route.[40] Second, and again in sharp contrast to 1919, the parade, a seven-minute march held a full week later, avoided Jasper and went directly to Churchill Square; there, the soldiers' families (few of whom had local roots) waited with national, provincial, and civic dignitaries for speeches and a wreath-laying at the Cenotaph. Third, angry at their own treatment as forgotten men rather than returning heroes after much longer and bloodier conflicts, many veterans of the Korean and Second World Wars refused to attend.[41] Their grievance is significant, suggesting that the First World War – even with the stirring display of military pomp along Jasper led by the city's 49th Battalion – generated no local memory or tradition that survived that one occasion to dictate future protocol.

That Whyte Avenue was seriously able to challenge Jasper Avenue as the preferred site for civic ritual and tradition further indicates that by the late twentieth century public memory was not especially attached to place in the downtown artery. Whyte had always sat on the edge of official consciousness, and parts of it, especially the western portion by the University of Alberta, had often figured in official itineraries. Also, before the tracks crossed the High Level Bridge in 1913, the Canadian Pacific extension from Calgary ended at Whyte, making some ceremonial role for Strathcona inevitable for visiting dignitaries arriving by rail. What thrust the avenue to the fore, however, was the decision in the 1970s, spearheaded by the Old Strathcona Historical Foundation, to preserve and transform its turn-of-the-century central section into a people-friendly heritage district. One result was a vibrant, bar-focused youth culture and reputation for late-night raucousness difficult to police. Most infamously, the 2001 Canada Day riot that destroyed property up and down the avenue, occurred when the beer tent on the Legislature grounds closed and revellers turned south across the High Level Bridge to Whyte, rather than north to Jasper, to continue the party. It was also here that Oilers fans, some of whom were newcomers to the avenue, converged at each game's end during the team's improbable "run for the Cup" in the 2006 playoffs. At times, Whyte Avenue and Old Strathcona usurped Jasper's earnestness, hosting independent marches against the Iraq War, for example.[42] But they were best known for being slightly quirky and anti-establishment, more bottom-up than top-down. Neither the summer Fringe Festival nor Canada Day's "silly" parade competed with official events across the river, and indeed they rejected the stuffy formality associated with Jasper. A sign of the different personalities and values that Whyte and Jasper symbolized, the city's gays and lesbians staged their first parade, in 1992, in Old Strathcona. Equally significant, when the parade eventually moved to Jasper Avenue, its organizers initially chose not the downtown core but a gay-friendly neighbourhood that formed part of a thriving street culture in the west end.[43]

What Mary Bothwell, Mah Yuen, and the two Ukrainian women with their clashing impressions of Jasper Avenue would think of it today can only be speculated. What the future holds for the street in the communal life and

Commemorations

identity of Edmontonians, as reflected in their shared rituals and memory (both formal and informal), is also difficult to say. The annual summer parade – kick off to the City Ex, as Klondike Days was rebranded – constitutes the only surviving and regular user of the space from decades past. Much, no doubt, depends on the success of various projects intended to breathe life into the city's centre. Much depends as well on how collective moments and points of identification binding its citizens are not only defined but also judged best celebrated or commemorated. That Churchill Square and Whyte Avenue displaced Jasper to the extent that they did points both to the erosion of the identification of memory with place and to the fickleness of memory itself. Maybe Edmonton was simply too young, its population too mobile and diverse, and its growth too rapid for ritual and tradition to take hold and attract deep loyalty. Whyte Avenue's specific emergence as an alternative symbolic space to Jasper also highlighted the independence and priorities of the grassroots, including rejection of the cold skyscrapers of downtown for the welcoming brick, human scale, and ambiance of Old Strathcona.

In conclusion, although the early history of Jasper Avenue substantiates a fundamental claim of this volume – namely, that place is made meaningful by memory and commemorative practice and that placing is critical to memory making – its more recent history does not. Rather, it substantiates another theme of the book, the mobility of memory, and attests especially to the flexibility of place, ritual, and memory when people have no deep emotional investment in the place itself. Jasper Avenue was first and foremost a commercial centre and traffic corridor, which precluded its becoming anything like a *lieu de mémoire,* static and nostalgic. Its great advantage as a site for commemoration and memory was that it allowed for moving spectacles connecting points along its length as well as maximum opportunities for viewing and participation. But the street was only periodically borrowed for such purposes, acting both to reinforce and to contest established boundaries and power relationships. Also, just as the choice of Jasper as the focus of community ritual did not recognize any formative event or place in the existing local collective memory, so were the commemorative performances subsequently staged on the street not tied to anything that happened in its space. Nor were the monuments and memorials that the street attracted deliberately commemorative in intent; rather, they were utilitarian structures that evolved into popular monuments and memorials that extolled "the local" but, like the street itself, were not immune to progress. Ultimately, Jasper Avenue was – and re-mains – a living street in constant flux, making tension and accommodation between its provision for present and future needs and its role as a place of memory a permanent facet of its character.

NOTES

1 Criminal Case Files, Provincial Archives of Alberta (PAA), Edmonton, Alberta, Records of the Department of the Attorney General, 72.26/805.

2 John Sokolowksi, conversation with author, 20 February 2005.

3 See Historic Sites Committee, Edmonton Historical Board, "Jasper Avenue," in *Naming Edmonton: From Ada to Zoie* (Edmonton: University of Alberta Press, 2004), 165.

4 The obvious debts here are to Eric Hobsbawm and Terence Ranger, eds., *The Invention of Tradition* (1983; reprint, Cambridge, UK: Cambridge University Press, 1992), esp. 1-14; and Benedict Anderson, *Imagined Communities: Reflections on the Origin and Spread of Nationalism,* rev. ed. (London: Verso, 2006).

5 On the potency of the street as public space, see Patrick Cotrell, "St. Patrick's Day Parades in Nineteenth-Century Toronto: A Study of Immigrant Adjustment and Elite Control," *Histoire sociale/Social History* 25 (1992): 57-63; and Ronald Rudin, *Founding Fathers: The Celebration of Champlain and Laval in the Streets of Quebec, 1878-1908* (Toronto: University of Toronto Press, 2003).

6 The current St. Barbara's Russian Orthodox cathedral dates from 1958. On the parish's history, see *Saint Barbara Forty-Third Anniversary Year Book* (n.p., n.d.), 6-7; *Canadian Orthodox Messenger* 1 (1979): 7-11; and *A Century of Faith: St. Barbara's Russian Ortho-dox Cathedral, Edmonton, Alberta, 1902-2002* (Edmonton: St. Barbara's Russian Ortho-dox Cathedral Book Committee, 2002), 12-15.

7 On the demolition of the tower, which camouflaged the water tank servicing the store's sprinklers, see *Edmonton Journal,* 27 August 1938. On the opening of the new store, see *Edmonton Journal,* 14 and 15 November 1939.

8 Photograph, PAA, B6736; and Photograph, City of Edmonton Archives (CEA), EA-10-812.

9 Both inauguration events and decorations along Jasper Avenue were well photographed. See Photographs, PAA, B6705-B6752; and Photographs, CEA, EA-10-187, EA-10-798 to 800, EA-10-806, and EA-10-2527.

10 *Edmonton Bulletin,* 31 August and 2 September 1905.

11 See the coverage of the governor general's two-day visit in *Edmonton Bulletin,* 23 Sep-tember – 2 October 1909 (quotations 1 October). For photographs of the Chinese arch (often misidentified), see CEA, EA-10-2809, EA-10-822 and 823; and PAA, A11210.

12 Photograph, PAA, B4956.

13 *Edmonton Bulletin,* 11 and 12 November 1918; and Photograph, CEA, EA-10-655.

14 Photograph, PAA, P6567.

15 See the postcard album *Souvenir of the Queen's Diamond Jubilee Celebration at Edmonton, N.W.T., June 22-23-1897* (Edmonton: n.p., 1897); and *Edmonton Bulletin,* 17 and 24 June 1897.

16 Brian Osborne, "From Patriotic Pines to Diasporic Geese: Emplacing Culture, Setting our Sights, Locating Identity in a Transnational Canada," *Canadian Journal of Communications* 31, 1 (2006): 154. Opp and Walsh also discuss Osborne's work in the introduction to this volume.

17 Crystal Willie, "Ethnicity and the Pioneer in Alberta's Community Museums" (MA thesis, Department of History and Classics, University of Alberta, 2003), notes the input of a local French elite in early historical initiatives in post-fur trade Alberta.

18 *Edmonton Bulletin,* 24 and 28 January and 1 February 1901.

19 *Edmonton Bulletin,* 21 May 1910; Photographs, PAA, B4859; Photographs, CEA, EA-10-1008 to 1011. Edmonton also commemorated happy royal occasions, staging, for example, Coronation Day parades along Jasper Avenue for George V in 1911 and George VI in 1937; see Clippings Files, CEA.

20 *Edmonton Journal,* 20 January 1936 (republished from 1919). See also *Edmonton Bulletin,* 12 September 1919, for the festive appearance of Jasper Avenue; Photographs, CEA, EA-160-203, EA-160-707, EA-160-1601, EA-160-1605; and Photographs (erroneously dated), PAA, A2178, A10637.

21 *Edmonton Bulletin,* 11 and 12 November 1918.

22 *Edmonton Bulletin,* 22 and 23 (quotation) March 1919. See Figure 3.4 and Photograph, Glenbow Museum (GM), Calgary, Alberta, ND-3-170.

23 *Edmonton Bulletin,* 17 (quotation) and 24 June 1897; Photograph titled "Indian loyalty – Chief Alexander and his Band, next day," in the postcard album *Souvenir of the Queen's Diamond Jubilee,* n.p.

24 *Edmonton Bulletin,* 28 and 30 (quotation) March 1911 (Chinese participation); *Edmonton Daily Capital,* 21 and 23 June 1911 (marchers and placement); Photographs of the parade, including the Chinese float, CEA, EA-10-819 to 821, EA-10-3066 to 3067.

25 See *Edmonton Bulletin,* 26, 29, and 30 (quotation) June and 3 July 1928; *Edmonton Journal,* 26, 27, 29, and 30 June and 3 July 1928; and *Zakhidni visty,* June and July 1928. The following decade, the 1898 arrival date that the anniversary celebrated was jettisoned with the "discovery" of Ivan Pylypiw and Vasyl Eleniak, living on homesteads in Alberta, who had come to Canada in 1891.

26 *Edmonton Bulletin,* 26 June 1928.

27 *Edmonton Journal,* 1 and 3 May 1937; Photographs, CEA, EA-160-1230 to 1251, EA-160-1292 and 1293.

28 *Edmonton Journal,* 15 April 1970.

29 *Edmonton Journal,* 16 February and 23 March 2003; both marches were organized by the Edmonton Coalition against War and Racism.

30 Photograph (parade), PAA, A10124-5; Photograph (barbeque), GM, ND-3-6348a to 6348d.

31 *Edmonton Journal,* 14-18 July 1955.

32 Discussion based on Andrew Pemberton-Pigott, "'A Solid Footing in the Commercial World': The Creation and Development of Edmonton's Klondike Days" (term paper, Department of History and Classics, University of Alberta, 1998).

33 See *Edmonton Journal*, 20-25 (22 quotation) May 1984; and *Edmonton Sun*, 1 and 3 June 1987.

34 Edmonton's original and "replaced" Chinatowns, the latter planned together with City Council, are discussed in David Chuenyan Lai, "Three Chinatowns," in *Edmonton: The Life of a City*, ed. Bob Hesketh and Frances Swyripa (Edmonton: NeWest Press, 1995), 256-66. On the Gibson Block, see records of the Society for the Protection of Architectural Resources in Edmonton, CEA.

35 See, for example, *Real Estate Weekly*, 21 September 2000; *Edmonton Journal*, 6, 8 (quotation), and 13 August 2008; and http://www.connect2edmonton.ca/forum. In the wake of the University of Alberta's appeal, and reflecting a compromise, the one-time Bay Station is now known as the Bay/Enterprise Station.

36 *Edmonton Journal*, May and June 1939; Photographs, PAA, B8641, B8642, A9041, A9042; Photographs, CEA, EA-160-1805.

37 *Edmonton Journal*, 28-30 June and 1-2 July 1983. See also, for example, coverage of the visits of Princess Margaret for Alberta's seventy-fifth anniversary in 1980 (*Edmonton Journal*, 25-26 July 1980); the Queen Mother in 1985, when the province took out an ad to say where and when she could be seen (*Edmonton Journal*, 15 July 1985); and Pope John Paul II, in his open Popemobile, which pleased onlookers, although the cavalcade from Namao to Jasper Avenue disappointingly exceeded its promised speed (*Edmonton Journal*, 4-18 September 1984).

38 The tradition of memorial services, however, persisted. George VI's death, for example, was marked with memorial services in All Saints' Cathedral, Edmonton public schools, and Edmonton Gardens, as well as with a drumhead service at the Legislature grounds. See Clipping File (George VI – death), CEA; and *Edmonton Journal*, 16 February 1952.

39 See *Province of Alberta and City of Edmonton Coronation Program*, 2 June 1953, Clipping File (Elizabeth II – coronation), CEA.

40 Gerald Parsons, "How the Yellow Ribbon Became a National Folk Symbol," *Folklife Center News* 13, 3 (1991): 9-11.

41 *Edmonton Journal*, 29-31 July and 8 August 2002; *Edmonton Sun*, 30-31 July and 9 August 2002.

42 *Edmonton Journal*, 27 October 2002, 21 March 2004.

43 See, for example, *Edmonton Journal*, 22 June 1983, 8 June 1984, and 11, 12, and 16 June 2003; and *Edmonton Sun*, 27 April 1989, 24, 26, and 28 June 1992, 27 June 1993, and 12 July 1998.

The Highland Heart in Nova Scotia
Place and Memory at the Highland Village Museum

ALAN GORDON

4

"I always thought you were a damn liar, Michael Eoin!" shouted Big Malcolm Stephen on hearing a tale of artificial refrigeration producing blocks of ice in the heat of summer.[1] Such things simply were not part of the simple and rustic life of the Highland Scots of Cape Breton Island at the turn of the twentieth century. This incident was captured nearly fifty years later when a more modern Scots descendant, the American-born journalist Neil MacNeil, published a loving reminiscence of ten childhood years spent living in Cape Breton with his grandfather, Michael Eoin MacNeil.[2] Told with both a sense of humour and real affection for the people of Washabuckt, Nova Scotia, *The Highland Heart in Nova Scotia* depicts Cape Breton's Scottish settlers as a traditional, rural community, clinging to the Gaelic culture of the Scottish Highlands they had refashioned in their own corner of the New World. MacNeil's depiction of the descendants of Clan MacNeil, who had left the Scottish island of Barra in the nineteenth century for Barra Bay in the centre of Cape Breton Island, reveals a community of hardy individualists who overcame a harsh climate with "a simplicity that is close to sublime."[3] Eschewing even the basics of effete modernity, the MacNeils carved out a proud existence in the rugged landscape of Cape Breton, "well-equipped to care for themselves," much as their ancestors had done for centuries across the Atlantic.[4] The semi-fictionalized Highland Scots of MacNeil's book are a quaint, superstitious, and romanticized folk of times gone by, deeply rooted in the land and in their communities.

Five years after the publication of *Highland Heart,* a group of three thoroughly modern men met in Halifax to plan a similar romantic, or even anti-modern, image of the Highland Scottish heritage of Nova Scotia. They dreamed up a memorial to the Highland Clearances in the form of a Highland Village Museum to be constructed somewhere in Nova Scotia. This museum was to be the finishing piece of provincial tourism marketing. It would both draw modern, international tourists to Nova Scotia and draw out local folk memories of Scottish ancestry in Atlantic Canada. Like MacNeil's book, the village was supposed to preserve memories of life in a time and place that were disappearing in the face of advancing modernity. It could preserve the Highland heart, the "Scottish essence" of Nova Scotian life that made it a unique place in the world. The museum's successes and failures, then, inform our understanding of the anchoring and re-anchoring of an ethnic collective memory through imaginations of place.

The history of this museum does not follow an easy linear narrative. It is at once connected to global, but imagined, Scottish ethnicity and yet equally rooted in a discrete locale. It is at once a celebration of a simpler time and makes ideological claims about material progress. Even the narrative of the museum's construction is fractured and in places contradictory. It was a product of two periods and reflected their prevailing ideologies. Conceived and designed in the years that straddled the Second World War, it was not built until the 1970s when economic decline gripped the region. The tensions between these different periods similarly confound efforts to simplify the tale. The story of the Highland Village Museum, like the story of Nova Scotia's Scottish identity, is a story of nuance, complexity, and even contradiction.

This chapter explores a well-known dimension of Nova Scotian tourism promotion from the theoretical perspective known as "imagined communities." Since Benedict Anderson first published the book by this name in 1983, the concept of imagined communities has come to dominate scholarly thinking about ethnicity and nationalism.[5] Many historians have cast such "imagined" ethnic communities as falsehoods, much like Big Malcolm Stephen when he denied the existence of artificial refrigeration. Perhaps the most notorious example is Hugh Trevor-Roper's belittling of Highland culture as pure invention.[6] But unlike artificial refrigeration, which demonstrably exists even though the "primitive folk" of *Highland Heart* could not accept it, ethnic identities are less easily demonstrated. Nevertheless, they should not be summarily dismissed, however easy it is to debunk their myths. Real or not, imagined communities operate on individuals and groups of individuals in ways that help to steer their worldviews. This focus on falsehood and truth diverts attention from other issues in the making of imagined communities that are worth exploring.

Certainly, there are many problems with applying Anderson's model of national-identity formation universally. There are chronological and empirical weaknesses in the book that are highlighted by Anderson's unwillingness to engage with exceptions to the rule. And in places – for instance, in his discussion of eighteenth-century newspapers – Anderson's depictions fail to capture past reality accurately. Indeed, although central to Anderson's argument, his history of print-capitalism raises too many questions to be convincing. For instance, Michael Lessnoff has pointed out that Anderson's argument focuses only on the production side of print-capitalism and that his understanding of capitalism itself lacks nuance and cannot explain why these new ideas reached beyond cultural elites.[7] More broadly, the tension in Anderson's accounts between elites, colonizers, and everyday people is never effectively resolved. Nevertheless, *Imagined Communities* has had exceptional staying power and is one of the most influential books of the late twentieth century. It offers not so much a model as a way of thinking about national identity. In this case of Nova Scotia's Scottish identity, Anderson's discussion of the map and memory suggests how time and place can be connected to a sense of community.[8]

Anderson's imagined communities are fundamentally territorial, as he makes clear in discussing the importance of drawing national borders. But they are also territorial in ways Anderson does not anticipate. *Imagined Communities* focuses on the effort to draw lines around nations, but the map is not the only possible geographical representation of national identity. Features of particular natural landscapes, such as the forests and lakes of the Canadian Shield, are sometimes taken for markers of "national" landscapes. This is not to imply that there is only one "national" geographical form in any nation. And certainly the Shield depicted by the Group of Seven is only a partial and regional depiction of Canada's landscape. However, as many authors have noted, specific cultural practices have produced an image of the Canadian Shield as emblematic of a kind of Canadian identity in ways that privilege its iconic features of geography.[9] As Simon Schama explains, people often connect their communities to ideas of landscape and associate geographical features with ethnic identities. Over the eighteenth and nineteenth centuries, landscape, a picturesque vista, idealized as much as real, evoked ideas of community and connections between populations and their modes of life. In this way, landscape, understood broadly, helps to embed a sense of place within particular local and ethnic identities.[10] One such example of this placing of identity in geography might be the link between Scottish identity and the bleak yet compelling landscape of northern Great Britain. Connections between the landscape, the "place" of Scotland, and its people crossed the Atlantic with Scottish migrants and their descendants and later became wrapped in the geography of Nova Scotia.

Place is not a simple concept. In its most basic construction, place is simply named space. Yet, despite the common tendency to see place in such terms, it is really an idea that encompasses not only geographical co-ordinates but also residents, landscapes, built environments, and ideas as an integral part of the imagination of community. Citing John Agnew, Tim Creswell has outlined a three-part understanding of place as "meaningful location." First, "locations" are geographical co-ordinates, the physical site in a material world. At the next level, "locale" represents the physical environment in which social relations are carried out, the material conditions of lived experience. And finally, there is a "sense of place," a concept that encompasses the emotional attachments people feel to those co-ordinates and physical environments.[11] Place brings together meaning and the material world in a particular location. It is a lived experience that is simultaneously material and abstract. Sense of place draws out the connection between the character or identity of locales and our own identities; it provides a sense of belonging to those places.[12]

The term "sense of place" imparts additional layers to the understanding of place. For one, it suggests that place is also imagined. David Harvey has discussed this notion of the imagined place in a paper first delivered in 1990 but published in 1993. For Harvey, "place," "in whatever guise, is like space and time, a social construct." Harvey's reaction to the racial politics of Baltimore directs him to see "place" as an attempt to mark boundaries that reinforce a social hierarchy, a sort of political economy of place. Like space and time, capital is mobile, but place offers what Harvey sees as the security of fixity or permanence for local communities.[13] Place, then, is an effort to fend off the anxieties of globalization by marking lines of inclusion and exclusion around communities.

As noted in the introduction to this volume, Doreen Massey sees things differently. In a paper that appeared alongside Harvey's in 1993, she imagines place as more inclusive and less reactionary. In what amounts to a reformulation of place as a process, Massey describes her own multicultural London neighbourhood as a site of diversity and progressive inclusiveness.[14] This is not merely a case of different examples producing contrasting conclusions. Setting aside the principal concerns of Harvey and Massey, this analysis explores how "place" links the local and the global in important ways. In contrast with Harvey's vision of place used to defend against globalization, Massey envisions a more hopeful interaction of global influences on local relationships as local people bring "outside" cultures to new places through their social interactions. In the Highland diaspora that helped to produce a Scottish community in Nova Scotia, social relationships and sense of place were fluid. The sense of place was envisioned across the Atlantic and at the same time rooted at home in North America. In this complexity of place as an imagined construct, scholars are offered a path to understand the emotive power of "place" in ways that are not necessarily bound to physical geography.

A second layer that sense of place adds to the understanding of place comes through memory. Place and time are deeply interconnected in this imagination. Indeed, it is the passage of time that gives place its emotional resonance with communities. Although Massey considers such a conception to be reactionary, many communities attempt to root their sense of place through an authenticity of memory. As Jeff Malpas puts it, "the sense of place, one might argue, is bound up intimately with a sense of heritage."[15] The Scottish ethnic identity imagined in the Highland Village Museum suggests the importance of the past in constructing a notion of community. Museums serve as an archive of memory. Living-history museums, such as village recreations, connect the past to specific places by demonstrating a semblance of the physical environment (the locale) of the past. And local people often donate artefacts that establish personal connections to the place archive.[16] The Highland Village Museum was built on a notion of connection to generations past and to their lives as members of the same community. Moreover, by drawing attention to the story of trans-atlantic migration, this imagination of the past connected in one mnemonic community people who lived in different times and in different locations. Here was a sophisticated understanding of community that linked local and international identities in important ways. This imagining allowed a sense of community to form beyond the geographical and temporal limits of a single place and time.

I'M NOT LOOKING FOR A NEW SCOTLAND

Ian McKay has argued that Nova Scotian "Scottishness" was invented, primarily through the efforts of Premier Angus L. Macdonald, in the years between 1933 and 1953.[17] In his view, the province's highly successful reimagining of itself as "New Scotland" in the mid-twentieth century was an elite-driven exercise that remembered "Scottishness" in a nostalgic fashion, romanticizing a pre-modern folk culture and paradoxically marginalizing the Gaelic roots of the population. The Highland Village Museum fits McKay's interpretation of Nova Scotian identity in important ways. It was Macdonald's initiative and located on Cape Breton Island, not far from his birthplace. In some ways, the museum was a tribute to Angus L. Macdonald. Celebrations at the museum portrayed Highland music, dancing, and the Gaelic language as an exotic "otherness" disconnected from modern life, much as McKay describes. Still, local citizens were not passive recipients of an official memory. Ordinary Cape Bretoners, in the personal memories they amassed, in their music and socializing, in their interpretation of landscape, and in the uses they made of the museum, helped to shape a collective memory of "Scotland" and forged their own imagined community. Even though the museum did not become the tourist attraction its designers hoped, locals found it a useful setting to celebrate their identity as "Highlanders" or Scots on special occasions.

Nova Scotia's Scottishness, despite its commonsense veracity, does not truly hold up to scrutiny, as McKay's article demonstrates. The historic name of Nova Scotia alludes to the 1621 Scottish charter granted by James I and VI to Sir William Alexander. In 1624 a small section of Edinburgh Castle was designated "Nova Scotia" so that some 150 baronets could take "possession" of their New World estates as part of Alexander's first serious plan for colonization. In 1629, a few settlements were established at Cape Breton and Port

112

Commemorations

Royal in the Annapolis Basin, but they lasted only until Britain returned the territory to France in 1632. This original Nova Scotia was far more ephemeral, and of less political or economic significance, than the French Acadia that overlapped it in the seventeenth century. This stillborn project of colonization cannot be construed as the origin of modern Nova Scotia, despite the name, or as representing the Scottish origin of its people. Perhaps, then, the province's Scottish character derived from the exodus of Scottish Highlanders during the Highland Clearances from about 1790 to the middle of the nineteenth century. By the end of this period, thousands of dispossessed people had arrived in Nova Scotia from Scotland, and in some counties, particularly on Cape Breton Island, Scots settlement accounted for a major proportion of the population.[18]

The demographic importance of Scottish people and their descendants in Nova Scotia is undeniable. However, it was too much to claim, as W.L. Fillmore once did, that Nova Scotia "is New Scotland ... with her own flag and a population predominantly of Scottish descent."[19] The 1921 census, at the start of McKay's period of emerging "tartanism," identified 148,000 people of Scottish origin in the province. This was not the largest provincial gathering of Scots; Ontario's population of Scottish origin stood at almost 400,000. Proportionately, the nearly 30 percent of Nova Scotians who declared themselves Scottish compared favourably to the 13 percent across Canada as a whole and represented the highest provincial concentration of Scots in the country. But this too is misleading. The Scots in Nova Scotia were outnumbered by the nearly 40 percent of the province who claimed "English origin" in the same 1921 census. The provincial identity, then, was more complex and nuanced than such promotional trappings as a saltire flag, a provincial tartan, and the piper at the New Brunswick border suggested to bus loads of tourists every summer.

Even within tartanism, there were further nuances that the Highland Village Museum helps to reveal. The museum that emerged in the 1970s was a living-history village that reflected more than a fantasy past and an imagined provincial ethnicity. It also told a story of migration and material improvement in the New World. In *Highland Heart*, MacNeil's portrayal of Washabuckt pointedly contrasts himself and his well-read and well-travelled grandfather with the simple folk among whom they lived. Similarly, the portrayal of a

Scottish and Nova Scotian folk history at the museum reveals a tension between a romanticized folk and a progressive people, both rooted in distinctive landscapes that connected them to the global Scottish diaspora.

AN CLACHAN GAIDHEALACH: THE 1950S AND THE POLITICS OF INNOCENCE

Nova Scotia's tartanism, including the origins of the Highland Village Museum, was part of a much broader, global Gaelic imagination. Although the Scots of the Enlightenment may have distanced themselves from a too close association with their "primitive" Celtic ancestors,[20] some Victorian Scottish nationalists began mythologizing a Highland past. Certainly, a romantic mythologization of the Highland *landscape* was evident early in Queen Victoria's reign. But Highland landscape painting built an iconography in which the historical and contingent human presence was lost to a tranquil, Arcadian natural wilderness.[21] The "repopulation" of the (imagined) Highlands was a longer process connected to the romantic writings of nationalists like Sir Walter Scott, the activities of antiquarians, and processes of modernity beyond the scope of this chapter. However, numerous historians have mused about the construction of Highland culture as a national imagery for all Scotland, including the Lowlands, during the course of the nineteenth century. Amid anxieties about the decline of Scottish identity, some nationalists saw a way forward through reference to the distinctive, imaginary Highland culture that earlier Victorians had dreamed up. By the early twentieth century, the outward trappings of Highland culture had become associated with Scottish national identity.[22]

Nova Scotia followed a similar pattern of decline, abandonment, and revival. For instance, use of the Gaelic language had declined in the province throughout the nineteenth century. Although the School Act of 1841 gave equal status to English, French, German, and Gaelic as languages of instruction, few communities took advantage. Like Nova Scotia's other minority languages, Gaelic came under increasing pressure. In the 1870s school inspectors commented on the pernicious influence of the language on accent and the pronunciation of English words. From the 1880s fewer and fewer parents encouraged their children to learn the ancestral language, preferring instead that they adopt English as the language of modernity.[23] As the twentieth century progressed, Gaelic in Nova Scotia seemed to many all but lost. Certainly, some continued to comment on Gaelic's survival in the early twentieth century, and no doubt people continued to speak it in some form. But such claims were most often made in the era of tartanism and reflected a romantic vision of Highland identity in Nova Scotia as it was in the process of invention.[24] Still, calls for a Gaelic revival began to be heard. Gaelic fit well with the culture of innocence that Nova Scotia used to promote itself as a "playground" for tourists.[25] Gaelic was promoted as the language of the simple Highland folk, whose lives were lived without the pressures of modernity. By 1938 James MacNeil could insist that Gaelic instruction was a "sacred right" for the Scots of Nova Scotia. But it was also something that needed nurturing and protection: "There are at least 140,000 descendants of our noble race in the Province whom we intend to arouse to a sense of duty in preserving their mother tongue that blossomed into eloquence and poetry thousands of years ago."[26] That same year, St. Ann's Gaelic College was founded by Rev. A.W.R. MacKenzie (a man who did not himself "have the Gaelic") as a school devoted to the study and preservation of the Gaelic language and Celtic arts and culture. Situated in the heart of the earliest Scottish settlement in Cape Breton, the college began as a school of Gaelic language in a small log cabin overlooking St. Ann's Bay. Even in its early days, MacKenzie had lofty ambitions for his program. And it was clearly connected to the broader program of promoting tartanism and innocence both as a tourist marketing tool and as an ideological imperative that reinforced liberal individualism.[27] But its organization amounted to barely more than MacKenzie's personal efforts, and it always looked greater on paper than in reality. Other aspects of Highland culture followed suit. Highland dancing, for instance, once popular in Cape Breton, declined in the twentieth century to be replaced by English square dancing and step dancing. In mainland Nova Scotia, it remained popular, especially around Antigonish, but had fallen out of favour on the island.[28] When the St. Ann's Gaelic College held its first Highland Games, dancers had to be imported from the mainland. Yet, in the span of half a decade, W.L. Fillmore boasted in 1955, between 400 and 600 authentic Highland dancers were active on the island.[29]

Much as Nova Scotians imagined their cultural connections to Scotland, the idea of a village museum was borrowed from Scotland itself. In 1938, at the British Empire Exhibition held in Glasgow, Premier Macdonald had seen a mock-up of a Hebridean village. For a separate fee, visitors to the exhibition could escape its triumphant modernity and slip back to the simpler times of a Highland clachan. Modelled on a similar exhibit at the Glasgow Exhibition of 1911, the clachan combined the real with the imaginary, the authentic with the false. Peopled by Gaelic-speaking Highlanders, it offered displays of household tasks undertaken in reproduced cottages from across the Hebrides, set around a meandering brook that disappeared into a painted backdrop of a generic Highland loch. The clachan was a controversial addition to the exhibition, with many critics arguing that it was neither historically accurate nor authentic. Others complained that it distracted from the modernist theme of Scotland's progress that underpinned the fair with its anachronistic, primitive, and pre-industrial caricature of the Scottish people. It was even lampooned by the popular *Sunday Post* comic strip "The Broons."[30] Yet, despite criticism and witticism, the clachan was at least influential, with over 1.5 million visitors willing to pay the supplement to have a look. Angus L. Macdonald was much taken with it and imagined building a copy for Nova Scotia both to promote tourism and to help inculcate his personal vision of the province as a New Scotland. However, world events put this dream on hold, as Macdonald moved from Halifax to Ottawa to serve in the wartime cabinet of Mackenzie King.

The Nova Scotia Highland Village, then, emerged from Macdonald's fertile imagination, combined with his "memories" of Scotland. A few years after returning to Nova Scotia as premier, he called a meeting at his Halifax home to discuss again the possibility of building a clachan or shieling in Cape Breton. There had been a "lone shieling," a single replica settler cabin, constructed in 1942 in the new Cape Breton Highlands National Park and associated with the opening of the Cabot Trail as a tourist draw. In 1925 the province began opening up Cape Breton's northern peninsula for motor tourists by constructing the Cabot Trail, a highway hugging the coast of the island. The park and the highway combined to create an attraction for motorists.[31] The lone shieling, essentially an empty home, was one of the early attractions placed in the park. Of course, the irony of building a fake abandoned home in a park made by expropriating settlers' properties was apparently lost on federal and provincial officials.

Macdonald's scheme was to be a grander tourist draw than a lone shieling. He envisioned a full Highland village almost exactly as he had seen in Glasgow. Although the premier passed away unexpectedly, and never saw the museum develop, the other men at his meeting, C.I.N. MacLeod and W.L. Fillmore, pushed the plan forward. They secured blueprints for the 1938 Glasgow clachan from the architect and presented them to the Nova Scotia Association of

Scottish Societies in 1954.[32] The following year, the association itself made a formal request to the province that it fund six initiatives to promote Scottish-themed tourism in the province, the first of which was "the establishment of a Highland Village at a place with a recognized Scottish environment."[33] What exactly a "recognized Scottish environment" might mean was unclear, but it demonstrates the connection of landscape and place at the heart of this identity.

Despite many protests from rival communities, including a strong argument for Pictou on the mainland, where the ship *Hector* had landed in 1773 carrying 189 Scottish passengers, organizers fixed early on a site known as Hector's Point near the village of Iona as the location for the museum.[34] Centrally located on Cape Breton Island, this site offered a number of justifications. It was relatively close to the birth place of Macdonald and even closer to the Washabuckt of MacNeill's bestselling *Highland Heart*. It was sufficiently inland to meet the goal of drawing tourists off the beaten track, which was a major imperative of official interest in the project.[35] And there was a convenient parcel of land for sale. This segment of the story clearly fit into the construction of tartanism outlined by McKay and reflected the period's major concerns. It combined the economic interests of the postwar tourism boom then unfolding in North America with an interest in citizen education. As Fillmore wrote in a 1955 justification of the museum, "the highland village should not only be looked on as a tourist attraction. There are many other advantages too long to go into here, one of which is to incorporate the educational angle."[36] It exploited an image of antimodernism and innocence, an imaginary simple life, to expand the thoroughly modern tourist industry in the province.

BUILDING THE HIGHLAND VILLAGE MUSEUM

Despite this quick initiation of the project, very little was accomplished before the early 1970s. Certainly, a Highland Village Society (HVS) was organized and incorporated by MacLeod and Fillmore, and local boards of trade and tourist associations traded notes on what the museum could accomplish for the local economy. But little in the way of construction was carried out. The HVS, a voluntary organization, relied on the free time and donations of residents of an economically depressed region of the country. The collapse of the Cape Breton steel and coal industries, already in progress in the 1940s and finally recognized with the appointment of a Royal Commission on Coal in 1960, hampered fundraising and dampened prospects for this new and untested venture. Starting in 1962, the HVS organized Highland Village Day, a gathering of pipe-band concerts held on the first Saturday in August. Until the 1970s this was the main fundraising opportunity, and it never produced sufficient revenue to carry out the full construction. After it opened to the public in 1966, the museum operated on a budget assembled from gifts, small donations, and the proceeds of its annual festival.

This financial insecurity changed only in the years that followed the creation of the Cape Breton Development Corporation, or DEVCO, in 1967. A product of yet another royal commission on the Cape Breton steel and coal industries, DEVCO initially concentrated on running the nationalized coalmines of the Dominion Steel and Coal Corporation. However, its mandate also included a gradual phasing out of coal and the diversification of the island's economy, with a special focus on tourism. Particularly after Liberal Party strategist Tom Kent took charge of DEVCO in 1971, the company turned to a policy of small grassroots enterprises linked to Cape Breton's natural resources and the service economy.[37] The Highland Village was a natural fit for this local, small-scale kind of development assistance. DEVCO first became interested in the Hector's Point site in 1972 when looking for suitable properties for a motel. With its scenic environs and proximity to pleasure-boating opportunities on Bras d'Or Lake, the Highland Village site was particularly attractive. DEVCO entered into an agreement with the HVS to build what became the Highland Village Inn and thus put itself in a position to be interested in the development of the village museum as well. By 1974 DEVCO's grant to the museum had grown to over $60,000. Although it never underwrote the entire venture, nor took an ownership stake, DEVCO's support permitted sufficient stability to develop the village.[38]

The original plan had called for a reproduction of a Scottish Highland village along the lines of those in the earlier Glasgow exhibitions. However, the next generation of planners turned this idea into a commemoration of their own particular history in the New World. Crafted with the help of Barry Diamond of the Technical Division of the provincial Department of Industry and Development, 1971's master plan helped to steer the museum in a new direction.[39] Instead of a series of Highland cottages, the village would represent the stages of material improvement the Scots had undergone once in Canada.

Figure 4.1 The Tigh Dubh or Highland Blackhouse as it appeared in the summer of 2004. Looking south across the open water of Bras d'Or Lake, low-lying clouds and the apparent emptiness of the distant hills help visitors to imagine this as a bleak, Hebridean landscape. Photograph by Alan Gordon.

Certainly, elements of Highland primitiveness remained in the finished development. The highlight of the village reconstruction was the Tigh Dubh, or Highland Blackhouse (see Figure 4.1). The Tigh Dubh had been projected as one of the first units of the village in its 1950s plan by Cameron MacLeod.[40] According to MacLeod, a "typical blackhouse" was a rough stone structure with a sod roof. The interior, at least at Hector's Point, was divided into three rooms. Usually, there was only one door and no windows, except perhaps for a skylight above the main living quarters. In the central room, a fireplace burned peat for warmth, and the smoke was vented, without benefit of a chimney, through the opening in the roof. The floor was earthen.[41] Here was the very stereotype of primitive living that fit nicely with twentieth-century imaginations. Although such primitive housing was common in the outer

Hebrides early in the nineteenth century, when many of the Clearance migrants left the Highlands, it significantly underplayed the development of Scotland and made the Highlands a romanticized place removed from history. The inclusion of the Tigh Dubh, and indeed its being featured at the beginning of the museum, connected Nova Scotia's Scottish essence – its "Highland heart"– to a primitive world separated from the challenges of twentieth-century modernity. It implied a connection between old and new Scotlands. Most obviously, the structure spoke to the ethnic origins of the people in Nova Scotia. It connected them to their ancestral homes in the Highlands and islands of Scotland and emphasized commonness. This was the root of the Cape Breton Highland culture that the village sought to memorialize. Yet the Tigh Dubh also represented a boundary. It separated life in the old country from the conditions of the new one. It pointed not to a heritage continued in the New World but to one that had been left behind in Scotland.

Throughout the 1960s the Tigh Dubh and the performance stage for Highland Village Day were the only structures on the site. However, in the 1970s the HVS was able to flesh out its plan of a multi-building village museum. New buildings were added gradually over the first half of the 1970s. As was typical for such reconstructed "villages" in Canada, some were period structures moved from original locations and others were new constructions modelled on the styles of the past. By 1975, when expansion halted, the museum had eleven of a planned twenty-six buildings in place and was hosting between 10,000 and 12,000 visitors a year.[42] What was less typical of living-history museums was the deliberate reference to historical change in the plan. Normally, pioneer-village museums attempt to portray a particular period of the past, such as Ontario's Upper Canada Village, which represents a "typical eastern Ontario village of the 1860s."[43] At the Highland Village, however, the museum was laid out so that visitors moved more or less clockwise through the decades of the nineteenth century. From the Tigh Dubh, visitors progressed to a log house of 1810, the centre-chimney house of 1829, the central-hallway house and school of 1865, and the 1920s general store. The message of progress was clear. As the generations passed, each built better and larger homes, formal educational institutions emerged, and by the 1920s a commercial complex had been added.

These were not the quaint folk of McKay's 1950s tartanism but a progressive people building on the labour of successive generations and improving themselves materially over time. This should not be surprising but is perhaps a demonstration of the operation of local memory in the project. Nineteenth-century Cape Bretoners were often conscious of their improved standard of living and sometimes wrote home to proclaim it.[44] Although, much as McKay's argument suggests, the Tigh Dubh might be seen to reify the folk in the past, this community envisioned a past of economic accomplishment and progression and separated itself from the primitive poverty left behind in the old country. Certainly, this could also reinforce the Darwinian individualism McKay caught in Nova Scotian tourist promotion. The emphasis on self-sufficiency supported a liberal interpretation of material improvement. People pulled themselves up by their own bootstraps. But such a message was contradicted by the museum's own dependency on DEVCO financing and by its increasing reliance on provincial and federal expert support. Indeed, its own story, one that was well known among locals, demonstrated the failure of a system of individual volunteerism and the importance of state support in building community institutions. The museum of the 1970s, as opposed to that planned in the 1950s, reflected changes and contradictions in the ideology of liberalism.

There were other myths built into the museum's message. The Highland Village ignored the religious discord of the nineteenth century. Until the relocation of an old Presbyterian church in 2003, there was no expression of religion whatsoever in the village. Animosities between Catholics and Protestants, both in the Highlands and in Nova Scotia, were left outside this expression of collective memory. Presbyterian and Catholic Scots in Cape Breton in the nineteenth century lived in proximity to one another but did not intermingle much. Separations of faith were reflected in institutional and cultural separations. People attached great importance to religious boundaries, and even within the Presbyterian faith, internal divisions crossed the Atlantic and continued to produce dissent and friction.[45] On the other hand, a secular, state education and commerce were central to this imagined past. The school and the general store – the state and private enterprise – represented the institutional life of the Highland heart. The Highland past on display for tourists presented memories of a simpler time and a united community.

Despite its genesis as a tourist attraction, the museum never really fulfilled its anticipated role in the provincial tourist industry. Financial records reveal the small scale of the project. At the 1974 Annual Meeting of the Highland

Village Society, a year described as the "best year to date," excluding government grants, revenue totalled less than $20,000.[46] In part, the village was simply too far off the beaten track of the Cabot Trail to draw scenery-loving motor tourists down Cape Breton's secondary roads. On the other hand, this remoteness suggests the Highland Village must be seen less as a typical tourist attraction and more as an expression of local community.

From the beginning, many Cape Bretoners felt connected to the museum project and made a number of donations of artefacts to appear in the village. There is no handy list of donations to the museum; artefacts began flowing into the collection before there was much of an organization to properly collect them, let alone catalogue the collection. By 1964 the museum had gathered nearly 800 artefacts from across the province, with an estimated value of nearly $5,000.[47] In 1968 the museum reported on its holdings to the provincial Department of Trade and Industry. Before describing, in general terms, the kinds of artefacts the museum had amassed, the curator offered an overview of the collection: "The contents of the Museum are made up [of] primitive tools used by the early settlers after they came to this country from Scotland … With very few exception[s] the articles in it were donated chiefly from Victoria and Cape Breton Counties."[48] This collection represented an archive of local and personal memories commemorating the life and labour of past generations. Memory does not function only through abstraction. Material traces of the past serve as prompts for memory and, alongside texts and narratives, can be mutually constitutive of shared or collective memories.[49] Local people felt connected enough to the mission of the village to entrust the care of personal heirlooms (although some items were no doubt just old junk) to the village staff. They identified their family histories with that of the wider Scottish identity proclaimed by the Highland Village Museum.

Another avenue for local people to use the village and its message of Scottish identity was Highland Village Day. Modelled on the Scottish National Mod, another innovated tradition of late-Victorian Scotland, the day was a festival of Celtic arts and crafts, music, song, and dance. Highland Village Day was the most popular feature of the village, and every year through the 1970s it drew half the annual visitors to the museum. This was a local day open to tourists but dominated by Cape Bretoners and attended prominently by community leaders, such as local Member of Parliament Allan MacEachen.[50] It was as much a community day as it was a commemorative or tourist festival, as well as helping to raise much needed funds from everyday people and government representatives. Highland Village Day spread local awareness of the project, keeping it and the community's Scottish identity in people's minds.

In this identity, the physical landscape of Cape Breton was of crucial concern. The allegedly "Scottish" landscape around Iona figured in promotions. The landscape of Cape Breton Island was central in this imagination of ethnicity and community. Back in the 1950s Hugh Mackenzie, secretary of the Grand Narrows Board of Trade, wrote Cameron MacLeod to promote the choice of Iona for the Highland Village over rival Pictou and Antigonish Counties on the mainland. His argument hinged on the "choice" made by the founding settlers of Iona: "Until the arrival of the ship *Harmony* in 1821, all who settled at Iona and the adjacent areas ... came from Pictou and Antigonish Counties. This, in itself, should be ample proof that then, as now, the scenery in this area was such as to please the most fastidious Highlander."[51] Time after time, specific reference was made to the similarities of the Cape Breton and Scottish landscapes. Every year at Highland Village Day, the sound of the pipes, the wearing of kilts and the tartan, the village, and the *land* blended to make an imaginary New Scotland. But the landscape of Cape Breton is not at all a Scottish landscape. Its Scottishness is imagined. The terrain at Hector's Point in particular is low lying, more heavily forested than the Scottish Highlands. Sitting an ocean apart, the climates of Scotland and Nova Scotia should contribute to distinct senses of place. John Gray has drawn attention to the at times ironic connection the Scots poet Tim Douglas drew between Scottish identity and Scotland's weather in the 1980s.[52] Although he wrote of the Borders, not the Highlands, there is a similar yet distinct irony captured in the imagination of Cape Breton's Scottishness. Nova Scotia, with much harsher winters and hotter summers than Scotland, supports different fauna and flora than one will find in northern Britain. Even the human influence on the landscape – whether the construction of buildings and houses, the surveying and parcelling of land into separate plots, or the techniques, crops, and livestock of farming – highlights the differences between Nova Scotia and Scotland. However much people might imagine that Bras d'Or Lake looks like a Scottish loch, Cape Breton's Scottish descendants lived and built in a New World environment with materials and conditions specific to the place. But in the imaginations of local residents, it felt Scottish. Even local, face-to-face communities are, to an extent, imagined.

CONCLUSION

Conceived in the 1950s, the Highland Village Museum came together in the 1970s as federal and provincial state expansion poured money into local development and expressions of ethnicity. The Highland Village Museum must be seen in this context. Born of the 1950s Celtic revival on the island, it gestated in the 1960s but flourished only in the 1970s culture of government support for multiculturalism and regional development. As liberalism changed to accommodate greater state intervention, so too did the inspiration behind the museum. What had been planned as a voluntarist venture was undertaken instead as part of state support for economic redevelopment and, by 1980, had been absorbed by the provincial state as an arm of the Nova Scotia Museum. Through it all, the Highland Village Museum blended elite ideals of antimodernism and folk innocence with local memories that helped to express an idea of the Scottish community of Nova Scotia.

Imagined communities are not entirely real, but nor are they lies or patent falsehoods of the kind that Big Malcolm Stephen accused Michael Eoin MacNeil of fabricating with his story of refrigeration. Imagined communities operate on individuals and groups of individuals by building connections to the world beyond immediate experience. In the case of an emigrant population, such as the Highland Scots of Nova Scotia, the "community" is imagined at multiple levels. Speaking more directly to an Irish experience, John Belchem has noted that "imagined communities, for those who leave home, become doubly important because the initial referent, the shaping community, is left behind and a further community, the new homeland, begins to shape the mental landscape."[53] Such a double, or perhaps multiple, importance was clearly at work in Nova Scotia in the twentieth century. As Paul Basu has noted, myths of a common origin help to unite diasporic communities. For Scots, whose diaspora is truly a global phenomenon, the sense of place of a Scotland left behind helped communities to reforge themselves in new environments. Despite the imprecision of the image, the remembered place was the mythic Highlands.[54] This chapter examines only one aspect of these multiple imaginations of community, that which linked together the Scots in the New World and bound them to their ethnic ancestry.

This chapter argues that the concept of place as connected to memory is complex and multifaceted. Nova Scotians looked back to Scotland for inspiration but not in false mimicry of their ancestors. Their imaginings of place and time were part of a negotiation between local and global Scottish identities. Seen from this perspective, the community was imagined as a Canadian way of being part of an ethnic identity that was also at once rooted in a place and roaming the globe. The Highland Village Museum connected a global Scottishness to a local narrative of migration as betterment. As much as the Scottish Highlands the community remembered was a fiction of the imagination, it was nevertheless integral to the memory of place in the community. Cape Breton Island itself might appear more real in this memory, but even it was, to a degree, altered by the imagination. Projected as a landscape similar to that in Scotland, it helped the people to remain connected to their ancestral ties, even as they abandoned their past way of life and found new ways to express their heritage. Place, then, is remembered in ways that reflect the complexity and nuance of the human imagination.

ACKNOWLEDGMENT

The research for this chapter was supported by a grant from the Social Sciences and Humanities Research Council of Canada. The author would also like to thank Pauline MacLean and Roger Chaisson of the Highland Village Museum for providing access to the museum's files.

NOTES

1   Neil MacNeil, *The Highland Heart in Nova Scotia* (New York: Charles Scribner's Sons, 1948), 48.

2   Neil MacNeil was born in Massachusetts in 1891 and attended St. Francis Xavier University in Nova Scotia before becoming a correspondent for the *Montreal Gazette* and later editor at the *New York Times*. In 1954 he became an assistant to Herbert Hoover. His papers are preserved at the Herbert Hoover Presidential Library in West Branch, Iowa.

3   MacNeil, *Highland Heart*, 34.

4   Ibid., 51.

5   Benedict Anderson, *Imagined Communities: Reflections on the Origin and Spread of Nationalism*, rev. ed. (London: Verso, 2006).

6   Hugh Trevor-Roper, "The Invention of Tradition: The Highland Tradition of Scotland," in *The Invention of Tradition*, ed. Eric Hobsbawm and Terence Ranger (Cambridge, UK: Cambridge University Press, 1983), 15-42.

7   Michael Lessnoff, *Ernest Gellner and Modernity* (Cardiff: University of Wales Press, 2002), 42. See also John Breuilly, "Approaches to Nationalism," in *Mapping the Nation*, ed. Gopal Balakrishnan (London: Verso, 1996), 160-61.

8   Anderson, *Imagined Communities*, 170-75, 187-203. See also Mark Hamilton, "New Imaginings: The Legacy of Benedict Anderson and Alternative Engagements of Nationalism," *Studies in Ethnicity and Nationalism* 6, 3 (2006): 73-88.

9 See especially Brian Osborne, "From Patriotic Pines to Diasporic Geese: Emplacing Culture, Setting Our Sights, Locating Identity in a Transnational Canada," *Canadian Journal of Communication* 31, 1 (2006): 147-75. Osborne instructs us that iconic landscapes employ mnemonic tropes in ways that reinforce past power structures. See also Brian Osborne, "Figuring Space, Marking Time: Contested Identities in Canada," *International Journal of Heritage Studies* 2, 1-2 (1996): 23-40; Claire Campbell, *Shaped by the West Wind: Nature and History in Georgian Bay* (Vancouver: UBC Press, 2005); Ross Cameron, "Tom Thomson, Antimodernism, and the Ideal of Manhood," *Canadian Historical Association Journal* 10 (1999): 185-208; and Dennis Duffy, "Algonquin Revisited: Biography to Hagiography to Label," *American Review of Canadian Studies* 32, 1 (2002): 67-96.

10 Simon Schama, *Landscape and Memory* (New York: Alfred A. Knopf, 1995), 6-19; Pamela J. Stewart and Andrew Strathan, eds., *Landscape, Memory and History: Anthropological Perspectives* (London and Stirling, UK: Pluto, 2003), 2-3.

11 Tim Creswell, *Place: A Short Introduction* (Oxford: Blackwell, 2003), 7-11.

12 Jeff Malpas, "New Media, Cultural Heritage and the Sense of Place: Mapping the Conceptual Ground," *International Journal of Heritage Studies* (May 2008): 199-200. See also Tim Creswell and Gareth Hoskins, "Place, Persistence, and Practice: Evaluating Historical Significance at Angel Island, San Francisco, and Maxwell Street, Chicago," *Annals of the Association of American Geographers* 98, 2 (2008): 393-94.

13 David Harvey, *Justice, Nature, and the Politics of Difference* (Oxford: Blackwell, 1996), 292-98; David Harvey, "From Space to Place and Back Again," in *Mapping the Futures: Local Cultures, Global Change,* ed. Jon Bird, Barry Curtis, Tim Putnam, George Robertson, and Lisa Tickner (London: Routledge, 1993), 3-29.

14 Doreen Massey, "Power-Geography and Progressive Sense of Place," in *Mapping the Futures: Local Cultures, Global Change,* ed. Jon Bird, Barry Curtis, Tim Putnam, George Robertson, and Lisa Tickner (London: Routledge, 1993), 59-69. See also Doreen Massey, "A Global Sense of Place," in *Reading Human Geography,* ed. Trevor Barnes and Derek Gregory (London: Arnold, 1997); and Doreen Massey, *For Space* (London: Sage, 2005), 315-23.

15 Malpas, "New Media," 199-200.

16 There is a substantial literature on the history of museums, and scholars are showing a growing appreciation for the distinct history of living-history museums. For a sample of the writing on the development of museums, see these classic works: Kenneth Hudson, *A Social History of Museums: What Visitors Thought* (London: MacMillan, 1975); Donald Horne, *The Great Museum: The Re-Presentation of History* (London: Pluto, 1984); Tony Bennett, *The Birth of the Museum: History, Theory, Politics* (London and New York: Routledge, 1995); Steven Conn, *Museums and American Intellectual Life, 1876-1926* (Chicago: University of Chicago Press, 1988); Susan Crane, ed., *Museums and Memory* (Stanford, CA: Stanford University Press, 2000). On living-history museums, see, for example, Jay Anderson, *Time Machines: The World of Living History* (Nashville: American Association for State and Local History, 1984); W. Leon and M. Piatt, "Living

History Museums," in *History Museums in the United States: A Critical Assessment,* ed. W. Leon and Roy Rosenzweig (Urbana: University of Illinois Press, 1989), 64-97; Jay Anderson, ed., *A Living History Reader,* vol. 1, *Museums* (Nashville: American Association for State and Local History, 1991); Richard Handler and Eric Gable, *The New History in an Old Museum: Creating the Past at Colonial Williamsburg* (Durham, NC: Duke University Press, 1999); and B. Goodacre and G. Baldwin, *Living with the Past: Recreation, Re-enactment and Education at Museums and Historical Sites* (London: Middlesex University Press, 2002). Obviously, neither list is intended to be exhaustive.

17 Ian McKay, "Tartanism Triumphant: The Construction of Scottishness in Nova Scotia 1933-1954," *Acadiensis* 21, 2 (Spring 1992): 5-47.

18 Stephen J. Hornsby, *Nineteenth-Century Cape Breton: A Historical Geography* (Montreal and Kingston: McGill-Queen's University Press, 1992), 48-53.

19 W.L. Fillmore to A.H. MacKinnon, 1 March 1955, Nova Scotia Highland Village Society Papers (NSHV), Early History.

20 On Scottish unease with the Celtic past, see Colin Kidd, "Gaelic Antiquity and National Identity in Enlightenment Ireland and Scotland," *English Historical Review* (November 1994): 1197-1214.

21 Trevor Pringle, "The Privation of History: Landscape, Victoria and the Highland Myth," in *The Iconography of Landscape,* ed. Denis Cosgrave and Stephen Daniels (Cambridge, UK: Cambridge University Press, 1988), 143.

22 The literature on the making of Scottish national identity is too vast to treat extensively here. See, for example, Peter Womack, *Improvement and Romance: Constructing the Myth of the Highlands* (Basingstoke, UK: Macmillan, 1989); M.G.H. Pittock, *The Invention of Scotland: The Stuart Myth and the Scottish Identity, 1638 to the Present* (London: Routledge, 1991); Ian Donnachie and Christopher Whatley, eds., *The Manufacture of Scottish History* (Edinburgh: Polygone, 1992); David McCrone, Angela Morris, and Richard Kiely, *Scotland the Brand: The Making of Scottish Heritage* (Edinburgh: Edinburgh University Press, 1995); and J.R. Gold and M.M. Gold, *Imagining Scotland: Tradition, Representation, and Promotion in Scottish Tourism since 1750* (Aldershot, UK: Scolar Press, 1995).

23 D. Campbell and R.A. MacLean, *Beyond the Atlantic Roar* (Toronto: McClelland and Stewart, 1974), 176-80. See also Jim Lotz and Pat Lotz, *Cape Breton Island* (Vancouver: Douglas, David and Charles, 1974), 153-56.

24 See, for example, Phosa Kinley, "Kennington Cove, Cape Breton," *The Maritime Advocate and Busy East* (May 1943): 25-26.

25 From the end of the 1920s, the Nova Scotia government used simplistic graphics and childhood metaphors to create an idea of innocence in its tourist promotions. The slogan "Canada's Ocean Playground" was in use from 1928.

26 James MacNeil to Angus L. Macdonald, 25 February, 23 March, and 22 July 1938, Angus L. Macdonald Fonds, vol. 1504, file 403, Nova Scotia Archives and Records Management (NSARM), MG2.

27 See Ian McKay, *The Quest of the Folk: Antimodernism and Cultural Selection in Twenti-eth-Century Nova Scotia* (Montreal and Kingston: McGill-Queen's University Press, 1994).

28 Kenneth Donovan, "Reflections on Cape Breton Culture: An Introduction," in *The Island: New Perspectives on Cape Breton History, 1713-1990*, ed. K. Donovan (Fredericton/Sydney: Acadiensis Press/University College of Cape Breton Press, 1990), 5-7.

29 W.L. Fillmore to Earl Clark, 17 January 1955, Nova Scotia Historic Sites Advisory Council Fonds, vol. 933 H, NSARM, MG20.

30 Perilla Kinchin and Juliet Kinchin, *Glasgow's Great Exhibitions: 1888, 1901, 1911, 1938, 1988* (Oxford: White Cockade, 1988), 156-57; Bob Crampsey, *The Empire Exhibition of 1938* (Edinburgh: Mainstream, 1988), 49-50.

31 See Alan MacEachern, *Natural Selections: National Parks in Atlantic Canada, 1935-1970* (Montreal and Kingston: McGill-Queen's University Press, 2001), 48-53.

32 Colin Sinclair to W.L. Fillmore, 14 June 1954, NSHV, Early History.

33 H.M. Macdonald, "A Submission of the Nova Scotia Association of Scottish Societies to the Premier and Members of the Nova Scotia Government," 3 May 1955, NSHV, Early History.

34 Hector's Point was named after a local settler, not the ship that had become symbolic of the origins of the Scottish settlement. In 1923 the province used the 150th anniversary of the *Hector*'s arrival to gauge the potential of history as a promotional vehicle for tourism. See Michael Boudreau, "'A Rare and Unusual Treat of Historical Significance': The 1923 Hector Celebration and the Political Economy of the Past," *Journal of Canadian Studies* 28, 4 (1993-94): 28-48.

35 Earl Clark to C.I.N. MacLeod, 13 January 1955, NSHV, Early History.

36 W.L. Fillmore to Earl Clark, 17 January 1955, Nova Scotia Historic Sites Advisory Council Fonds, vol. 933 H, NSARM, MG20.

37 James P. Bickerton, *Nova Scotia, Ottawa, and the Politics of Regional Development* (Toronto: University of Toronto Press, 1990), 249. See also Tom Kent, "The Cape Breton Development Corporation: One Canadian Case of Planning on the Spot," in *Canadians and Regional Economic Development at Home and in the Third World*, ed. Benjamin Higgins and Donald Savoie (Moncton: Canadian Institute for Research on Regional Development, 1988), 87-116.

38 "Report on Highland Village, Iona," February 1975, Nova Scotia Department of Tourism Fonds, vol. 621, NSARM, RG66. The Highland Village Inn is still in operation.

39 Barry Diamond to R.C. MacNeil, 8 October 1971, NSHV, 1971 Correspondence.

40 *Weekly Cape Bretoner,* 7 September 1957.

41 C.I.N. MacLeod, "The Hebridean 'Tigh Dubh,'" NSHV, Early History. See also Hayden Lorimer, "Ways of Seeing the Scottish Highlands: Marginality, Authenticity, and the Curious Case of the Hebridean Blackhouse," *Journal of Historical Geography* 25, 4 (1990): 517-33.

42 Rick Young to Jean Ross, 13 August 1975, Nova Scotia Department of Tourism Fonds, vol. 621, NSARM, RG66.

43 "Upper Canada Village Press Kit, 1961," Administrative Records of the St. Lawrence Parks Commission, file 4, Ontario Archives, RG5-54. See also Beryl Way, "Upper Canada Village," *Canadian Geographical Journal* (June 1961): 219.

44 Hornsby, *Nineteenth-Century Cape Breton*, 71.

45 Lucille Campey, *After the Hector: The Scottish Pioneers of Nova Scotia and Cape Breton, 1773-1852* (Toronto: Natural Heritage Books, 2004), 148-50.

46 Highland Village Society, Annual Meeting, 21 December 1974, NSHV, 1974 Correspondence.

47 "Report on Highland Village, Iona," February 1975, Nova Scotia Department of Tourism Fonds, vol. 621, NSARM, RG66.

48 S.R. MacNeil to S.R. Fraser, 3 February 1968, NSHV, 1960s Correspondence.

49 Katharine Hodgkin and Susannah Radstone, "Introduction: Contested Pasts," in *Contested Pasts: The Politics of Memory*, ed. Katharine Hodgkin and Susannah Radstone (London: Routledge, 2003), 11.

50 R.C. MacNeil to Albert MacLeod, 20 July 1974; Albert MacLeod to Allan MacEachen, 16 August 1974, both in NSHV, 1974 Correspondence.

51 Hugh MacKenzie to C.I.N. MacLeod, n.d. (likely spring 1956), NSHV, Early History.

52 John Gray, "Iconic Images: Landscape and History in the Local Poetry of the Scottish Borders," in *Landscape, Memory and History: Anthropological Perspectives*, ed. Pamela J. Stewart and Andrew Strathan (London and Stirling, UK: Pluto, 2003), 34.

53 John Belchem, "The Irish Diaspora: The Complexities of Mass Migration," *Review of Studies in the Polish Diaspora* 31, 1 (2005): 92.

54 Paul Basu, *Highland Homecomings: Genealogy and Heritage Tourism in the Scottish Diaspora* (London and New York: Routledge, 2007), 16-19. See also Tom Devine, *The Scottish Nation, 1700-2000* (London: Allen Lane, 1999), 231.

"That Big Statue of Whoever"
Material Commemoration and Narrative in the Niagara Region

RUSSELL JOHNSTON AND MICHAEL RIPMEESTER

A small white church stands just outside of downtown St. Catharines, Ontario. Its location is the post-industrial landscape of a small city, where canals and railways that no longer exist once anchored factories that are no longer open, where neighbourhood homes and businesses have been converted into diners and taverns, garages and second-hand shops. The location is faithful to the church's origins. Nonetheless, its location might seem anticlimactic, perhaps even disconcerting, to the many pilgrims it now draws each year – historical tourists who know what the church represents. This is Salem Chapel, built in the 1850s to serve former African American slaves who had travelled the Underground Railroad to its end in Upper Canada. Among them was Harriet Ross Tubman, a figure now celebrated as a courageous leader in the railroad and the fight against slavery in the United States. Members of white society in the city may have condemned slavery, but they did not always welcome its refugees. The modest chapel was not built on stately Church Street downtown, near the leading parishes of the city's other denominations, but on the fringe of the commercial core.

More than a century later, Salem Chapel is a highly celebrated city church. It is marked by five historical plaques. One was erected by the Canadian

Figure 5.1 Salem Chapel, St. Catharines, Ontario. Photograph by Michael Ripmeester.

federal government to honour the church itself, one by the Province of Ontario to honour Tubman, and one by the city to honour the first local church for African Canadians, while two more celebrate the chapel's designation as a national historical site – one each from the city and the current congregation (see Figure 5.1). A sixth plaque, one block south, was raised by the city to mark the Underground Railroad.

Salem Chapel provides an intriguing example of how mnemonic narratives become articulated. As the other chapters in this volume make clear, specific narratives can be invested with differing levels of significance by different groups of people. We also know that the appeal of any one narrative waxes and wanes with changes in society, culture, and politics. In this case, we are also reminded that a single narrative has been interwoven simultaneously with the master narratives that four different agencies want to tell. Each has adopted the chapel as a tangible reminder of its own proud history. Such dense overlapping commemoration of a single narrative indicates that this is a site that not only prompts local memory and pride but also reinforces self-perceptions on a provincial, national, and perhaps international scale.

These observations introduce the concept of place into a consideration of mnemonic narratives. Scholars once perceived the landscape as a reflection of human endeavour. Recently, however, scholars have conceptualized it as both the product of, and context for, human life. Building on this, geographers argue that the landscape is much more than its physical presence.[1] Nuala Johnson contends that "treating the landscape as a theater or stage broadens the imaginative scope of interpretation by suggesting that life gets played out as social action and social practice."[2] In the same vein, Arturo Escobar suggests that "place, more an event than a thing, is characterized by openness rather than by a unitary self-identity."[3] The emphasis here on interpretation and openness is important. Although all features of a landscape are loaded with significance and meaning, the extent to which any one feature figures in a "staging" or "event" depends on the context of its use. The landscape offers a stock of elements that reflect and guide the actions of everyday life, but the significance and meaning of these elements can shift into or out of discursive consciousness.

Implicit in these considerations of place are considerations of agency. When scholars examine mnemonic narratives and commemorations, they usually focus on "memory entrepreneurs" – those members of a community who work to have a particular version of the past accepted as common knowledge.[4] If our goal is to understand popular memory, we must consider the dialogue between memory entrepreneurs and their audience, the general public. Does the general public embrace the messages crafted by memory entrepreneurs? Does the general public even receive them?

St. Catharines provides an excellent ground to assess the power of place in the dissemination of mnemonic narratives. It is the largest city in the Regional Municipality of Niagara and lies roughly twenty kilometres west of Niagara Falls, the American border, and New York State. The area was part of the Iroquois Confederacy at the time of European contact. The first white settlers were Loyalists during the American War of Independence, and they established farms along Twelve Mile Creek where it drains into Lake Ontario. Later, they would be followed by Irish peasants fleeing the Potato Famine and former American slaves who followed Harriet Tubman to freedom. Throughout these decades, the region's situation on the border with the United States also made it a strategic location during international conflicts. British, Native, and American troops marched through the area during the War of

1812, and Laura Secord's fabled trek ended at a home overlooking the future city. William Lyon Mackenzie's rebels used New York as a base to raid Upper Canada during the Rebellions of 1837, just as the Fenian Brotherhood did in 1870 to advance Irish independence. The city's economic importance grew thanks to entrepreneurs like William H. Merritt. He promoted the first Welland Canal in the 1820s and its expansion twenty years later. After the first hydro-electric power generators were completed under the eye of Adam Beck at Niagara Falls, the city experienced industrial growth to rival the region's agricultural production; General Motors built two plants in St. Catharines. Since 1980, however, manufacturing has been eclipsed by service industries – especially tourism – anchored by the international appeal of Niagara Falls.[5]

Socially and culturally, St. Catharines today is shaped by people, goods, and media that flow into the city from other places. Among neighbouring cities, Buffalo, New York, is forty minutes away by car, while Toronto lies eighty minutes away. Both serve as destinations for employment, entertainment, and shopping, and both supply major media services to St. Catharines, particularly television. Although the city has one daily newspaper and one talk radio station, it does not have a television station of its own. CHCH-TV, located forty minutes west in Hamilton, Ontario, is the only station that considers St. Catharines part of its news-coverage area. It is challenging, therefore, to articulate and popularize any local narratives, let alone mnemonic narratives. Despite a past that is rich in military, economic, and societal events of national consequence, residents live in a mediascape that privileges mnemonic and contemporary narratives from outside the region.

Monuments can be considered both media and part of the human landscape. Much of the literature on commemoration describes its function as aggressively didactic and acutely hegemonic; it encourages readings that support asymmetrical power relations.[6] Pierre Nora contends that *lieux de mémoire* became a repository of meaning for a French society that seemed keen on forgetting, a link between elite and vernacular narratives.[7] This function is identifiable during moments of intense communal feeling and is particularly effective during periods of "hot nationalism." In other places and contexts, scholars have arrived at similar findings, noting for example that officially prescribed memoryscapes in Scotland and Ireland were effective in getting the people to "know themselves" as distinct societies and that the memorialization of the World Trade Center has had a profound effect on

American nationalism.[8] That said, memory entrepreneurs cannot force a populace to internalize narratives. Tension over meaning can meet or even precede the unveiling of a memoryscape.[9] Michael Heffernan, writing of Great Britain, and Hamzah Muzaini and Brenda Yeoh, writing of Singapore, describe how war memorials in both countries became "battlefields" over form and symbol.[10] Even long-established memoryscapes can become centres of tension. During "irruptions of memory" – when suppressed memories boil to the surface – mnemonic landscapes become lightning rods for action. They bear the brunt of political upheavals, the demise of a despised regime, or broad social changes.[11]

These findings must be qualified. While researching a St. Catharines war memorial, we discovered that survey respondents drawn from the local area knew nothing of the specific soldier or event it marks. Nonetheless, our respondents still grasped its generic message. They readily told us that the figure of a soldier valorizes qualities such as courage, duty, and sacrifice.[12] The figure may convey this message because it exists within a dense web of memory work that valorizes Canadian military service in precisely these terms. Memory entrepreneurs across Canada hail this image of the soldier through channels both official (e.g., coins, stamps, Remembrance Day rituals) and popular (e.g., newspapers, magazines, film, television, song). The pervasive presence of these symbols is taken for granted, a fact often lamented by veterans groups. That said, Michael Billig reminds us that not every symbol needs to make an emotional impact every time it is seen in order to have an impact.[13] Not every flag is waved or saluted, for example. In St. Catharines the war memorial serves as a visual argument, a sign that viewers need only glimpse to comprehend.[14]

Here, we return to place as staging or event. The socio-spatial world is crafted from an almost infinite number of potentially significant material artefacts and symbolic associations. Memoryscapes are only one such feature. In writing of identities in the modern world, Manuel Castells contends that individuals and groups create identities out of available resources:

> from history, from geography, from biology, from productive and reproductive institutions, from collective memory and from personal fantasies, from power apparatuses and religious revelations. But individuals, social groups, and societies process all these materials, and rearrange their meaning,

according to social determinations and cultural projects that are rooted in their social structure and in their space/time framework.[15]

In sum, we are selective and can make choices within certain constraints. Anthony Giddens likens this selection process to making sense of a newspaper:

> A newspaper ... presents a collage of information, as does, on a wider scale, the whole bevy of newspapers which may be on sale in a particular area or country. Yet each reader imposes his own order on this diversity, by selecting which newspaper to read – if any – and by making an active selection of its contents.[16]

The landscape in both material and symbolic form constitutes a similar re-source. Individuals draw on the landscape – they use what is materially and symbolically present – within the constraints of discursive mores and the circumstances of everyday life. The literature on place abounds with examples, but two may suffice here. A Stockholm dockworker, moving through an everyday world, creates a meaningful world for himself in ways that are at times commensurate and at other times antithetical to elite desires.[17] Simi-larly, activists in West Virginia added new layers of meaning to the Bunker Hill Monument by using it to commemorate children lost to urban violence.[18] Given different actors, different contexts, or different times, a single landscape may be conceived in multiple ways.

This point brings us back to the dialogue between memory entrepreneurs and their audiences. Research on mnemonic devices typically focuses on memory entrepreneurs and the objects of their concern, the narratives they feel ought to be preserved. Such research explores the motives, conflicts, and compromises that lay behind the creation of public rituals and memorials, and it is well served by traditional historical methods such as archival docu-ments and oral-history interviews. We must be cognizant, however, of the intended audience for memorials, the general public. It is necessary to ask how the public think about and use memorials once they are unveiled, and this question informs the work of John Bodnar, Charlene Mires, and Roy Rosenzweig and David Thelen.[19] Examining heritage activities in the United States, Bodnar argues that commemoration is never a simple imposition of elite perspectives on submissive publics. Memorials are subject to a process of interpretation that forces compromise between the perspectives of memory entrepreneurs and their audiences. Mires reveals how this occurs through time in her study of Philadelphia's Independence Hall. She isolates key moments in the building's history to explore its changing status in the American imagination. For contemporary publics, however, comparable archival documents are not available. To examine contemporary publics, we take a cue from historians Rosenzweig and Thelen. They conducted a national telephone survey to explore the popular uses of history in the United States. They found that every individual participates in the creation of popular memory by drawing on multiple sources and mnemonic narratives. The work of any one group of memory entrepreneurs remains active only insofar as it remains relevant and consistent within a wider mix of intellectual resources. Again, Rosenzweig and Thelen's goal was not to see how memory entrepreneurs represent the past but to see how a representative sample of the American public actually conceives of and engages with the past in daily life.

Eviatar Zerubavel provides a way to explore the dialogue between memory entrepreneurs and the general public.[20] If every commemoration within a community marks a specific date, then the date associated with each commemoration can be tabulated on a timeline. In most communities, commemorations tend to cluster around certain dates. The result is a bar chart that graphically reveals the investment made by memory entrepreneurs in each era of their history. Zerubavel calls this chart a "commemogram." A similar chart can be developed for contemporary popular memory. If individuals are prompted to supply a list of people, events, places, or things that represent their community, their answers too can be tabulated on a timeline. A comparison of the two commemograms should reveal the extent to which memory entrepreneurs and popular memory share the same priorities.

In a previous paper, we constructed two such commemograms for the Niagara region. The first graph established that Niagara's memoryscape, as articulated through plaques, is heavily weighted toward foundation stories, the War of 1812, the building of the Welland Canal, the Underground Railroad, and local participation in the two world wars. The second graph found that participants from St. Catharines drew almost exclusively on contemporary people, places, things, and events as key signifiers of the region. This was unexpected. Sir Isaac Brock and Laura Secord had recently ranked very high in a CBC poll for the "Greatest Canadian."[21] The apparent rift between the CBC's national audience and the survey's local participants prompted a more focused examination of the links between national narratives articulated at local historic sites and local popular memory. Hypothesizing that local and supralocal understandings of Niagara may be nested or otherwise intertwined, this study explores the links between national and local mnemonic narratives by introducing the national sphere as a consideration for our participants. Their responses offer insights into the ways individuals respond to, and use as a resource, mnemonic narratives and commemorations.

In this chapter, the research again compares two sets of data: the inventory of historical plaques in the Niagara region and a sample of popular opinion on Niagara's mnemonic narratives. First, the inventory of historical plaques provided a representative and quantifiable measure of the work of memory entrepreneurs. We chose plaques because they are the most salient aspect of memory work at all levels, be they local, provincial, or national. Memorials take many forms, but plaques often serve as the main channel through which a selected mnemonic narrative is articulated. For each plaque, the inventory notes the subject, location, dates marked, memory entrepreneur, and date of unveiling. This set of data should indicate how memory entrepreneurs have distributed resources to mark each period of the community's past. A greater concentration of memorials dedicated to people, places, events, and things during any one decade should indicate that greater significance has been invested in its mnemonic narratives than in those of other periods.

The plaque inventory was developed by combining two pre-existing lists and then adding details through field work whenever necessary. The Special Collections unit of the St. Catharines Public Library maintains the first list. This list incorporates photographs, archival documents, and newspaper clippings documenting memorials across Niagara. The second list is maintained by amateur historian Wayne Cook and is available on his website, which is recognized as authoritative by educational bodies, municipal governments, and History Television.[22] These inventories have one distinct advantage. Their thematic approach is comprehensive; they do not focus on a particular place, type of event, or memory entrepreneur. This is underscored by the compilation process itself. Library staff review local periodicals continually and systematically to maintain clippings files on Niagara history. This ensures that their lists are current; indeed, the most recent additions included a municipal plaque unveiled while our research was in progress. Cook solicits submissions from the general public and is assisted by many contributors who have identified and transcribed local plaques. In both cases, the lists provide detailed information on each plaque.

The second component of the research was a survey conducted among pedestrians in St. Catharines during May 2008. As the largest city in the region, it serves as a commercial and administrative hub for the surrounding cities and towns. It is home to municipal, provincial, and federal government offices, and its economy is dominated by retail and service establishments catering to residents. The authors and two research assistants staked out public sidewalks and courtyards around the downtown core on weekdays between the hours of 10:00 a.m. and 2:00 p.m. The locations provided a mix of commercial and institutional sites: the farmers' market, the regional court building, the main library, one popular commercial street, and a second street with banks and professional offices. The month, in mid-spring, provided weather that was sufficiently warm to foster participation but also ensured that most passers-by were locals rather than tourists. The time of day was selected to provide the most demographically diverse set of pedestrians, when both those who work downtown and residents from across the city run errands.

The questionnaire had two parts. The first part sought simple demographic information that allowed us to compare our pool of participants with the most recent census of St. Catharines. The second part collected opinions regarding the participants' personal engagement with the past and their sense of Niagara's place in a national narrative. Specifically, we asked about their level of interest in history, the resources that supply their knowledge of local and national history, the extent to which historic sites and monuments are one such resource, and the extent to which Niagara contributes to Canada's national identity.

Participants were recruited as they walked past a member of the research team. All members of the team wore name tags identifying them as employees of the local university. All pedestrians were approached with the exception of two groups. First, we avoided parents and guardians in the company of small children as a courtesy. Second, we avoided any youth who appeared to be under the age of eighteen. Our goal was to measure the enduring impact of material commemorations on individual consciousness of historical narratives and personal identity, and we believe that schooling has a direct bearing on this consciousness and identity. Including participants who were still in school would have incorporated participants for whom the learning of national mnemonic narratives is a required task. More pragmatically, it would have been difficult if not impossible to obtain informed consent from the parents of these minors during the sidewalk interview process.

With both sets of data in hand, a commemogram was plotted. Every person, place, thing, and event marked by a plaque or identified by a survey response was associated with a key date. For example, Laura Secord is best known for her trek in 1813. We then sorted all plaques and survey responses by the decade in which their key dates fell. It must be noted that the number of plaques reflects a finite number of artefacts, whereas there was potentially an infinite number of survey responses. To produce comparable data, we used proportional rather than absolute figures. Each decade's share of the total number of plaques and responses was calculated. These shares rather than the absolute figures were then plotted on the graph. The completed graph should provide a quantitative description of local memory work. Specifically, it should indicate how memory entrepreneurs have distributed resources to mark each mnemonic narrative in the region's past in relation to the others, and it should indicate the extent to which these narratives are predominant in the minds of local residents when considering the region's contributions to national narratives.

In all, our inventory included 261 plaques. The resultant commemogram is displayed in Figure 5.2. Three peaks immediately stand out: the 1790s (associated most often with foundation narratives), the 1810s (War of 1812), and the 1910s (First World War). There are also smaller peaks associated with the 1820s (construction of the Welland Canal), the 1850s (Underground Railroad), and the 1940s (Second World War). Other decades are interesting because of the absence of commemoration. For example, the period prior to European arrival gets but faint mention, as do the 1920s, the 1930s, and the period after 1960.

The inventory and its commemogram produced several insights. First, commemorations are dispersed geographically in predictable ways. The greatest share of plaques is in St. Catharines, the largest community in Niagara. The greatest concentration of plaques, however, is along the Niagara River, where most of the sites associated with the War of 1812 and contemporary tourist activities are found. Second, local memory entrepreneurs were responsible for almost half of the plaques in our sample (see Figure 5.3). They do

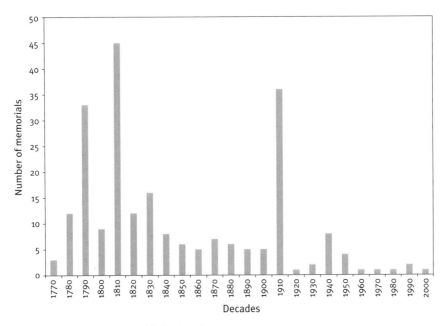

Figure 5.2   Niagara memorials by decade

not represent a single-minded or unified mass; we identified over thirty different categories of local memory entrepreneurs, and in many cases their efforts were supported by voluntary subscriptions. Taken together, these two facts suggest there is significant popular support for memory work. By contrast, the federal and provincial governments were responsible for far fewer plaques despite the presence of powerful mnemonic narratives with supralocal implications.

Third, there is little disagreement over which narratives are most important in Niagara (see Figure 5.4). Among the most active memory entrepreneurs, all identified foundation narratives, the War of 1812, the canal, and the Underground Railroad as significant. There is one noticeable difference: Canada and Ontario have commemorated very few local narratives that transpired after 1890, even though local memory entrepreneurs have devoted significant resources to the First and Second World Wars.[23] The two wars, however, represent a special case since the federal government directly financed only two memorials in Canada. Federal policy dictated that local memorials such as cenotaphs, arches, and buildings were the responsibility of local memory entrepreneurs.

Commemorations

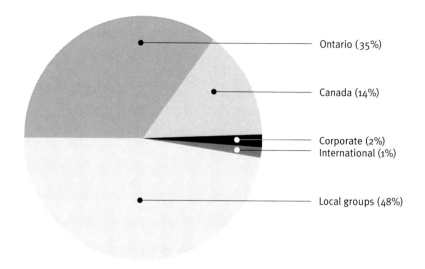

Figure 5.3   Memory entrepreneurs in the Niagara region

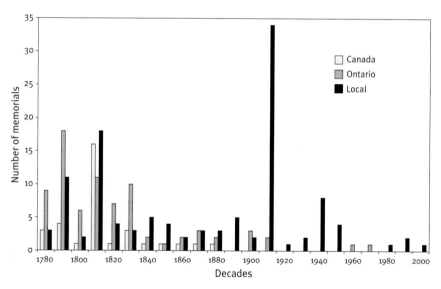

Figure 5.4   Memory entrepreneurs' efforts by decade

This qualification reminds us that the sheer quantity of plaques is not always a clear indication of mnemonic investment by any one agency. The federal government may mark fewer sites in Niagara than do local memory entrepreneurs, but the scale of its commemorations (seen in the maintenance of Fort George, Fort Erie, and Brock's Monument at Queenston Heights) clearly indicates the significance it lends to the 1812 narrative. It should not be surprising that local memory entrepreneurs have erected the most plaques since it is likely that locals in any jurisdiction will find more of interest in their area than will outsiders. Locals are aware of and more inclined to honour the everyday (such as notable buildings), the odd (notable feats), and the simply old (notable relics).

The survey gathered information from 173 participants over the last two weeks of May 2008. The demographic profile of the sample was reflective of the population of St. Catharines as measured by the most recent census in 2006. The gender and age composition of the sample closely followed the census data, while its ethnic and occupational composition matched less precisely but followed broad trends. The sample was skewed toward the employed workforce; whereas roughly 60 percent of city residents were employed, roughly 70 percent of our sample was. This can be explained in part by the

Table 5.1

Participant responses

People		(%)	Places		(%)
Sir Isaac Brock	19	9.8	Niagara Falls	71	27
Laura Secord	14	7.3	Local wineries	38	14.4
William Hamilton Merritt	8	4.1	Welland Canal	31	11.8
Harriet Tubman	4	2.1	War of 1812 sites	27	10.3
No one	3	1.6	Niagara-on-the-Lake	24	9.1
Paul Bernardo and Karla			General historical sites	13	4.9
Homolka	2	1	No place contributes	3	1.1
Other	13	6.7	Other	20	7.6
No answer	130	67.4	No answer	36	13.7
Totals	193	100	Totals	263	100

Events and things		(%)
War of 1812	44	22.8
Local festivals	27	14
Underground Railroad	16	8.3
Auto industry	2	1
No events contribute	1	0.5
Other	6	3.1
No answer	97	50.3
Totals	193	100

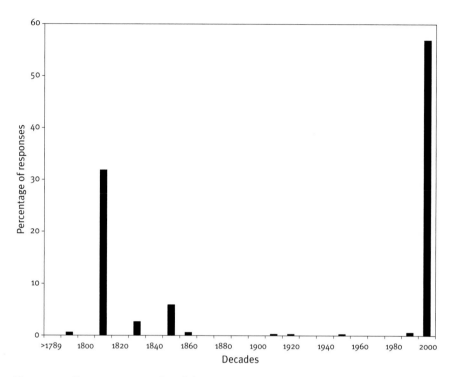

Figure 5.5   Commemogram of participant responses

high number of participants who worked in educational, government, or religious organizations, likely a side effect of conducting the survey in the downtown core. Nonetheless, the responses of these participants to our analytical questions did not vary from the responses of the other occupational groups. Thus we are confident that this sample produced a reliable body of data.[24]

The central question had two parts. First, we asked participants whether or not Niagara has anything to contribute to Canada's national character. We expected the question to trigger civic pride, and indeed 91 percent of participants affirmed that Niagara does contribute something to the national character. Second, when participants responded in the affirmative, they were asked to name specific examples of Niagara's contribution. If they sought a prompt, they were asked to consider people, places, things, or events. Their specific examples are summarized in Table 5.1 and Figure 5.5.

The second set of answers revealed a greater feeling of ambivalence than was evident in the first set of answers. Every participant answering the second question believed that Niagara contributes to Canada's national character, but the majority could not name a single person, event, or thing as an example. After our question was posed, one participant replied, "Certainly, but let's not do examples." Another stated, "I would hope so! But I can't think of anything specific." A third commented, "Strangely enough, I cannot think of anything. History is harder to come to grips with than the present." Yet another tried to explain her apparent lack of memory: "Yes [significant things happened here], but I'm not a history buff. I don't know." Her reply suggests that the retention of mnemonic narratives is important only to those with an interest in the subject. When participants did name specific examples, the results were skewed toward geography: 85.2 percent of respondents named local places they believed are significant to Canadian history, but 69 percent did not name a person and 50.8 percent did not name an event or thing. Further, participants rarely made connections between their examples. One participant identified Fort George but did not mention the War of 1812, Sir Isaac Brock, or Laura Secord. Similarly, another participant stated, "I remember reading about when Brock [Monument] was put up. I also read about Merritt and Adam [Beck]. I read about that on a plaque in the park." In other cases, some participants were simply unsure of their history and/or geography. Certain participants associated Pierre Elliott Trudeau and Terry Fox with the Niagara region, identified St. Catharines as a First Nation reserve, and placed the Plains of Abraham in Niagara.

A comparison of the two sets of data yields clear results. Despite modest parallels between the priorities of memory entrepreneurs and survey respondents, the two commemograms reveal startling differences (see Figure 5.6). If memorials promote specific values and foster common knowledge of the narratives they mark, then we should expect the narratives championed on local plaques to reappear in the answers of our respondents. They do not, and in this our survey responses in 2008 did not differ from those in 2005.[25] Both sets of responses indicate that local residents call to mind present-day people, places, things, and events rather than those of the past when thinking of Niagara. Yet there are modest parallels between the two commemograms. As noted above, memory entrepreneurs have invested considerable resources in the celebration of the War of 1812, Welland Canal, Underground Railroad, and First World War. And these are the mnemonic narratives on which our participants drew. We will consider this further below. For the most part, however, our survey participants identified the region's tourist destinations (Niagara

Falls and Niagara-on-the-Lake), prominent industries (the canal and wineries), and opportunities for recreation (local festivals). Those who included the canal are instructive here. Many did not note its historic importance in the development of industry in Upper Canada but rather its present-day role in Great Lakes shipping and its own appeal as a tourist destination. Our respondents thought first of the present, lived reality of the region rather than of the past celebrated by memory entrepreneurs.

This insight was articulated by many participants in their own words. When asking for examples of local contributions to the national character, we were repeatedly told things like, "There is the Grape and Wine and icewine, and Niagara-on-the-Lake has quaint buildings"; "The wine, the falls, Niagara-on-the-Lake"; "Tourism; there's the falls and Niagara-on-the-Lake ... that's it for history, historical tourism"; "Niagara Falls, that's the one place I know"; "Well, Niagara Falls are a wonder of the world. I'm not sure if people come to the area for historical places." References to Niagara-on-the-Lake were not tied to its War of 1812 sites but to its refurbished (some might say "Disney-fied") streetscape, which is anchored by the Shaw Festival – a summer theatre that features the work of George Bernard Shaw. One individual offered a

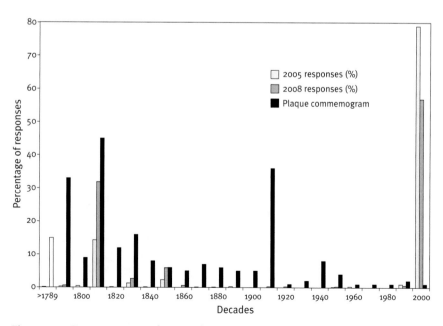

Figure 5.6 Commemogram of 2005 and 2008 participant responses

particularly comprehensive reply: "Aren't we famous for being the doughnut capital of Canada and for fat people? There's also the auto industry, the War of 1812, the falls, and the wine industry."[26] This response suggests that local mnemonic narratives may have national importance, but they are no more important than the realities of contemporary Niagara. Another believed that "Laura Secord and people like that" are historically significant, but "people don't identify with them nationally. There's the Grape and Wine, it attracts a lot of people ... And Niagara Falls. You say you're from Niagara Falls and everyone knows where that is." Although participants acknowledged local mnemonic narratives, many individuals dismissed their significance in relation to contemporary Niagara's place in the national consciousness.

One important difference emerges when the survey responses from 2005 and 2008 are compared. Participants in 2005 were asked to name important contributions to local identity, and only 20 percent of their responses drew on mnemonic narratives. Participants in 2008 were asked to name important local contributions to the national character, and 42.5 percent drew on such narratives. Placing the question of local significance in a national frame, therefore, produced a dramatic increase (110 percent) in the proportion of respondents who thought in historical terms. Thus, for example, one of our participants noted, "The settlement of the Loyalists, 1812, building of the canal. These are things that affect the local region but also the province and the nation." Another made the connection between 1812 and Canadian sovereignty: "Canadians are not reminded of the greatness that happened here ... In 1812 and 1837 we kicked the Americans' freakin' asses back over there." The difference between the two sets of survey data can be traced to three specific narratives named by participants: the War of 1812, Welland Canal, and Underground Railroad (see Figure 5.5). Together, they accounted for 18 percent of all responses in 2005 and for 31.6 percent of all responses three years later. This suggests that the context within which individuals remember narratives is indeed an important factor.

This reading is reinforced by our participants' level of engagement with material commemorations. Two questions in the survey probed our participants' thoughts and habits with respect to local history. First, when asked where they learn about local history, only 11.8 percent of participants referred to historic sites and monuments (see Table 5.2). Second, when asked to what extent they learn about local history from this source, 32.4 percent of partici-

Table 5.2

Use of local history resources

		(%)
Mass media	153	48.9
Historic sites and monuments	37	11.8
Passive learning	33	10.5
Formal schooling	29	9.3
Interaction with others	42	13.4
Not interested	6	1.9
Other	10	3.2
No answer	3	1
Totals	313	100

pants stated that they learn "quite a lot." The seeming contradiction in these responses might be easily explained. If participants have little interest in local history, the information found at historic sites and monuments may represent the sum total of their local-history knowledge because they do not seek it elsewhere. One person explained, "I remember the material on the monuments. But I don't commit it to deep memory." Another explained that their interest in local history was trumped by the overall presence of national and provincial interests: "I know where the big things are, but really know them? I notice more when I am travelling." It is worth noting that the second question itself may have prompted participants to think about monuments. Nevertheless, only a minority identified historic sites and monuments as a source of information on local history.

Participants often felt apologetic about their lack of engagement with material commemorations, and most offered justifications for their answers. More than one participant asserted that monuments and plaques are things one "doesn't do" here. One person commented, "Monuments don't tell me much. I take it for granted. I feel like I know it all. I'm more interested in statues ... where I am [travelling]. We live here, but don't do what's here." Another saw engagement with monuments as an unexpected outcome of planned outings: "Monuments provide passive knowledge. You go there for some other reasons – say it's a beautiful park – and then say, 'hey, what's that?'" Another mentioned the tourists' investment in monuments: "For the tourists, monuments are good. If you take an interest, you will go see it. I'm not sure if local people visit them or know much about local history." Another had a similar response: "Monuments are a minor source of local history. Maybe it would be more if I had time. It is difficult if you are just driving by." Again, material commemorations did not figure largely in local place making for local residents.

There are two ways to explain this situation. First, we might view material commemoration as an anachronistic artefact of the pre-automobile city. The automobile city produced two interrelated consequences that are germane here: the urban-gridiron plan and the decline of the public individual.[27] Together, they fostered cities where efficiency and goal-oriented tasks trump leisure and the pauses necessary to engage monuments.[28] Thus, as our participants made clear, they tightly managed their time in the city both in transitory space and at their destinations. Many participants suggested that they were far too busy to engage monuments on a day-to-day basis. One person related, "I don't pay attention to monuments. I'm too busy trying to make a living. I do notice quite a few of them, but too many flowerpots get in the way."

Second, we may explain a reluctance to engage with material commemorations with reference to tourism. As noted above, the most heavily plaqued area in Niagara outside of St. Catharines is defined by the Niagara Parkway, which parallels the Niagara River (see Figure 5.7). Many local residents avoid this area because of its association with tourist sites, a point supported by scholarship on international tourist landscapes and the complicated relationships that locals have with them.[29] Although many locals acknowledge the economic benefits of tourism, they also realize that the commoditization of landscapes can diminish or destroy local attachment to place. Traffic, busyness, crowding, and the overexploitation of area resources are among the consequences of commercialization. Clare Mitchell and her colleagues describe this "creative destruction" in the context of Niagara-on-the-Lake, which sits at one end of the parkway.[30] The argument can be applied to the parkway's entire length.

There is a certain irony in the participants' responses to tourist areas. If residents know that the parkway is a tourist area, they also know that it is dense with material commemorations. Mnemonic narratives are part of its publicity profile. The promiscuity of narratives in this part of Niagara may form the core of a "vernacular-culture region," a regional self-identity that grows out of an amalgam of economic, historical, political, and cultural factors and may be the outcome of sustained promotional or publicity campaigns. It bears repeating, then, that those participants who identified mnemonic

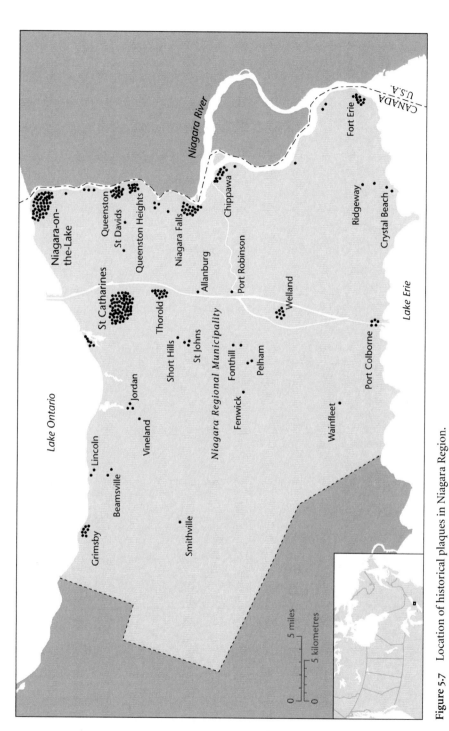

Figure 5.7 Location of historical plaques in Niagara Region.

Note: Each dot represents one historical plaque.

narratives may have been drawing on tourism brochures and newspaper articles rather than on the material commemorations themselves. Mnemonic narratives have been woven into efforts to market the falls, wineries, and several other people, places, things, and events identified during the survey. If we return to the metaphor of the landscape as "stage," we might argue that to make Niagara meaningful to themselves, participants use these mnemonic properties no differently than they are used in the marketing – or, indeed, that they are inspired by the marketing. Their avoidance of the parkway and its monuments may be driven by tourism advertising and its promotion of the monuments, in which case regional self-promotion may have fostered active non-engagement with local mnemonic narratives.

Last, we return to the modest parallel between the two commemograms. Despite our participants' lack of engagement with material commemorations, they did recall three of the most commonly marked mnemonic narratives: the War of 1812, Welland Canal, and Underground Railroad. If our participants' knowledge of these narratives was not derived from commemorations, then presumably it came from other sources. When participants were asked where they had learned about local history, the mass media emerged as the most common source of information (48.9 percent of responses). By contrast, visits to historic sites and museums accounted for only 11.8 percent of responses. Such visits were rivalled by the participant's social circle (13.4 percent), formal schooling (9.2 percent), and what we categorized as "passive learning" – several participants told of absorbing information randomly from whatever persons, texts, or sites they happened to encounter (10.5 percent). A pattern emerges when we consider these sources in relation to the three mnemonic narratives identified by participants. They have all been commemorated by all three levels of government. They also appear in school curricula and event programming (e.g., re-enactments, Black History Month, permanent museum exhibits). They inform local toponomy through the names of local streets, neighbourhoods, institutions, and businesses (e.g., medical clinics, auto dealerships, hotels). Physically, they form the backdrop to everyday experience, particularly for those who regularly encounter the canal and its many bridges or the 1812 forts and battlefields. In the recent past, the Underground Railroad gradually acquired similar status as local memory entrepreneurs restored former safe houses and plotted a Freedom Trail linking sites throughout the region – including Salem Chapel. Tourism promoters have also invested heavily in these narratives to cast Niagara as a geographically unique destination. In short, participants recalled those narratives that are highly intertextual – that is, those narratives that have been told through multiple channels beyond material commemorations.

Participants referenced these multiple sources of information and noted when they had learned particular narratives in two or more different contexts (particularly their school days). As one person stated, "the War of 1812 was drummed into us at school. We visited a lot of historic places when I was young. Particularly the role they played in the development of Canada." Another participant noted, "I learn some things about Canadian history from monuments. We live in a very historical area. But my national history is kind of weak. I haven't thought about it since Grade 10." Yet another professed an interest in plaques but only as a secondary source of information: "They're putting more money into plaques [pause]. It's always interesting, so I'm interested. So, I'm drawn into monuments, but I'm more driven to go to the library." Some participants suggested that historic sites and monuments best served as prompts to acquire more knowledge elsewhere. One noted, "We get general impressions from monuments, not detailed knowledge. It is important to get a sense of where things happen, otherwise they remain abstract." The purpose of monuments, then, may be to serve as a spatial marker more than as a source of knowledge. Enduring knowledge, if held at all, is found elsewhere.

Somewhere, at some point in time, our participants were told that the narratives marked by these plaques are important. Now, however, these narratives are taken for granted or entirely forgotten. One person was sure that commemorations are a significant source of information on local history but demonstrated some difficulty in coming up with details: "Monuments do contribute to my knowledge of Canada. In Niagara-on-the-Lake, there's that big statue of whoever – the general who fought against the Americans. Then there's the Moses of her people ... the Underground Railway. I can see her, she's rather severe looking, I remember from the photos ... [a passer-by helps out] Oh yes, Harriet Tubman." Participants believe that commemorations are meaningful and significant, but they do not know why and doubt their impact on daily life. They may see plaques, statues, and stones on a daily basis, but these commemorations do not spark a thunderclap of recognition or a directive to action. Rather, for most of our participants, their cursory glances of commemorations register on an unconscious level that is sufficient to maintain vague memories of narratives they already know.[31]

We began this chapter with a series of questions about the relationship between memory entrepreneurs and their audiences, between the intent of material commemorations and their actual operation as ideological resources for individuals. Our current questions were prompted by a 2005 survey in which local residents did not reference frequently marked mnemonic narratives when contemplating local identity. In response, we conducted a second survey to discover whether local residents would reference these narratives if they were asked to consider them in a national context rather than in a strictly local context. Asking our survey participants to think of Niagara consciously in terms of national narratives made a noticeable difference in the frequency with which local mnemonic narratives were identified. We must take care, however, in assigning a definitive influence to material commemorations. It may be that participants were responding to accounts in the mass media, their schooling, or contemporary promotional work within the tourism industry more than they were responding to memory work.

Our argument maintains that places can be read as events or stages where people create meaning in the course of everyday living. Elements of the landscape are resources or properties on which people draw to construct this meaning; based on the context of their use, the meaning of these resources can change. Material commemorations operate as resources; they can reinforce narratives within any context, from a local to a national scale, depending on their use. This situation is evident from the Niagara plaque inventory, as most memory entrepreneurs have commemorated the same four narratives: the War of 1812, Welland Canal, Underground Railroad, and First World War. The Salem Chapel provides one clear example of this phenomenon in St. Catharines itself. The survey responses, meanwhile, indicate that the general public draw on a rich variety of resources to conceive a local identity. Material commemorations are simply one resource among many and occupy a relatively modest position well behind the mass media.

It appears, then, that the landscape shaped by memory entrepreneurs is less influential than they may hope – that material commemorations play only a minor role in the identity of Niagara residents. Nonetheless, their influence cannot be dismissed entirely. There are two reasons. First, the latent messages they convey can be as influential as their manifest content. Our survey participants, in 2005 and 2008, indicated that monuments can make powerful visual arguments. Second, any seeming silence may not be permanent. Like Salem Chapel in St. Catharines, Brock's Monument at Queenston Heights provides a good example of the shifting mnemonic priorities of local residents. It was the site of an enormous fete when erected in 1824, sparked renewed interest in 1844 when destroyed by an Irish patriot, and did so again in 1856 when a new monument was unveiled. The bicentennial of the Battle of Queenston Heights and the death of Brock occurs in 2012. Will the monument's significance be restored? Local residents may well embrace it once again if local, provincial, national, and commercial memory entrepreneurs promote the anniversary through every available channel. However, any renewed interest in the monument would therefore be sparked not by the messages that the monument itself communicated but by its narrative's ubiquity in other media. The monument would not serve to prompt popular memory of the narrative; rather, the narrative would prompt popular memory of the monument.

ACKNOWLEDGMENTS

This project was funded by a Standard Research Grant from the Social Sciences and Humanities Research Council of Canada held by the Popular Culture Niagara Research Group. Our thanks to Kim Randall and Kirby Calvert for their enthusiastic survey work.

NOTES

1   Doreen Massey, "Places and Their Pasts," *History Workshop Journal* 39 (1995): 182-95; Tim Cresswell, *In Place/Out of Place: Geography, Ideology, and Transgression* (Minneapolis and London: University of Minnesota Press, 1996); Tim Cresswell, *Place: A Short Introduction* (Oxford: Blackwell, 2004); Nuala Johnson, "Public Memory," in *A Companion to Cultural Geography,* ed. James Duncan, Nuala Johnson, and Richard Schein (Malden: Blackwell, 2004), 87-116, 316-28.

2   Johnson, "Public Memory," 322.

3   Arturo Escobar, "Culture Sits in Places: Reflections on Globalism and Subaltern Strategies of Localization," *Political Geography* 20 (2001): 143.

4   Elizabeth Jelin, *State Repression and the Labors of Memory,* trans. Judy Rein and Marcial Godoy-Anativia (Minneapolis: University of Minnesota Press, 2003).

5   Niagara Economic Development Corporation, "Top St. Catharines Employers," 2007, http://www.stcatharines.ca/forbusiness/ecodevt/eco_dev_employers.asp.

6   Ian McKay, *The Quest of the Folk: Antimodernism and Cultural Selection in Twentieth-Century Nova Scotia* (Montreal and Kingston: McGill-Queen's University Press, 1994); Iain Hay, Andrew Hughes, and Mark Tutton, "Monuments, Memory and Marginalization in Adelaide's Prince Henry Gardens," *Geographiska Annaler* 86B, 3 (2004): 201-16.

7   Pierre Nora, "Between Memory and History: Les Lieux de Mémoire," *Representations* 26 (1989): 7-24.

8   Charles Withers, "Place, Memory, Monument: Memorializing the Past in Contemporary Highland Scotland," *Cultural Geographies* 3 (1996): 325-44; Nuala Johnson, "Cast in Stone: Monuments, Geography, and Nationalism," *Environment and Planning D: Society and Space* 13 (1995): 51-65; Brian Graham, ed., *In Search of Ireland: A Cultural Geography* (London: Routledge, 1997); Neil Leach, "9/11," in *Urban Memory: History and Amnesia in the Modern City,* ed. Mark Crinson (London: Routledge, 2005), 169-94.

9   John Bodnar, *Remaking America: Public Memory, Commemoration, and Patriotism in the Twentieth Century* (Princeton, NJ: Princeton University Press, 1992); Roy Rosenzweig and David Thelen, *The Presence of the Past: Popular Uses of History in American Life* (New York: Columbia University Press, 1998).

10 Michael Heffernan, "For Every England: The Western Front and the Politics of Remembrance in Britain," *Ecumene* 2, 3 (1995): 293-323; Hamzah Muzaini and Brenda Yeoh, "War Landscapes as 'Battlefields' of Collective Memories: Reading the Reflections at Bukit Chandu, Singapore," *Cultural Geographies* 12 (2005): 345-65; Hamzah Muzaini and Brenda Yeoh, "Memory-Making from 'Below': Rescaling Remembrance at the Kranji War Memorial and Cemetery, Singapore," *Environment and Planning A* 39 (2007): 1288-1305.

11 Alexander Wilde, "Irruptions of Memory: Expressive Politics in Chile's Transition to Democracy," *Journal of Latin American Studies* 31, 2 (1999): 473-500; Sanford Levinson, *Written in Stone: Public Monuments in Changing Societies* (Durham, NC: Duke University Press, 1998); Brian Osborne, "Constructing Landscapes of Power: The George Etienne Cartier Monument, Montreal," *Journal of Historical Geography* 24, 4 (1998): 431-58; Yvonne Whelan, "The Construction and Deconstruction of a Colonial Landscape: Monuments to British Monarchs in Dublin before and after Independence," *Journal of Historical Geography* 28, 4 (2002): 508-33; Jonathan Leib, "The Witting Autobiography of Richmond, Virginia: Arthur Ashe, the Civil War, and Monument Avenue's Racialized Landscape," in *Landscape and Race in the United States,* ed. Richard Schein (New York: Routledge, 2006), 187-212; Russell Johnston and Michael Ripmeester, "A Monument's Work Is Never Done: The Watson Monument, Memory and Forgetting in a Small Canadian City," *International Journal of Heritage Studies* 13, 2 (2007): 117-35.

12 Johnston and Ripmeester, "A Monument's Work."

13 Michael Billig, *Banal Nationalism* (London: Sage, 1995), 40.

14 M. Christine Boyer, *The City of Collective Memory: Its Historical Imagery and Architectural Entertainments* (Cambridge, MA: MIT Press, 1996); David Birdsell and Leo Groarke, "Toward a Theory of Visual Argument," *Argumentation and Advocacy* 33, 1 (1996): 1-10; J. Anthony Blair, "The Possibility and Actuality of Visual Arguments," *Argumentation*

and *Advocacy* 33, 1 (1996): 23-39; Cara Finnegan, "The Naturalistic Enthymeme and Visual Argument: Photographic Representation in the 'Skull Controversy,'" *Argumentation and Advocacy* 37 (2001): 133-39; Cara Finnegan, "Recognizing Lincoln: Image Vernaculars in Nineteenth Century Visual Culture," *Rhetoric and Public Affairs* 8, 1 (2005): 31-58.

15 Manuel Castells, *The Information Age: Economy, Society and Culture,* vol. 2, *The Power of Identity* (London: Blackwell, 1997), 7.

16 Anthony Giddens, "Modernity and Self-Identity: Tribulations of the Self," in *The Discourse Reader,* ed. Adam Jaworski and Nikolas Coupland (London: Routledge, 1999), 415-27.

17 Allan Pred, *Making Histories and Constructing Human Geographies: The Local Transformation of Practice, Power Relations, and Consciousness* (Boulder, CO: Westview Press, 1990).

18 Sarah Purcell, "Commemoration, Public Art, and the Changing Meaning of the Bunker Hill Monument," *Public Historian* 25, 2 (2003): 55-71.

19 Bodnar, *Remaking America*; Charlene Mires, *Independence Hall in American Memory* (Philadelphia: University of Pennsylvania Press, 2002); Rosenzweig and Thelen, *Presence of the Past.*

20 Eviatar Zerubavel, *Time Maps: Collective Memory and the Social Shape of the Past* (Chicago: University of Chicago Press, 2003).

21 Mark Starowicz and Susan Dando, executive producers, *The Greatest Canadian,* video recording (Toronto: CBC Television, 2004), http://www.cbc.ca/greatest; Russell Johnston and Michael Ripmeester, "'I haven't read it, but I will some day': Historic Plaques and Public Memory in a Small Canadian City," paper presented at the Canadian Communication Association Annual Conference, Saskatoon, May 2007.

22 Wayne Cook, "Wayne Cook's Genealogy and Historic Plaques Page," http://www.waynecook.com.

23 See Jonathan Vance, *Death So Noble: Memory, Meaning and the First World War* (Vancouver: UBC Press, 1997); Robert Shipley, *To Mark Our Place: A History of Canadian War Memorials* (Toronto: NC Press, 1987).

24 Statistics Canada, "St. Catharines, Ontario," table, in *2006 Census: 2006 Community Profiles,* Statistics Canada Catalogue no. 92-591-XWE (Ottawa: Ministry of Supply and Services, 2007); Statistics Canada, "Profile of Ethnic Origin and Visible Minorities for Canada, Provinces, Territories, Census Divisions and Census Subdivisions," table, in *Census of Canada, 2006,* Statistics Canada Catalogue no. 94-580-XCB2006001 (Ottawa: Ministry of Supply and Services, 2008).

25 Johnston and Ripmeester, "'I haven't read it.'"

26 The respondent is referencing statements made in André Picard, "St. Catharines leads the fat parade," *Globe and Mail,* 21 July 2001, A1.

27 Richard Sennett, *The Conscience of the Eye: The Design and Social Life of Cities* (New York: W.W. Norton, 1990); Richard Sennett, *The Fall of Public Man* (New York: W.W. Norton, 1990); Bernard Rudofsky, *Streets for People: A Primer for Americans* (New York: Van Nostrand Reinhold, 1982).

28 Paul Fotsch, *Watching the Traffic Go By: Transportation and Isolation in Urban America* (Austin: University of Texas Press, 2007); Patrick Joyce, *The Rule of Freedom: Liberalism and the Modern City* (London: Verso, 2003); Grady Clay, *Real Places: An Unconventional Guide to America's Generic Landscape* (Chicago: University of Chicago Press, 1994).

29 Peter Korca, "Resident Perceptions of Tourism in a Resort Town," *Leisure Science* 20 (1998): 193-212; Clare Mitchell, R. Greg Atkinson, and Andrew Clark, "The Creative Destruction of Niagara-on-the-Lake," *Canadian Geographer* 45 (2001): 285-99; David Snepenger, Ryan O'Connell, and Mary Snepenger, "The Embrace-Withdraw Continuum Scale: Operationalizing Residents' Responses Toward Tourism Development," *Journal of Travel Research* 40 (2001): 155-61; K. Evans, "Competition for Heritage Space: Cairo's Resident/Tourist Conflict," in *Managing Tourism in Cities,* ed. Duncan Tyler, Yvonne Guerrier, and Martin Robertson (Chichester, NY: J. Wiley, 1998), 179-92.

30 Mitchell, Atkinson, and Clark, "The Creative Destruction," 285-99.

31 Johnston and Ripmeester, "A Monument's Work."

Part 2

INSCRIPTIONS: RECOVERING PLACES OF MEMORY

Placing the Displaced Worker
Narrating Place in Deindustrializing Sturgeon Falls, Ontario

STEVEN HIGH

To tell a story is to take arms against the threat of time, to resist time or to harness it. The telling of a story preserves the teller from oblivion; a story builds the identity of the teller and the legacy he will leave in time to come.

– Alessandro Portelli

The identity of places is very much bound up with the histories which are told of them; how these histories are told, and which history turns out to be dominant.

– Doreen Massey

Language becomes the force that binds people to places. It is through language that everyday experiences of self-in-place form and mutate; moreover, it is through language that places themselves are imaginatively constituted in ways that carry implications for "who we are."

– John Dixon and Kevin Durrheim

Figure 6.1 The Sturgeon Falls Paper Mill. Photograph by David W. Lewis.

The "displaced worker" entered our everyday language in the 1940s with the economic upheaval that accompanied the Second World War. One of the earliest published references that I have uncovered was a July 1942 article in *Barron's* that spoke of the US government's efforts to assist people displaced in the conversion to a war economy.[1] Displaced workers took on new prominence in the early 1960s with the upheaval that accompanied trade liberalization. Government programs in the United States and Canada were created to assist long-service workers who lost their jobs to imports. Since then, the "displaced worker" label has come to apply to all those caught up in layoffs and in mill or factory closings.[2] The US Department of Labor, for example, has sponsored biannual Displaced Workers Surveys since 1984.[3] These statistics and others generated like it in Canada are sifted through by economists and social scientists for significant patterns. Displacement is almost always measured in narrowly economic terms. Who was displaced? How many? How long were they unemployed? What were their earnings once re-employed? The numbers are then broken down into the usual categories of sex, race, age, occupation, and region. In my view, the reliance on the aggregate and the abstract has contributed to an impoverished view of dis*place*ment that equates worker

dis*location* with an event (a mill or factory closure) and the subsequent absence of paid employment rather than with a social and spatial process that is highly meaningful.[4]

Life-history interviewing provides an opportunity to explore the cultural meaning of displacement from the vantage point of those most directly involved: workers themselves. Until recently, I have interviewed displaced workers decades after their mill or factory "went down." Some of these men and women found new jobs. Others never found steady work again. Despite the time that had passed, these interviews were highly emotional undertakings. Anger and loss punctuated many of the stories told. Yet nothing prepared me for the raw emotions encountered in the Sturgeon Falls project. Sturgeon Falls is a town of 6,000 located between Sudbury and North Bay in northern Ontario. We began interviewing displaced workers within a year of Weyerhaeuser's closure of the corrugated-paper mill in December 2002 (see Figure 6.1). Life-history interviewing continued as efforts to reopen the century-old mill petered out and it was pulverized into dust and trucked away. By 2005 I and my research assistants had interviewed over sixty people. Several interviewees demanded to know whether we had any connection to the company before agreeing to participate. A number of others declined to be interviewed out of fear that they would not be able to control their emotions. To deepen the conversation further, I conducted follow-up interviews with fifteen of the mill workers in 2006. Most interviewees were still in mourning, and their profound sense of loss permeated everything spoken. The resulting interviews record some of the thoughts, feelings, and attachments that workers had *at the time* of displacement or shortly thereafter.

It should come as no surprise that mills and factories are highly meaningful places for those who toiled there. This is particularly true of long-service workers who have spent twenty, twenty-five, or even thirty years in a given workplace. All of the industrial workers whom I have interviewed in the past decade have used home and family metaphors to describe their attachment to people, place, and product. Their intent is clear: the job meant more than a paycheque. Other historians have found much the same thing. In their now classic study of the Amoskeag textile mill published thirty years ago, Tamara Hareven and Randolph Langenback wrote that textile workers exhibited a "highly developed sense of place" and formed tightly knit groups.[5] Place attachment is a complex phenomenon that involves affect, emotion, feeling, and memory. Places are thus seen, heard, smelled, felt, experienced, and imagined.[6]

My own thinking on place identity and attachment has been profoundly influenced by British geographer Doreen Massey. In her brilliant essay "Places and Their Pasts," which appeared in *History Workshop Journal* in 1994, Massey argued that place identity is constructed out of a particular constellation of social relations meeting and weaving together. Places don't just exist on a map but *in time* as well. According to Massey, "places as depicted on maps are places caught in a moment; they are slices through time."[7] One might say that places are products of constantly shifting social relations. The identity of any place is thus temporary, uncertain, and in process.[8] For Massey, the local is always a product of the global, at least in part. Larger social, economic, and political forces are thus integral to the making of places. Yet the past of a place is "as open to a multiplicity of readings as is the present. Moreover, the claims and counter-claims about the present character of a place depend in almost all cases on particular, rival interpretations of its past."[9] Places are thus products of history that exist in time and space.[10]

What is largely missing from the scholarly discussion of place making, however, is its flip-side: the unmaking or demolition of place. What happens

Figure 6.2   Ken and Bruce Colquhoun, Summer 2005. Photograph by David W. Lewis.

when places are lost to us and these ties are forcibly broken? If place attachment is a symbolic bond between people and place, this bond is often severed in times of sudden social or economic crisis such as a mill closing. People then attempt to re-create these attachments by remembering and talking about these places.[11] How was the mill spoken of during the interviews? Do former paper workers define themselves as displaced? Or do they display a heightened attachment to mill and factory? Are these two reactions mutually exclusive?

In responding to these questions, I will listen to many voices but most deeply to those of Hubert Gervais and Bruce Colquhoun, the two worker-historians at the Sturgeon Falls mill. They are the keepers of the "mill history binder," a memory book in photographs and documents. The binder (one of the biggest that I have ever seen) was first put together by Hubert Gervais in 1995, was updated in 1998 for the mill's centennial, and has been revised since then by Bruce Colquhoun (see Figure 6.2). What is interesting here is how the two men and others treated the binder in the months and years that followed the closure: it was spoken of with great reverence, in a whisper. It was as though the mill history binder had become a surrogate for the mill itself.[12]

MILL/TOWN

The bonding of people with their workplaces ensures that periods of major economic and social change are periods of major spatial change as well.[13] The power of place was everywhere apparent in our conversations with displaced workers and their families. It infused their language and structured their stories. Mine, mill, or factory closings challenge our sense of place at the deepest level: "Workers lose a social structure in which they have felt valued and validated by their fellows."[14] The mill's closure therefore hit interviewees hard. Randy Restoule spoke for many when he said, "I felt a deep loss. The fact that everyone else was leaving ... All your friends are gone. And like I said before, the reason that you keep going in a job is because of friends."[15] In the beginning, people spoke of the mill in the present tense as part of their "today" but soon shifted to the past tense. As you can imagine, the mill's demolition unleashed strong emotions. Bruce Colquhoun related this story:

> When I stopped by on Ottawa Street on the far side of the mill and I take some pictures. I met with some of the older guys there who are retired. One guy looked up at me who was sitting in his car. I went over and talked to him and he says, "you know Bruce. I never thought I'd live to see the day that they'd tear that mill down." Then, tears are coming down. He says, "I gotta go." He took off. I never thought I'd see that place taken down either.[16]

Places exist at varying geographic scales in the plant-shutdown stories recorded. At times, displaced workers attached themselves to a particular department inside the mill (like the paint line) or to the mill as a whole. At other times, they identified more strongly with the town, region, or nation. All of these local and translocal identifications provided the men and women interviewed with a sense of belonging in a time of catastrophic change. In this section, we focus on people's strong attachment to the mill community and their sense of distance from the larger local community.[17]

Sturgeon Falls was a single-industry town like many others. The corrugated-paper mill was the town's largest employer and offered the best wages. Most of the interviewees went to work in the mill straight out of high school.

At its peak in the 1950s and 1960s, it employed 700 people and provided revenue to farmers in the surrounding rural areas who supplied the mill with much of its wood supply. Nearly every family in the town was once connected to the mill in some way. Over the years, however, employment levels dropped off until there were only 150 left. The mill's conversion to recycled paper from virgin wood in the early 1990s and the closure of the hardboard mill cut the plant's ties with farmers. As a result, the shrinking circle of "mill families" became increasingly isolated from other residents.[18]

With the mill's social and economic dominance fading, it became possible for residents to imagine the town's future without the mill. Sturgeon Falls' identity as a mill town thus eroded over the years of decline. It remained the town's largest private-sector employer but not by much. The mill's unfortunate closure in 2002 and its subsequent demolition only confirmed this new reality in the minds of many. There was no going back. For mill workers and their families, however, the town's indifferent response to the mill's closure came as a stunning blow.

One of the remarkable discoveries of our project is that the plant-shutdown stories told by unionized production workers, salaried staff, and locally recruited managers follow the same narrative path. They all call the mill "home" and co-workers "family." They are all rooted in place. There are differences, of course, although these are never consistent. Several former mill managers, for example, seemed more forgiving of the company. The mill was old and it was small. The free market must be respected. Yet the "we" in their narratives consistently referred to the mill workers and their families regardless of workplace hierarchies. This cross-class attachment to place was also evident in the frequent use of "our mill" in the interviews. "All of those people that I worked with at that mill for twenty-five years," recalled Mike Lacroix, "are people that I went to school with, people that I knew ... their families. I knew their fathers. I knew their kids. I knew them all. They were 'born and raised.' We worked together. I spent more time with the boys at the mill than I spent with my own family." He called it a "little family."[19]

The reason for this submergence of difference within the mill is twofold. In part, it was a product of the shared experience of displacement. Locally rooted managers were in much the same boat as unionized production workers. The old differences between unionized "staff" (or "company people") and the "shop floor" (or "workers") blurred once the mill closed. The closure appeared to pit residents against a non-resident company and Canadians against Americans (Weyerhaeuser was United States-owned). The second factor that needs to be considered relates to the web of kinship ties that connected many of the mill employees. Almost all of the Sturgeon Falls mill workers whom we interviewed listed other family members, past and present, who worked at the site. "Some families had three or four brothers working in the plant at the same time," recalled Percy Allary.[20] It was commonplace. Several interviewees could name three generations of mill workers in some local families. Bruce Colquhoun's father and grandfather, for example, worked in the mill before him. Family memories of the mill often went back generations. To mill managers brought in from the outside, it quickly became apparent just how tightly knit the workforce was. "The first thing I learned," said mill superintendent Gerry Stevens, was "don't say anything about anybody because they are probably related."[21]

Most interviewees were hired on at the mill with the help of their fathers or, in a few cases, their mothers. Mike Lacroix's father and two uncles worked at the mill, and it was his father who got him in. But he did so on the condition that his son work hard and be on time: "Back then, the old man, he said 'you know, if you are getting in there, you better not screw up. If you screw up you will have to deal with me' ... You didn't want to make your dad look bad."[22] This informal practice, common everywhere, was eventually formalized. It became plant policy to hire summer students on the basis of the seniority of their mill-working father or mother as well as their level of education. Otherwise, the hiring issue risked causing bad blood. "I always hated to play God," recalled a relieved Ed Fortin, the mill's long-time personnel director.[23] No distinction was henceforth made in the hiring of the children of mill managers or production workers. "It was easy after that," he said. Other students in Sturgeon Falls, however, were out of luck. The mill's hiring policy made it a very closed shop indeed.

The mill therefore loomed large in the oral narratives of former employees, casting its shadow over the town. For more than a century, the rising smoke from the stack was a reminder of the jobs that the mill provided. Smoke signalled prosperous times, and its absence has always been a danger signal in industrial towns and cities.[24] We were repeatedly told that the mill's smokestack and water tower could be seen from anywhere in Sturgeon Falls. In actuality, the mill was set apart from most of the town by the Sturgeon River and its high embankment. One could therefore see these physical landmarks only in certain areas and not at all from downtown streets. These remarks are therefore more an indication of the mill's local social and economic dominance, and its centrality in the lives of mill workers and their families, than a realistic assessment of its physical presence. They need not be taken literally.

Yet Sturgeon Falls was a colonized landscape. The mill had several distant owners over its 104 years of operation. The Spanish River Pulp and Paper Company (1920s), Abitibi (1929-79), MacMillan Bloedel (1979-99), and Weyerhaeuser (1999-2002) were all multi-site producers of newsprint and other paper products. Until the final years, the English-speaking mill managers were recruited from outside the locality. They once lived in "the compound," a residential section of company-owned houses adjacent to the mill. Most are reputed to have promptly left Sturgeon Falls on retirement, if they had not already been transferred to another site.[25] Few Franco-Ontarians, who constituted the bulk of the locally recruited workforce, made it into management – although this began to change in the final decade. The social structure of the town therefore resembled that of other mill towns in northern Ontario and Quebec during the 1950s and 1960s. In fact, one of the superintendents interviewed had worked in Chicoutimi until Quebec's Quiet Revolution made life difficult for a unilingual anglophone.[26] He initially found a familiar social landscape in Sturgeon Falls, but the language issue followed him across the Quebec-Ontario border when a fight erupted in the town in 1970 over French-language schooling. Until then, the town's only high school was English. In this regard, the mill changed much more slowly than the town itself.

THE MAKING OF THE "MILL HISTORY BINDER"

At the time of the mill's closing, I was teaching history at Nipissing University in North Bay, a twenty-five-minute drive east of Sturgeon Falls. I closely followed the efforts to reopen the mill in the local newspaper. Much of what I read was familiar to me. The workers and their union wrapped themselves in the Canadian flag in the hopes of forcing Weyerhaeuser to sell the plant as a going concern. The old opposition between "American bosses" and "Canadian workers," however, did not bring province-wide or national attention to this local struggle.[27] So the workers went to court. It was while these efforts to re-open the mill were continuing that we began to interview workers about the closure. It was our hope that the story would have a happy ending, as sometimes occurs.[28]

I first met Bruce Colquhoun in late 2003 at the Action Centre, a job-assistance centre operated by the paper workers' union for the former mill workers. Dave Hunter, a local resident who assisted with this research project in its early days, first told me about the "mill history binder" – the largest binder he had ever seen. I really *had* to see it. He also told me that everyone he approached to be interviewed told him to first talk to Bruce, one of its compilers. I of course agreed. We met one wintry day in the Action Centre, a big room with tables arranged end-to-end in long rows. There were three or four other men in the room when I was introduced to Bruce and his huge black binder.

Bruce Colquhoun and the others treated the mill history binder as a sacred text or shrine to the mill: their voices lowered to a whisper, and Bruce turned the pages with loving care. I instinctively did the same, as it was immediately apparent to me that this binder meant a great deal to these men.[29] It was a giant memory book, with clippings of old news stories, photographs, and photocopied material on the mill found in the old *Abitibi Magazine.* Over the next two hours, Bruce told me stories as he slowly turned the pages. A soft-spoken man, Bruce noted that the mill history binder was treasured by the mill workers and their families. He related how he would sometimes get requests to borrow the binder to show a visiting family member or a grand-child. Sometimes, former mill workers just wanted to revisit their old lives inside the mill.

Rereading my field notes from that day's meeting, I am reminded that this was a highly significant encounter in my own intellectual journey. It was the catalyst for a book-length project on the mill's closing. At that moment, I knew that the mill history binder would be the subject of a full chapter. You might wonder why it appealed to me. For starters, it provided an opportun-ity to explore one personalized response to the economic crisis facing Canada's forest-dependent communities.[30] The mill history binder can be read as a deep expression of place attachment. Historians sometimes look down on "amateur" historians or "collectors." They are usually untrained – in the sense of not having graduate degrees in history – and are said to produce flawed research that is sentimental, celebratory, excessively detailed, or lacking in

Figure 6.3 Hubert Gervais at the old plant. Photograph by David W. Lewis.

analysis. The mill history binder could be criticized on any one of these counts. Yet, to do so would be to ignore what it is: a storehouse of memories from and for a workplace community that was shattered by a decision made far away. How displaced workers related to this memory book in the months and years following the closure tells us a great deal about the hold that the mill had on them.

The visual language of the mill history binder reminds me of a school yearbook, a family photograph album, or scrapbook – each image has a story attached to it. In her book *Suspended Conversations,* art historian Martha Langford asks what makes the photograph album so special: "Well, memories of course."[31] The album "preserves the life story of the departed within a concrete and bounded report."[32] The mill history binder serves much the same function, keeping its main protagonist, the mill itself, alive. In so doing, the binder came to symbolize the mill workers' continuing connection with the past. People's attachments to specific places are not constant; we are most conscious of the sense of belonging that we derive from place when this connection is most at risk. Place attachment is often "activated retrospectively."[33] Yet the mill history binder differs from a yearbook or photograph album insofar as its very openness, the refusal to "close" the meanings or additions, suggests that the binder serves a function very different from that of Langford's albums.

We know a great deal about the making of the mill history binder from a series of interviews that we conducted with the two worker-historians involved, Hubert Gervais and Bruce Colquhoun. Hubert grew up in the nearby village of Field before starting to work at the mill on 29 April 1963 as an "office boy."[34] He worked in the mill's offices for the next thirty-five years. Bruce, by contrast, followed his father – who had been one of the first workers hired when the mill reopened in 1947 after being shut for fifteen difficult years – onto the mill's shop floor. He worked in the maintenance department as an "oiler," oiling and greasing machines all over the plant. The job took him everywhere. The two men – one francophone and the other anglophone; one an office worker and the other a production worker – thus neatly mirrored the social structure of the mill, albeit in reverse. They were interviewed on several occasions, alone and together, between 2003 and 2006. In all, there are probably ten hours of recorded conversations. We also asked our other interviewees about the binder.

In an interview over lunch at a popular local restaurant, I asked Bruce and Hubert why they undertook the mill history project. Why was it important to them? To this, Bruce answered, "I like history too, like Hubert. I wanted to know about the mill. I had always looked around and seen the old stuff in the mill. I don't know. I was doing my family history too. Hubert would help me out at the time, and he showed me what he had done until 1976."[35] Bruce asked whether he could take the story up to the present. At this juncture in the interview, Hubert piped in to say that Bruce had been after him for a few years to do so. Hubert explained, "I was retiring. I wanted to give it to somebody who was interested."[36] Bruce therefore became the mill's historian on Hubert's retirement in 1998.

That year, Bruce Colquhoun inserted a full-page tribute to Hubert Gervais and the making of the mill history project in the binder itself (see Figure 6.3). He divides its development into three phases. It originated in Hubert's passion for the mill and its long history. "Like a few people working here," wrote Bruce, Hubert "wanted to know the history of our mill. So, he took it on himself to find out what made our mill tick."[37] When asked, Hubert credited a co-worker for pushing him to put together the first mill history binder in time for the town's centennial in 1995. One of the women who worked with Hubert in the mill offices encouraged him to gather his historical materials in one place. "I had to put them someplace," he told me. The text that introduces each chapter of the binder was typed by her. She worked on it every time she had fifteen or twenty minutes to spare. In this first effort, Hubert provided a brief history of the mill from 1898 until 1976.

The first history binder's existence was announced in the mill's newsletter, in a story entitled "Our Mill – Way Back Then." Employees were told that Hubert had "compiled a book of old photos and articles from the old *Abitibi* magazine dating from 1949-1969" and advised that "anyone interested in looking at this book may do so in the main office lobby."[38] There appears to have been only one or two copies made. That month, the town's weekly newspaper, the *Tribune,* published a piece by Hubert Gervais entitled "1898-1947: A Bit of the Sturgeon Falls Mill's History."[39] It consisted of a chronology of the mill's development in the first half-century.

These efforts to tie the mill's history to the town's centennial, however, were overshadowed by the publication of *Sturgeon Falls, 1895-1995,* a book commissioned by the Sturgeon Falls Centennial Committee as a "salute to over 100 years of life in Sturgeon Falls." Authored by local journalist and historian Wayne LeBelle, this 173-page book, generously illustrated with over 500 photographs, was released to great fanfare.[40] All 500 copies of the book were sold in the first four days. Asked why, LeBelle was quoted as saying, "I think this is a family photo album of the Town of Sturgeon Falls." Centennial celebrations are "really family reunions," he said. Indeed, readers of the *Tribune* were informed that the book "portrays many of our families, special times, important events and interesting people who have made Sturgeon what it is today."[41] Although it celebrated the place identity of the town as a whole, the mill and the forest industry loomed large in LeBelle's narrative. "Wood has been the lifeblood of the community for the last 100 years," he wrote.[42] Yet the "constitutive narrative," or foundational myth, of the town – the founding families and so on – is largely missing from the mill history binder, which provides a surprisingly dispassionate description of the early years.[43]

If the first mill history binder failed to reach much beyond those who flipped through its pages in the mill's offices, it still resonated with Bruce

Colquhoun. On his retirement in 1998, Hubert agreed to let Bruce bring the history of the mill up to date. In August the two men were approached by the mill manager to finish the history in time for the mill's centennial later that year. Bruce shared:

> It was in August or September of that year, that mill management approached him [Hubert] and asked him if he would write a complete history of the mill, and if he could do it by October. It was on that date back in 1898, that our mill was born, and they wanted to put out a book to commemorate the first 100 years. It would be a monumental task to get the history written in time for the 100th anniversary, but, Hubert took up the challenge. The result of his hard work is one extremely well written and documented history book, with lots of old photos included.[44]

Twenty copies of the second history binder were made, one for each department in the mill. "Hubert kept one, and since I am now the designated mill historian, I too received a copy," noted Bruce. "Everyone here loved it. He had done a wonderful job," said Hubert. Copies of the 1995 and 1998 binders were eventually donated to the local museum and to the public library by the mill manager as a lasting contribution to the history of the town.[45]

After 1998 the mill history binder continued to evolve under the stewardship of Bruce Colquhoun. I will discuss its contents in the next section, but Bruce explained its production this way:

> Later that year, Hubert called me to say that he had about 200 *Abitibi* magazines ranging in years from 1947-69. Each of them had a page or two on our division in them. He gave them to me, and what I saw was "FANTASTIC." Here was a pictorial and written history of our mill, during some of the years that Abitibi owned it. I showed some of them to Marc Coté, Mechanical Superintendent. He was amazed with them. Marc and I photo-copied each and every page that had something to do with Sturgeon Falls. Since there were 20 copies of Hubert's book, we decided to make 20 copies of each page. We put them in plastic sheet protectors, then in 3" binders, and distributed them the same way as was done with Hubert's book. Everyone loved them. They saw pictures of their fathers, mothers, grandparents, aunts, uncles,

brothers, sisters, and even some of themselves. There is well over 200 pages of pictures and history. I combined Hubert's book and the *Abitibi* pages, and, together, they filled a 5" binder. I am continuing on with the history, and Hubert is helping me with it. Every once in a while he calls me to say that he has found another picture or a historical fact. If it wasn't for Hubert, we wouldn't know what we now know about our mill. I would like to take this opportunity to say, on behalf of everyone at the mill, a heart-felt THANK YOU to Hubert.[46]

The mill history binder's very existence is an act of defiance in the face of the erasure that accompanied the mill's closing. Hubert Gervais had begun to collect historical and pictorial materials in the 1970s and gathered them into an "archive" kept in the old transformer building that once stood at the base of the mill's water tower. By the time the mill closed, the space was filled with boxes dating back to Spanish River days. The mill's records were shredded or shipped off to destinations unknown after the closure. I managed to get into the mill on two occasions while the demolition company was "preparing the site" by stripping the interior. I saw hundreds of blueprints piled high on the floor in the engineering offices, ready for destruction. Some of these plans dated back to the 1920s. I asked the Weyerhaeuser official onsite if it would be possible to save this heritage, offering to go through the materials myself. He refused, albeit politely.

The company, however, did not succeed in destroying everything. Through Hubert's perseverance, and the clandestine help of another staff member, he spirited a box filled with the mill's newsletter – the *Insider*[47] – out of the closing plant. It had to be done quietly, as the mill manager had earlier turned down their request for the materials in a fit of pique. One day when the mill manager was out of town, Hubert was told to drive his vehicle up to the door where the contraband was delivered.[48] In interviewing people, we discovered that many others had secreted away documents as well: a file here or a box there. Whenever possible, I copied the material – filling twenty-eight large and small binders of my own – and urged the rescuers to donate the originals to the local museum. There should be a law against companies stripping industrial communities of their pasts. Weyerhaeuser owned the mill for only three years, yet it destroyed a century-long record of work and production without hesitation.

NARRATING PLACE IN THE MILL HISTORY BINDER

The mill history binder takes a biographical approach to the history of the mill. Its twenty-eight chapters closely follow the linear stages in its century-long development. The resulting meta-narrative can be divided into four periods: the early days from 1898 until 1930 (Chapters 1-5), the "depression years" from 1930 to 1947 (Chapter 6), the "good years" from 1947 until 1990 (Chapters 7-25), and the "trying years" from 1990 to 2002 (Chapters 26-28). Many of the chapters consist of a few pages of text and a handful of photographs. Other chapters are longer. The visual and textual narrative provides a unifying image of the memory of place. The mill history binder is a manifestation of "constitutive memory": it is both an expression of a shared history and identity and a builder of it. These proud memories were brought into question with the mill's closing in December 2002.

Hubert Gervais' original version of the binder was focused on corporate ownership, work process, natural disasters, and the mill's physical structures. There are therefore chapters dedicated to the mill managers, utilization of sawmill waste, the primary treatment plant, renovations to the main office, as well as the floods of 1928, 1951, and 1979.[49] The focus is resolutely on the mill buildings and machines, not the mill workers themselves. It therefore resembles the kind of institutional history that one would expect to find from seeing the corporate logo of MacMillan Bloedel on the binder's front cover. This would be a mistake, however, as Hubert's narrative details the history of the mill itself, not those corporations that would claim it. It is the story of the making of the Sturgeon Falls paper mill – its industrial processes, production records, and other significant moments.

After 1998 the mill history became less a narrative of "the mill" and more a yearbook that was peopled with mill workers and their families. With Hubert's help, Bruce Colquhoun inserted two hundred pages from *Abitibi Magazine* that recorded the social world tied to the mill.[50] An open invitation to the mill workforce produced other photographs and documents. These new additions were organized year by year within the existing chapter structure, but the years were marked. These pages revealed the social world that existed in and around the mill. Many of the photographs marked ritualized moments: production records, retirement parties, service awards, scholarships to the children of employees, and the like. Anniversaries and other commemorative

Figure 6.4 The layers of time that were embedded in the mill's physical structures. In the foreground are the foundations for the old "grinders" – several of which continue to do service as hydro-electric turbines. Photograph by David W. Lewis.

activities were now included. In 1968, for example, Abitibi Price commissioned a ten-by-fourteen-foot mosaic of the mill in the high school, composed of 15,036 one-inch tiles, based on the sketch by the school's principal, Frank Casey. Other celebrations now appeared, including photographs of mill workers and their families.

Bruce Colquhoun opened the binder to other workers, appealing for help in the *Insider* newsletter. The wording of the public call noted that Bruce was "compiling a historical book of the mill" and that he was looking for "pictures and/or information about this division starting in 1976." He specifically asked for "old articles from newspapers or pictures about the people of the industry."[51] Other mill workers appear to have responded to the call. People submitted a variety of things: "I got guys with their moose in there. Little girls. New babies. One guy got mad at me. He says, 'how come my picture is not in there?' I said, 'well you didn't give it to me.'" Newly inserted documents included a photocopy of the "First Board Made No. 2 Hardboard Machine, October 16, 1963." The board had a number of signatures on it. Finally, Bruce included lists of local union-executive members and shop stewards as well as other union milestones.

During one of our interviews, I asked Bruce Colquhoun and Hubert Gervais how they decided what to include in the binder. Both men insisted that everything went in: "It's all history. It's the past." Bruce stated, "The mill is not just the mill. It is all of Sturgeon and West Nipissing." As a living memorial to the mill, the binder's evolving contents reflected the interests of the two co-authors. With the inclusion of visual and textual sources related to the mill workers and their families, the mill history binder changed substantially in the years that followed. This subtle shift occurred during a period of heightened conflict within the workplace and the uncertainty that accompanied Weyerhaeuser's 1999 purchase of MacMillan Bloedel and with it the Sturgeon Falls mill.

It took Bruce Colquhoun hours to prepare each of the twenty copies of the binder. A three-inch binder was no longer sufficiently large, however, so he had to buy a five-inch binder. He went and saw Marc Coté, his superintendent, for permission to purchase these binders, which cost $35 apiece. "I was very shy about asking for stuff," he said. Bruce got two. When the mill's communications officer later asked to see the binder, Bruce agreed to bring it in. The man then said that he wanted to take a look at it, but Bruce refused. The man insisted, saying that it was "mill property." Only then did Bruce relent and agree to show the binder to him.

Once recovered, these old stories were a hit on the shop floor. Several interviewees expressed fond memories of the binder: "Everybody likes to read about the mill. We photocopied all the Sturgeon papers there and brought them into the mill and guys were freaking out. 'Oh my God there is my dad.' 'There's my grandfather.' 'My aunt and uncle.' And that's because of Hubert and [inaudible] that they have the *Abitibi Magazine*."[52] While the mill still operated, Randy Restoule used to lug the binder into the operator's booth where he worked. He noted that the mill workers looked at it "when they could." The mill history resonated most with Ruth Thompson. One of the few women employed at the mill, she loved to look at the binder while on the job: "Something like that I related to because I love to hear stories of just things that happened, people's lives ... What it was like ages ago. It showed the pictures of the logging operations and the old trucks. The clothes the old guys wore. I loved that book." Thompson particularly liked to see the photographs of her co-workers from "ages ago when they were young" and liked to see the clothes that they wore in the 1950s and 1960s, especially during the "hippy times."

Those family stories that risked being lost, as few people had cameras in those days, were now being recovered. Bruce explained his family's deep connection to the mill: "I worked [there] for twenty-nine years. My dad worked there for forty-one years. My grandfather worked there." In these comments, we see that the mill history binder was very much a family album like any other. One photograph showed Bruce's own father in 1952. But Bruce was amazed to find his grandfather there as well: "My dad's dad. He worked there as an electrician." Joseph Colquhoun was congratulated on the birth of a baby boy. Later, he was honoured for saving the life of another worker. He received a gold watch and a commendation. A proud grandson, Bruce included a copy of the Spanish River Medal for merit with blue ribbon, a certificate of commendation, that was awarded to his grandfather, Joseph Colquhoun, for saving the life of a co-worker in July 1924.

What are the politics of the mill history binder? Is it another case of "smokestack nostalgia"? The mill history binder was institutionally sanctioned, but it differs from the slick image-making typically found in corporate publications of all kinds. First, the binder was never a public relations exercise. In fact, it was self-consciously produced by and for the mill workers themselves. Its loose format, a binder, and the nature of its distribution within the mill ensured that nobody could possibly confuse it with Weyerhaeuser's glossy commemorative book *Tradition through the Trees*, published on its corporate centennial in 2000.[53] The mill history binder therefore acted as a rear-view mirror for mill workers and their families, relating the history of the place.

These galleries of work and friendship provided a sense of pride in their work and in their shared history. The mill's production records were their collective achievements, as were the photographs of smiling retirees and service-award recipients. There is none of the anger or loss that was so apparent in the interviews. Yet it is not a joyful history – the mass layoffs and eventual closure of the mill ensured that the mill workers flipping through its pages had a nostalgic reaction to its contents. Without question, the two worker-historians felt empowered by the existence of the binder. Their special status within the mill community was widely acknowledged. People constantly advised us to "ask Hubert" or "go see Bruce" when we asked questions about the history of the mill. "Have you seen the binder?" – was our constant companion.

During one of our meetings, I asked Bruce and Hubert whether mill managers had ever attempted to influence what went into the binder. It turns out they had. Both men, however, expressed some delight in recounting how they overcame these hurdles. For example, Bruce told us this story:

> Scott Mosher [the mill manager at the time, said,] "I want to see everything before you put it in that book. I want to approve it." And I said, "I work eight hours a day and I don't have time to run in here, 'Is that okay?' And next day, 'Is that okay?' We are not having classified secrets ... I am not going to bad-mouth you ... It is just the facts of the history of the mill." He said, "Don't go to extremes, we will pay for the ink and that for your cartridge, but don't go to extremes. Don't go out and buy a $500 printer." I said, "I got a printer."[54]

In the end, Mosher agreed to pay for the paper and cartridges. With this recollection, Bruce shifted to a more conciliatory posture, adding: "He was good. I didn't like the idea that he wanted to control everything there for awhile." This story was followed by an account of another confrontation – this one with the mill's final manager when Bruce was again told to hand over the binder:

> He said, "I've seen that binder." He says, "I want it."
> "No."
> [Hubert laughs.]
> He says, "Why not? It's the mill property ... That paper is my paper." He says, "Yes we'd pay for the paper."

"You didn't pay for the paper," I said. "That paper is my paper."

He said, "We'd paid for the binder."

"Fine, I'll give you the binder back."

He'd say, "We'd pay for the ink."

I said, "I'll buy you a cartridge. You're not getting that binder."

He says, "That's mill property, Bruce."

I said, "No it isn't! It's at my place. You are going to need a court order to get it out of my yard." [Laughs.] I said, "You're not touching that binder."[55]

It was at this moment that the mill manager decided that Bruce and Hubert would not get their hands on the mill's newsletter. As already mentioned, the whole run of the *Insider* – which was produced throughout the 1990s – was rescued anyway. Both men took some joy from their belief that an earlier plant manager now wanted "to see the binder bad." But it was not "*for him*"; it was theirs. The contents of the mill history binder are thus an expression of Bruce's and Hubert's profound attachment to the mill and the people who worked there. In many ways, it has been their personal response to the mill's closing.

A LIVING MEMORIAL

One thing that I have wanted to know from my very first meeting with Bruce Colquhoun at the Action Centre is why he and Hubert hadn't updated the binder to include the mill's closure and aftermath. Every time I ask the question, I get the same answer: to do so would have been to admit that the mill was dead and their workplace community with it. Both men feared that this would signal the end of their efforts. It was still "too soon." They "weren't ready." Much the same thing happened when I asked whether they intended to publish the binder in some way. Bruce told me that this would make it impossible for him to continue to add to its contents. It would freeze it forever. He did not want this – not now. It would stop being a living memorial to the mill and to the mill families. To my knowledge, Bruce Colquhoun still has not inserted the news stories, photographs, and other materials documenting the closure (such as a photocopy of the last roll of paper produced at the mill, signed by the workers) that he has collected. It remains a living memorial to the past, a book frozen in time.

"Voices must be heard for memories to be preserved," notes art historian Martha Langford. For the family photograph album to fulfill its function, it must continue to live: "Ironically, the very act of preservation – the entrusting of an album to a public museum – suspends its sustaining conversation, stripping the album of its social function and meaning."[56] Langford's words made sense to me the first time that I read them, largely because I had heard Bruce Colquhoun and Hubert Gervais make much the same point on several occasions. The mill history binder, like the photo albums Langford speaks of, has its roots in orality – workers remember by visual association. "The showing and telling of an album is a performance," writes Langford.[57] As long as the mill history binder continues to be interpreted for others through such a performance, the conversation continues and the old connection to place remains. Yet in not taking the story up to the mill's closing and the painful aftermath, Colquhoun and Gervais have detached the mill history binder from its present context. The conversation contained in the binder may not be "suspended," but it is certainly circumscribed. Everyday patterns of remembering, and place making, are of course politically charged. In her study of the working-class Hillesluis district of Rotterdam, sociologist Talja Blokland asks how place making becomes a shared endeavour. The process of shared remembering begins, she says, when people ask, "do you remember when?" These conversations mark places as "theirs."[58]

We asked our interviewees about the memory book. Almost everyone knew what it was. It was a "great big binder," recalled Raymond Marcoux. Ray Lortie likewise remembered the book well, covering as it did the mill's entire lifespan. Several interviewees had their own copies – whisked away, no doubt, from the closing mill. "They showed them to me," declared student interviewer Kristen O'Hare. Others had little to say about the memory book. A few had never heard of it. For his part, Lawrence Pretty told us that one of his children recently used the binder for a school project on the history of the mill. He was not alone.

Once the mill closed, Hubert Gervais shifted his focus to documenting the demolition with his own camera. Over the six months that it took the company to completely demolish the mill, leaving the mill's hydro-electric plant and a big hole in the ground, Hubert took an astonishing 1,400 photographs of the mill.[59] He began taking pictures from outside the fence in July 2004, returning each day. One day he entered the mill property through the front gate. The security guard, who had been there while the mill was active, let him through after he explained that he was taking pictures for "the book."

Yes, the mill history binder. "Sure go ahead, take all the pictures," she replied. As he walked onto the site, a contractor's truck came up to him and he was asked his business. Hubert was then invited to trade access to the site for the right to use these images in company promotion.[60] He accepted: "I was there everyday. From the [time] they started to the time they quit [in November 2004]." Hubert observed that the demolition company seemed to work "back in time" – dismantling the newest parts of the mill before tackling the oldest parts. He decided not to go the day that they demolished the main office but had someone take pictures for him. On the day that the giant stack was toppled, Hubert took a piece of the rubble as a souvenir. There were always five or six cars parked outside the fence as others watched at a distance.

CONCLUSION

All blue-collar workers, to some degree, are attached to locality by ties of family and friendship, by work ties, or by affect.[61] The act or process of displacement, or the putting out of place, is thus an integral part of "industrial restructuring," "globalization," or whatever other label we want to apply to economic change. Capitalism destroys the old in order to make the new.[62] The urge to reaffirm and celebrate industrial history in the face of the crisis in North American manufacturing and the resource sector is not limited to Sturgeon Falls, Ontario. In Pittsburgh, for example, the impulse to commemorate steelworkers – "to fix their historical identity forever in a didactic monument – arose from the demise of a living industrial culture that could nourish such memory from within."[63] What is different about the mill history binder is the insistence on keeping it open to additional materials and available to other mill workers. It serves to keep the mill alive in their memories, even as the mill itself has been erased from the physical landscape.[64] A sense of place would be impossible without memory.[65]

Place is more than a static category, an empty container where things happen. It must be understood as a social and spatial process, undergoing constant change.[66] Place is therefore contingent, fluid, and multiple. Like the piece of rubble picked up by Hubert Gervais during the mill's demolition, the binder has become a last vestige, or remnant, of the past, a site of memory "in which a residual sense of continuity remains."[67] Yet the place being remembered is fixed to happier times before the mill's closing. Like the makers of other commemorative monuments, the co-creators of the mill history binder aim to "create a stable and coherent past sealed off from the vicissitudes of change."[68] The place that was the Sturgeon Falls mill, an active industrial site for more than a century until it closed in December 2002, is thus forever frozen in time. Doreen Massey's notion of place as existing in time and space is thus made manifest.

ACKNOWLEDGMENTS

I would like to thank all of the men and women who agreed to be interviewed for this project. I would especially like to thank Hubert Gervais, Bruce Colquhoun, and Wayne LeBelle. Dave Hunter and Kristen O'Hare provided invaluable research assistance. Finally, I would like to thank David W. Lewis for letting me use his photographs of the Sturgeon Falls paper mill and the mill workers.

NOTES

Epigraphs: Alessandro Portelli, "'The Time of My Life': Function of Time in Oral History," *International Journal of Oral History* 2, 3 (1981): 162; Doreen Massey, "Places and Their Pasts," *History Workshop Journal* 39 (1995): 185; John Dixon and Kevin Durrheim, "Displacing Place-Identity: A Discursive Approach to Locating Self and Other," *British Journal of Social Psychology* 39 (2000): 27-44.

1 Albert Fancher, "Placing the Displaced Worker," *Barron's,* 27 July 1942.

2 According to the US Bureau of Labor Statistics, "displaced workers are defined as persons 20 years of age and older who lost or left jobs because their plant or company closed or moved, there was insufficient work for them to do, or their position or shift was abolished." See United States Bureau of Labor Statistics, "Displaced Worker Summary," *News,* 15 September 2006.

3 Steven Hipple, "Worker Displacement in the Mid-1990s," *Monthly Labor Review,* July 1999, 15.

4 Charles Koeber makes this last point. See his "Corporate Restructuring, Downsizing, and the Middle Classes: The Process and Meaning of Worker Displacement in the 'New Economy,'" *Qualitative Sociology* 25, 2 (Summer 2002): 217-46. See also Gary McDonogh, "The Geography of Emptiness," in *The Cultural Meaning of Urban Space,* ed. Robert Rotenberg and Gary McDonogh (Westport, CT: Bergin and Garvey, 1993), 3-9.

5 Tamara Hareven and Randolph Langenback, *Amoskeag: Life and Work in an American Factory City* (New York: Pantheon Books, 1978), 12. See also Jacquelyn Dowd Hall, James Leloudis, Robert Korstad, et al., *Like a Family: The Making of a Southern Cotton Mill World* (Chapel Hill: University of North Carolina Press, 1987).

6 Historian Joy Parr is conducting some of the most interesting research into the senses. See her "A Working Knowledge of the Insensible: Radiation Protection in Nuclear Generating Stations, 1962-1992," *Comparative Studies in Society and History* 48 (2006): 820-51.

7   Massey, "Places and Their Pasts," 188.

8   Ibid., 189. People produce places not under circumstances of their own choosing. See Allan Pred, *Making Histories and Constructing Human Geographies: The Local Transformation of Practice, Power Relations and Consciousness* (Boulder, CO: Westview Press, 1990), 9-10.

9   Massey, "Places and Their Pasts," 183.

10 In her study of the working-class Hillesluis district of Rotterdam, sociologist Talja Blokland asks how does place making include and exclude. The process of shared remembering engaged in by long-time residents in the ice cream parlour and in other public spaces served to define these places as theirs. In so doing, this process and the stories told by white "regulars" powerfully excluded recent immigrants from the conversation and from the venues themselves. See Talja Blokland, "Bricks, Mortar, Memories: Neighbourhood and Networks in Collective Acts of Remembering," *International Journal of Urban and Regional Research* 25, 2 (June 2001): 279.

11 Dixon and Durrheim, "Displacing Place-Identity," 27-44. Rituals and storytelling are important in establishing and maintaining the symbolic bond between individuals or groups and physical sites; see Setha M. Low and Irwin Altman, "Place Attachment: A Conceptual Inquiry," in *Place Attachment*, ed. Irwin Altman and Setha M. Low (New York: Plenum Press, 1992), 2; and Yi-Fu Tuan, "Place: An Experiential Perspective," *Geographical Review* 65, 2 (April 1975): 151-65. For a seminal critique of "experience," see Joan Scott, "The Evidence of Experience," *Critical Inquiry* 17 (1991): 773-97.

12 Social psychologist Setha M. Low suggests that we treasure these memories all the more, "recreating" them through memory. See her "Symbolic Ties That Bind," in *Place Attachment*, ed. Irwin Altman and Setha M. Low (New York: Plenum Press, 1992), 167.

13 Doreen Massey, *Spatial Divisions of Labour: Social Structures and the Geography of Production* (London: Macmillan, 1984), 11. Scholars increasingly view spatiality as actively produced and "as an active moment within the social process"; see David Harvey, *Spaces of Global Capitalism* (London: Verso, 2006), 77. Henri Lefebvre's tripartite division of space as material (i.e., space of experience and perception), as conceptual (i.e., space as conceived or represented), and as lived (i.e., sensation, imagination, emotion) has been particularly influential in this regard; see Henri Lefebvre, *The Production of Space* (Oxford: Blackwell, 1991); and his *The Survival of Capitalism: Reproduction of the Relations of Production* (London: Allison and Busby, 1976).

14 Kathryn Marie Dudley, *The End of the Line: Lost Jobs, New Lives in Postindustrial America* (Chicago: University of Chicago Press, 1994), 47.

15 Randy Restoule, interviewed by Kristen O'Hare, 5 August 2004.

16 Bruce Colquhoun, interviewed by Kristen O'Hare, 2004. For more on the phenomenon of former workers watching the demolition of their former mills or factories, see Steven High and David W. Lewis, *Corporate Wasteland: The Landscape and Memory of Deindustrialization* (Toronto: Between the Lines Press, 2007), ch. 1.

17 John C. Walsh and Steven High, "Rethinking the Concept of Community," *Histoire sociale/Social History* 32, 64 (1999): 255-74.

18 For more on this divergence, see High and Lewis, *Corporate Wasteland,* ch. 4.

19 Mike Lacroix, interviewed by Kristen O'Hare, 4 February 2004.

20 Percy Allary, interviewed by Kristen O'Hare, 9 June 2004. See also the follow-up interview conducted by Steven High, June 2005.

21 Gerry Stevens, interviewed by Kristen O'Hare, 2 June 2004.

22 Mike Lacroix, interviewed by Kristen O'Hare, 4 February 2004.

23 Ed Fortin, interviewed by Kristen O'Hare, 5 August 2004.

24 Having grown up in a forestry town (Thunder Bay) myself, I remember my economics teacher dramatically throwing open the windows of our school classroom to let the mill's sweet sulphur scent waft in. "Smell that," he said. "That is the smell of money." The point was not lost on us.

25 Local historian Wayne LeBelle had a great deal to say on this point in the various interview sessions.

26 Gerry Stevens, interviewed by Kristen O'Hare, 2 June 2004.

27 For more on collective responses to mill and factory closings, see Steven High, *Industrial Sunset: The Making of North America's Rust Belt, 1969-1984* (Toronto: University of Toronto Press, 2003).

28 Two regional cases stand out in this regard, at least within the forestry sector: Kapuskasing, Ontario, and Temiscaming, Quebec. See Thomas M. Beckley and Naomi T. Krogman, "Social Consequences of Employee/Management Buyouts: Two Canadian Examples from the Forest Sector," *Rural Sociology* 67, 2 (2002): 183-207; and Martin Duckworth, dir., *Temiscaming, Québec,* documentary film (National Film Board of Canada, 1975).

29 It mattered to me, too. I had never come across anything quite like it in fifteen years of research into mill and factory closings.

30 For more on personalized industrial heritage, see Robert Summerby-Murray, "Interpreting Personalized Industrial Heritage in the Mining Towns of Cumberland County, Nova Scotia: Landscape Examples from Springhill and River Hebert," *Urban History Review* 35, 2 (Spring 2007): 51-59.

31 Martha Langford, *Suspended Conversations: The Afterlife of Memory in Photographic Albums* (Montreal and Kingston: McGill-Queen's University Press, 2001), 3.

32 Ibid., 63.

33 Low, "Symbolic Ties That Bind," 167.

34 Hubert Gervais, interviewed by Kristen O'Hare, 12 March 2004.

35 Bruce Colquhoun and Hubert Gervais, interviewed by Steven High, 18 December 2004.

36 Ibid.

37 Bruce Colquhoun's full-page tribute to Hubert Gervais and the compilation of the mill history is located in the part of the binder that deals with 1998.

38 "Our Mill – Way Back Then," *Insider,* May 1995. In the possession of the author. My copy of these documents will be donated to the Sturgeon Falls House Museum at the project's conclusion.

39 Hubert Gervais, "1898-1947: A Bit of the Sturgeon Falls Mill's History," *Tribune*, 30 May 1995.

40 The activities can be followed in the town's weekly newspaper, the *Tribune*; see 14 March 1995, 4 April 1995, 11 April 1995, 25 April 1995, 2 May 1995, 30 May 1995, and 15 August 1995.

41 Wayne F. LeBelle, *Sturgeon Falls, 1895-1995* (Field, ON: WFL Communications, 1995), 1.

42 Ibid., 23.

43 For more on the founding myths of industrial towns and cities, see Sherry Lee Linkon and John Russo, *Steeltown USA* (Lawrence: University of Kansas Press, 2002), 2; and Daniel James, *Dona Maria's Story: Life History, Memory and Political Identity* (Durham, NC: Duke University Press, 2000), 186.

44 Bruce Colquhoun and Hubert Gervais, "Mill History Binder" (2005 version). In the possession of the author of this chapter as well as in that of it authors.

45 Bruce Colquhoun and Hubert Gervais, interviewed by Steven High, 18 December 2004.

46 Colquhoun and Gervais, "Mill History Binder."

47 The *Insider* was published during the 1990s.

48 Bruce Colquhoun and Hubert Gervais, interviewed by Steven High, 18 December 2004.

49 For more on photographic-image worlds, see David E. Nye, *Image Worlds: Corporate Identities at General Electric, 1890-1930* (Cambridge, MA: MIT Press, 1985).

50 The mother of one of the Sturgeon Falls workers had been the magazine's editor, so he had the originals. It took Bruce three nights, staying late, to make all the photocopies. There were twenty binders. "I put them all in binders and plastic sleeves. We made twenty copies of each page." From Bruce Colquhoun and Hubert Gervais, interviewed by Steven High, 18 December 2004.

51 *Insider*, 18 September 1998.

52 Bruce Colquhoun and Hubert Gervais, interviewed by Steven High, 18 December 2004.

53 Joni Sensel, *Tradition through the Trees: Weyerhaeuser's First 100 Years* (Seattle: Documentary Book Publishers, 2000).

54 Bruce Colquhoun and Hubert Gervais, interviewed by Steven High, 18 December 2004.

55 Ibid.

56 Langford, *Suspended Conversations*, 5.

57 Ibid.

58 Blokland, "Bricks, Mortar, Memories," 279.

59 Hubert Gervais, interviewed by Steven High, 22 June 2005.

60 The photographs can be found on the demolition company's website: http://www.environmentalhazards.com/demolition/weyerhaeuser.htm.

61 Andrew Herod, "Workers, Space and Labor Geography," *International Labor and Working Class History* 64 (Fall 2003): 112.

62 David Harvey notes that place attachment and displacement are an integral part of capitalism; see his *Spaces of Global Capitalism*, 81. The term "creative destruction" was coined by Joseph A. Schumpeter, *Capitalism, Socialism and Democracy* (1942; reprint, New York: Harper, 1975).

63 Kirk Savage, "Monuments to a Lost Cause: The Post-Industrial Campaign to Commemorate Steel," in *Beyond the Ruins: The Meanings of Deindustrialization,* ed. Jefferson Cowie and Joseph Heathcott (Ithaca, NY: Cornell University Press, 2003), 248.

64 Its closure and subsequent demolition destroyed this spatial fix, leaving people without a "framework for memories." The destruction of the steel mill had this effect in Homestead, Pennyslvania, say Judith Modell and John Hinshaw, "Male Work and Mill Work: Memory and Gender in Homestead, Pennyslvania," in *Gender and Memory,* ed. Selma Leydesdorff, Luisa Passerini, and Paul Thompson (Oxford: Oxford University Press, 1996), 133-50.

65 Joan M. Schwartz makes precisely this point in "Constituting *Places of Presence:* Landscape, Identity and the Geographical Imagination," in Marlene Creates, *Places of Presence: Newfoundland Kin and Ancestral Land, Newfoundland 1989-1991* (St. John's, NL: Killick's Press, 1997), 11.

66 Walsh and High, "Rethinking the Concept."

67 Pierre Nora, "General Introduction: Between Memory and History," in *Realms of Memory: The Construction of the French Past,* vol. 1, ed. Pierre Nora (New York: Columbia University Press, 1996), xv.

68 Savage, "Monuments to a Lost Cause," 238.

Capital Queers
Social Memory and Queer Place(s) in Cold War Ottawa

PATRIZIA GENTILE

In 1963 the Royal Canadian Mounted Police (RCMP) relied on a map of Ottawa marked with red dots to track homosexual activity in the city. As their information expanded, the map finally became covered with so many red dots that it was practically useless. In light of this, the RCMP turned to detection tests, seen at that time as more "reliable" in locating queer social-sexual networks for the purpose of surveillance. A year earlier, in 1962, the RCMP had commissioned the chair of Carleton University's Psychology Department, Dr. Frank Robert Wake, to research and design such a detection device.[1] This "Special Project" also failed to produce desired results: Ottawa's queer communities continued to create vibrant and dynamic spaces even as they were forced to exist underground and to endure increased surveillance.[2]

Although this map was a useless tool in locating queers in Cold War Ottawa once it was saturated with red dots, it does show how queer place was "plotted" by the security state as it attempted to understand and construct queer space for surveillance purposes. From the perspective of the police, the red dots played a central role in the use of visual cues to flag buildings, streets, parks, and houses as potential sites of queer activity, but these very sites were also *evidence* of the growth of queer communities and networks. The map was both a surveillance tool *and* a visual reminder of how queer place en-croached on and literally *surrounded* spatial manifestations of the security state, such as the Parliament Buildings. Whereas the security state conceptual-ized and defined these spaces in opposition to the interests of national secur-ity, these sites of queer place and the memories forged in and around them played a critical role in Ottawa's queer social formation.

This chapter details the impact of such Cold War security campaigns against queers in re-configuring and re-organizing queer communities from the late 1950s to the 1980s in Ottawa, a time and place in which the majority of people worked either directly or indirectly for the federal government. In this discussion, the meanings associated with the event of the Cold War and the security concerns attached to this historical moment are integral to under-standing how the local was imbued with geographies of vulnerability based on sexuality and gender specific to the nation's capital. Mapping the boundaries of queer communities during the Cold War period in Canada's capital, what David Churchill calls an "imagined gay geography," is a story of identifying enclaves and sanctuaries where queers could socialize and strategize as they resisted the persistent scrutiny of the national security state and the geograph-ies of vulnerability that it introduced.[3] These boundaries consist of the network of buildings, parks, bus and train terminals, houses, organizations, and organ-ized dances recognized by members of queer communities as social-sexual space (see Figure 7.1). Acts of resistance or non-cooperation allowed for those boundaries to grow and shift toward a larger, more cohesive network of as-sociations, meetings, and organizations especially in the 1970s and 1980s. However, I will show that these acts of resistance and non-cooperation against the national security state and its surveillance tactics were not always as suc-cessful in creating sanctuaries, or even safe havens, in the 1950s and 1960s, when the boundaries of queer communities in a government town were less stable. In the context of the Cold War and the security state, the Ottawa land-scape was a veritable geography of vulnerability for people who lived "out of place" vis-à-vis the normalized ideals of respectability and loyalty.[4] National security ideology imposed a particular meaning of "normalcy" in the nation's capital that significantly affected the lives of queers. The context of the police surveillance practices buttressed by the security regime of the Cold War per-iod made queer space in Ottawa a contested place where the lines between

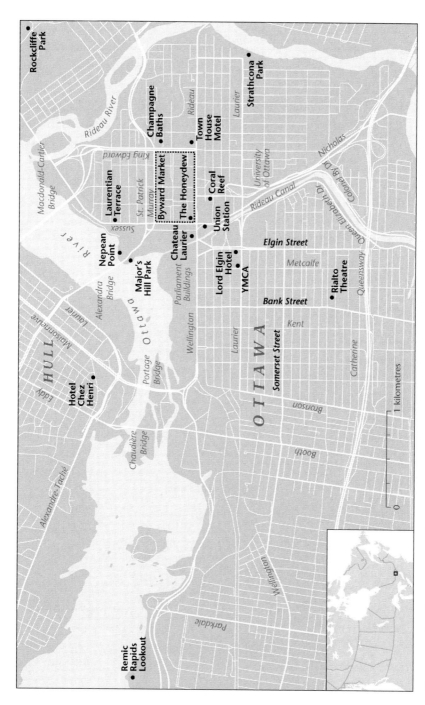

Figure 7.1 Popular queer spaces in Ottawa, 1960s-1970s.

sanctuary and danger were blurred but the possibilities of resistance always present. It was precisely in this contested and liminal space that most queer communities emerged, or as Tim Cresswell suggests, a "permanent heretical geography" developed.[5]

Queer place in Ottawa both produced and produces memories complicated by the fear and trauma of being "caught," as well as a sense of finally feeling "at home." Seeking out other queers – whether that meant sharing a drink at a bar, having sex in a park or public toilet, or meeting at a rally – constituted memory *in* place through the emergence of queer communities. In particular, the cultural memories, as recounted in the narratives outlined below, of queer networks and sites occupying this space between sanctuary and danger were linked to the local. In other words, the physical space, whether it was a bar or park or house, became associated with being a "queer site" because of the memories and the social relations created there. Once a memory is forged, space ceases to be defined by the physical alone and becomes understood as place. In the context of the purges against queers in Cold War Ottawa, the memories of these places are shaped by the active surveillance and interrogation practices of the local and federal police forces.

The mapping of queer space(s) is a significant area of study for queer historians and scholars.[6] John D'Emilio's 1981 essay on the rise of gay politics and community in San Francisco marked an entry point into not only the writing of queer space but also the beginnings of queer historiography.[7] In his remarkable study on gay culture and life in New York from 1890 to 1940, George Chauncey traced what can be said to be one of the most complete spatial accounts of a gay district in queer scholarship. Chauncey also drew from oral histories to illuminate the life of gay culture and identity in the Bowery. Chauncey's *Gay New York* was followed by David Bell and Gill Valentine's collection *Mapping Desire: Geographies of Sexualities,* a book exploring historical and theoretical issues regarding queers, space, and place. In both of these books, the author and editors were interested in not only documenting the existence of gay culture and communities but also mapping the relationship between community-building and the making of queer space(s).

The book on which this chapter is based, *The Canadian War on Queers,* does not foreground the making of queer space but follows in the tradition of exploring how community-building for queers is connected to the social relations of resistance and surveillance. At its core, it is an institutional eth-nography of the security purges against queer communities in urban centres, the federal civil service, and the military.[8] *The Canadian War on Queers* intro-duces a methodology that enhances our ability to queer the Cold War by highlighting how the writing of Cold War history is an exercise in legitimizing security practices and sexual regulation through the silencing of subaltern voices. This chapter takes this methodology a step further by using memories created by the locality of Cold War Ottawa to reveal a hidden queer cartography of the nation's capital.

In order to reveal this queer cartography, I draw on a similar theoretical principal used in *The Canadian War on Queers,* namely, the attempt not to forget the development of human and social capacities for agency, creativity, and resistance.[9] Privileging official texts, even critical readings of them, can trap us in the discursive processes of reification whereby social practices and relations between people get transformed into relationships between things, variables, categories, or concepts, preventing us from remembering past struggles and compromises. As Theodor Adorno and others have stressed, "all reification is a form of forgetting" – that is, a forgetting of the human, social practices involved in creating our past, present, and possible futures.[10]

The mapping of queer space(s) is a critical undertaking because it subverts meta-narratives driven by what we call "the social organization of forgetting," especially the annihilating of queer social and historical memories. It also leads to the wholesale acceptance of social mythologies that assert that the Cold War, for example, was "necessary" and that the nation and national se-curity are unproblematic. This social organization of forgetting is a crucial way that ruling relations and social power work in our society.[11] Forced to forget where we come from, our histories have never been recorded and passed down in the traditional archives, and we are denied the social and historical literacy that allow us to remember and relive our pasts and, therefore, to grasp our present.

Mapping Ottawa's queer cartographies through collective memory is a strategy toward "archiving" this past in the present. The memories drawn on in this chapter, and even the act of writing itself, are examples of what Ann Cvetkovitch calls an "archive of feelings," where memories based in love, guilt, shame, or trauma function as monuments to the unrecorded pasts of subaltern peoples and the formation of public cultures.[12] Although I am interested here in showing how gays and lesbians formed communities and networks connected to locality as they engaged in resistance or non-cooperation against the surveillance and interrogation practices of the RCMP, it is equally important that we recognize that these narratives were forged during a time of heightened political and social anxiety. Resistance and non-cooperation formed the core of queer communities especially in the 1950s and 1960s, but these actions were born from the necessity to challenge the hegemonies of national security discourse, which constructed homosexuality as a threat. Consequently, memories are more than just a product of a subject's ability to remember and forget experiences. They are also highly political and cultural in that such memories record the collective acts that help to establish, in this case, a map of a queer geography and the social memory that sustains it. The permanence of this "heretical geography" is forged by these traumatic/anxious/joyful/sexual memories that become acts of transgression in response to the "topographies of power" deployed by the hegemonic discourses of heterosexuality and by the gender codes that are implicit in national security ideology.[13]

CONTEXTUALIZING THE PURGES

This particular story of the formation of queer space begins in 1946 with the defection of Igor Gouzenko. Gouzenko's defection revealed a complex and wide-reaching spy ring active throughout North America.[14] The federal government took action by forming the Security Panel, a powerful interdepartmental body that actually determined Canada's security policy until the late 1960s. It was on the Security Panel's advice and recommendations that the prime minister's cabinet issued directives to the RCMP, which, in turn, enforced the investigations and surveillance work that dogged the gay and lesbian community during the height of the anti-homosexual security purges in the 1950s and 1960s and well into the 1970s and 1980s, when the gay liberation movement began to organize.

In the name of national security, homosexuals were constructed as a security problem because of their "character weakness." According to official texts, this character weakness made them unreliable and thus vulnerable to blackmail and subversion from the Soviet Union's agents. Throughout the Cold War, the RCMP collected the names of thousands of gay men and lesbians, using a classification system in which people were organized as either "suspected," "alleged," or "confirmed" homosexuals. The security classifications used to categorize hundreds of gay men and lesbians into "problems" and "threats" had severe consequences. Such classifications led to the loss of public service and military jobs or to demotions to less sensitive positions within the federal public service. In addition to the wide surveillance net that was spread over the gay and lesbian community, the Security Panel even initiated and funded research into a means to detect homosexuals, a project dubbed the "fruit machine."[15]

The social relations created by such national security campaigns played an important role in the sexual regulation of homosexuality and are responsible in part for how gay and lesbian communities and queer spaces in particular were established either as sanctuaries or as sites of danger.[16] By advocating that homosexuals were suffering from a character weakness that automatically put their loyalty into question, the state was able to maintain heterosexuals' social-sexual activity as normative and hegemonic. In some ways, heterosexual hegemony is a foundational concept of national security because it emphasizes the use of cultural (and sometimes physical) coercion to enforce heterosexuality within the imaginary boundaries of what we understand as Canada, as well as manufacturing heterosexuality as the *national sexuality*. Therefore, whereas heterosexuality was considered safe and a pivotal component of nation-building, homosexuality was abnormal, problematic, and proof of an unstable personality. The ideology of national security enabled the state to create homosexuals and queers as potential security risks and then to go about organizing surveillance networks and interrogation procedures to ensure that homosexuals were identified, especially in Ottawa. In effect, the security state was not just about the supposed protection of Canadian borders and secrets from counter-espionage; it involved the active practice of constructing and sustaining an image of the Canadian state as a rational (i.e., "masculine") and effective (i.e., "heterosexual") entity.

Interviews conducted with the men and women who were directly affected by the security campaigns show how social standpoint informs the interrogation of security regime practices and provides the entry point for exploring security regime relations. It also reveals an important disjuncture between official national security discourse and gay/lesbian accounts of the national security campaigns. The narratives and memories collected and the experiences they expose are the filters through which the social organization of the national security campaigns is interrogated. A major orienting question for this chapter in Canadian history, therefore, is how this national security campaign created problems and difficulties in the daily lives of queers in Cold War Canada.

SECURITY AND THE COMMUNITY IN THE 1950S AND 1960S

The security regime against gays and lesbians in Ottawa involved a vast surveillance system sustained by the RCMP and the Ottawa Police. Surveillance practices included interrogations, park sweeps, taking pictures of gay men in bars as well as following them, and opening mail and listening to phone conversations of suspected homosexuals. In the civil service, and especially in the military, there were many more opportunities for surveillance. Here, security forces could exert greater powers to maintain social-sexual regulation. Queer networks in the civil service and the military had an awareness of RCMP security strategies, but they adapted and reacted to this surveillance by establishing a collective response characterized by moments of resistance, non-cooperation, and the formation of communities. In other words, the very existence and formation of these networks and social-sexual sanctuaries can be documented as a collective response against security measures and heterosexual hegemonic space.

For example, during the 1950s and 1960s, several bars, restaurants, hotels, and parks constituted a complex web of queer social-sexual space(s) in Ottawa, and yet they can only be described as limited queer space. Important constraints on the development of these social-sexual spaces included the policing of gay sex in the city, the national security campaigns themselves, the social organization of housing, the regulation of bars and establishments, as well as the character of the city as the seat of Canada's capital. These regulatory practices and policies were actively deployed in marking "moral geographies" critical to the construction of the closet, or living a "double-life," in Ottawa given that it was a government town and the centre of national security activities.[17] Those who lived a double-life, making a conscious choice to pass as heterosexual even as they sometimes engaged in homosexual activity, were a key focus of the national security regime. Living in the closet as a survival strategy could be considered a transgressive place or location used by queers. In this way, the closet becomes another location from which the centre (Cold

War Ottawa) begins to mark heretical boundaries. The invisibility afforded by the double-life and the closet meant that the RCMP could use the threat of exposure to family members in order to help maintain and employ security and interrogation practices. In turn, this shaped the particular character of the city and the formation of its queer communities. Bushes and the cloak of the night's darkness meant that parks became a central focal point of gay-male space. Invisibility, in all its permutations, was organized by secrecy imposed by heterosexual hegemony and the threat of being caught in the surveillance nets.

Notwithstanding this enforced invisibility, members of Ottawa's queer communities still established queer places. Some of the more popular establishments were located in hotels and restaurants considered hetero-social/sexual spaces, such as the Lord Elgin Hotel or the Chateau Laurier, two Ottawa landmarks near the Parliament Buildings and the Byward Market. Gay men co-opted some areas of these hetero-social/sexual spaces and used them to carve out a queer space. The basement tavern at the Lord Elgin and the lower level of the Chateau Laurier (located on Wellington Street and connected to Major's Hill Park, a major cruising ground) were two central places where visitors and gay men could enjoy social time and casual sexual encounters.

A veritable bathhouse, the Chateau Laurier sauna and steam rooms were in proximity to Major's Hill Park and Mackenzie Street, a male prostitute thoroughfare, making the Chateau Laurier a convenient place for sexual encounters. Historically, however, the Chateau Laurier has also been a major meeting place for the social and political elite because of its proximity to the Parliament Buildings and other government institutions, including the US Embassy. According to one narrator, for gay men the Chateau Laurier "was one of the most notorious places in Ottawa at the time [1950s and 1960s]," and "it was a very, very, very popular sexual place."[18] Robert, a regular at the Chateau Laurier, confirms this assessment in the following exchange:

[Robert]: There was a masseur, there was a steam room, there was a sauna, there was an exercise area. But there was a weird – you know, a door, and it was about the size of a phone booth with a little bench. That was it. You dressed in there and left your clothes, and you locked it. But of course, you could also sit there and cool off, and people would walk by and people would walk in.

[Patrizia]: It was just like a bathhouse [...]

RC [Robert]: Just like a bathhouse. And it had a steam room that was extremely long. It was almost the length of this room, which is about twenty feet. And when you entered the front door, you couldn't see the back at all. You couldn't see the back wall, but as you started walking through, there were benches all, like a U-shape, and there was stuff going on in the back of the room and in the showers.

[Patrizia]: Men having sex ...

[Robert]: Yeah! No crew would raid the Chateau Laurier. Nobody.[19]

Indeed, because the Chateau Laurier was a symbol of political and social wealth and power, it was in many ways the perfect cover while also allowing the same members of the political and social elite access to potential same-sex sexual play. As places frequented by the Ottawa political elite and middle and upper classes, hotels like the Chateau Laurier and the Lord Elgin were pivotal in instituting another element of geographies of vulnerability for queers not politically connected or from the lower classes. In this sense, Cresswell's notion of "out of place" also applies to queer cartographies when class is foregrounded. In Robert's words, "no crew would raid the Chateau Laurier [or the Lord Elgin]" as long as the men who frequented these elite hotels to engage in sexual play did not seem "out of place" based on definitions of class, which introduced another level of exclusionary practices characterized by an outsider/insider epistemology.

The Lord Elgin was built facing Confederation Park in 1941. Located at the corner of Elgin and Laurier, it was a two-minute walk from the YMCA, a popular cruising spot at the corner of Laurier and Metcalfe.[20] Robert recounted that the washroom cubicles in the basement of the Lord Elgin had "glory holes" and were particularly "active."[21] In his interview, Marvin confirmed that the Lord Elgin was frequented by gay-male civil servants: "They loved to see the old World War II buildings were still being used then, and they were in that area and lot of guys would go in there in the afternoon and have a few drinks [...] So you'd see a lot of those people in there."[22]

The RCMP targeted the basement tavern of the Lord Elgin. Implicated in the surveillance net when his name was given by someone caught in an RCMP park sweep, David recounted how an RCMP officer he knew, about to be cashiered, was shown pictures of men sitting and drinking in the basement tavern in the Lord Elgin. According to David, RCMP surveillance of the Lord Elgin soon became common knowledge and sometimes resulted in resistance:

> We always said when you saw somebody with a newspaper held up in front of their face [...] usual thing was somebody would take out something like a wallet and you ... sort of ... do this ... [picks up a wallet and pretends he is taking a picture] ... and of course everybody would then point over to the person, you see. And of course, I'm sure that the person who had the newspaper knew that they'd been found out. But that was sort of the thing, you take out a wallet or pack of matches or something like that or anything [...] I mean it was always a sort of joke. You'd sort of see somebody and you would be looking around the table and catch everybody's eye [...] We all knew we were ... that they were taking pictures.[23]

This memory is remarkable because it not only highlights a moment of resistance but also reveals how queer space was contested. Gay patrons of the Lord Elgin tavern knew this space as a place for social networking, laughter, camaraderie, and even potentially for sexual encounters, but it also presented the possibility of danger or, at least, of being "caught."[24] However, in this instance, the basement tavern, despite being another geography of vulnerability for queers, can also be understood as a site where the undercover police officer is "out of place." Although Cresswell's concept is meant to refer to acts, people, and behaviours constructed as not "natural" to a place, if the basement tavern was occupied by queers, then non-queers or elements that posed a threat to queer social relations were in turn vulnerable. Bruce Somers, involved in the Canadian Council on Religion and the Homosexual, reported that members of the community started to talk about "police watching" and began swapping stories about police informants. He talked about a general unease regarding entrapment:[25] "We were constantly on guard against strangers or against people we suspected of being snoops because they weren't gay, they weren't there to cruise, nobody knew them from sexual contact."[26]

The Cold War surveillance practices against queer communities prevalent throughout the 1950s and 1960s exacerbated the regular routine of harassment and fear tactics already in place. Peaches Latour, a drag queen who lived in Ottawa during this period, shared a story about one encounter with an Ottawa police officer that made him particularly afraid:

The '50s were a very violent time. We were petrified of everybody, and I remember an incident on Bank Street, and I believe I would be in my late teens or early twenties [...] Bank Street was the cruising area, and I was walking with a friend and we were looking in the window, and some big cop came to say something and I answered just as sarcastically, and he grabbed me by the throat and he raised me up like that, you know ... It was a very unpleasant experience, and he called me a "fuckin' queer."[27]

In other parts of the interview, Peaches used the word "unpleasant" to describe the police harassment and violence against homosexuals while also describing how "you always seemed to go out on the cover of night and always liked to stay in little groups. And you always watched for each other, you were afraid to stay in the park alone ... it was always too dangerous." Here, Peaches revealed an important incongruence between the telling of a memory and the details of that memory. In this example, the word "unpleasant" understates the level of fear that the atmosphere of police harassment, homophobia, and surveillance created and consequently how it framed queer space(s) in Ottawa. In this memory, we see how violence and fear as social relations enabled local police to "put queers in their place" in an attempt to establish Bank Street, a major Ottawa thoroughfare that cuts through the core of the city, as a normative space.

The Chez Henri on Rue Principale in Hull (see Figure 7.2), a city in Quebec about a five-minute drive from Ottawa's core, stayed open later in the evening and was known as "the original gay bar:"[28]

When you went into the Chez Henri, you had to go on the left side. The right side was straight and on the left side was gay. We had to wear ties and we had to be seated. You couldn't go in without a shirt and tie, and that's why I think it was a way at the time of controlling.

As the designated entrance to the "gay section," the door on the left side of the Chez Henri gave patrons access to the upstairs level, where Peaches and other female impersonators would perform for mixed audiences:

Upstairs ... and we had as many responses from the straight population because we filled the place up. Whenever we had a show, we had posters downstairs and you couldn't get in upstairs. The straight people used to think it was wild. Men dressed up as women. You know, they weren't on television, and people like to see.

The popularity of the Chez Henri drag shows in the late 1950s and 1960s offered a level of visibility that allowed queers a "legitimate" space to congregate. This legitimacy, however, was based on the entertainment factor that drag shows provided non-queer audiences interested in having a "gay experience." Drag queens embody a transgressive location within queer communities and thus introduce a different "heretical reading" of place from within queer communities. In this sense, drag queens performing at the Chez Henri in Cold War Ottawa were questioning and resisting "the 'way things are' by (mis)using and appropriating already existing places by crossing boundaries that are often invisible."[29] In this one memory, Peaches recalls a time when the Chez Henri figured as a place where people and fellow performers were able to have fun and enjoy each other's company even if it meant having to share this space with non-queers. He also described the Chez Henri, however, as "very, very tough in the '50s and '60s. Extremely dangerous. You needed the help of the bouncers. A lot of the clients were very aggressive." Reading these conflicted memories as simply contradictory does not capture how the atmosphere of fear, harassment, homophobia, and surveillance meant that businesses that catered to a queer clientele could nonetheless occupy a liminal space that was potentially hostile and vulnerable.

The Honeydew, described by Peaches as the "original meeting place where we were all accepted" in the late 1950s, was also a popular hangout for gay men. Located next to Union Station, Ottawa's old train station and a place where men met for sex in the bathrooms, the Honeydew and the train station faced the Chateau Laurier, Major's Hill Park, and Mackenzie Street. Nepean Point (a park behind the National Art Gallery located at the end of Mackenzie Street and just south of a bridge to Hull) and the Byward Market, each in the vicinity of the Chateau Laurier, the Honeydew, and Union Station, were also known as areas where men could meet potential sexual partners. Not far from this area, on King Edward Avenue near St. Patrick Street, another queer landmark was the Champagne Public Baths, also frequented by gay men in the 1950s and 1960s.

Figure 7.2 Exterior of Chez Henri Hotel, 15 January 1954. Photograph by Andres Newton.
Source: City of Ottawa Archives, Ottawa, MG393/CA4618.

Not only was Major's Hill Park (also known as Mackenzie Park) well known and well used by men looking for outdoor sex with other men, but it was also the place to pick up male prostitutes (see Figure 7.3).[30] Other queer sites in proximity to these hotels and the park included a gathering place above a bar named Snow Goose and the Rialto, an old movie theatre located on Elgin near Cooper.[31] Robert identified parks other than Major's Hill as queer sites, including Strathcona Park (in Sandy Hill), the Rideau Canal (along the pathways), and Rockcliffe Park.[32] By the 1970s, Remic Rapids Lookout, a green space between the Prince of Wales and Champlain Bridges accessible from the Ottawa River Parkway, functioned as another place to engage in

Inscriptions

Figure 7.3 A view of Major's Hill Park from Nepean Point, n.d. Photograph by D.A. McLaughlin. *Source:* City of Ottawa Archives, 79 D 6/CA6307.

public sex. After its construction, this park became a favourite among gay men but was heavily patrolled by RCMP officers.[33]

Parks were of particular interest to the municipal and federal police forces. Park sweeps and entrapment tactics were the most effective ways that police corroborated information.[34] Unlike many clients of establishments such as the Lord Elgin, Chez Henri, or the Honeydew, the majority of the men who frequented parks to find sexual partners were living double-lives. This allowed the police to blackmail these men into revealing the names of people they knew to be homosexual, thereby helping the RCMP to expand its lists. In the 1950s and 1960s men caught in park raids were interrogated by the RCMP regarding other members of the queer community. Albums filled with pictures of men, some taken at the various venues mentioned above, were used to identify who was homosexual. David recounted his experience with these albums when he was picked up and interrogated:

> At first, they just ask me to list everybody; they didn't have a list of their own. Later, they came out with what appeared to be just family photo albums with people's pictures and names and asked me to run through and identify the people who I knew in their albums. I just felt the best thing to do was to say nothing because if I said, "these people are definitely not," and then another person, [if] I refused to give information about this [other] person, they'd surmise that that person was. And so I felt the best thing [was] to stay with a blanket statement, "I will not give any information whatsoever." However, they kept after me; every so many months, they would be after me again and always led by one person ... I don't remember his rank, but his name was Lapointe ... and none of these were pleasant interviews whatsoever. They were, frankly, scary. But the whole idea was not to let them know you were scared, and I just tried to remain as calm as I could under the circumstances.[35]

Ironically, the Security Panel and the RCMP found this system to be inefficient even though informants were perhaps the best vehicle through which the RCMP were able to track queers in the city. Memories and knowledge of queer geographies became part of the security practices used by the state to identify other queers and to make queer place visible. But not everyone who was caught and forced to confirm the identities of other queer people complied. Peaches brought his *own* pictures *of friends* to his interrogation, effectively stifling any attempts to force him to identify individuals in pictures by turning the tables on the RCMP surveillance practices.

These public spaces – hotels, restaurants, coffeehouses, train stations, parks, washrooms, and movie theatres – afforded a visibility that house parties did not. House parties also came under surveillance by the RCMP, but they proved more difficult to monitor and identify. These parties took place almost every weekend and were the "safest" sites for gay men to congregate not because they were organized in people's "private" homes but because learning the location of these parties meant that the RCMP had to have access to "insider" information. Space arbitrarily constructed as private/public was subverted by the social-organizing force of the visible and invisible. More important, the resources needed to conduct surveillance of these house parties probably outstripped the RCMP's budget.

Many more social-sexual spaces were available for gay men than for lesbians in the 1950s and 1960s, but lesbian spaces did emerge. One person we interviewed suggested that in 1967 she found lesbians and lesbian networks easily but that cultural habits and financial considerations made it difficult for them to establish networks similar to those described above. For queer women, class and gender sharpened the edges of geographies of vulnerability. Notions of respectability and women's lack of access to public spaces at night meant that lesbian women were less likely to establish the same network of bars and parks available to men. In addition, the growing bureaucracy and its insatiable need for an army of cheap labour led to a particular disciplining of female bodies and space, including dress codes and forms of presentation of the body.[36] Employment possibilities in government service at the lower-paid end and the social organization of housing for single women were particularly challenging for lesbians living and working in Ottawa.

SINGLE WOMEN AND LESBIAN SPACE

The boundaries of Ottawa's queer communities during this period had a gendered component. This gendered component complicated queer geographies in Ottawa, and it also caused considerable frustration for the RCMP. In Cold War Ottawa, women created a queer community that encompassed hybrid social-sexual space(s) consisting mostly of house parties, a few bars, housing for single female government workers, and organizations. Unlike queer space formed by some gay men, female social-sexual spaces were practically invisible. Not only were women restricted by notions of propriety and public space and by financial consideration (it was less likely that women could afford to buy drinks), but also the sexual activities afforded to men frequenting places designated as gay sites were even less available to women. This invisibility meant that this community and the spaces it forged were smaller and insular, making it easier for women to escape the peering eyes of RCMP surveillance.

Government housing for single women, such as Laurentian Terrace, formed part of what Becki Ross calls the "ripening methodological opportunity to examine the queer reconstitution of space outside bar culture."[37] In the context of a government town like Ottawa, establishing and maintaining a lesbian community supported by a network of lesbian bars was practically non-existent. Of course, this does not mean that lesbians did not find places to congregate, socialize, or meet for erotic experiences. The challenge, then, lies with excavating possible sites of lesbian networking in a city where discretion in one's behaviour, relationships, clothing, and appearance was central to keeping a job in the civil service regardless of one's sexual orientation. Indeed, the "government girl's" location as an insider was precarious at the best of times and highly restricted to her *work as a government employee*.[38] An exploration of Laurentian Terrace, an all-female residence for women roughly between the ages of eighteen and twenty-five built in 1946, offers a possible space for Martha Vicinus' call for historians "to retrieve a richer past, but also to understand the complex threads that bind women's actions and desires to the larger world."[39]

Ross's cue "to examine the queer reconstitution of space" and Vicinus' position that "lesbianism can be everywhere without being mentioned" and that "the sustained withholding of the name can actually be the very mechanism that reinforced its existence as a defined sexual practice" have led me to conceptualize this extensive network of same-sex residences as a possible rich source for lesbian space and history.[40] In fact, Vicinus argues that it is only when we conceive lesbians as historical agents that we will be able to "recognize the sheer variety and richness of women's sexual desires and actions."[41]

Interviews are indispensable in this project of mapping women's social-sexual geography. For example, Sue identified a few hotels where lesbians and gay men congregated, as well as several women's sports networks.[42] Sports networks offered relief for some lesbians from the gendered disciplining of female bodies, especially since this usually meant adhering to strict codes of femininity. I have come across many pictures of women involved in the sports leagues for female civil servants sponsored by the Recreational Association throughout the 1950s and 1960s where the obligatory shirts, blouses, and pumps have been discarded for jeans, baseball caps, and baseball jerseys.[43]

Barbara also offered some valuable insights into the lesbian networks within the civil service and into the social networks that developed in the larger Ottawa community. Barbara moved to Ottawa in the mid-1970s and worked in various government departments. In addition to providing information about the continuing security issues that lesbians and gay men had to contend with well into the late 1970s and early 1980s, Barbara confirmed that lesbians did have extensive social-sexual networks, which mostly took the form of house parties and the bar scene over the bridge in Hull. Due to the security and financial risks involved in "getting found out," invitation to the private parties that Barbara mentioned were limited strictly to women known to at least one other person in the group: "A lot of it was private parties, but you had to know someone to be invited somewhere. So I mean, if you were a stranger, you couldn't go anywhere until someone got to know you. Sort of our own little security system because we wanted to make sure [everything] was on the up and up."[44] These tightly knit groups were also characteristic of the networks that formed within some government departments. For example, according to Barbara, certain sections of the Department of Veterans Affairs and Superannuation had close networks of gays and lesbians. And yet socializing was still kept to a minimum for fear that fellow workers who were not part of the queer network would develop suspicions that might identify their queer co-workers as "out of place" and that might therefore be disastrous for the group.

Barbara also mentioned the weekly dances held at the Townhouse Motel on Rideau Street (near the ByTowne Cinema) organized by Lesbians of Ottawa Now (LOON). The Coral Reef, however, was a main lesbian bar in Ottawa in the 1970s. A Caribbean club located on Sparks Street from 1962 to 1968, the Coral Reef became a gay and lesbian bar in 1968 when one of the owners, a lesbian, was convinced by a friend to open its doors to the gay community. According to Homer, an owner of the Coral Reef, the bar was a "gay bar" on Monday, Tuesday, and Wednesday and a black/Latin club on Thursday, Friday, and Saturday.[45] When people who went to the Coral Reef from Thursday to Saturday became aware of its "gay nights," they stopped coming to the Reef. At this point, the switch in 1968 to a gay/lesbian bar every day of the week was complete, with regular drag shows. Thursday nights became designated lesbian-only in the mid-1970s. The sheer numbers of women attending on Thursday nights prompted Homer to mark Friday night as lesbian nights too.

When asked whether civil servants were among the people who held membership cards to the club (obligatory in the 1970s), Homer responded that most of the women worked for the government in some capacity, making a point to mention that in the 1970s coming down to the Coral Reef (twenty-one steps to the basement) was a risky trip for these civil servants. It was especially difficult to get these women to sign membership cards since it entailed revealing names and addresses. Like most queer bars in Ottawa, the Coral Reef was also known to the RCMP and the local police. Barbara recalled a particular "routine" where Homer warned customers of imminent police surveillance practices:

> [After] a couple of years of being here, I started seeing someone who was under the drinking age, and we would walk into the bar – we were regulars. Homer knew our names [...] and he'd get up to me and say, "Barb, get Lorrie out of the bar by eleven o'clock. So we'd trundle out about a quarter to eleven, and then we would come back at 11:30 after the police had been there checking the IDs. So obviously, he had an in and he was warned.[46]

These regular intrusions by the police contributed to the atmosphere of being watched. Barbara recounted that at these moments patrons stopped dancing and returned to their tables, patiently waiting for the police to leave the premises. This memory illustrates the way that topologies of power underscored by surveillance and heterosexual hegemony enabled the state's regulatory practices to be re-affirmed as the centre by encroaching on the heretical geography of this queer place. There was still a sense that the tracking of people by local and federal police forces could result in a series of events that would very likely include losing one's job or being outed to family and friends.

Notwithstanding the longevity of bars like the Corel Reef, lesbian social networks remained largely confined to house parties. Whereas gay men had more accessibility to a wider choice of bars and cruising areas, lesbian socializing mostly took place in people's homes. This afforded some "invisibility," making it more difficult for the RCMP and other police corps to easily locate and identify lesbians. These transitional queer sites were, nonetheless, a central survival strategy that lesbians used to protect themselves from exposure.

SURVEILLANCE AND GAYS/LESBIANS IN THE 1970S AND 1980S

The partial and limited decriminalization of homosexual sexual acts in 1969 did, however, create more space for lesbian/gay organizing and movements and for community formation. Despite its limitations, the 1969 reform and the profound social transformation of the 1960s helped to create the social conditions for the expansion and visibility of gay and lesbian networks.[47] This increased possibilities for resistance and non-cooperation against the national security campaigns and also created the basis for further expansion of community formation. The ideology of the national security state and its security practices had "the unintended consequence of making space a means of control [by] simultaneously [making sites] of meaningful resistance" for queers.[48] Gay activists in the 1970s attempted to use the 1969 law reform as a strategy to eliminate national security policies against homosexuals. A particularly important gay-rights document titled "WE DEMAND," submitted to the federal government in 1971, was used to end surveillance policies and practices against homosexuals.[49]

These activists challenged the basis of national security campaigns against queers, which hinged on the secrecy and shame that surrounded homosexuality. Radical actions and queer visibility began to unravel the discourse and practice of the national security regime. This new movement directly challenged the practices of the national security regime itself as well as broader discriminatory practices in employment and the social organization of the relations of the closet. What the RCMP in one document refers to a change in "attitude" meant that many gay men and lesbians were not as afraid of public exposure, a development the RCMP was less likely to encounter in the 1950s and 1960s. The surveillance strategies of the RCMP during these heady times developed in relation to the movement and activism. Undercover officers or informants were present at these meetings and often wrote reports on the proceedings as well as demonstrations. In some cases, this surveillance involved taking pictures at these events.

Barbara recounted that it was common knowledge that the offices and members of LOON and of Gays of Ottawa (GO) were watched by the RCMP.[50] GO was formed in Ottawa in 1976 by a lesbian who felt that LOON was not meeting all of the community's needs. Marie Robertson, one of its founders, remembered that outside one of the main gay activist's households, there would often be undercover cops in unmarked cars apparently keeping the house and the people who came in and out of it under surveillance. She reported that on at least one occasion, a visitor approached the car, knocked on the window, and told the occupants to "fuck-off." Robertson also remembered being told stories by people "who knew they had been under RCMP surveillance," including civil servants and former civil servants.[51]

The RCMP encountered a new breed of gay and lesbian political activists in the 1970s who affirmed that "gay is just as good as straight" and were willing to publicly proclaim their pride in being gay and lesbian. In so doing, they re-configured topologies of power that enforced certain geographies of vulnerability by revealing the hidden through the "knowable" despite the ideology of the national security state in Cold War Ottawa. In other words, they destabilized the centre from the margins of heretical geography. The national security state adapted to this shift so that surveillance and monitoring were now aimed not only at individuals but also at gay and lesbian organizations. Whereas queer sites in the 1950s and 1960s were sanctuaries established to facilitate social-sexual relations and to forge queer sites, the gay-liberation activists of the 1970s and 1980s wanted to reach beyond the creation of havens and dismantle geographies of vulnerability. The queer cartography that existed and flourished underneath/around/within/outside of respectable and normative space as defined by the ideological imperatives of the Cold War security state meant that queer sites are *remembered* as monuments of resistance and non-cooperation against the sexual and geographic regulation of queer existence and that they are *monumental* for queer activism. These memories of place continued to motivate queer activism in the context of the social and political upheavals of the late 1960s and the 1970s.

Unlike other major cities such as Vancouver, Toronto, and Montreal, Ottawa does not have a designated series of streets or a neighborhood known as a "gay village." Indeed, given the extensive changes respecting queer visibility in Canada, the absence of such a "village" is jarring. However, this history of the formation of queer communities through the memory of place offers some important clues as to why Ottawa lacks a clearly delineated space even though it is the home of many queer people. The queer communities described here were not located in "low" spaces as described by Churchill in his essay on Toronto.[52] The invisible but active network of queer geographies that included social and sexual relations, for instance, was situated in the heart of what we can arguably describe as the centre of Canada's political power. All the major sites of social-sexual activity, the Lord Elgin, the Chateau Laurier, Major's Hill Park, Union Station, Nepean Point, Chez Henri, and the Byward Market, even the location of the Corel Reef in the parking garage of Rideau Mall (located at the corner of Rideau and Sussex Streets), surround the Parliament Buildings. This proximity to the seat of respectable political power meant that, unlike Toronto, queer sites were located in the midst of places often categorized as "respectable." The geography of these queer sites, however, also meant that the people who frequented them were connected in some way to the government and thus aware of the potential dangers associated with state surveillance, such as being found out and possibly losing their jobs or being revealed to family members. The legacy of the security campaigns against queers and of the fear that these surveillance strategies created continues to be felt in Ottawa's queer communities even though local queer businesses such as the Centretown Pub, Wilde's, and After Stonewall are a major presence at the core of Ottawa's downtown (Somerset and Bank Streets).

Queer place continues to be contested at the local level across Canada, but its boundaries are now less likely to be forged in the urgency of finding a place to escape heteronormativity or police and state surveillance. These new boundaries delineating the sanctuaries of contemporary queer space are the direct legacy of the re-configuration forged through resistance against the regulatory state practices of the gay-liberation era. The stories and memories showcased in this history of queer geographies in Ottawa during the Cold War reveal how place and social memory intersect, thus furthering our understanding of how experience and feelings form critical archives for recording queer pasts and locating queer place.

ACKNOWLEDGMENTS

I would like to thank James Opp, John Walsh, and Pauline Rankin for their insightful comments on earlier drafts of this chapter and Gary Kinsman for his tireless support. I am also grateful for the stimulating conversations generated at the 2008 Placing Memory and Remembering Place Workshop organized by the editors. Some of the material for this chapter is drawn from collaborative work undertaken with Gary Kinsman; see Gary Kinsman and Patrizia Gentile, *The Canadian War on Queers: National Security as Sexual Regulation* (Vancouver: UBC Press, 2009). The interviews used in this chapter were conducted as part of the research for that manuscript. All of the narrators' names, except in cases where we received permission, are pseudonyms.

NOTES

1 Wake's document, entitled "Special Report," suggested that the most "productive line of research which might be undertaken" consisted of three tests: the Hess-Polt pupillary test; the McCleary Palmar Sweat Test, a measurement of skin perspiration; and the plethysmograph, with a modification to measure pulse rate. F.R. Wake, "Report on

Special Project," December 1962 Canadian Security Intelligence Service (CSIS), AIR 91-008.

2   Communities never represent monolithic identities. Indeed, throughout the Cold War period, it is fitting to describe the queer community in Canada as diverse in a variety of ways, including in terms of race, gender, and class. Although the RCMP and the Security Panel did not view homosexuals as having a community, they did understand homosexuality in a monolithic fashion.

3   David Churchill, "Mother Goose's Map: Tabloid Geographies and Gay Male Experiences in 1950s Toronto," *Journal of Urban History* 30, 6 (September 2004): 830.

4   The notion of being "out of place" is developed by Tim Cresswell. Cresswell shows how people seen as behaving or acting contrary to a particular cultural meaning, sometimes described as "common sense," ascribed to a place or site are classified as "out of place" because of the contradictory meaning-making associated with that behaviour. Cresswell argues that "out of place" acts are often described as a type of contagion or plague. See his *In Place/Out of Place: Geography, Ideology, and Trangression* (Minneapolis: University of Minnesota Press, 1996), 24.

5   Ibid., 175.

6   The historical literature and contemporary scholarship on queer space is always expanding. For historical works that include oral history to help construct the development and growth of queer space in urban communities, see George Chauncey, *Gay New York: Gender, Urban Culture, and the Making of the Gay Male World, 1890-1940* (New York: Basic Books, 1994); Ester Newton, *Cherry Grove, Fire Island: Sixty Years in America's First Gay and Lesbian Town* (New York: Routledge, 1997); and Elizabeth Lapovsky Kennedy and Madeline D. Davis, *Boots of Leather, Slippers of Gold: The History of a Lesbian Community* (New York: Routledge, 1993). For work in the Canadian context, see Elise Chenier, "Rethinking Class in Lesbian Bar Culture: Living 'The Gay Life' in Toronto, 1955-1965," *Left History* 9, 2 (Spring/Summer 2004): 85-118; and Steven Maynard, "Through a Hole in the Lavatory Wall: Homosexual Subcultures, Police Surveillance, and the Dialectics of Discovery," *Journal of the History of Sexuality* 5, 2 (October 1994): 207-42. For a history of gay and lesbian spaces in Montreal, see Line Chamberland, *Mémoires Lesbiennes: Le lesbianisme à Montréal entre 1950 et 1972* (Montreal: Éditions du remue-menage, 1996); and Ross Higgins, "Des lieux d'appartenance: Les bars gais des années 1950," in *Sortir de l'ombre: Histoires des communautés lesbienne et gaie de Montréal,* ed. Irène Demczuk and Frank W. Remiggi (Montreal: VLP éditeur, 1998), 104-28. Several anthologies examine historical or contemporary issues and queer communities/sites, such as Gordon B. Ingram, Anne-Marie Bouthillette, and Yolande Retter, eds., *Queers in Space: Communities/Public Space/Sites of Resistance* (Seattle: Bay Press, 1997); and David Bell and Gill Valentine, eds., *Mapping Desire: Geographies of Sexualities* (London: Routledge, 1995).

7   Some of John D'Emilio's major contributions to the writing of queer history have been reprinted in his *Making Trouble: Essays on Gay History, Politics, and the University* (New York: Routledge, 1992), including the article I am referring to in the text, "Gay Politics,

Gay Community: San Francisco Experience," *Socialist Register* 55 (January-February 1981): 77-104. A little more than a decade later, Elizabeth Lapovsky Kennedy, Madeline D. Davis, and George Chauncey published some of the first full-length manuscripts documenting the existence of queer communities in urban centres. Kennedy and Davis not only offered a history of butch-femme relationships in Buffalo from the 1930s to the 1950s but ultimately also produced a book that focused on the local through the lens of a series of oral histories, among other sources. See Chauncey, *Gay New York*; and Kennedy and Davis, *Boots of Leather*.

8   In *The Canadian War on Queers*, Gary Kinsman and I rely on Dorothy Smith's work on institutional ethnography; see her *The Everyday as Problematic: A Feminist Sociology* (Toronto: University of Toronto Press, 1991). We demonstrate how the official texts authored by government officials were central to establishing national security as a form of sexual regulation. The interviews we conducted with over forty people who were either involved with or directly affected by the purges show how official texts and security practices were mediated through a particular understanding of national security as the security of capitalist and hetero-patriarchal hegemony.

9   For a fuller development of this notion of human capacities and their social and historical character, see Philip Corrigan, *Social Forms/Human Capacities* (London: Routledge, 1990).

10   David McNally, *Bodies of Meaning: Studies on Language, Labor, and Liberation* (Buffalo: State University of New York Press, 2000), 195. On how reification takes place in the writing of sociology and within sociological theory, see Dorothy Smith, "Sociological Theory: Methods of Writing Patriarchy into Feminist Texts," in *Writing the Social: Critique, Theory, and Investigation* (Toronto: University of Toronto Press, 1999), 45-69.

11   On memory and the social organization of forgetting, see Philip Corrigan and Derek Sayer, eds., *The Great Arch: English State Formation as Cultural Revolution* (Oxford: Basil Blackwell, 1985); Roxanne Dunbar-Ortiz interview, "The Opposite of Truth Is Forgetting," *Upping the Anti* 6 (Spring 2008): 47-58; Kristin Ross, *May '68 and Its After-lives* (Chicago and London: University of Chicago Press, 2002); and the companion volumes by Susannah Radstone and Katharine Hodgkin, eds., *Regimes of Memory* (London and New York: Routledge, 2007), and *Contested Pasts: The Politics of Memory* (London and New York: Routledge, 2007).

12   For a remarkable investigation and exploration of memory and queer studies, see Ann Cvetkovitch, *An Archive of Feelings: Trauma, Sexuality, and Lesbian Public Cultures* (Durham, NC: Duke University Press, 2003), esp. the introduction and Chapter 7.

13   On transgressive acts and topographies of power, see Cresswell, *In Place/Out of Place*, esp. Chapter 7.

14   For more on Gouzenko, see Reginald Whittaker and Gary Marcuse, *Cold War Canada: The Making of a National Insecurity State, 1945-1957* (Toronto: University of Toronto Press, 1994), esp. Part 2.

15   The infamous "fruit machine" highlighted a long and established history of the manipulation of gender stereotypes by the medical community. Under "methods for

detecting homosexuality," Wake included a word association list with 147 terms, designating certain words as "homosexual." The use of masculinity/femininity tests was one of the ways that gender assumptions entered into the research. This was based on the coding of male homosexuals with "effeminacy" and of lesbians with "masculinity."

16 For an example of policing and sexual regulation in the Canadian context, see John Grube, "'No More Bullshit': The Struggle for Democratic Gay Space in Toronto," in *Queers in Space*, ed. Ingram, Bouthillette, and Retter, 127-45. This article also traces the growth of the "gay" district in Toronto.

17 Chauncey uses the term "double-life" to describe how some men in the early twentieth century moved between heterosexual and homosexual practices "as a reasonable tactical response to the dangers posed by the revelation of their homosexuality to straight people"; see Chauncey, *Gay New York*, 273-80 (quotation 273). For a brief discussion of "moral geography," see Cresswell, *In Place/Out of Place*, 149.

18 Peaches Latour, interview by Gary Kinsman, August 1994.

19 Robert, interview by Patrizia Gentile, October 1996.

20 The YMCA/YWCA is now located on Argyle and O'Conner Streets facing the Museum of Nature (the National Museum in the 1960s).

21 Robert, interview by Patrizia Gentile, October 1996. For more on the critical role of washrooms and gay-male sexuality, see Maynard, "Through a Hole in the Lavatory Wall."

22 Marvin, interview by Gary Kinsman, May 1998.

23 David, interview by Gary Kinsman, May 1994.

24 In his essay on Toronto's imagined gay geography, Churchill offers important insights about the bar being "the most fully developed and articulated gay site while being the least sexually explicit." This is critical in the context of the Lord Elgin since its importance in the imagined Ottawa gay geography was precisely due to the fact that it was a place where "respectable" bureaucrats met to socialize. See Churchill, "Mother Goose's Map," 848.

25 The Canadian Council on Religion and the Homosexual was an organization created in the 1950s with chapters in the United States and Canada. According to Bruce Somers, Wake approached this organization with questionnaires that may have been the masculinity/femininity scale used for Wake's "Special Report."

26 Bruce Somers, interview by Gary Kinsman, June 1994.

27 Peaches Latour, interview by Gary Kinsman, August 1994.

28 Peaches also mentioned a coffeehouse called Le Petit Souris, located next to the RCMP's headquarters in Ottawa. Its doors opened in 1968-69, and "it was the first open gay-positive place." None of the other narrators mentioned this bar.

29 Cresswell, *In Place/Out of Place*, 175.

30 In 1999 the US Embassy moved from a building located directly in front of the Parliament Buildings on Wellington to its present location between Mackenzie Street and Sussex Drive. With the embassy's barricades, mounted cameras, and security presence, Mackenzie Street is no longer a popular area to hire male prostitutes.

31 Robert mentioned the Snow Goose in his interview. He also mentioned a place that turned into a bathhouse after midnight located on Slater near the Esplanade Building on Laurier. According to Robert, after hours the club owners would draw the drapes, and it would become a bathhouse.

32 Robert, interview with Patrizia Gentile, October 1996.

33 The park is under the jurisdiction of this federal police force because it was built by the National Capital Commission, a federal government agency.

34 For a discussion on why parks were a popular choice for gay men, see Churchill, "Mother Goose's Map," 841.

35 David, interview by Gary Kinsman, August 1994.

36 For more on proper gender codes in the civil service, see my "'Government Girls' and 'Ottawa Men': Cold War Management of Gender Relations in the Civil Service," in *Whose National Security? Canadian State Surveillance and the Creation of Enemies,* ed. Dieter Buse, Gary Kinsman, and Mercedes Steedman (Toronto: Between the Lines Press, 2000), 131-41.

37 See B. Ross, "Destaining the (Tattooed) Delinquent Body: The Practices of Moral Regulation at Toronto's Street Haven, 1965-1969," *Journal of the History of Sexuality* 7, 4 (1997): 594.

38 For more on the role of the "government girl" and gender anxiety in Cold War Ottawa, see my "'Government Girls' and 'Ottawa Men.'"

39 Martha Vicinus, "Lesbian History: All Theory and No Facts or All Facts and No Theory?" *Radical History Review* 60, 57 (1994): 58.

40 Ibid., 59. Examples of other government-built and -funded residences for women in Ottawa include the Canadian Women's Army Corps (CWAC) accommodations at Kildare House on Chapel Street, the former residence of the late J.W. Woods; and Immaculate College at 312 Laurier Avenue, once the home of the late George Goodwin. The government also acquired in 1942 the former Ottawa Ladies' College for the CWAC. The Navy women's corps residence was located on Laurier Avenue East, and the personnel of the Royal Canadian Air Force, Women's Section were lucky enough to have a $250,000 building constructed for housing accommodations.

41 Ibid., 66.

42 Sue, interview by Gary Kinsman, February 1996.

43 See my "Searching for 'Miss Civil Service' and 'Mr. Civil Service': Gender Anxiety, Beauty Contests and Fruit Machines in the Canadian Civil Service, 1950-1973" (MA thesis, School of Canadian Studies, Carleton University, 1996).

44 Barbara Bain, interview by Gary Kinsman and Patrizia Gentile, 14 July 1997.

45 Homer, interview by Patrizia Gentile, 1997. All references to Homer are taken from this interview conducted via telephone. Sadly, I do not have his family name.

46 Barbara Bain, interview by Gary Kinsman and Patrizia Gentile, 14 July 1997.

47 See Kinsman, *Regulation of Desire: Homo and Hetero Sexualities,* 2nd edition (Montreal: Blackrose Books, 1996), 288-93.

48 Cresswell, *In Place/Out of Place,* 163.

49 August 28th Gay Day Committee, "We Demand." This document is in the author's possession. An edited version is included in *Flaunting It! A Decade of Gay Journalism from the Body Politic,* eds. Ed Jackson and Stan Persky (Vancouver/Toronto: New Star Books/Pink Triangle Press, 1982), 217-20.

50 Barbara, interview by Patrizia Gentile and Gary Kinsman, July 1997.

51 Ibid.

52 Churchill, "Mother Goose's Map," 843.

Archive and Myth
The Changing Memoryscape of Japanese Canadian Internment Camps

KIRSTEN EMIKO McALLISTER

ARCHIVAL MEMORY

A small rectangular window lets pale stretches of light into the dimly lit archive. Inside its walls there is a deathly stillness, with only the sound of paper shuffling and the distant clicking of the museum assistant's keyboard. Removed from the world of family secrets and political machinations, saved from creeping mould and the acidic oil of curious fingers, everything that enters the archive is inducted into another temporal order. The archive is a space where time accumulates and condenses in stacks of worn documents, pencil-drawn sketches and maps, fading photographs and film reels, ink-stained diaries, and carefully composed letters.[1] It is a repository for the material of memory haunted by the myths of places and people who have long since disappeared.

I had been at the Japanese Canadian National Archive and Museum (JCNAM) all morning, poring over its collection of photographs. It was January 2000 and I had just begun my research project on photographic records of the incarceration camps built by the Canadian government in the mountainous terrain of British Columbia during the 1940s. The government interned thousands of Japanese Canadians in these isolated camps from 1942 to 1946. Claiming they posed a threat to national security, Prime Minister Mackenzie

Figure 8.1 Japanese United Church, Lemon Creek, BC, 1 April 1945. *Source:* Courtesy of Japanese Canadian National Museum, 1995/126.1.5.

King's cabinet used the War Measures Act to strip them of their rights and to remove them from their homes along the Pacific coastline. The internment camps were part of a systematically deployed plan aimed at removing over 22,000 "people of Japanese racial origin" from the province of British Columbia and, eventually, from Canadian territory.[2]

Against the drive to remove this racially undesirable segment of the population from the province's social landscape, the photographs in memoriam have imprinted the presence of Japanese Canadians in its rugged heartland.[3] With so little left of the vibrant prewar communities along the Pacific coastline and almost nothing remaining of the internment camps, it is astonishing to see thousands of Japanese Canadians – youth, adults, young children, the elderly – assembled together in the internment camps located in isolated

Inscriptions

mountain valleys in the interior of British Columbia.[4] The photographs capture that four-year span of time before the federal cabinet extended its powers under the War Measures Act to force almost everyone to leave the province for either war-torn Japan or unfamiliar destinations scattered across the rest of Canada.[5]

As a community-based archive, the Japanese Canadian National Archive and Museum (now the Japanese Canadian National Museum [JCNM]) is different from other archives with records about the internment camps. In contrast to Canada's national archives in Ottawa where the majority of the records about the camps are stored, most of the JCNAM's holdings have been donated by former internees and their families. Unlike the masses of government records in the national archives, these records are what internees decided to save from the internment camps. They are personal documents that trace their lives inside the camps, sites of order and control where the government stripped them of their identities and rights, reducing them to their "racial" origins. On the one hand, their photographic records vividly document their removal from the historical landscape of British Columbia, from small towns, fishing ports, and urban neighbourhoods. But at the same time, these photographs also record their temporary presence in the province's remote mountainous valleys and ghost towns in British Columbia.[6] They provide insights into how internees visualized these sites and how they inhabited them during their four years of incarceration. Over the years these images have taken on new meanings for Japanese Canadians. Now used as family as well as community records, as I will argue, these images function to secure the camps as ambivalent mythic sites in the community's memoryscape.

The meaning of photographs, their power of signification, as Roland Barthes argues, takes shape in their contexts of use.[7] In this case, as mentioned, the photographs belong to the JCNM, a community-run archive that opened in 2000. It is one of the few sites of memory over which the Japanese Canadian community maintains jurisdiction. The archive offers one means for the community to secure as well as mediate its relation to the many places from which Japanese Canadians were displaced during the 1940s. The significance of place in this archive is reflected in the importance that the archive grants to the locations where photographs were taken (as well as to whether they were taken before, during, or after the Second World War). All items in the database can be searched using the names of internment camps and prewar settlements.

These places are particularly important because Japanese Canadians identify themselves by the places where they lived before the war, where they were interned in the 1940s, and where they were relocated after the war. Place has thus become central to the history as well as the collective identity of Japanese Canadians.

One of the challenges researchers face with the archive is the power of what Diane Taylor calls "archival memory," which "exists in documents, maps, literary texts, letters, archaeological remains, bones, videos ... all those items that are supposedly resistant to change."[8] Taylor argues that "what changes over time is the value, relevance, or meaning of the archive [and] how the items it contains get interpreted, even embodied ... Bones might remain the same, even though their story may change, depending on the paleontologist or forensic anthropologist who examines them."[9] Archival memory "separates the source of 'knowledge' from the knower – in time and space."[10] In contrast, Taylor approaches items in the archive as a "repertoire" of embodied practice/ knowledge that includes "all those acts usually thought of as ephemeral, non-reproducible knowledge ... performances, orality, movement, dance, singing ... As opposed to the supposedly stable objects in the archive, the actions that are the repertoire do not remain the same. The repertoire both keeps and changes the choreographies of meaning."[11] In this chapter, I try to release the grip that archival memory has on the camps, on the stories resistant to change, so that I might explore the photographs in their changing choreographies of meaning.

THE POWER OF MYTH AND VISUAL ACTS

The photographs of the camps bear a heavy burden of witnessing, or "meaning," in a community where for many years, very few people publicly spoke or wrote about what happened in the camps. After 1945 most Japanese Canadians focused on the struggle to rebuild their lives and reunite members of their families who were scattered across Canada and Japan. Although there were organized attempts in the 1950s to request compensation from the government, which led, for example, to the Bird Commission, it was decades later, in the 1980s, when activists began to mobilize Japanese Canadians across the country in the movement to seek redress from the Canadian government for violating the wartime generation's rights.[12] As Roy Miki argues, Japanese Canadian activists, artists, and writers had to create a new language with which to navigate the humiliation, the social and material losses, and the psychic scars and create a political language as citizens whose rights had been violated.[13]

During the years when there was no collective language and no public forums in which to speak about the war years, in many homes the photographic records of the camps could be found in family albums, pasted beside snapshots of family picnics and Christmas trees or they were stored in shoe boxes and biscuit tins in closets and basements along with other family memorabilia. There they sat innocently, images that bore witness to what few would speak about. These images began to enter the public realm in exhibitions and publications during the 1970s when young activists began to research what many of their families refused to speak about. With radical nisei, issei, and new Japanese immigrants, they launched projects like the *Dream of Riches* photography exhibit, which explored Japanese Canadian history.[14] In the 1980s photographs of the camps began to circulate more widely when redress activists used these images in political briefs and press stories. But during the 1970s and 1980s, the photographs acted primarily as illustrations, documenting the community's history and the violation of their rights. The use of photographs, in other words, was based on the assumption that they were records with fixed meanings. There was little exploration of these photographs as part of the community's changing memoryscape.

As I searched through the photographic collection in the JCNM, I was surprised by what I found.[15] At first glance, most of the photographs of the internment camps could be mistaken for life in small rural towns. What is thus remarkable about the photographs is what they do not (directly) reveal. They do not reflect any of the accounts I had heard and read about the cramped, uninsulated living quarters, insufficient food supplies, intolerable summer heat and icy winters, depression and suffocating boredom, as well as fear and debilitating humiliation. Nor do the photographs capture the magic of nostalgic recollections about illicit autumn hikes high up the mountain slopes to harvest matsutake mushrooms, romances and heartbreaks, relations with indigenous people and Doukhobors who lived near camps, or hiding casks of homebrew when the Mounties conducted their regular inspections. But both expectations reveal the pervasive community myths shaping my view of the camps.

The camps are mythic sites in the memoryscape of Japanese Canadians. For some, they symbolize communal life. Since the late 1980s, during the reunions of former internees and in novels like Terry Watada's *Daruma Days,* the camps have been nostalgically remembered as the last sites where everyone lived together as a community.[16] For others, the camps symbolize "the end of the community." Redress activists have amply documented how the camps were part of the plan implemented by the government to dissemble the intimate as well as institutional foundations of Japanese Canadians' prewar communal life, banning political and economic organizations and separating family units.[17] Novelists like Joy Kogawa and Kerri Sakamoto explore these sites as damaging psychic spaces that continue to trouble the community today.[18]

The expectation that the photographs would illustrate stories about the camps as nostalgic communal places or damaging psychic spaces rests on the assumption that photographs are transparent realist records of an already determined if contradictory "reality." To examine the photographs as a visual medium and consider what they "do" rather than simply assess how accurately they represent what is in fact a mythic "reality" of the camps requires another approach. As particular types of spaces, the camps can be described, using the work of de Certeau, as a rigidly delineated series of sites that were designed, ordered, and controlled through abstract master plans administrated by hierarchically organized governmental bodies under multiple systems of surveillance and policing.[19] Designed to extract people of Japanese racial descent from the population, the camps were part of a systematic plan that controlled the factors necessary for the biological and economic reproduction of the Japanese Canadian social body.[20] At one level, by controlling the factors necessary for their reproduction as a community, this plan was designed to control the "contingency of time": the unknown direction of their social body's unfolding future. More specifically, by controlling these factors, the government sought to remove the very possibility of a future, to destroy it.[21]

In this chapter, although I describe how these photographs visualized the camps as sites of systematically deployed racial eradication, I am also interested in these photographs as personal records saved by the internees. Here, I approach the photographs as a changing repertoire of embodied knowledge whose meanings change according to their use and enactment. Over time, through the acts of collecting, exchanging, and finally donating these records to the JCNM, these photographs have become memory objects with the potential to re-image and re-member Japanese Canadians back into the landscape of the province. Though, as I will argue, as acts of memory they do not secure the geographic origins of Japanese Canadian identity as much as they affirm the ambivalent presence of Japanese Canadians in places that no longer exist.

I focus on the photographs that make up the majority of the collection in the archive: officially sanctioned photographic records of the institutional life in the camps. Many of these images appear mundane and repetitious. Although the images of school children and church groups might appear to reassure viewers that "life goes on" in the camps, this chapter examines how they impose institutional camp order on the men, women, and children lined up in rows waiting for the photographs to be taken. Drawing on the work of photography scholars influenced by Michel Foucault's work, like John Tagg, as well as on the work of feminist scholars like Annette Kuhn and Marianne Hirsch, I argue that photographs are "acts" that impose institutional order on the spaces and bodies contained in the camps.[22] But as personal documents saved by internees, these photographs also have another valence of meaning. They have come to mean something other than containment and systematic control. As I suggest, they have become a means for internees to remember their lives together in the camps before they were forced apart when the government shipped thousands to Japan and forced the rest to resettle in scattered locations east of the Rocky Mountains. In this context, these photographs elicit memories of the camps that paradoxically transform the camps into mythic places of communal existence. I am particularly interested in the symbolic power of the camps for the surviving internees, most of whom are second generation Japanese Canadians who were adolescents in the camps.

In the last section of the chapter, I thus explore how group photographs of high school students paradoxically enact this myth. Through the students' stylish clothing and playful Hollywood poses, these photographs, I argue, capture their youthful dreams of belonging to larger society. For this new generation, the camps were places where they collectively enacted and shared this dream. At the same time, their dreams paradoxically transported them out of the camps, defying the spaces of incarceration where they were treated as a threatening alien race. As I conclude, the potency of this generation's myth of communal life in the camps is tied to the very fact that today, looking back, we know that their dreams were never fulfilled, that they were impossible dreams.[23] The government had already planned their future. As I argue, the photographs mark the locations of former internment camps throughout the province as sites of ambivalent, uneasy memory that move between the collective dream of belonging and the destruction of the very communal body where this dream could be played out and performed.

HABITS OF MEANING AND THE HABITUS OF PLACE

> [The] miniature is a world of arrested time; its stillness emphasizes the activity that is outside its borders. And this effect is reciprocal, for once we attend to the miniature world, the outside world stops and is lost to us. It resembles other fantasy structures ... even sleep.[24]

During my first visits to the archive, the sheer mass of imagery overwhelmed me. I looked through the rows of black binders filled with photocopies of the 3,000 accessioned images, wondering how I was going to make sense of so many records. It is amazing that even though cameras were confiscated from internees, the JCNM currently has 1,234 photographic records of camp life.[25] With only the name of the donor, the date and location of the photograph (in most cases), and sketchy information about the events and people they document, it is as if the photographs are shorn of meaning.[26] As records of migrant families, these images once narrated a history of places that were intimately tied to each family's settlement in British Columbia. Tracing these families' histories of residence and employment across a series of towns, urban neighbourhoods, fishing ports, mining and mill towns, and agricultural centres, the photographs of each family follow their moves, whether they were forced to move because of the hostility of local inhabitants, legal restrictions on their livelihoods, employment problems, or natural disasters or whether they moved in search of better networks of support, business prospects, or educational opportunities for their children. Over time and through these families' movements, the photographs also trace their integration into the social and cultural life of the province, despite their racial segregation, as they embraced the habitus of each locale by adapting the local forms of comportment, styles of clothing, types of camaraderie and friendships, local foodways, workplace skills, and leisure activities in what was then, as it is now, a diverse multicultural society.[27]

In the archive, although most of the personal family meanings are lost, other meanings emerge. As Allan Sekula argues, even though archives strip objects of their everyday meanings and re-order them into abstract systems of classification, this process is not simply a negation.[28] He argues that archives have the potential to generate new meanings. He claims that "the meaning of the objects in archives is liberated from the actual contingencies of their use in the everyday world and while this liberation is ... a loss, an abstraction from the complexity and richness of use, archives tend to suspend meaning and use."[29] With the suspension of meaning, artefacts and documents "[exist] in a state that is both residual and potential. The suggestion of past uses coexists with a plentitude of possibilities."[30] When photographs are removed from the taken-for-granted order of everyday life and habitual patterns of use, it becomes possible to understand individual photographs and documents in new ways. Thus in the archive, photographs donated by Japanese Canadians are no longer confined to the domestic domain as intimate records of an individual family.

How was I going to begin? I wondered whether I should examine all the photographs from a particular camp or whether I should examine the photographs donated by a particular family. But this would deny the possibilities of the archive outlined by Sekula where, liberated from the systems of meaning that locked them into specific narratives, the photographs from different fonds could be compared and analyzed in relation to other photos in new ways. The attempt to reconstruct the narrative of a particular family, for example, could result in "archival memory," in a return to conservative forms of autobiography that reproduce linear historical narratives common in the Japanese Canadian community. As I pored over the pages, taking notes and drawing rough sketches of the types of photographs, patterns began to emerge that, as Sekula suggested, would not have been apparent if I had restricted myself to one or two families' records.

With photographs from almost every camp donated by different individuals and families, I began to identify common genres. In addition to, for example, the aerial photographs of the camps, the postcard images, the landscape

shots, and a small handful of family portraits, most of the photographs recorded the institutional life of the camps.[31] There were group portraits of
elementary students and high school students, training classes for cooking
and sewing, social clubs, church congregations, and picnics for ikebana clubs
as well as photographs of sporting events, evening entertainment, and the staff
working for the British Columbia Security Commission. Photographs from
each camp had the same types of institutional group shots.

To gain insight into the types of photographs taken in the camps, as well
as how internees got around the ban on photography, I interviewed historian
Midge Ayukawa, who was an elementary school student in the camps, and
Marie Katsuno, a young teacher who created photo albums of Tashme from
her own snapshots drawing on her experience as an avid recreational photographer before the war.[32] They both explained that although the government
confiscated cameras, along with motor vehicles, radios, fishing boats, firearms,
and explosives, a number of Japanese Canadians who were professional photographers were designated official photographers in the camps.[33] They were
permitted to bring their camera equipment with them, and the Department
of Labour provided darkroom equipment. According to Ayukawa, the camp
photographers were responsible for recording officially sanctioned events,
such as school graduations, United Church gatherings, and concerts in the
Buddhist halls.[34] In addition, some internees managed to smuggle their cameras into the camps, and as restrictions began to slacken, others ordered in-
expensive brownie cameras to snap photos of friends and events, which they
mailed in to get the film developed (see Figure 8.1).[35]

It is unknown whether the government kept the negatives of the official
photographers, but no researcher has yet reported finding them in the Library
and Archives Canada. The only government documents that I have found thus
far that refer to photographs of the internment camps involve correspondence
regarding the itineraries of special inspection tours for officials from the
International Red Cross or the Spanish Counsel. Usually, arrangements would
be made for a photographer from the National Film Board to accompany the
entourage and take pictures that would illustrate the inspectors' reports.

Although documents regarding the official camp photographers have yet
to be found, it is possible to trace their activities by examining the photos that
have been donated to the archive. Examining the photographs as part of the

archive's larger collection of prewar and wartime images rather than focusing on individual family records or photographs from one camp provides new ways to understand the photographs. After I had viewed and re-viewed the collection, it became apparent that the photographs adhered to already existing photographic conventions practised before the war. There appears to be continuity between prewar and wartime photography practices. I found group photographs of church groups and school children, landscape shots, photojournalistic records, recreational snapshots of friends and social gatherings, and family photographs in the collections of images from the period before the war. Thus, rather than focusing on what the photographers did or did not record in the camps, another way to approach the photographs is in terms of the continuity and discontinuity of genres within photography as a social practice.[36]

As a social practice, photography, as scholars like Marianne Hirsch, Annette Kuhn, and Jo Spence have argued, is, in the words of Hirsch, one of the "family's primary instruments of self-knowledge and representation – the means by which family memory would be continued and perpetuated, by which the family story would henceforth be told."[37] So even though the government confiscated cameras from Japanese Canadians supposedly because of concerns regarding espionage, this policy also restricted an important social practice through which Japanese Canadians as modern subjects constituted their individual, family, institutional, and communal identities.

A recognition of the importance of photographs as a social practice is suggested by the very fact the government permitted professional Japanese Canadian photographers to keep their equipment and to record officially sanctioned activities. This was a concession. The government wanted the cooperation of the Japanese Canadians, and the photographs, like films of the internees, were a way to assure them that family members and friends in other camps were being treated well. A number of the same institutional photographs can be found in different fonds, especially the group photographs of students, such as "Catholic High School, Slocan City, 1944-45" (see Figure 8.2).

The multiple copies of these institutional photographs suggest that they were produced *for* the internees, who could purchase them from the photographers. That so many Japanese Canadians collected photographs of their group life in the camps, whether their children's school classes or memorable

Figure 8.2 Catholic High School, Slocan City, 1944-45. *Source:* Courtesy of Japanese Canadian National Museum, 1995/126.1.69.

evening performances, and when possible took recreational photographs of landscapes and snapshots of friends, underlines how integral photography had become as a social practice in constituting the self in relation to others in the locations where they lived. Of particular significance are the photographs of internees that place them in the local environments. In contrast to the prewar photographs, images from the camps show that Japanese Canadians rarely took part in the recreational and cultural activities specific to the town or region where they were incarcerated, whether parades, dances, or visiting agricultural fairs. Instead, there are images of their work activities, for example, as members of logging and highway crews as well as images of their recreational activities in the camps, whether picnics, sporting events, or evening performances of dance and theatre. These images situated them in the landscapes where the camps were located. In this context, the acts of taking as well as collecting photographs (and very likely exchanging them after they were dispersed) suggest that internees continued prewar photographic practices that reiterated collective identities, articulating them, even if tenuously, with reference to particular places. But as I argue below, the photographs also trace the emergence of new types of postwar identities as well as post-redress identities.

REMOVED FROM THE SOCIAL LANDSCAPE

As indicated above, from every camp, there were the same types of photographs of institutional life. At first, the institutional photographs seem to suggest there is continuity with prewar life: internees continued to practise Buddhism and Christianity, children went to school, and so on. Yet if one more closely compares the camp photographs to the prewar photographs, there are many key community institutions missing. For example, there are no photographs of Japanese Canadians' powerful political organizations and economic associations, such as their affluent farm co-operatives and the Japanese Fishermen's Association, which challenged the federal government's legislation that restricted the areas where Japanese Canadians could fish.[38] Although there were camp committees that represented the internees' interests, with a number of them hiring lawyers to challenge the government's attempts to "deport" them to Japan, there are almost no photographic records of their activities.[39] At one level, the lack of photographs recording political as well as economic organizations reflects the government's ban on political organizations and its attempt to destroy the community's prewar leadership.[40] At another level, it could be argued that prewar photographs of economic and political organizations were symbolically replaced by camp photographs of British Columbia Security Commission staff, who now controlled the life (and fate) of Japanese Canadians (see Figure 8.3).

Among the camp photographs, there is also an absence of family homes and businesses, leisure activities like visiting the Capilano Suspension Bridge, social events like picnics in city parks, and occasions that included non-Japanese Canadian co-workers, neighbours, and friends. Nor are there any photographs showing their participation in public events like parades and royal visits. These types of prewar photographs integrated Japanese Canadians into the social landscape and to some degree into the public life of the province, despite the exclusionary legislation that denied them the right to vote, run for office, take up various professions, and so on. In contrast, when one looks at the camp photographs, there are few signs of other British Columbian residents and activities. It is peculiar to see so many Japanese Canadians congregated in such barren landscapes where there is a marked absence of other BC residents and no signs of the towns, cities, fishing ports, sawmills and mines, as well as agricultural settlements where they previously lived. With

Figure 8.3 Staff of the Slocan British Columbia Security Commission Hospital, Spring 1945. *Source:* Courtesy of the Japanese Canadian National Museum, 1994/76.011.

the exception of the government staff and a few white teachers, in contrast to the prewar photographs, the only children and adults present, even in the background, are Japanese Canadian. Most groups of internees are photographed outside. They are standing or sitting on wooden benches on the barren ground or snow. Behind them, most buildings are rudimentary constructions of either logs or unpainted wooden boards. If the photographs are taken inside schools or community halls, the interiors are makeshift, with light bulbs hanging from wires and bare wooden walls and floorboards. In many photos, Japanese Canadians are surrounded by distant mountain slopes, with no sign of cars, trains, or buses. Whereas in the prewar photographs their lives were set in urban centres as well as in canneries and mining towns and there were wealthy business families as well as individuals and families struggling to earn enough to purchase the bare necessities, in the photographs of the camps everyone was reduced to the same primary identity: enemy aliens of "Japanese racial origin."[41] In the camps, what had socially differentiated individual Japanese Canadians had been removed, whether it had been their homes or their belongings, and there was also little to indicate their education,work skills, and social capital.[42]

The group photographs thus place Japanese Canadians outside of the province's social and economic life. Ironically, many of the camps were located in "ghost towns." Once prosperous "boom" towns dependent on mining, they went "bust" when the world markets dropped for whatever ore was being mined. In other words, Japanese Canadians were placed in the economically and socially "dead" zones of the province.[43] But at the same time, given the shortage of wartime labour, the government used Japanese Canadian labour in these dead zones to ensure, for example, that there was a sufficient supply of fuel wood for the province. In addition, the government used able-bodied men to build what are now some of the province's major highways (as well as entire families as labourers on prairie sugar-beet farms).[44] In these dead zones, their labour was thus used to reproduce the lives of the province's population rather than their own lives.

These dead zones have been profoundly important in the formation of identity for wartime Japanese Canadians. In the camps, they had very restricted opportunities to engage in any kind of "productive human activity" where they had any determination over and ability to partake in re/producing their lives in their own terms.[45] Their lives were determined primarily by government regulations, whether the housing they were assigned, their employment opportunities, or access to schooling. But paradoxically, the very sites where their collective lives were dismantled and their identities reformed are the sites that they have reappropriated for their postwar community identities. As mentioned, Japanese Canadians now openly identify themselves both by the settlement where they lived before the war and by the camps and sugar-beet towns where they or their families were interned.[46]

As can be expected, given the government's control over the photographs taken in the camps, as I have discussed elsewhere, there are few "evidential" shots documenting more generally the difficult living conditions.[47] It is interesting to note, however, that the camp photographer Tak Toyota took photographs of Japanese Canadians as they were leaving the camps en route to Japan. This was a very distressing period for many, especially for the children whose parents had "signed up" the family to go to Japan as well as for those who felt they had no other choice, given that the other "choice" was to relocate to unknown areas east of the Rocky Mountains that were possibly just as hostile as British Columbia.

Toyota took a series of "arrival" and "departure" shots, which echo a genre of photographs that would have been familiar to many Canadians with families in other countries – the "welcome to a new life" and the "bon voyage" photographs of Canada as a settler society in which boats arrive and leave with relatives and immigrants from England, Europe, and Asia. Although Toyota may have meant simply to document the forced removal of Japanese Canadians from their country's soil, his photographs map painful experiences into a familiar genre. Insofar as these photos were donated to the JCNM, it is evident that internees kept them. Perhaps they offered both those leaving Canada and those staying behind a way to integrate the events into their understandings that reduced the harshness of the reality that they were being finally and completely stripped of all of their rights of citizenship and expulsed from the country.

I now return to the photographs of institutional life in the camps. At one level, as I have suggested above, the photographs seem to suggest normalcy, reassuring internees that to some degree there was some continuity with regular life. This could be viewed as an ideological strategy to provide reassurance while at the same time misrepresenting the government's ultimate plans for the internees. But this conclusion precludes an examination of these images' potency. The pervading sense of normalcy is disquieting. There is a certain tedium about these photographs, which becomes especially evident in the archive, where the majority of the camp photographs are of groups of people, organized in rows, facing the camera – row after row of school children, church congregations, and training classes. There is a certain anonymous feel to these shots in part because they are "institutional": everyone's identity is primarily marked by the fact that each is a member of a particular institution. Except for the organization's administrative heads, whether teachers (many of them are non-Japanese Canadian) or chairmen, no one is supposed to "stand out." In addition, in the photographs where the photographer had to position the camera at a distance in order to fit everyone into the frame, it is difficult to discern the individual characteristics of the internees, further inducing anonymity (although over the past two decades at reunions for former internees, someone usually brings group photos and asks others to identify

Figure 8.4 "Sports Day in Tashme," c. 1943-45. *Source:* Courtesy of the Japanese Canadian National Museum, Marie Katsuno collection, 2001/05.01.008.

the unknown individuals). Everyone sits or stands in a similar pose, with a similarly appropriate expression. They are lined up to conform to a predetermined pattern. Given that these groups are state-sanctioned, there is a sense that the institutional order of the camp is being imposed on the internees' social and individual bodies. The museum's collection of prewar photographs also includes group shots, but in contrast to its collection of camp photos, the prewar collection contains a larger array of other types of images, including more spontaneous snapshots and records of Japanese Canadians involved in diverse activities. After examining photo after photo, one is left with the impression that in the camps Japanese Canadian bodies were always under control, posed, and choreographed according to the new institutional order, which is reiterated through the endless group photographs.

MOVING IMAGES

As I looked through the photographs in the museum, amid the regimented group photos, a smaller number of photographs of youth participating in sport events, evening performances, and dances caught my eye. In contrast to the group shots, in these photographs everyone's body seems full of movement and life (see Figure 8.4). The bodies are expressive and have character, even though they are also styled according to the lines of movement particular to the activity, whether baseball, high jumping, or cheerleading. Most of the events typify the period's popular culture. As they stylishly dance or leap in the air, the youth seem to enter a form of play, trying on the style and mood of the era as though they were open and accessible to everyone.[48] Here, style moves them outside the reductive institutional order of the camps and positions them in the mood of the era, which is not necessarily a space of freedom according to Lauren Berlant, as I discuss below.[49] Yet this mood continues powerfully to captivate the wartime generation today.

These photographs made me look with more care at the photographs of youth in camps, particularly the group photographs of high school students from the Lemon Creek camp. Lemon Creek was the second-largest camp, with over 2,500 internees. It was located in the Slocan Valley, where there were three other camps: Slocan (which consisted of Bayfarm, Popoff, and Slocan City), New Denver (which consisted of New Denver, Harris Ranch, Trite Ranch, and Rosebery), and Sandon. Among the photographs in the archive, although the largest number of photos are from Tashme (781, of which 706 are snapshots taken by one donor, Marie Katsuno) and from Slocan (112), given my desire to read these photographs in terms of a "repertoire" of embodied knowledge, I am especially interested in the Lemon Creek photographs (54) because of the large number of reunions by former internees from this camp. I am interested in one photograph in particular: "Lemon Creek High School, January 1946" (see Figure 8.5). Ruby Truly used this image in her video documentary of the "Lemon Creekers'" first reunion in 1992, which included a bus tour back to the sites of the internment camps.[50] This is when I first encountered the photograph. I accompanied Truly on the bus tour as her sound person and remember finding the way she incorporated wartime photographs in the documentary emotionally powerful. In one of the documentary's scenes, as an elderly man shares a few words in memory of his wife, Truly's camera gently hovers over her snapshot, a photo that the man took out of his wallet to show us. Although he says little, the camera slowly zooms in and, with a slight tremble, focuses on her image, which the man has carefully propped up on a picnic table. Then the camera floats upward, past the man to the magnificent mountain range. It is almost as though she were present, quietly accompanying her husband back to the site where they were interned.

Truly's camera work also animates photographs of students from Lemon Creek as she slowly pans over row after row of their youthful faces. Again, with the tiny trembles of the handheld camera, it is almost as though she were reaching out to gently touch their small and vulnerable youthful faces. On the sound track, a woman who was a teacher in Lemon Creek sings in Japanese. She devotes the song to "the mothers" who "struggled for four years." As she sings, the other participants, many of whom were students in the camps, fall silent. Her voice has an odd, ethereal quality. She sings along to recorded music that, because of her earphones, only she can hear, as though she were accessing another reality, preserved on her electronic device. In her thin, fragile voice, she follows the melody with determination, recalling the fragile security that mothers were determined to create for their children. Whether as memory objects of their long-departed loved ones or as mementos of their classmates from so many years ago, the photos stand in for the lost youth of the now-aging internees as they look sadly and lovingly back to those days when they thought a future full of promise was before them.

As mentioned, I am interested in these photographs, particularly the photograph of "Lemon Creek High School, January 1946," in terms of their place within the repertoire. Although I was first introduced to the photographs through the Lemon Creek reunion, I saw them again sixteen years later, while I was conducting research for this chapter, in the JCNM. I am interested in how memory is enacted and embodied through the use of these images, which circulate both outside and inside the archive as memory objects at reunions, in video documentaries, and now, in my own study.

Photographs of adolescents in the camps capture them at a particular point of identity formation. They are on the cusp of adulthood yet still supposedly "children" under the care of their parents. School was one of the few places where there was any sense of another world, a future that took them beyond the camps. The provincial government, which had jurisdiction over education, refused to extend services to 5,500 Japanese Canadian children in the camps. One year later, the federal government decided it would provide education to elementary students until Grade 8.[51] In addition to using trained teachers, teacher training was set up for Japanese Canadians with high school

Figure 8.5 Lemon Creek High School, January 1946. *Source:* Courtesy of Japanese Canadian National Museum, 1995/100.1.4.

Figure 8.6 High School – Lemon Creek, BC, April 1944. *Source:* Courtesy of Japanese Canadian National Museum, 1995/103.1.2.

　　　　　　　　　　　　　　　　　　　　　　　Inscriptions

and university degrees.[52] High school students were left to fund their own education through correspondence courses until the Anglican Church and United Church decided to staff and finance their education.[53]

Education thus symbolically and actually became a place of determination that offered the possibility of a future, even if that future remained full of uncertainty. For high school students, however, this place was not as secure as it was for younger students. The oldest children were often expected to forgo high school education and assume responsibility for the care of the younger members of the family as well as find work to help cover the cost of rent, food, and other necessities for which the government expected the internees to pay. They were also temporally closer to the reality of their future, to what awaited them when they graduated. But in the camps, there was no future. There were no regular jobs or training opportunities,[54] nor was there the opportunity for parents to save earnings in order to improve their circumstances – for example, by financing the further education of their children. In other words, there was no possibility for the students of taking up the narrative of adulthood that in the heteronormative sense meant getting married, having a family, and contributing to one's community.

Yet, in the photographs of high school students, it is the youth who seem to capture the possibility of a future most poignantly (see Figures 8.5 and 8.6). Annette Kuhn describes in detail the relation of the temporality of photographs to what she calls their "poignant" quality.[55] In seizing a moment in time, photographs always assume loss in the very act of attempting to instil hope. The photograph as a record "looks towards a future time when things will be different, anticipates a need to remember what will soon be past."[56] Poignancy comes from the failure to have fulfilled the hope that things would be different. In the camp photographs, the students are almost adults, as tall as or taller than their teachers. As mentioned, being youth, they still had the liberty of dreaming, of entering the fantasy space of popular culture. Stylishly dressed in fitted jackets, the young women, no longer "girls," have glamourously swept up their hair like Rita Hayworth and Lana Turner, while the young men sport cardigans with crests and baseball jackets and have combed back their abundant black hair in Bogart-like styles. Their stylish poses and clothing are at odds with the rural settings of the photographs. In fashioning themselves after style icons, they signalled that they wanted to belong to urban,

Figure 8.7　Detail of Lemon Creek High School, January 1946. *Source:* Courtesy of Japanese Canadian National Museum, 1995/100.1.4.

cosmopolitan locations. They thus reject the camp, the isolated rural location, and the institutional order that reduced them to compliant subjects.[57]

Here, despite the requirements of the group photograph, where everyone poses in conformity, the exuberance of youth's style breaks out most evidently in the bodies of two youth sitting on the benches in the front row (see Figure 8.7). One youth juts his knee forward, resting his elbow on it, his arm across his chest. While he looks into the camera, engaging the viewer and a future not yet known, the light strikes his face, which is tilted slightly to the left, giving the impression of a cautious yet perhaps also cocky assessment of what lies ahead of him. This cautious-cocky look is reinforced by the arm defensively positioned across his chest and by his hands, which are loosely clenched in fists. To his left, two youth sit confidently, squarely facing the camera, arms resting on their widespread knees. The young man in the light-coloured jacket stands out. His arms are crossed as though defensively and somewhat defiantly, with one hand in a fist and the other hand cradling his

Inscriptions

arm, supporting it, suggesting a need for reassurance. His head lowered, he looks up at the viewer with the hint of a daring smile. Both young men seem to be trying on the style of masculinity circulating in Hollywood at the time, Cagney-esque. There is little submissive about them, although there are hints of vulnerability: the hand that cradles an arm; the ambiguously defensive-defiant/cautious-cocky looks. They suggest individuals with determination, with pent up energy. The youth with one knee jutting forward looks like he is in a sprinter's position, suggesting he is literally ready to charge into his future. But the date of the photograph is significant. The photo was taken in 1946, which means that many of the students in the photograph had possibly been signed up to be shipped to Japan.

The government moved everyone relocating to central Canada to the Kaslo camp. Those being shipped to Japan were sent to Lemon Creek, Rosebery, Slocan, and Greenwood before they were all deposited in the Tashme camp on their way out of the country, which was just 100 miles away from the coast.[58] Given the organized efforts to halt the government's attempt to ship Japanese Canadians overseas, it is likely that not all of the students in the photograph would end up struggling for survival in war-torn Japan, which for many of the nisei was a foreign country where they had limited knowledge of the language and society. Although 10,000 initially were signed up to be shipped to Japan, eventually 5,000 were sent.[59] Thus the final fate of most of the students in this high school graduation photograph was in the hands of the government, which provided their parents with two (insufficiently explained) "options" *for leaving* the province. What we do not see in the photographs is what awaited them in the near future: shipment to Japan paid for by the government or self-funded relocation to unknown settlements across Canada. In the photographs, they still embrace the dream world promised by popular culture.

Knowing the context gives these school graduation photographs another level of meaning. Students will not be saying goodbye to their schoolmates as they begin their journeys to establish their lives as contributing adults. Instead, they will be saying goodbye quite possibly forever, as each goes forth into unscripted futures where, as "Japanese" in central Canada and as "Canadians" in war-torn Japan, they will be neither welcome nor offered much in the way of opportunities and support. This context gives the poses of these young men an even more daring, and retrospectively tragic, air.

Figure 8.8   Detail of High School – Lemon Creek, BC, April 1944. *Source:* Courtesy of Japanese Canadian National Museum, 1995/103.1.2.

In "High School – Lemon Creek, BC, April 1944," it is again a student sitting in the front row of the photograph who breaks out into a stylish pose, defying the conformity of the institutional group shot (see Figure 8.8). Since she is sitting in the front row, like the young men in the photo discussed above, her entire body is exposed, rather than being partially hidden by other students standing or sitting in front of her. Second in from the right side of the photo, she faces the camera squarely, her ankles crossed, her flared skirt draped over her legs above bare knees. She confidently rests her left elbow on the back of her bench but she folds her other arm across her waist and clasps the left hand in her right, suggesting a movement of restraint. Around her neck, she wears a patterned kerchief, and her hair is swept up in a long curly coif. She is smiling with open lips, her head slightly tilted to her right. The smiling young woman to her left leans toward her, more modestly holding her hands in her lap. By contrast, the kerchiefed young woman looks relaxed and rather jaunty, rather Katharine Hepburn-like with her casual sporty look. Again, like the

Inscriptions

young men in the photograph discussed above, by taking up the style and mood of the era, she moves outside of the space of regimentation. Unlike the young men, she would not yet have known her fate, as it was 1944. But the poignancy is just as strong.

These young adults take up the style or what Berlant calls the "cliché" of an era that offers a dream that in fact is never to be realized. In her discussion of the film *Now Voyager* (1942), Berlant argues that the clichéd style of femininity – which includes everything from the way one coyly tilts one's head and flirtatiously returns a look to one's clothing and the treble of one's laughter – promises the heterosexual fantasy of love, a fantasy that can never be realized.[60] Likewise here, these youth embrace the possibilities of flight offered by the stylish poses and fashions of Hollywood. Hollywood transports them out of the rigid regimentation of the camps, the non-place of administrative control, and the government's imposition of a new form of social order that breaks apart and fragments the habitus of their community.[61] Yet this posturing is profoundly poignant not just because, as Kuhn notes, we now know that the future will fail to fulfill their hopes but also because the youth are literally looking into the future, into our eyes, as we look back at them from today, which we know *has already* been taken away from them. It is a future where Mackenzie King's cabinet had scripted their postwar identities, ensuring that if they chose to stay in Canada, there would be no possibility for them to continue to exist as people of "Japanese racial descent."

THE MEMORYSCAPE OF THE ARCHIVE

To conclude, in the archives, removed from their domicile in family albums and personal records, photographs of the internment camps take on new meanings. Once bearing witness to events that had no language and whose weight was too much for any one family to carry alone, the photographs enter a collective of images in the archive, a memoryscape where it becomes possible to understand the photographs from the internment camps in multiple ways. But even as the photographs are removed from the social contexts of meaning that narrate the lineage of individual Japanese Canadian families into a series of places of residence as well as document their displacement and loss of identity as Canadian citizens, the archive has its own "archival memory," which can fix the photographs' meanings. In the Japanese Canadian community, archival memory is articulated in an ambivalent fashion through contradictory myths about the camps, on the one hand, as the last sites of communal existence and, on the other hand, as sites of destruction.

Insofar as the camps are the basis of identity for Japanese Canadians whose families were interned during the war, I explore what the photographs of the camps reveal about this double process of communal identification/destruction. Although it is astounding to see so many Japanese Canadians gathered together, it is also shocking to see them extricated from the province's social landscape. Vulnerable and exposed in the barren sites, the group photographs are part of the process by which Japanese Canadians were rearranged into a new institutional order. The repetition of order in the group photographs, for example, and the conformity of the rows of subjects formally posing for the camera, suggests a loss of identity. In contrast to the prewar photographs in the archive, which locate Japanese Canadians in the social, economic, and cultural landscape of the province, the camp photos locate them in the dead zones of the province, where they have been extricated from their homes, their work, and the social activities that once integrated them into the local habituses of towns, fishing ports, and urban neighbourhoods.

Yet, as I argue, despite the imposition of institutional order, the photos also show that not everyone conforms. The group photographs of the youth are particularly poignant. On the cusp of adulthood, their futures would normally lie open, holding possibilities yet to be discovered. The photographs capture their youthful dreams of Hollywood heroes and heroines, taking them beyond the confines of the camp, beyond the isolated rural terrain, into a more cosmopolitan world, where rugged individuals can craft their own futures. They remake a future tenuously scripted after Hollywood's dreamscape with echoes of the urban life that many nisei lost when the government sent them to internment camps. Approaching the photographs as part of a repertoire of embodied knowledge, especially for nisei who were adolescents in the camps, I describe how the camp photographs paradoxically capture the moment when they could still be transported by these dreams beyond the reality of the camps. But looking back to this time, they now know, as we know as viewers, that beyond the camps there was no future for them in Canada as "people of Japanese racial origins." They had to leave Canada and give up what it was to be Canadian, or if they stayed, they had to give up what it was to be Japanese Canadian. Although their glamourous dreams allowed them to break out of the regimentation of institutional order (symbolized by the group photos), we know as viewers looking back that they understood there was nowhere, except perhaps in the camps with other youth, where they could escape into that fantasy. Today, this gives the sites of the camps significant meaning in the memoryscape of Japanese Canadians. The photographs of youth incite nostalgia, the stylish poses capturing the era's cocky and jaunty air of confidence. But they also evoke the pain of loss and denial. In the broader context of Canadian society, the racialized bodies of these youth would exclude them from even the pretence of belonging to the world of their fantasy.

As I have argued, in the archive images can be released from archival memory and take on new meanings when they enter new choreographies that are generated by tracing their movement through repertoires where they are re-imagined and re-narrated in multiple ways. The Lemon Creekers who donated the photographs regather and re-enact what it meant to be youths in internment camps located throughout the isolated, barren, economically dead zones of the province. They lovingly embrace the vulnerability of their youthful dreams, which in the camps had not yet been dashed by the harsh postwar realities. But there is a sense of sadness as they look back, knowing the rejection they would face when they were forced to relocate across the rest of Canada and to Japan. Through the camp reunions and through documentaries like Ruby Truly's *With Our Own Eyes,* the photographs of the camps retrospectively reimage and rework the meaning of these sites. In this new choreography, the meanings of these places do not become fixed; rather, their paradoxical nature becomes apparent. The photographs show that what the youth embraced was the dream they shared rather than the reality of the camps. But this dream necessitated a denial of the places where they collectively enacted the dream: the incarceration camps. Years later, as nisei and younger generations return to the sites of internment in search of this surplus of poignant meaning, the sites of internment now hold memories of this generation's lost youth.

The archive in this context thus becomes an important site of memory. It is a site where it becomes possible to prize open the "archival memory" that has been institutionalized through systems of cataloguing and data retrieval. It is a site that privileges place in the narrative of Japanese Canadian identity and dangerously overlooks the ambivalent meanings of the camps. But by examining the way that items enter and exit the archive's collections and become part of repertoires that enact multiple meanings, it is possible to examine how the archive can be a place to explore the camps as poignant and painful places of identity. The potency they continue to have in the memory-scape of Japanese Canadians, as I argue in this chapter, lies in the camps' association with an ambivalent, unresolved dream that both embraces and denies place.

ACKNOWLEDGMENTS

I would like to acknowledge the incredible work and innovation of James Opp and John Walsh in bringing scholars together in dialogue first in the 2008 Placing Memory and Remembering Place Workshop at Carleton University and then in this volume to explore issues of place and memory in the Canadian landscape. Their insights and generous suggestions have been essential for the development of this chapter. I would also like to gratefully acknowledge the support I have received in the form of a Postdoctoral Fellowship and a Standard Research Grant from the Social Sciences and Humanities Research Council of Canada. My work on photography and visual culture in particular is indebted to the support of Annette Kuhn and Jackie Stacey at Lancaster University, where I did my postdoctoral studies.

NOTES

1 This draws on Luciana Duranti's idea about archives' holdings being "the documentary by-productions of action." See Luciana Duranti, "Archives as Place," *Archives and Social Studies: A Journal of Interdisciplinary Research* 1 (2007): 450.

2 Ken Adachi, *The Enemy That Never Was* (1976; reprint, Toronto: McClelland and Stewart 1991); Ann Gomer Sunahara, *The Politics of Racism: The Uprooting of Japanese Canadians during the Second World War* (Toronto: James Lorimer, 1983).

3 I have reversed the heartland-hinterland dichotomy so that the interior of the province, historically the source of livestock and many primary resources as well as the vast territories of numerous First Nations, becomes "the heartland."

4 There are a few exceptions, including settlements like New Denver, where the Kyowakai Society built the Nikkei Internment Memorial Centre to mark the site where many of its members were interned during the 1940s and continued to live after the war.

5 Sunahara, *Politics of Racism*, 142.

6 The term "ghost towns" refers to depopulated mining towns.

7 Roland Barthes, *Image, Music, Text* (London: Fontana Press, 1977).

8 Diane Taylor, *The Archive, The Repertoire: Performing Cultural Memory in the Americas* (Durham, NC, and London: Duke University Press, 2003).

9 Ibid., 19.

10 Ibid.

11 Ibid., 19-20.

12 Cassandra Kobayashi and Roy Miki, *Justice in Our Time: The Japanese Canadian Redress Settlement* (Vancouver: Talon Books, 1991); Roy Miki, *Redress: Inside the Japanese Canadian Call for Redress* (Vancouver: Raincoast Books, 2004).

13 See Miki, *Redress*.

14 Japanese Canadian Centennial Project (JCCP), *A Dream of Riches: Japanese Canadians, 1877-1977* (Vancouver: JCCP Redress Committee, 1978).

15 Kirsten Emiko McAllister, "Stories of Escape: Family Photographs from World War Two Internment Camps," in *Locating Memory: Photographic Acts,* ed. Annette Kuhn and Kirsten Emiko McAllister (Oxford and New York: Berghahn Books, 2006), 81-110.

16 Kirsten Emiko McAllister, "Confronting Official History with Our Own Eyes: Video Documentary in the Japanese Canadian Community," *West Coast Line: Colour. An Issue* 13, 14 (1994): 66-84. Watada mythologizes the camps, modelling them after Japanese villages and using plot lines from Japanese folktales; see Terry Watada, *Daruma Days: A Collection of Fictionalized Biography* (Toronto: Ronsdale, 1997).

17 Adachi, *Enemy That Never Was;* Sunahara, *Politics of Racism;* Kobayashi and Miki, *Justice in Our Time;* Audrey Kobayashi, "The Uprooting of Japanese Canadians after 1941," *Tribune* 5, 1 (1987): 28-35.

18 See Joy Kogawa, *Obasan* (New York: Penguin, 1983); Kerri Sakamoto, *The Electric Field* (Toronto: Alfred A. Knopf Canada, 1998).

19 Michel de Certeau, *The Practice of Everyday Life* (Berkeley: University of California Press, 1988).

20 Michel Foucault, *The History of Sexuality,* vol. 1 (New York: Vintage Books, 1990).

21 de Certeau, *Practice of Everyday Life,* 40, 94.

22 John Tagg, *The Burden of Representation* (Minneapolis: University of Minnesota Press, 1993); Annette Kuhn, *Family Secrets: Acts of Memory and Imagination* (London: Verso, 1995); Marianne Hirsch, *Family Frames: Photography, Narrative and Postmemory* (Cambridge, MA: Harvard University Press, 1997).

23 Kuhn, *Family Secrets;* Lauren Berlant, *The Female Complaint: The Unfinished Business of Sentimentality in American Culture* (Durham, NC: Duke University Press, 2008).

24 Susan Stewart, *On Longing: Narratives of the Miniature, the Gigantic, the Souvenir, the Collection* (Durham, NC, and London: Duke University Press, 1993), 67.

25 There are 781 photographic records from the Tashme camp, but 706 are snapshots taken by Marie Katsuno. There are more photographs from Tashme, Lemon Creek, and Slocan and fewer from camps like Greenwood, Kaslo, and Sandon. More investigation is needed, but it is interesting to note that whenever there are camp reunions in Vancouver, they seem to be followed by donations to the JCNM. In the largest camps, like Tashme and Lemon Creek, there were probably more people taking as well as saving photographic records. In addition, former internees from camps like New Denver, Greenwood, and Kaslo might have donated their records to the museums in those locales rather than to the JCNM.

26 Allan Sekula, "Reading an Archive: Photography between Labour and Capital," in *Visual Culture: The Reader,* ed. Jessica Evans and Stuart Hall (London: Sage, 1999), 181-91.

27 Adele Perry, *On the Edge of Empire: Gender, Race and the Making of British Columbia* (Toronto: University of Toronto Press, 2001).

28 Sekula, "Reading an Archive."

29 Ibid., 184.

30 Ibid.

31 Thus far, I have written on the family photographs, the landscape photographs, and the postcard images. See McAllister, "Stories of Escape"; Kirsten Emiko McAllister, "Photographs of Japanese Canadian Internment Camps: Mourning Loss and Invoking a Future," *Visual Studies* 21, 2 (2006): 133-56; and Kirsten Emiko McAllister, "Held Captive: The Postcard and the Icon," *West Coast Line: Special Issue on Photography, Autobiographical Memory and Cultural Literacy,* ed. Jerald Zaslove and Martha Langford, 35, 1 (2001): 20-40.

32 Midge Ayukawa, interview by Kirsten McAllister, Vancouver, 2001; Marie Katsuno, interview by Kirsten McAllister, Burnaby, BC, 2001.

33 Ibid.

34 Ayukawa, interview.

35 Ayukawa, interview; Katsuno, interview.

36 McAllister, "Stories of Escape."

37 Hirsch, *Family Frames,* 6-7; Kuhn, *Family Secrets;* Patricia Holland, "Introduction: History, Memory and the Family Album," in *Family Snaps: The Meaning of Domestic Photography,* ed. Jo Spence and Patricia Holland (London: Virago, 1991), 1-15.

38 Mas Tasaka, interview by Mari-Jane Medenwaldt and Kirsten Emiko McAllister for the Japanese Canadian Citizens' Association's Oral History Project, Steveston, BC, 1990. The government quickly and efficiently removed issei leaders who could have informed and organized the community using their communication networks across various coastal communities. Able-bodied men were also picked up by the Royal Canadian Mounted Police with as little as twenty-four hours' notice, leaving their confused and terrified families behind. For months, many families did not know that these men had been sent to road camps throughout British Columbia, with the more outspoken men being sent to prisoner-of-war camps in Ontario. See Sunahara, *Politics of Racism.*

39 Sunahara, *Politics of Racism,* 135.

40 There are large numbers of letters in the national archives addressed to government officials by women (likely nisei) asking after their husbands and demanding their release from prisoner-of-war camps.

41 This is not to say that there weren't distinctions between the camps as well as within the camps. Japanese Canadians who had enough capital to pay directly for the costs of their internment were in what were called the "self-support" camps, whereas those in government camps did not directly pay for their costs (although they did pay "rent" for the shacks they were assigned, and the government liquidated their properties along the Pacific coastline and used the funds to cover the costs of the internment camps); see Miki and Kobayashi, *Justice in Our Time.* In addition, certain camps received

higher numbers of Buddhists (e.g., Sandon), whereas others received higher numbers of Catholics (e.g., Greenwood).

42 Andrea Walsh, "Re-placing History: Critiquing the Colonial Gaze through Photographic Works of Jeffery Thomas and Greg Staats," in *Locating Memory: Photographic Acts*, ed. Annette Kuhn and Kirsten Emiko McAllister (Oxford and New York: Berghahn Books, 2006), 21-52.

43 See Mona Oikawa, "'Driven to Scatter Far and Wide': The Forced Resettlement of Japanese Canadians to Southern Ontario, 1944-1949" (MA thesis, Department of Sociology, OISE, University of Toronto, 1986).

44 Ibid.

45 This stands in contrast to self-support camps like Lillooet, where internees grew agricultural products such as melons and tomatoes to support themselves and constructed infrastructure to ensure a supply of fresh water (wooden water flews were built to bring each shack water from the Fraser River, which each household then filtered with charcoal).

46 See Oikawa, "'Driven to *Scatter*.'"

47 McAllister, "Stories of Escape"; McAllister, "Photographs."

48 Berlant, *Female Complaint*.

49 Ibid.

50 See Ruby Truly, dir., *With Our Own Eyes: A Trip to Lemon Creek*, video documentary (Vancouver: Video Out, 1991). The reunion took place immediately following the National Association of Japanese Canadians' "Homecoming Conference" in Vancouver, which marked the fiftieth anniversary of the internment camps.

51 Adachi, *Enemy that Never Was*, 263-64.

52 Ibid.; Frank Moritsugu and the Ghost Town Teachers Historical Society, *Teaching in Canadian Exile* (Toronto: Ghost Town Teachers Historical Society, 2001).

53 Adachi, *Enemy that Never Was*, 264.

54 Japanese Canadians were already a skilled workforce. The main barrier they faced was legislation that restricted their access to professions like the law. There were classes in the camps that Japanese Canadians taught, such as cooking and sewing, which most treated as recreational activities. Obviously, more training opportunities were available before the war. The one exception was teacher training for high school graduates and university students. Teachers were needed to teach the children in the camps.

55 Kuhn, *Family Secrets*, 19.

56 Ibid.

57 Although the students in these photographs are restricted to practical "oxford" shoes for the classroom, women and men just a few years older – for example, those working for the Slocan British Columbia Security Commission Hospital (see Figure 8.3) – are even more stylishly fashioned in other group photos. Women wear high heel shoes and crepe dresses and suits with wide bodices and flared skirts. One man even sports white shoes and a double-breasted suit – all in stark contrast to the matronly white female staff in their practical cotton dresses and lace-up shoes.

58 T.B. Pickersgill, "Re: Carrying Out Segregation," 12 June 1945, Records of the British Columbia Security Commission, vol. 16, file 622, part 1, Library and Archives Canada (LAC), RG36.

59 Segregating Japanese Canadians who were being sent to Japan had a corrosive social and political impact. Already divided over the best strategy and misinformed by government officials (e.g., many believed that if they signed up for Japan, which meant the government would permit them to continue working in British Columbia, they could later remove their names from the list and stay in Canada), there were families in which some members selected the option to relocate to assigned locations across Canada while the others selected the option to be shipped to Japan (or were signed up by their parents for shipment). When this happened, the government physically separated families and sent members to different camps. The government saw the separation of those staying in Canada and those going to Japan in strategic terms. In response to a request from Mr. Collins, the commissioner of Japanese placement, for advice on the implementation of the removal of Japanese Canadians from British Columbia, R.A. Davidson stated that segregation "will break these Japanese up, preventing them from gathering in groups and discussing the pros and cons of the War and of the affairs of Japanese in Canada, thus avoiding much unrest and dissension"; see R.A. Davidson, Memorandum to Geo. Collins, Commissioner of Japanese Placement, re: Change of Policy – Japanese, 31 August 1944, Records of the British Columbia Security Commission, vol. 16, file 622, part 3, LAC, RG36.

60 My use of "cliché" as a concept draws heavily from my notes from Lauren Berlant's public lectures, and on the discussions that followed them, while she was a visiting scholar at Lancaster University in the spring of 2002.

61 Marc Augé, *Non-Places: Introduction to an Anthropology of Supermodernity* (London: Verso, 1995), 78-79.

Immersed
Landscaping the Past at Lake Minnewanka

MATTHEW EVENDEN

Lake Minnewanka, located in the upper Bow River Basin in Banff National Park, is most frequently viewed from the south, where tourists stand on a road built over a dam (see Figure 9.1). Concrete pylons, barbed wire, and metal fences ensure that they don't fall backward over the dam's face. In the warmer months, tourists leave their cars in small lots at either end of the dam while they picnic and hike around the lake; others boat, fish, and scuba dive. Panels orient visitors, offer concise histories of the site, and set out rules to observe: where to park, how to catch fish, and when and how to scuba dive. The lake's surface reflects imperfectly the forested slopes and impressive folds of Rocky Mountain sandstone that rise like walls, north, east, and west. Less visible is a canal that cuts southeast from the lake, carrying water to a small power station located on the north slope of the Trans-Canada Highway. Completely invisible below the lake's surface is a flooded town and an old dam, both of which disappeared under the lake's rising waters in 1941, when the larger dam, on which the road is built and the tourists stand, was constructed as a war project.

A historical plaque built in the late 1960s and located at one of the viewpoints tries to make sense of the presence of a dam in a national park by describing Lake Minnewanka as "a compromise with nature."[1] In carefully chosen

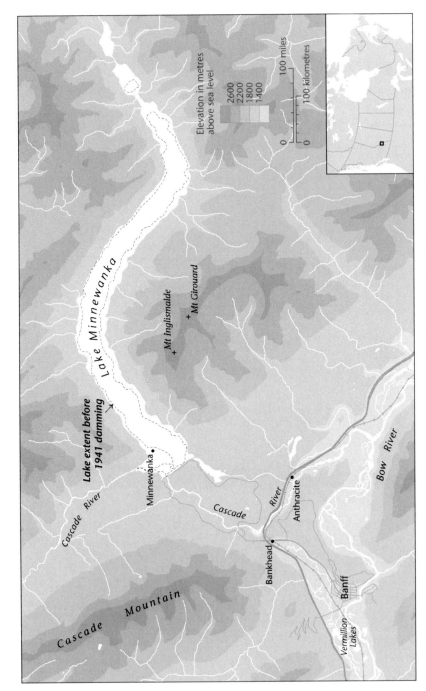

Figure 9.1 Lake Minnewanka showing the water level before and after the construction of the storage dam, 1941.

language, the plaque acknowledges that "the natural scene has been altered but nature has done much to heal the scars wrought by man." There is no reference in this text to the fact that the dam was built as a war project, although the date of completion is provided. More recent signage refers to the wartime origins of the dam, while also providing details about the cultural and natural heritage that it flooded. The text and the accompanying photographs contain a strong vein of nostalgia for what was lost. A display panel devoted to Minnewanka Landing, before the dam, bears the name "Minnewanka Memories." The display of photographs in sepia tones suggests an old and well-worn photo album. The signage at the lake points to shifting official interpretations, ranging from no comment to uneasy acknowledgment to regret and nostalgia – all variously placed on the lakeshore to greet the inquiring gaze of visitors.

Tourists seem not to be overly troubled by the dam's presence in the park. The loop road to the lake from the Banff townsite carries steady traffic in the summer months. Boating and fishing remain popular activities, and the lost town has become a destination for scuba divers who enjoy swimming about the ghostly sub-aqueous remains. Some have sought to leave their mark, vandalizing the old dam or leaving objects under water, including "propane bottles, bath tubs, road signs, plastic pink flamingoes, plastic daisies, plaques of dubious commemorative value, and even a toilet ... carefully riveted in to one of the spillways."[2] Visitors to the lake experience a certain delight in the thoroughly mixed-up place that Lake Minnewanka has become – a hidden cultural heritage site, an industrial landscape constructed as natural, and a functioning power reservoir.

Lake Minnewanka's contemporary landscape is a bricolage, the layers and elements of which appear unrelated, confused. Pink flamingoes lie next to penstocks. If landscape features can "act as points of reference for communicating tacit knowledge," as Julie Cruikshank argues, then what forms of tacit knowledge does Lake Minnewanka communicate?[3] Although the answer to this question would involve a study of contemporary reception, which lies beyond the scope of this chapter, it is possible to retrieve some of the historical foundations of this lake as a flooded town, a park scene, and a power reservoir. By examining the decisions made to transform this lake during the Second World War, and the arguments conducted over its appearance and use, one comes closer to understanding how the lake was constructed as a point of reference, as a landscape to prompt memories and tacit knowledge of a certain kind.

The design of the lake sought to produce a scene suggesting a timeless and untouched nature, a primeval wilderness, befitting an important national park. This framing drew on well-developed design principles and aesthetics but sought to define them particularly for a future of post-war automobile tourism in which the lake and the scene would be increasingly viewed, appreciated, and consumed from behind a windshield.[4] What remained less apparent or hidden in this rendering, however, was the functionality of the space as a dam and reservoir site, holding back waters to generate hydro-electricity. Even less evident was the lost town, which once bordered the lake in an earlier era of tourist development, or the meanings given to the place by Nakoda (formerly known as Stoney) peoples who had frequented Lake Minnewanka before it was folded into a national park. To be effective and to remain coherent, the natural landscape of memory produced at Lake Minnewanka had to hide and flood other pasts.

Lake Minnewanka was, of course, fundamentally re-designed in this process. Apart from the aims of parks officials and landscape architects, the lake was re-plumbed and dammed, its waters diverted. A supposedly public landscape enshrined in a national park was, for the purposes of its water powers, practically alienated. The train of events that led to this outcome emerged entirely beyond the lake and its vicinity. For hydro developers what mattered about this lake was not its history or cultural meanings, its scenic qualities, or its expression of a wilderness ideal. What mattered, rather, was its position within a water basin, its connection to dam sites downstream, and its proximity to an urban electricity market that was rapidly expanding. Lake Minnewanka was understood less as a place and more meaningfully as a location, defined in abstract terms according to the rationality of engineering principles and system development. Developers understood that, owing to the politics of this lake's location, certain aspects of design and landscaping would have to be accepted and paid for; but, as we shall see, they did not accept unconditionally that wilderness values ought to trump functionality.

Although a considerable body of work in the place and memory tradition invokes the national as the primary frame of reference, this chapter proceeds from the understanding that places of memory must be located somewhere.[5]

Even as places of memory are bound up in broader processes of regional, national, or multi-scalar significance, they exist at particular sites.[6] My aim is not to prioritize one scale over another or to treat the local as though it somehow stands apart. But looking at one lake closely makes it possible to ground observations about national policies, hydro development, and aesthetic traditions at points where the social relations that constitute them come into view.[7] Seen in this way, the local is not only a meeting ground but also an important place where changes happen, broader forces are mediated, and places of memory conflict with landscapes of use and consumption.

Lake Minnewanka sat within the original reservation placed on the cave and basin hot spring in 1885 by the federal government to protect a scenic mountain spring from private commercial development. When the Rocky Mountains Park was established two years later, Lake Minnewanka lay at its centre, a few miles north of the Banff townsite, to which it was connected by a carriage road that brought travellers from the railway to lakeside accommodations.[8] Known initially as Devil's Lake (a normative reconstruction of the Nakoda toponomy, Spirit Lake, or Minn-waki), the lake served as an accessible site for park visitors, offering comfortable quarters, boating and fishing, as well as scenery that met the emerging aesthetic ideals of sublime nature borrowed from European Romanticism.[9] The separation of people from the landscape lay implicit in this aesthetic, and in this case the past and recent use of the lake by Nakoda was neither advertised nor recognized.[10] To the contrary, throughout the early period of park development, parks officials, supported by sport and game clubs, sought to exclude Nakoda as unprincipled animal killers.[11] The surviving guest books from the Lake Minnewanka Hotel and the Beach House Hotel in the late nineteenth century record an international clientele including British officers on holiday from India, American professors, and well-heeled railway tourists from eastern Canada. Many of the guests' comments refer to the plentiful bull trout and give voice to the casual pleasures of boating in the mountain air.[12] In the era before automobile tourism in the mountain parks, visitors experienced a genteel natural landscape, peopled by servants and guides as well as by other wealthy tourists. Lake Minnewanka played an important role in this early park era as a suitably scenic, amusingly rustic, but nevertheless exclusive space of leisure.

Lake Minnewanka's exclusive qualities began to break down in the 1910s with the arrival of automobiles. Although automobiles had been explicitly banned from the park, pressure from drivers and auto clubs caused parks officials to reassess their defence of the railway's transportation monopoly to the park and the dominance of outfitters within it. In 1911 parks officials bowed to what they perceived to be the inevitable. After the First World War, this reorientation continued as parks officials worked actively to improve roads, build new ones, and establish car camps in the name of increased public access.[13] Given its proximity to the Banff townsite, Lake Minnewanka became a favoured destination of automobile tourists, and the lakeside town grew as a result. Alongside the Hotel and Beach House, businesses emerged to service the higher number of tourists coming to boat and fish – despite the dwindling number of trout.

At about the same time that Lake Minnewanka opened to automobile tourists, parks officials made the decision to dam it. Built in 1912 by Calgary Power, the regional utility, to enhance storage for downstream power generation on the Bow River at Seebe, the dam raised the level of the lake by twelve feet and forced the partial relocation to higher ground of several buildings around the Hotel and Beach House. By the mid-1920s, parks staff had built a generating station to deliver power from the dam to the Banff townsite, changing the dam's function and adding another layer of infrastructure to the scenery – exposed pipe works, transmission wires, and a generating station. Although the dam had important effects in this early period, parks officials did not see it as antithetical to their mandate in protecting the park and neither, apparently, did residents or visitors who took the new dam and raised lake in stride. In the early 1920s, there was still an operating coalmine in the park at Bankhead, close to the lake, and the idea that the park should exclude industrial activity was only beginning to emerge. In this era, the dam did not cause tourists to recoil but gained acceptance as a necessary utilitarian addition to the recreational landscape. This reception of the dam, however, would be placed in a different light as plans emerged to expand the works and flood the town.[14]

As part of its developmental program in the interwar period, Calgary Power sought permission to dam upper-basin tributaries in the Bow Watershed. Both locations at Lake Minnewanka and on the Spray River were contained within the boundaries of the Rocky Mountains Park. Such a program promised additional power generation sites as well as storage facilities to allow for a staged water-release schedule for dams downstream. What looked like rational efficiency to the power company, however, provoked an unprecedented backlash from parks officials and recreational groups.

Beginning in the early 1920s, a new perspective on the role of parks emerged that placed a higher priority on recreational use. Within the parks system, officials increasingly viewed industrial activity as intrusive and potentially damaging to the tourist trade. When the Bankhead mine closed after a bitter strike in 1924, for example, parks officials took the opportunity to dismantle the townsite and close the mine.[15] Recreational groups, for their part, began to attach a rhetoric of democratic values to park use that aligned tourism with the people and industrial development with corporate exploitation. In the background, an increasingly popular wilderness aesthetic, which parsed the world into the wild and the civilized, made the presence of resource development in the parks appear out of place and difficult to justify. Recreation, within this view, held a different status and imposed almost no burden on the scenery.

Calgary Power's development proposal ran headlong into this opposition. A range of groups coalesced to question and attack the company's proposal, including the Calgary Automobile Club, the Alpine Club of Canada, and a new organization, formed in part to block the dam, the Canadian National Parks Association. After several years of conflict, the federal government imposed a compromise in 1930: opening the opportunity to develop the Spray River while protecting Lake Minnewanka. To do so, it re-drew the park's boundaries, removing the Spray and the surrounding lands so that the company might gain development rights from the Province of Alberta. The company would not, however, gain access to Lake Minnewanka, the more important tourist site. In the short term, this partial victory for the power company rang hollow. With the decline in economic conditions in 1929, the company found its regional market hard hit, removing any incentive to pursue development projects.[16]

Although the immediate effects of the debate seemed therefore muted, it nevertheless contributed to a more general shift in parks policy. After the conclusion of the controversy, the federal government passed a new National Parks Act (1930), which in its statement of general purpose highlighted the centrality of recreation: "The Parks are hereby dedicated to the people of Canada for their benefit, education and enjoyment ... such Parks shall be maintained and made use of so as to leave them unimpaired for the enjoyment of future generations."[17] The timing of the new legislation probably had more to do with the final resolution in 1930 of the natural-resources question between the prairie provinces and the federal government.[18] Nevertheless, the debate over the Rocky Mountains Park, renamed Banff National Park in 1930, had been important and suggested the new direction of parks policy as well as the role of park advocates in the process.

If the protection of Lake Minnewanka from further development appeared certain in 1930, it did not a decade later. The Second World War transformed the context, propelled economic expansion, and drove up electrical demand across the country. After the fall of France, as the Canadian government moved to convert the economy to a wartime footing, the newly created Department of Munitions and Supply let contracts for a whole range of military goods and materials.[19] In some locations these contracts placed an enormous new burden on the electricity supply.

Calgary was one of these locations. Although most military contracts were let in Ontario and Quebec using established industries and manufacturers, Munitions and Supply sited an energy-intensive explosives plant making ammonium nitrate in Calgary for the British government. Although Calgary Power had met the needs of the depression-era city and region handily, the growth in economic activity after 1939 and the unanticipated needs of a large military plant that would account for about a quarter of the existing electrical demand in the city suggested the need for new generation.[20] Although Calgary Power might have been expected to develop its Spray River property at this stage, its executives demurred, citing the slow building schedule (two to three years), while also pouring cold water on another alternative, coal-based steam power, which was said to be prohibitively expensive.[21] In the midst of the wartime crisis, Calgary Power approached the federal government seeking rights to dam Lake Minnewanka, as the only reasonable opportunity to produce more power in under a year.[22]

As of August 1940, the federal government had imposed a new regulatory structure over power generation across the country in view of threatening shortages in key industrial regions. A power controller, within the Department of Munitions and Supply, oversaw the power outlook and held sweeping authority to command generation projects, cancel developments, and impose conservation restrictions. As it turned out, the individual chosen for this position was Herbert J. Symington, a well-connected Montreal lawyer who served as general counsel for Royal Securities, sat on the Board of Directors of one of its important Canadian investments, Calgary Power, and held stock in the western utility.[23]

This is not the place to describe the political machinations that led the federal government to approve Calgary Power's request, although it is worth noting that the Parks Bureau disagreed and tried furiously to steer the company and senior ministers toward alternatives.[24] Prime Minister Mackenzie King noted in his diary that the damming of the lake would be a sad destruction of scenery that should be avoided, but his colleague, Minister of Munitions and Supply C.D. Howe, saw matters differently and carried the issue.[25] The Parks Act would simply be circumvented by an order-in-council, made possible by the wartime emergency.[26] Little public protest arose around the proposal. In Banff local workers looked forward to the employment opportunity after a difficult decade.[27] Both the advisory board in Banff and the municipal government in Calgary wrote to the federal government in favour of the dam project. Selby Walker of the Canadian National Parks Association made a concerted, but ultimately lonely, effort to discredit the project as a conspiracy of eastern capitalists exploiting the wartime emergency for private gain. "Perhaps the possibility of having the project constructed as a war measure at public expense and becoming available salvage after the war is less patriotic than alluring to St. James Street," Walker wrote in a typical salvo to J. Smart of the Department of Mines and Resources in October 1940.[28] Other groups, such as the Alberta Fish and Game Association and members of the National Geographic Society, raised concerns, but this was not the broad coalition that had arisen in the 1920s to defend the park against power.[29]

By late 1940 there was little doubt that a new dam would be built at Lake Minnewanka. The federal cabinet had approved the matter in principle, as had the premier of Alberta, William Aberhart.[30] Surveys at the lake had already commenced.[31] Because of the wartime emergency, work would proceed and legislation would follow.[32] When in December 1940 Thomas Crerar, the minister of mines and resources, responsible for national parks, announced the licence to Calgary Power in a press release, he acknowledged that the project represented a "drastic departure" from past practice but insisted that parks staff would monitor the building carefully: "Every effort will be made to ensure the least possible disfigurement of the beauties of Lake Minnewanka and the surrounding area and to protect and safeguard all other interests of the Park."[33]

For parks officials who had lived through the protests of the 1920s, and tried to block the current proposal with stirring memoranda, the only option now was to accommodate a massive object that they deemed profoundly out of place. This then was the challenge of the Lake Minnewanka Dam: how to flood a town, raise a lake, and build a functional dam while integrating the resulting scene into an aesthetic of parks wilderness.

For Calgary Power, the Minnewanka project was a political and engineering problem. The war context and the co-operation of the federal government had, for all intents and purposes, solved the political problem. But not entirely. The licence granted to the company also sought to insert some constraints on how the development would proceed.[34] As the envisioned dam would flood Minnewanka Landing, the company agreed to pay a settlement to existing owners and relocate cottages to equivalent properties. There is almost no record of protest from those who had to vacate, perhaps owing to the financial settlement and the fact that businesses had the option of restarting operations later. Although these arrangements took some time to work out and explain, affected interests raised no quarrel.[35] It may be that the transience of the community, which included summer workers as well as the annual draw of automobile tourists, provided a weak base for local resistance or regret.[36] Another important constraint in the interim licence referred to the appearance of the project and the need to maintain scenic values. By the terms of the licence, the park's bureau would not only oversee construction closely with an inspecting engineer but would also retain (at the company's expense) a landscape architect to advise on beautification.

The engineering problem at Lake Minnewanka was comparatively straightforward. The dam would rise sixty feet and flood an additional 1,900 acres around the lake. A control structure on the lake's southeast corner would release flows through a canal and penstock network to pass through a power generator above the Banff-Calgary road (later the Trans-Canada Highway) before water entered the Bow River. An additional tail race allowed for water releases into the Cascade River if water levels rose too quickly. Beyond the power-generating function, the dam had a higher purpose in controlling seasonal flows so that Calgary Power's major dam facilities downstream at Seebe, the Ghost River, and Horshoe Falls received as steady a flow as possible throughout the year to provide for a higher mean generating capacity. This was the dam's primary function as a control structure within a wider system

Figure 9.2 Disassembling Minnewanka Landing, 6 May 1941. Note the tree stumps in the foreground and the breakwater in the background. *Source:* National Parks, accession 1970-226, neg. no. C-035040, Library and Archives Canada.

of hydrological and power flows linking the demands of an urban electricity market with the rationalized seasonality of a river.

As the dam served only the purpose of water raising, its design was comparatively simple. Below the outlet of the lake, a canyon with good foundations existed that served as the new dam site. The dam contained a clay core and stone-and-earth fill. A quarry just south of the dam on the road to Banff provided the necessary gravel. The plans contained no stone or reinforced concrete on the face, for the simple reason that it was unnecessary. The crest of the dam also included a roadway for service vehicles that would later provide a link in the Minnewanka loop scenic drive. When publicly explaining the project, Calgary Power officials sought to capitalize on this new "scenic road," which they claimed would add value to the park.[37]

The re-engineering of the lake rapidly replaced the existing townsite and park facilities. In the winter of 1941, a labour camp of tents was inserted among the rustic hotel and surrounding buildings. Construction began in earnest, and one lake gave way to another. As the dam came to completion in late 1941, the water levels rose, immersing the traces of the former landscape.

It is at this stage that the deliberate place-making activities surrounding Lake Minnewanka come into view. Faced with the unstoppable demands of the power corporation and the federal government, parks officials in Banff took on the task of observing the construction process, regulating it and placing demands on the appearance of things. They saw the dam as a necessary evil, which with some effort at disguise might be accommodated.

In the early stages of construction, as surveyors worked on the site and placement of the dam, construction contractors began the long and gruelling process of clearing the surrounding area for the expanded reservoir. Whereas most of the existing townsite was removed, the old dam remained in place. Figure 9.2 shows one of the last remaining buildings, partly dismantled, standing starkly against a future lakebed of stumps. What concerned officials more was the possibility that flooded trees, lying along the lake's shoreline, would rot and surface in the lake, creating dead heads, snags, and visual eyesores. A timber cruise noted the presence of thousands of board feet of commercial timber, in addition to much scrub and brush.[38] Alongside the dam-building project would be a small timber-felling and brush-burning operation. To make a clean, beautiful lake, safe for boating, the forest had to go.

Clearing the reservoir of trees and brush was a labour-intensive activity, and despite the formerly poor employment market in depression-era Banff, by 1940 local workers were in short supply. The construction firm who assumed the clearing contract therefore looked for ready alternative workers and found them downriver, a short distance from Banff, at Morley on the Nakoda reserve. Twenty-five men were engaged as a result. Although a rational business decision from the viewpoint of the construction company, the move raised flags for parks officials monitoring the construction. They seemed chiefly concerned that the Nakoda would set up camp within the park, bring in their families, and hunt animals on the side. "There is considerable game in the area," P.J. Jennings, superintendent of the park, noted in a letter to superiors, "and it is felt that temptation to trap might exist."[39] When C.M. Walker, the park's inspecting engineer, discovered that the Nakoda had encamped a mile within the park's boundary, he forced them to relocate to the park's eastern edge (leaving the workers with a five-mile hike to the lake through rough bush) and warned superiors of the possible risk to wildlife.[40] After some debate pitting the parks staff who did not want the Nakoda in the park against the Indian Agent at Morely and the local member of Parliament who begged for some reasonable accommodation, the Nakoda and their families were allowed to camp near their worksite, although under the watchful gaze of the Indian Agent who was dispatched to ensure no hunting occurred.[41] Although the disagreement caused no major delay, its substance reminds us of the profound importance for officials of maintaining a boundary between the Nakoda and the park, of blocking or suppressing the indigenous presence, and of denying any Nakoda claim of connection or rightful access.

The close attention of parks officials to the clearing process presaged their level of involvement in the final stages of the dam construction. Clearing stumps had fixed one problem; hiding a dam would be more difficult. Rather than leave matters simply to Calgary Power, the parks branch engaged Stanley Thompson, a landscape architect based in Toronto, whose consulting firm specialized in golf course designs.[42] Thompson had earlier overseen the redesign of the Banff golf course, near the Banff Springs Hotel, as well as the course at Jasper. His experience and understanding of the parks context suggested that he would be ideal for the position. Calgary Power hired their own outside consultant, the chief engineer of Ontario Hydro, Thomas Hogg, to ensure that aesthetic demands did not unduly increase project costs.[43] Thompson visited Banff in the early stages of the construction process, took in the site, and returned to Toronto to draft a report recommending a series of landscape features that might soften the dam in the tourist gaze. His forty-five-page report, complete with architectural drawings, emphasized two basic points: that the infrastructure must be covered as much as possible with vegetation, or with locally sourced materials such as wood or stone, and that the scene must be imagined from the perspective of the automobile tourist and shaped to direct views toward the scenic beauty and away from the dam and canals.[44] Although the costs involved caused consternation for the power company, parks officials welcomed his suggestions and sought to implement them closely.

As the design called for a road to cross the dam, Thompson paid considerable attention to the problem of greening the dam and directing the point of view of tourists toward the lake. As a man whose medium of choice was grass, it is not surprising that Thompson's primary suggestion to hide the dam

Figure 9.3 Stanley Thompson's "suggested treatment road along top of dam looking northwest." *Source:* Stanley Thompson, "Report on Features Affecting Landscape at Lake Minnewanka and Cascade River, Banff National Park," February 1941, vol. 501, file B39-5, Library and Archives Canada, RG84.

involved vegetation. On the dam face, he proposed a covering layer of top soil and the generous planting of native plants and shrubs. Near the dam's crest, he called for a series of low shrubs and native trees to be planted in an irregular fashion to block the view over the barren sections of the dam's face. Figure 9.3 reveals Thompson's plan to give the road over the dam a curving bridge effect, with the lake drawing the viewer away from the dam face. On the lake side, rip rap would be used to cover the larger boulders, which might be exposed during draw downs. Any exposed reinforced concrete would need to be covered, he suggested, in a roughly cut rock, placed in an asymmetrical pattern. In this way, Thompson's design de-emphasized the straight lines, exposed surfaces, and industrial materials of the dam and imposed a facade of carefully chosen natural materials to suggest a rough-hewn landscape of

Figure 9.4 Stanley Thompson's "suggested type lookout areas west end of lake." *Source:* Stanley Thompson, "Report on Features Affecting Landscape at Lake Minnewanka and Cascade River, Banff National Park," February 1941, vol. 501, file B39-5, Library and Archives Canada, RG84.

forest and meadow opening onto a vast lake scene. At either end of the dam, Thompson inserted generous parking spaces to capitalize on the best viewpoints over the lake. Figure 9.4 reveals the centrality of automobiles and parking spaces to Thompson's understanding of the lake as a tourism site.

Thompson also took seriously the new road that would be built in conjunction with the dam in a wide loop, connecting the Banff townsite and the lake and running along the power canal south and east toward the penstocks and power generators. Chiefly, he worried about what the motorists would see. Because the infrastructure ought to be hidden, he reasoned, the loop road should be set back from the canal as much as possible, depending on the grade, and intercepted by a wide band of forest. He also advised erecting symbolic stone cairns on the road to greet visitors and mark their entry to the lake.

Figure 9.5 Stanley Thompson's "suggested treatment of power house." *Source:* Stanley Thompson, "Report on Features Affecting Landscape at Lake Minnewanka and Cascade River, Banff National Park," February 1941, vol. 501, file B39-5, Library and Archives Canada, RG84.

The massive infrastructure of penstocks, a surge tank, and a power generator (to be placed on the side of the road entering Banff from the east) posed some greater challenges. Figure 9.5, showing the design for the powerhouse, suggests Thompson's best effort to break up smooth surfaces with irregularly mounted rundle rock, to blur the sharp definition between the structure and its surrounding with a cluster of trees, and to limit the building's angularity with curving corners and a rounded roof. The surge tank presented a bigger problem, as it was a sharp, vertical structure to be placed on a high ridge above the power house in plain view of the road to Banff. Thompson proposed moving it to a nearby depression: "This will help to conceal it with a minimum of planting."[45] His aesthetic criteria, however, did not take into account the engineering rationale for placing the surge tank at a high point to take advantage of the resulting gravity. He left the matter open for further consideration but thought that the tank should probably be painted in some fashion.

The landscaping of the Minnewanka project threatened to become a farce in the following months as parks officials doggedly pursued what might be the right colour to paint the surge tank. On a recommendation from Mines and Resources officials in Ottawa who had heard of the visit of a Royal Air Force expert on camouflage paints, a Mr. C. Ironside, they took it on themselves to request his advice about how best to hide the surge tank, towering on a hillside, with paint. With a number of photographs of the site before him, Ironside offered his views, which were reported to staff in Banff by R.M. Gibson, director of the Parks Bureau. Given the surrounding context, he argued that a green paint used on the bottom side of military aircraft might work, or would, at any rate, be better than a grey shade – used with poor effect, he judged, on many water towers in England. His preference, however, was somewhat surprising. "From the artist's point of view the structure should be painted a [matte] white, which would make it more artistic: by using white the object does not become inconspicuous but is more pleasant to look at."[46] Just what the Banff parks officials made of this advice is unknown, but the surge tank duly received a coat of grey, not white, paint. Ironside's vision did not take into account the primary aim of erasing the surge tank's visual presence.

All of the attention given to paint shades, to plantings, and to Thompson's irregular rock and road rails suggested the close adherence of the design to interwar American ideals respecting the construction of naturalistic parks and rustic buildings. Although there is no record that directly suggests the design influences on Thompson's work or that points to the level of collaboration with parks officials, his choices mimicked and reassembled design perspectives outlined in Albert Good's three-volume *Park Structures and Facilities* (1938), which quickly became a canonical text in American park design and influenced Canadian parks planning and architecture as well. Good's advice to subordinate "structure to environment" might have served as the leitmotif of the Lake Minnewanka project.[47] The strong current of nostalgia that informed both this naturalistic program and the designs for rustic buildings that sought to capture pioneer styles by using local materials reveals the extent to which the hiding of Lake Minnewanka's dam aimed to produce a landscape of memory befitting a national park in the North American style.

Unfortunately for parks officials, no amount of landscaping could cover the operational downsides of the dam. As early as 1942, they complained that Calgary Power did not honour its early commitment to maintain spring and summer water levels, which led to exposed mud flats and stumps. For all of Thompson's efforts to promote lake views, the mud flats made for poor scenery. Selby Walker had seen this problem coming well before construction began. In one of his letters of protest, published in the *Calgary Herald*, he asked, "Why in the name of common sense should Lake Minnewanka be ringed with an unsightly mud girdle ... which will smell and the smell will be very different from the pleasant odor of the pines?"[48] Correspondence sailed back and forth between the Parks Bureau and Calgary Power, but power considerations consistently overrode aesthetic concerns.[49] In 1944, owing to power shortages in southern Alberta, the federal power controller explained that power for ammonium nitrate production far outweighed "any possible offence to the eye of any tourists who may go there."[50] It was not until after the war, when in 1947 Calgary Power sought to renew its interim licence, that the company agreed to a different monitoring process under the authority of the minister in which a sliding rate would be paid depending on the water level.[51]

Lake Minnewanka was transformed into a modern power reservoir during the Second World War, and reluctant parks officials sought to limit the collateral damage on the tourist experience of the lake by hiding the dam and beautifying its infrastructure as much as possible. Their actions were justified as a defence of scenic values against industrialism and of the protection of public over private interests. The particular construction of nature that resulted from this process, however, bore the markings of a "windshield wilderness," to borrow David Louter's evocative phrase.[52] The scenery was not preserved in and of itself but rather to be consumed by a modern automobile-based tourism trade. All of Stanley Thompson's landscape drawings assumed the primacy of the automobile public and the view from the driver's seat. As a result, aspects of the previous tourism landscape were unimportant to save in the dam-raising. The town at Lake Minnewanka could be lost without much effect, or notice, and former roads could be rebuilt and improved. Some parks practices revealed themselves in new forms, however, as when the Nakoda came under scrutiny for camping in the park even as they worked on the dam. The reconstruction of the site imposed a new landscape of memory while deleting the recent past of Minnewanka Landing and continuing to deny a deeper past of Nakoda presence.

Whether viewed as a power reservoir or tourism site, the management and use of Lake Minnewanka continue to rewrite the memory of this place and to subvert the landscape scripted for the post-war economy and automobile tourist. Although Lake Minnewanka remains a functioning element in the hydrological system now run by TransAlta utilities, it operates only on an occasional basis as a power generator. Much of the southern Alberta system currently depends on coal-based thermal power. The dam's future may depend on its presumed value in the new era of climate change in which hydro power is frequently cast as a green, carbon-neutral energy source.

As a tourism site, Lake Minnewanka remains a popular stop in the Banff circuit. Uses of the lake have changed over time, and understandings of the lake's past have, too. In the late 1960s parks officials erected a plaque to explain how the lake represented a compromise with nature, whereas more recent signage seeks to signal a long-standing indigenous presence and bears witness to the lost town of Minnewanka Landing. No attempt is made to explain the process by which a Nakoda place became a tourism resort, and the dam's origin in the war is simply noted as fact. These signs therefore prompt certain ways of seeing the lake that provide yet another layer of contested and partial meaning to the bricolage that Lake Minnewanka has become.

Beyond the signs and beneath the lake's surface, the collection of objects that scuba divers have placed on the lakebed presents a different response and perspective on changes to the lake. The addition of things, the range of household and exotic objects, suggests that place, memory, and nature are playfully understood as conditions both valuable and malleable, forgotten and rediscovered. All the objects are brought together in a postmodern land-scape of colliding forms, different period markers, and plastic pink flamingoes.

ACKNOWLEDGMENTS

I first learned of the Minnewanka Dam several years ago from Christopher Armstrong, who had written a lengthy chapter on the dispute over the lake during the war for an unpublished manuscript entitled "Wilderness and Waterpower" based on research that grew out of an earlier collaboration with H.V. Nelles on the history of public utilities in Canada. His work informed my own understanding of the politics of Lake Minnewanka and introduced me to the comic episode with the surge tank, recounted here. I owe a debt to Chris for sharing his unpublished work and some research notes as well as for commenting on a draft. Further research at Library and Archives Canada and the Whyte Museum and Archives as well as a visit to the lake were supported by grants from the Social Sciences and Humanities Research Council of Canada. Thanks to Kirsty Johnston and Maggie Skye Evenden for accompanying me to the lake and to Kirsty for commenting on a draft of the paper. My student Emma Norman pursued the problem of the dating of the "compromise with nature" plaque with the Banff parks staff, for which she has my thanks, as do the researchers at the park who shared their time and expertise, especially Marjorie Huculak, Stakeholder Relations, Banff Field Unit, Parks Canada Agency. Thanks also to members of the 2008 Placing Memory and Remembering Place Workshop, especially John Walsh and James Opp, for their constructive comments.

NOTES

1   The dating of the plaque is somewhat approximate. No record seems to exist of when it was created. The late 1960s or early 1970s is the best guess provided by research staff at Banff National Park. Emma Norman, personal communication with author, 8 July 2008.

2   Quoted from the highly amusing description of this scuba diving site by Charles Moore, "Underwater Archeology," http://www.saveontarioshipwrecks.on.ca/News/newsletter_moore.html.

3   Julie Cruikshank, *Do Glaciers Listen?: Local Knowledge, Colonial Encounters, and Social Imagination* (Vancouver: UBC Press, 2005), 11.

4   On the connections between automobiles, tourism, and parks, see David Louter, *Windshield Wilderness: Cars, Roads and Nature in Washington's National Parks* (Seattle: University of Washington Press, 2006); and in the Canadian context, Alan MacEachern, *Natural Selections: National Parks in Atlantic Canada, 1935-1970* (Montreal and Kingston: McGill-Queen's University Press, 2001).

5   See, for example, Karen Till's exploration of the geographical literature on place and memory, which treats memory as *national* memory, in her "Places of Memory," in *A*

   Companion to Political Geography, ed. John Agnew, Katharyne Mitchell, and Gerard Toal (Oxford: Blackwell, 2003), 289-301.

6   Doreen Massey, "Places and Their Pasts," *History Workshop Journal* 39 (1995): 182-92.

7   Laura Cameron, *Openings: A Meditation on History, Method and Sumas Lake* (Montreal and Kingston: McGill-Queen's University Press, 1997); Massey, "Places and Their Pasts."

8   On the early development of Lake Minnewanka as a tourist destination, I have relied in part on R.W. Sandford's beautifully illustrated book *Lake Minnewanka: The Spirit and the Waters* (Banff: Lake Minnewanka Boat Tours, 1999), as well as on E.J. Hart, *The Place of Bows* (Banff: EJH Literary Enterprises, 1999).

9   The name was changed to Lake Minnewanka in 1888. See Aphrodite Karamitsamis, *Place Names of Alberta,* vol. 1, *Mountains, Mountain Parks and Foothills* (Calgary: Alberta Culture and Multiculturalism and University of Calgary Press, 1991), 166.

10   Theodore Binnema and Melanie Niemi, "'Let the Line Be Drawn': Wilderness, Conservation, and the Exclusion of Aboriginal People from Banff National Park," *Environmental History* 11, 4 (2006): 724-50.

11   Ibid.

12   Guest Book Lake Minnewanka Hotel, 24 June 1890 to 14 October 1906, Whyte Museum and Archives (WMA), M265/V394, accn. 2961; Beach House Register, 1887-92, Lake Minnewanka, Rodney Touche Papers, M377, WMA.

13   Christopher Armstrong and H.V. Nelles, "The Influence of Automobile Tourism on Banff National Park," draft paper (2008), 3-4; and Amy Larin, "A Rough Ride: Automobiles in Banff National Park, 1905-1918," *Alberta History* 56, 1 (2008): 2-9.

14   Sandford, *Lake Minnewanka,* 31.

15   Ibid.

16   Pearlann Reichwein, "'Hands off Our National Parks': The Alpine Club of Canada and Hydro-Development Controversies in the Canadian Rockies, 1922-1930," *Journal of the CHA/Revue de la SHC,* n.s., 6 (1995): 129-55.

17   The National Parks Act, *Statutes of Canada,* 20-21, George V, ch. 33, assented to 30 May 1930, in *Documenting Canada: A History in Modern Documents,* ed. Dave De Brou and Bill Waiser (Saskatoon: Fifth House, 1992), 299.

18   Ibid., editors' commentary, 299.

19   Robert Bothwell and William Kilbourn, *C.D. Howe* (Toronto: McClelland and Stewart, 1979); J. de N. Kennedy, *History of the Department of Munitions and Supply* (Ottawa: King's Printer, 1950); Robert Bothwell, "'Who's Paying for Anything These Days?' War Production in Canada, 1939-1945," in *Mobilization for Total War: The Canadian, American and British Experience, 1914-1918, 1939-1945,* ed. N.F. Dreisziger (Waterloo, ON: Wilfred Laurier University Press, 1981), 59-69.

20   "Power at present available for Calgary District, Alberta, from Calgary Power's own facilities and through interchange agreements and interconnections," 20 November 1940, stamped Director, Surveys and Engineering. Library and Archives Canada (LAC), RG84, vol. 502, file B39-5. The plant's anticipated power demand was outlined in Gaherty to Gibson, 10 October 1940, LAC, RG84, vol. 502, file B39-5.

21 C.M. Walker to T.S. Mills, 9 September and 30 September 1940; and J.M. Wardle to Gibson, 1940 report discussions with Gaherty, President of Calgary Power, both in LAC, RG84, vol. 502, file B39-5.

22 Calgary Power Application for licence, 14 November 1940, LAC, RG84, vol. 502, file B39-5.

23 Power Control, 24 May 1943, Votes and Proceedings #65, page 1, Subject: Power Controller, LAC, RG28, vol. 54, file 1-1-98; "Symington, Herbert James," in *The Canadian Who's Who*, vol. 2, ed. Sir Charles G.D Roberts and Arthur Leonard Tunnell (Toronto: Murray Printing, 1937), 1048; "H.J. Symington Early Chief of TCA Held Key War Posts," *Globe and Mail,* 29 September 1965.

24 See, for example, Director to Deputy Minister, 21 November 1940; Gibson to Camsell, Deputy Minister, 20 November 1940; and Gibson to Smart, 14 November 1940, all in LAC, RG84, vol. 502, file B39-5. A fuller discussion of the politics of this episode may be found in Christopher Armstrong, Matthew Evenden, and H.V. Nelles, *The River Returns: An Environmental History of the Bow* (Montreal and Kingston: McGill-Queen's University Press, 2009), 136-42.

25 Mackenzie King Diaries, entry for 15 November 1940, LAC, MG26-J13, available at http://www.collectionscanada.gc.ca/king/index-e.html.

26 P.C. 7382, 13 December 1940, LAC, RG84, vol. 502, file B39-5.

27 Jennings to Smart, 2 December 1940, reporting the views of workers in Banff; J.M. Millar, City Clerk, Calgary, to Prime Minister Mackenzie King, 10 December 1940; and Secretary of Banff Advisory Council to Andrew Davison, Mayor, City of Calgary, 27 November 1940, all in LAC, RG84, vol. 502, file B39-5.

28 Walker to Smart, 1 October 1940; and Crerar, Minister of Mines and Resources, to C.D. Howe, Minister of Munitions and Supply, 13 November 1940, both in LAC, RG84, vol. 502, file B39-5.

29 R.A. Rooney, Alberta Fish and Game Association, to Gibson, 22 November 1940; and House of Commons *Debates,* 4 June 1941, Mr. Harris, MP for Danforth, reporting on letters of protest received from Canadian members of the National Geographic Society, both in LAC, RG84, vol. 502, file B39-5.

30 Aberhart to Crerar, 5 December 1940, LAC, RG84, vol. 502, file B39-5.

31 P.J. Jennings to F.H.H. Williamson, 30 September 1940; Smart to Gibson, 1 October 1940; and Jennings to Williamson, 30 September 1940, all in LAC, RG84, vol. 501, file B39-5.

32 Bill 60 to Amend the Alberta Natural Resources Transfer Act, as Passed by the House of Commons, 4 June 1941, Second Session, Nineteenth Parliament, 4-5, George VI, 1940-41, LAC, RG84, vol. 502, file B39-5.

33 Crerar Press Release, 17 December 1940, LAC, RG84, vol. 502, file B39-5.

34 Canada, Department of Mines and Resources, "Interim License for Storage and Water Development at Lake Minnewanka and Cascade River, Banff National Park," 13 December 1940, LAC, RG84, vol. 502, file B39-5.

35 A.S. Mather, Manager, Bow River Boat House Ltd., Banff, to Superintendent, Banff, 4 January 1941; and Jennings to Mather, 4 January 1941, both in LAC, RG84, vol. 502, file B39-5.

36 Although this outcome contrasts with notable post-war examples of dam development and displacement, such as on the Nechako River and the Arrow Lakes, it is well to remember the different scale and consequences. On the Arrow Lakes, for example, 25,000 arable acres were lost, and fourteen lakeshore communities encompassing 2,000 people were displaced. See Tina Loo, "People in the Way: Modernity, Environment, and Society on the Arrow Lakes," *BC Studies* 142-43 (Autumn 2004): 161-96, and Joy Parr, *Sensing Changes: Technologies, Environments, and the Everyday, 1953-2003* (Vancouver: UBC Press, 2009), 103-35.

37 "New Scenic Road to Minnewanka When Dam Built," *Calgary Herald,* 3 May 1941, LAC, RG84, vol. 502, file B39-5.

38 Holman, District Forest Officer, "Report of Cruise and Estimate of Timber Involved in Raising Level of Lake Minnewanka," Banff National Park, March 1941, LAC, RG84, vol. 502, file B39-5.

39 Childs for P.J. Jennings, Superintendent to F.H.H. Williamson, Control, National Parks Bureau, 21 February 1941, LAC, RG84, vol. 503, file B39-5.

40 C.M. Walker Memo to J.M Wardle, Director of Surveys and Engineering Branch, 21 February 1941, LAC, RG84, vol. 503, file B39-5.

41 J.N.R. Iredale, Acting Indian Agent, Morley, to Harold McGill, Director, Indian Affairs, 26 February 1941; Iredale to C.P. Schmidt, Inspector of Indian Agencies, 26 February 1941; and Gibson to Wardle, 22 February 1941, quoting letter from MP Edwards, all in LAC, RG84, vol. 503, file B39-5.

42 Letter [signature illegible] to Gibson, 19 December 1940; and "List of Operations of Mr. Stanley Thompson," n.d., both in LAC, RG84, vol. 502, file B39-5.

43 Gibson to Smart, 7 December 1940; and Gaherty, President of Calgary Power, to Camsell, 2 January 1941, both in LAC, RG84, vol. 502, file B39-5.

44 Stanley Thompson, "Report on Features Affecting Landscape at Lake Minnewanka and Cascade River, Banff National Park," February 1941, LAC, RG84, vol. 501, file B39-5.

45 Ibid.

46 Gibson to Wardle, 4 May 1942, LAC, RG84, vol. 504, file B39-5.

47 Albert Good quoted in Linda Flint McClelland, *Building the National Parks: Historic Landscape Design and Construction* (Baltimore, MD: Johns Hopkins University Press, 1998), 433.

48 W.J.S. Walker, Executive Secretary, Canadian National Parks Association, Letter to Editor, *Calgary Herald,* 5 September 1940, LAC, RG84, vol. 502, file B39-5.

49 Wardle, Director of Surveys and Engineering Branch, to Deputy Minister, 2 May 1944; Camsell to Symington, 28 April 1944; and Gaherty, President of Calgary Power, to Wardle, 24 April 1944, all in LAC, RG84, vol. 501, file B39-5.

50 Herbert Symington to Charles Camsell, Deputy Minister, Mines and Resources, 29 April 1944, LAC, RG84, vol. 501, file B39-5.

51 Memo from Smart to Gibson, 21 August 1946; and Memo from the National Parks Bureau to Smart, 9 September 1946, both in LAC, RG84, vol. 504, file B39-5.

52 David Louter, *Windshield Wilderness: Cars, Roads, and Nature in Washington's National Parks* (Seattle: University of Washington Press, 2006).

Finding the View
Landscape, Place, and Colour Slide Photography in Southern Alberta

JAMES OPP

An old colour slide from 1970 documents a family visit to Writing-on-Stone Provincial Park (Figure 10.1), located near the Alberta-Montana border. The image offers a wide view of the unique sandstone rock formations, which on closer inspection are marked with centuries-old petroglyphs and pictographs. The photograph was carefully framed by the photographer, my father, who purposely layered the foregrounded hoodoos in front of the meandering river of the middle ground and the low hills behind. As a result, the image offers a sense of depth and expansiveness that simultaneously speaks to a prairie aesthetic of open space and to a longer tradition of landscape paintings and photographs, which dictate the "correct" way to picture such scenes.

It might be easy to dismiss such photographs as straightforward visual appropriations of place, touristic views destined for the occasional (and occasionally dreaded) home slide show. But the context for producing this image of Writing-on-Stone offers a more complex reading. My parents, Don and Frankie Opp, did not simply visit the park on vacation but rather were participating in a photographic outing with around twenty other shutterbugs from the Chinook Camera Club (CCC).[1] Over its venerable fifty-year history, the club, based in the small town of Claresholm, Alberta, produced a steady stream of photographs that "pictured place."[2] Through regular summer outings, usually day trips to areas surrounding Claresholm in the foothills of southern Alberta, members of the club rendered a remarkable visual catalogue that both shaped and appealed to a collective "sense of place."

Founded in 1957 as a local chapter of the Color Photographic Association of Canada, the club was established to help members improve their photographic skills at a time when colour slide photography required a high level of technical expertise. Membership grew from nine original members to a robust thirty-four when my parents joined in the fall of 1966. From the late-1960s and through the next three decades, the CCC occupied a strategic place within the community as the dominant supplier and arbiter of photographic scenes. It routinely organized photographic competitions at the local fair, occasionally offered continuing-education courses on photography, and arranged numerous slide shows for viewing at local events and service-club meetings. Through the 1960s and 1970s, the Chamber of Commerce, the Town of Claresholm, and even the provincial tourist bureau for southern Alberta submitted requests to the CCC for images to serve as publicity and advertising.[3] As visual ambassadors for their community, the CCC's members also participated in multiple exchanges of slide shows (often including taped commentary or music) with other amateur photography clubs, some as far away as Australia and New Zealand.

When the CCC visited Writing-on-Stone in 1970, my father had just completed two years as its president, my mother had served as its secretary, and I was along for the ride at only a few months old.[4] It was the first of countless similar outings throughout my childhood and early adolescence, which involved not only taking photographs in the field but also endless meetings with other club members to judge slides, sort slides into shows, and learn what makes a picture "good" or "beautiful."

In reflecting on the intricate relationship between memory and place, I am drawn back to these camera club excursions of my childhood in part because in my parents' vast archive, "place" emerges as paradoxically both purposeful and accidental. If the aesthetic and artistic demands of colour slide photography drove camera clubs to stress the "universal" aspects of their images, they could not avoid reasserting the local in their work.[5] In Figure 10.1 the scene is composed around traditional landscape elements, yet the

Figure 10.1   Untitled, Writing-on-Stone Provincial Park,
Alberta, 4 October 1970. Photograph by Don Opp.

Figure 10.2 *Road to the Mountains*, August 1988. Photograph by Frankie Opp.

distinctiveness of the rock formations "place" it for those who know and experience the local topography. But if there is tension between the ideal landscape and the depictions of local place, where then lies the memories and histories of place that this volume seeks to address and uncover? Certainly at times elements of "nostalgia" were framed within the picture, but in situating these spatial representations, it is important to consider the wider social practices associated with colour slide photography. Through a close reading of selected slides from my parents' archive, I trace the manifold possibilities of memory that enwrap depictions of place. Despite the aesthetic demands of landscape and nature photography to produce pictures that are supposedly "timeless," it is the very bindings of images to temporal dimensions that bestow meaning. In their broad orientation, amateur camera clubs often sought to produce images that were essentially without or outside of place and time, but rather than accept this premise, I want to interrogate and invert it.[6] The multiple inscriptions of memory, although not always visible within the frame, are the sinews that link the pictured place to the picture itself. The thousands of slides that fill dozens of boxes in my parents' basement offer many representations of place, but they are also material artefacts of a wider social practice of envisioning, evaluating, displaying, narrating, and circulating.[7] Through these acts, memory and place emerge as deeply interdependent aspects of even the prettiest of pictures.

LOOKING EAST, LOOKING WEST

Claresholm's local-history book, first published in 1974, is entitled *Where the Wheatlands Meet the Range*, and the label offers an unofficial motto for the town and surrounding community.[8] Located on Highway No. 2 between Calgary and Fort Macleod, the road (and the railway before it) symbolically divides the wider rural area between farmers and ranchers, prairies and foothills. Although my parents farmed eight kilometres east of the town, their cameras and the outings of the camera club more often pointed west. Driving toward the mountains seemed to offer more creative possibilities for picture-taking, whether focusing on flowers, fauna, or landscape scenes. Large stretches of Crown land, forestry roads, and the nearby presence of Waterton Lakes National Park also encouraged this westward pull, in contrast to the surrounding prairie, which was, with a few exceptions, almost entirely held in private hands.

Although highways were usually hidden from view in my parents' photographs, occasionally more "rustic" routes could serve as distinguishing features of the landscape. In my mother's photograph *Road to the Mountains* (Figure 10.2), the strong vertical lines of the gravel road that allowed access to the "back country" abruptly intersect the blue mountains and sky. Such pictures, even without actually portraying the town of Claresholm or any notable local features, nevertheless spoke to the community's own identity and "place-ness," imagining itself to be of two worlds, literally where "wheatlands," marked by square-mile grids of 640 acres, met the "range." The illusion of proximity between these two spaces is achieved through the use of a long telephoto lens, flattening the perceived distance between the rolling hills and dramatic mountains.

Road to the Mountains proved to be one of my mother's more popular pictures, and copies of it were sold locally. However, the picture was not taken near Claresholm, or even within the surrounding Municipal District of Willow Creek. It was instead captured on a late-summer daytrip along a road north of Cowley, a small town almost 100 kilometres west and south from Claresholm. But such images still felt "local" in nature, expressing a deep "sense of place."[9] The same could not be said for travelling eastward, even for distances of half that length. Camera club members rarely organized outings that travelled this direction.[10] When the CCC hosted other photography clubs who belonged to the group Prairie Regional Photographic Arts in 1968, 1974, and 1980, the tours they organized for these occasions all led westward from town.[11] Claresholm itself sits on flat prairie, a town that owes its very birth, layout, and location to the economics of the Calgary and Edmonton Railway Company (later purchased by the Canadian Pacific Railway). And yet, pictorially, the local is firmly centred on the foothills.[12]

The prairie view is not absent in my parents' archive; wheatfields, scenes of rustic homestead buildings, trees covered with hoar frost, and dramatic skies are plentiful. Many of the "prairie" pictures, however, are connected directly to our family farm, which was established in 1905 by my mother's paternal grandfather. Bathed in the warm autumn light of dusk, *Harvest Time* (Figure 10.3) shows my grandfather driving a tractor with a pull-type combine harvester in 1975. The image would have likely remained a personal memento of our own family history if not for circumstances that transformed its circulation. The CCC had a long-standing agreement with the Claresholm Rotary Club to

Figure 10.3 *Harvest Time*, 1975. Photograph by Frankie Opp.

Figure 10.4 *Honey Coulee*, November 1980.
Photograph by Frankie Opp.

supply them with a yearly image to illustrate their annual "birthday calendar." Chosen through a special competition each year, *Harvest Time* was a featured calendar picture, transforming the personal into a symbol of locality.

Although technically *Harvest Time* might have been representative of any rural location on the Prairies, the physical proximity of our farm to the town signalled its acceptability as representative of the local. Such allowance would not have been granted for modern agricultural scenes from further afield. Five years later, Frankie Opp produced another calendar picture, *Honey Coulee* (Figure 10.4). Reiterating a familiar westward view, no one questioned the suitability of using this foothills landscape (with its location named in the title), located fifty kilometres west of town, as a visual signifier for the "imagined geography" of the local community.

In broad terms, looking "east," or close to town, represented economic progress, modernity, and more obviously peopled places. Looking "west" covered a wider geographical sweep, in part because images could be framed more clearly as representations of unpeopled, unchanging "wilderness."[13] Perhaps more accurately, the western foothills offered a "middle landscape" between city and wilderness that resembled "nature" more than the agrarian views of the east side of the highway, even though both areas were the sites of agricultural production.[14] When cows, fences, barns, or ranchers emerge in scenes from the west, they are usually framed in terms of western, cowboy nostalgia rather than pictured as features of a "modern" rural commercial enterprise. Being "where the wheatlands meet the range" offered an imaginative geography that grounded prairie soils in time, marked by the modern methods that tilled the land, and liberated the foothills as timeless in orientation or, if temporally bound, then it was to the previous century rather than the present one.

VIEWFINDERS AND FINDING VIEWS

Growing up with two photographers for parents, my brother and I found ourselves on countless trips to the foothills, sometimes as part of an organized camera club outing and sometimes just for a Sunday drive, which always involved picture-taking. Over time, I too learned to "see" like a photographer, at first by tracking down rare flowers in the forest for my parents and later by taking pictures on my own. Single-lens-reflex (SLR) cameras enabled the photographer to use a viewfinder to see directly through the lens, allowing the eye to carefully frame the scene to be captured on film. This act of seeing through the camera was important because unlike prints from black and white negative film, which could be adjusted within certain limits after the fact (size, tone, use of different papers, enhancing or reducing contrast through filters), colour slides do not allow for such alterations. Producing positive transparencies that project directly onto a large screen, slide photography offers no escape from incorrect exposures, fuzzy pictures, or crooked horizons. Film speed, shutter speed, and aperture settings had to be carefully calculated manually; light meters and tripods were essential tools for any serious amateur photographer. However, these technical aspects were only part of the photographic process. Using a viewfinder literally required that the photographer find the view, "composing" the scene artistically at the very moment that the picture was taken.

While the summer months were used to explore local spaces through organized and informal outings, over the rest of the year camera club members spent just as much, if not more, time judging and evaluating pictures as taking them. Every monthly meeting offered an opportunity for Roll Call, when members were asked to submit one image for judging. Every three months, a competition for the Tupper Cup was held, focusing on a pre-selected theme. The judging of pictures for both competitions was broken down into three categories, each worth five points: subject interest, composition, and technical quality. One detailed explanation of the judging system produced in the late 1960s explained that the picture's composition should be "in balance," with not too much sky or too much foreground. Photographers were advised that the "horizon should cut the picture in a one-third or two-third portion – never one-half," and that there should never be an even number of flowers pictured. Roads could be included in the image if they "lead into the picture," but "telephone and telegraph wires in pictures are taboo!" The category of "subject interest" was judged according to such criteria as "impact," whether or not one's "eye stays in the picture," and notably, the admonition that "each picture should tell one story."[15]

My father's photograph from the early 1970s titled *The Corner Post* (Figure 10.5) offers a sense of how judging criteria and the aesthetics of colour slide photography shaped the views of what was and was not captured on film. The close study of a log fence west of Claresholm epitomizes the criteria of

Figure 10.5 *The Corner Post*, c. 1973. Photograph by Don Opp.

Figure 10.6 *Autumn Leaves,* 1975. Photograph by Don Opp.

"balance," the weight of the strong vertical corner post offset by the horizontal logs that lead away from it. The foregrounded fence does not overwhelm the picture, being held in check by the thick foliage that surrounds it. The strong converging lines lead the eye to the centre of the picture. *The Corner Post* tied for first place at a Roll Call competition in 1973, accumulating a total of twelve points out of a possible fifteen.[16]

The weathered log fence of *The Corner Post* serves as more than simply a play of intersecting lines, although these angles were carefully considered. It also stands as a marker of history, of human activity and land use in the midst of "nature." The temporal roles here are practically reversed, as the log fence appears frozen in time, while the changing season is marked by the fall colours. The fence, although quite possibly still in use judging by the relatively new barbed wire that enwraps the post, speaks to a wider settler narrative of "old stock" families and their place on the range.[17]

Such evocations of a "sense of place" are also abstractions of place. Unlike *Honey Coulee*, the generic title given to *The Corner Post* dislocates the scene from its actual surroundings and environment. As much as the camera club situated itself within the community, its aspirations extended far beyond the local, and the aesthetics it pursued were deemed to be "universal." Members not only competed within the club but also submitted photographs for judging in regional and national competitions. In this wider context, place mattered far less than the formal elements of composition.

If *The Corner Post* spoke to a local sense of place through its depiction of an identifiable and familiar feature of the foothills, many other images spoke to a "purer" sense of nature that seemed both placeless and timeless. *Autumn Leaves* (Figure 10.6) was taken in the fall of 1975 and was awarded the Tupper Cup in June 1976. It reflects the dominant shift in the camera club's focus toward nature photography and scenic landscapes as the "serious" work of competitive amateurs. Although portraits and pictures with human subjects were still submitted for judging, it is clear from the minutes that by the mid-1970s, photographs of birds, animals, flowers, and "natural" landscapes and scenes dominated the top results. Nature photography in general seemed to be on the rise, popularized in Canada by photographers such as Freeman Patterson and Courtney Milne.[18] Over the years, my parents attended various seminars led by both photographers and owned copies of their books. Serious amateurs soon discovered that within this field, their work compared favourably with that of professionals, and many club members competed in regional and national competitions with impressive results.[19]

Such presentations of "nature" evoked the sublime. As William Cronon notes, the use of spiritual language to describe wilderness also reflects a temporal dimension, allowing us to "escape from history" and to "make a new cathedral not in some pretty human building but in God's own creation, Nature itself."[20] There was little question that religious values were viewed as intrinsic to the viewing of such scenes as *Autumn Leaves*. Indeed, in 1974 the CCC designed a collective show, using two slide projectors with a makeshift dissolve unit, entitled *A Sense of Wonder*. The show was matched with music and a commentary that drew on a book of verse owned by my parents entitled *God So Loved the World: Reflections on the Beauty of God's Creation*, which included colour photographs matched with quotations from Genesis through to Wordsworth and Rachel Carson.[21] Displayed at a number of events and places, the collective compilation was also entered into the regional competition that pitted clubs against each other for "showmanship." The project echoed the earlier work of Eliot Porter, whose colour photographs had been paired with the writings of Thoreau in the book *In Wildness Is the Preservation of the World*, published by the Sierra Club in 1962.[22] A similar show, although with less overt religious overtones, was *A Summer Stroll*, which took first place in the regional showmanship competition in 1976.[23]

Curiously, William Cronon makes the claim:

> The dream of an unworked natural landscape is very much the fantasy of people who have never themselves had to work the land to make a living – urban folk for whom food comes from a supermarket or a restaurant instead of a field ... Only people whose relation to the land was already alienated could hold up wilderness as a model for human life in nature, for the romantic ideology of wilderness leaves precisely nowhere for human beings actually to make their living from the land.[24]

What then, are we to make of the romantic and wilderness sublime presented in the colour slides of my parents? Is their presentation of nature and wilderness different because of their own relationship to the land, both as farmers and local inhabitants, or are they simply following "urban" or metropolitan artistic influences in adopting a particular aesthetics of wilderness?

Perhaps we should rethink the meaning and value of the pursuit of nature for those who live in and near such spaces. Why wouldn't local inhabitants express their own forms of "topophilia," which Yi-Fu Tuan defines broadly as "all of the human being's affective ties with the material environment," or, in short, "the human love of place"?[25] The adoption of a particular aesthetics of composition may have been directed by wider artistic influences, but for local photographers, their labours certainly offered a "human love of place," even if the overarching visual narrative directed attention away from the photographic construction and onto a divine transcendence. Indeed, hidden in the aesthetics of visual representation is the intimate knowledge of place accrued over years of picture-taking in the foothills in all seasons. Such scenes as *Autumn Leaves* and *The Corner Post* were marked by histories of view-finding, years of repeated photographic outings to the foothills; their very creation was, in part, premised on a local knowledge of the landscape, even if the compositional techniques framed the scene for a wider audience. Amateur photographers did not forsake their own economic relationship to the land in presenting local spaces as "wilderness" but rather sought to deepen it.

RAINBOW'S END

In 1974 a camera club outing to the foothills was cut short by a summer storm. On the drive back toward town, members of the club were treated to a dramatic scene of a rainbow splashed across the dark sky, above a series of grain elevators at Pultney, a few miles north of Claresholm. If the conditions for taking the picture, later entitled *Rainbow's End* (Figure 10.7), were fortuitous, the composition was hardly accidental. My father drove miles (in the opposite direction from our home) in order to produce the exact angle that would place the rainbow directly above the Alberta Wheat Pool elevator on the far left side.

In January 1975 the Tupper Cup competition theme was "Picture of a Song Title, with music." The entry from Don Opp, *Somewhere over the Rainbow* (almost certainly a re-titling of *Rainbow's End*), scored second place with a total of twelve and three-quarter points out of a possible fifteen, a bare quarter point behind the first-place winner. Although the club's records show only the results and point totals of those pictures that ranked in the top three of any competition, at the club meeting a commentary would have been offered for each photograph, providing constructive criticism to help the photographer improve. "Correct" composition and the ability to visualize images so that they could "tell one story" were as much artistic standards as they were technical ones. The imposed values reinforced a traditional landscape aesthetics, pushing club members to literally "frame" their work in relation to this wider idealization. My father's long drive to find the "right" angle improved the "balance," arranged the image so that only an odd number of elevators were shown, and, arguably, improved the "impact" demanded by the judging criteria. Undoubtedly, some would likely fault it for an abundance of sky and the forfeiting of the "rule of thirds" since the horizon is set low to accommodate the height of the rainbow.

If, as the judging criterion suggests, "each picture should tell one story," what narrative does *Rainbow's End* present to us? Is it an allegory that links the golden colour of grain to a mythical pot of gold, as inferred by the title, which directs our attention to the very point where rainbow and elevator meet? Is it primarily an aesthetic statement of "place," composed around symbolic icons of a prairie landscape? Do the elevators stand, as one observer suggests, as symbols of a "peaceful cohabitation with the prairie, a way of marking human presence and harmony with nature"?[26] How do the stories change, depending on whether or not the view is "local"? Patricia Vervoort argues that "grain elevators permeate the 'collective Canadian consciousness,'" standing at the centre of a constellation of symbolic meanings that are local, regional, and national in nature, but the meanings and readings of this landscape are hardly homogenous or stable.[27]

When *Rainbow's End* was taken in 1974, Pultney was little more than three elevators. By this time, they had stopped taking grain directly from nearby farmers and served as storage facilities for grain companies. In 1980 the buildings were torn down and erased from the landscape, marking the onset of globalizing economic forces that would dramatically reshape prairie agriculture.[28] Grain companies started to concentrate their holdings, building larger concrete terminals in key regional centres rather than reinvesting in the more dispersed geographical distribution of elevators that had been the pattern in the early twentieth century. By 2003 the number of "primary" elevators had dipped to 382, from a peak of close to 6,000.[29] By the end of the century,

Figure 10.7 *Rainbow's End,* 1974. Photograph by Don Opp.

Figure 10.8   Untitled, Writing-on-Stone Provincial Park, Alberta, 4 October 1970.
Photograph by Don Opp.

Claresholm too had lost not only its elevators but also the railway line that was responsible for its birth.

In the 1970s and 1980s my father used *Rainbow's End* to extend his photographic interests, experimenting with printing colour Cibachrome prints in our basement darkroom. The picture was framed, hung on display at our home, and became one of the most popular pictures that my father sold. For some, it was a lost visual landscape that they wished to recover. But *Rainbow's End* also spoke to a deeper insecurity about the very nature and future of the family farm. As the scales of agricultural production steadily increased, small landholders found it difficult to compete. The decade of the 1970s marked the emergence of a neo-liberal restructuring of the agricultural economy.[30] The full thrust of this transformation and the effects of globalization would not be felt until the 1980s, when drought, recession, and low commodity prices combined to ravage prairie producers. If *Rainbow's End* presents a romantic vision of the prairie landscape, it was not because my father was unaware of the deeper economic pressures faced by farmers like himself. Grain elevators were the point of exchange between local producers and a global market. In many ways, the economic intersections between local and global mirror the photographic tension between a local investment in place and a larger aesthetic aspiration.

In *The Lure of the Local*, Lucy Lippard contends that "photographs are about memory – or perhaps about the absence of memory, providing pictures to fill voids, illustrating our collective memory. So they are an excellent means with which to trigger concern and soothe anxieties about history and place, even when the means they employ resemble conventional landscape art."[31] The peaceful aesthetics of *Rainbow's End* mask a series of local anxieties that stretch through time. From the point at which the picture was taken (the rainbow marked the aftermath of a devastating hailstorm for local producers) to its later reprinting as an artefact of memory, the photograph refracted multiple concerns that complicated any clear dividing line between farmer/photographer, work/leisure, and commercial use of the land/personal contemplation of the landscape.

REVISITING LANDSCAPES LOST

My mother's picture *Road to the Mountains* (Figure 10.2) was taken in 1988, but the landscape it pictures no longer exists. The rolling hills depicted in the foreground were already designated as part of the basin for the Oldman River Dam, which was then under construction and would start to fill in 1991. Controversial since its site was chosen in 1984, the dam was built to provide water for the Lethbridge Northern Irrigation District (LNID). When construction started on the project in 1986, landowners, environmentalists, anglers, and the Piikáni Nation launched protests and court actions. The legal manoeuvrings exposed the slippages between federal and provincial jurisdictions over waterways and the environment. At the height of the protests against the dam, a standoff developed when a Piikáni group known as the Lonefighters threatened to build a diversion around the LNID weir, which was located on the reserve. A year after the dam was completed, a Federal Environmental Assessment Panel reported that the project was not environmentally sound and recommended that the dam be decommissioned. The federal government, which had resisted ordering a federal environmental review until finally ordered to do so by the Supreme Court, flatly refused to follow through on this advice.[32]

Although certainly aware of the dam controversy, my parents' photographic interest lay in capturing the scenic rather than engaging the politics of place. The view from the viewfinder, guided by artistic notions of a "proper" landscape perspective, did not leave room for accommodating the real debasement of the land. As Matthew Evenden points out in the previous chapter, Lake Minnewanka was remade in order to hide its industrial purpose, offering visitors a pleasant view through the windshield. My parents sought to capture the view before it disappeared, an act that was far more aesthetic than political. And yet, in hindsight and re-situated as the scene of an actual, if submersed, place, *Road to the Mountains* does offer the potential to speak back. In presenting a place as it once was, even in its picturesque guise, the image historicizes the landscape for those who know how to "place" it. The very portability of this photograph, signalled by its generic title, depoliticizes it, but this act in itself does not erase the visual inscription of a place that is past and not present. Certainly, such memories of place are not uniform or universal and always compete with other narratives of place. Indeed, the flood basin of the Oldman River Dam is viewed very differently by the Piikáni, for whom the landscape of memory was marked by cottonwood willows, traditional sacred sites, and long-standing material traces of past land use, from tipi rings to buffalo kill-sites.[33]

If the view captured in *Road to the Mountains* was directed by the aesthetic concerns of traditional landscape photography, the image also takes on new meanings when situated as part of a larger archive. By the early 1980s, faced with an almost unmanageable collection of thousands of slides, my parents started to systematically order their work in specialized metal boxes, numbering each box and each slide within it. Some were set apart specifically for personal and family use, many were culled altogether, and those remaining were given sequential numbers that grouped clusters of pictures taken at the same time and place. A hand-written book offers a rough guide to either the subject matter ("flowers") or place ("Waterton").[34] Retracing *Road to the Mountains* through the archive presents a wide range of alternative images, showing the different angles and perspectives that my parents attempted. These extra shots appear to reveal the presence of digging equipment on the margins of the frame. Although the choice of *Road to the Mountains* purposely erased these elements in order to maintain the proper harmony and "balance" of the picture, within the archive a different narrative lurks, one that speaks to the disruptions about to be unleashed. In her chapter, Kirsten McAllister aims to "release the grip" of archival memory over photographs of Japanese internment camps in order to explore changing "choreographies of meaning," but we can also reverse the direction by viewing archives as spaces of unexpected and unintended performance.

An indigenous presence in this landscape was rarely acknowledged in the archive of colour slides in my parents' basement.[35] One of the few exceptions was the visit to Writing-on-Stone Provincial Park, which lay too far east and south to serve as a definitive marker of the "local" community. Nevertheless, the visible marks on the sandstone rock formations reasserted the Prairies as a peopled place. The provincial park surrounding the site was created in 1957 in part to protect the pictographs and petroglyphs from vandalism, but the act of preservation increased damaging traffic from campers while restricting access and further alienating First Nations peoples from a place considered sacred.[36] The archaeological discourse that dominated official interpretations of the rock art preferred to focus on the "prehistoric" nature of the site and on the formalistic qualities of the rock art, temporally and spatially disconnecting its meaning from the surrounding Niitsitapi (Blackfoot) and Shoshone peoples. Until recently, little attention had been paid to the continuities of Aboriginal presence.[37] However, park strategies shifted in the 1990s, when consultations for a new management plan resulted in a series of important meetings with First Nations. As a result, the park name was amended to include Áísínai'pi ("it is pictured/written"), Niitsitapi stories were given prominence in the new visitors' centre, and the Aboriginal right to access the park for ceremonial and educational purposes was recognized.[38] And yet tensions still remain between the park as a site for camping or recreation and its role as a site for preservation.

Within my parents' archive, the eighteen colour slides of Writing-on-Stone taken in 1970 follow a strict division between artistically framed landscapes, such as Figure 10.1, and flattened, "straight" images of the petroglyphs themselves (see Figure 10.8). Only one slide mixed these views, capturing both the marks on the rock face along with the nearby rodeo grounds that, even today, remain within the park on a long-term lease to the chagrin of parks staff, who have long recommended the rodeo's removal. This visual strategy separated landscape from document, a discourse reinforced and valued by other experts in the field. In 1982 a researcher from the Provincial Museum of Alberta wrote to the CCC requesting to borrow old pictures of Writing-on-Stone in order to determine how much the petroglyphs and pictographs had eroded over time.[39] Traditional archaeological practices focused on the form and style of rock art, and similarly distinguished the scientific importance of straight, documentary views from the artistic rendering of the wider landscape. More recent scholars, however, suggest that this separation is problematic. Michael Klassen argues that rather than focusing on classifications of style, archaeologists need to reconsider "ritual performance, sensory experience and sacred landscape" as important factors in the production of rock art.[40] Understanding the "experience of place" is particularly vital at Áísínai'pi, where the petroglyphs are "clearly subordinate in function and meaning to the location itself."[41] Reframing scholarly attention on the sensory experience of place "situates" rock art as part of a wider cultural performance, one that speaks to the very human interaction with the surrounding environment.

Writing-on-Stone/Áísínai'pi carries the marks of multiple layers of memory and the scars of contested meanings. My father's view of this place was guided by long-standing artistic notions of landscape: in his scenic photographs, the rock formations add texture to the foreground of the picture but do not speak as, in the Niitsitapi tradition, animated "medicine rocks."[42] And yet, as with *Road to the Mountains,* the politics of place confront us in unexpected ways. In composing the "documentary" pictures of the petroglyphs, my father clearly tried to frame the images away from the modern graffiti that defaced the stone. However, no artful angle or perspective could avoid the bullet holes that pock the rock face visible in Figure 10.8.[43] No picture could retrieve or adequately represent the complex and multiple layers of meaning that Aboriginal peoples associated with this place. But as a visual documentation of acts of erasure, the image speaks loudly to the contested politics of place at Áísínai'pi. Grouped together in the archive, such images pull at us, stitching together landscape and document, overspilling the borders of separation that guided the framing and view-finding.

CONCLUSION

Lucy Lippard complains that "conventional landscape photography tends to overwhelm place with image. It is usually presented in fragments rather than in grounded sequences." This is perhaps true when outsiders or professional photographers exhibit their work with other "unrelated or loosely related landscapes," creating a "false image of unity."[44] However, the view from the centre of this flurry of amateur photographic activity, conducted over the course of four decades and circulated within the local community in a wide variety of venues, suggests that "place" in the local imagination also has a role in determining the image.

The fragments of landscape pictured by the CCC were framed by the artistic demands that guided their creation. And yet such pictures are both *de*-placed and *re*-placed within the local memory. Abstracted from their actual, specific locations, they are nonetheless recognized as being "of" a distinctive place and speak to a particular local memory. Space and time were deeply entwined in constructing the imagined geography of the local, even within images that were presented as timeless and placeless.

For more than forty years, my parents produced multiple narratives of place through their activities within the CCC. The photographs that circulated in competitions, on calendars, and in slide shows offered a visual catalogue of place that contained more than just the formal elements required to make a picture "beautiful." At the edges of the frame, in the stories of place they invoke, and in the archival remains of pictures that were never circulated or seen, the landscapes of locality emerge as deeply contested.

Colour slide photography offered a visual medium that thrived on the chromatic depth encountered through the projection of a positive transparency. Its technical qualities made it eminently suitable for nature photography, but the timelessness of nature captured on film is now subjected to the rampages of technological progress, which have consigned the slide to history. My parents had started to move toward digital photography in the 1990s, and even the CCC, after a great deal of debate, closed the door on colour slides in 2007, fifty years after its founding. An earlier attempt to preserve the large, collective slide shows of the late-1970s led to the production of a series of VHS video-recordings in the early 1980s. Yet this transfer from one technology to another did not alleviate the problem of obsolescence – it only delayed the inevitable.

Although serious amateurs using high-end digital cameras still look through a viewfinder, what one sees is no longer what one gets. Digital manipulation in Photoshop, such as re-cropping, correcting for exposure, altering horizon lines, adding sharpness, and so on, is now as much a part of the photographic process as actually taking the picture. In a curious reversal, digital photography software programs are designed to replicate the particular colour casts, characteristics, and grain of distinctive colour slide films. Such visual enhancements offer a retro veneer that invokes a particular nostalgic *mood*, but they ignore the wider *mode* of how such technologies and the active pursuit of photography shaped the view.

On the surface, the archive of slides in my parents' basement might appear to offer little more than a collection of views, a stock image bank of nature and landscape photography defined by particular styles and visual form. If, however, we look *through* rather than *at* such images, they reveal a great deal more about the social practices of amateur photography and the role of camera clubs in shaping, and reflecting, local "views" of place. Remembering is at the heart of these productions of place, whether or not the fragments of memory are visible within the frame.

ACKNOWLEDGMENTS

This chapter could not have been written without the active support and encouragement of my parents, Don and Frankie Opp, who tracked down club records and opened their slide collection to me without hesitation (or hovering). I wish to thank Finis Dunaway, Carol Payne, Michael Klassen, and Elizabeth Edwards for their comments on earlier drafts. Special thanks to John Walsh, who is single-handedly responsible for my interest in "place," who steadfastly encouraged me to write myself into this narrative, and who continues to be a remarkable colleague, collaborator, and friend. Research for this project was supported by the Social Sciences and Humanities Research Council of Canada, and final revisions were undertaken while serving as a Visiting Research Fellow at the Calgary Institute for the Humanities, University of Calgary. A version of this chapter was presented as the 2008 Alex Johnston Lecture. My thanks to the family, friends, and former club members who attended and welcomed me home.

NOTES

1   *Chinook Camera Club Bulletin,* October 1970, 2.

2   This phrase is explored in much greater depth in Joan M. Schwartz and James R. Ryan, eds., *Picturing Place: Photography and the Geographical Imagination* (London: I.B. Taurus, 2003).

3   See, for example, Chinook Camera Club (CCC) Minutes, April 1968, Claresholm Public Library. As early as 1959, the club was working on a slide show entitled *This Is Claresholm* in order to showcase the community. See CCC Minutes, June 1959 and November 1959, Claresholm Public Library.

4   It should be noted that my own familial ties to the CCC run deeper than just my parents. Bill Laing, who was elected president of the club in 1958, was my maternal grandmother's brother. And for a short time in the mid-1960s, my paternal grandfather, Bill Opp, was also a member of the club.

5   The tension between the (artistic) universal and (lived) local is embedded within the very complicated etymology of the word "landscape," which, according to Kenneth R. Olwig, held two competing definitions, namely, landscape as region, or a specific inhabited place, and landscape as abstract space, which appealed to artists. See his "The 'Actual Landscape,' or Actual Landscapes?" in *Landscape Theory,* ed. Rachael Ziady Delue and James Elkins (New York: Routledge, 2008), 158-71.

6   Elizabeth Edwards offers a method of looking *through* pictures, rather than *at* them, in order to understand the "performances of space, identities and power." Inspired by the work of Greg Dening on the possibilities of performance and the theatrical in reading photographs, she suggests that "this approach might enable us to spatialize the historical narrative"; see her "Negotiating Spaces: Some Photographic Incidents in the Western Pacific, 1883-84," in *Picturing Place: Photography and the Geographical Imagination,* ed. Joan M. Schwartz and James R. Ryan (London: I.B. Taurus, 2003), 278. Due to the nature of the photographic archive with which I am dealing, I consider this reflection predominantly an effort to "temporalize the spatial narrative," a process that entails its own set of cultural performances, both past and present.

7   W.J.T. Mitchell suggests that landscape itself "*circulates* as a medium of exchange, a site of visual appropriation, a focus for the formation of identity"; see his "Introduction," in *Landscape and Power,* 2nd ed. (Chicago: University of Chicago Press, 2002), 2, emphasis in original. A number of recent works stress the significance of considering the

materiality of photographs, including Elizabeth Edwards and Janice Hart, eds., *Photographs Objects Histories: On the Materiality of Images* (London: Routledge, 2004).

8   The phrase was originally submitted to an earlier contest to develop a slogan for the town and appeared for a time on the masthead of the local paper. It was revived for the local-history book project. See *Where the Wheatlands Meet the Range* (Claresholm, AB: Claresholm History Book Club, 1974), 3.

9   On the relationship between collective memory and a "sense of place," see David Glassberg, *Sense of History: The Place of the Past in American Life* (Amherst: University of Massachusetts Press, 1991), ch. 5. For a synthesis of the vast amount of geographical reconsiderations of "place," see Timothy Cresswell, *Place: A Short Introduction* (Oxford: Blackwell, 2004).

10 Occasional camping trips and photography courses did draw members to eastern locales, such as Cypress Hills on the Saskatchewan border, but these pictures were not usually presented as "local" representations of place.

11 Maps of these outings are available for 1968 and 1980, and both show only westward loops through the foothills. The exception may have been an organized outing to a local Hutterite colony, probably in 1974. Frankie Opp, personal communication with author, August 2008.

12 Even the highway signs for the town feature a layering of the landscape that positions prairie and foothills in front of mountains, reinforcing the dominant perspective of looking from east to west rather than the reverse.

13 As Yi-Fu Tuan notes, "'Wilderness' cannot be defined objectively: it is as much a state of the mind as a description of nature. By the time we can speak of preserving and protecting wilderness, it has already lost much of its meaning." See Yi-Fu Tuan, *Topophilia: A Study of Environmental Perception, Attitudes, and Values,* 2nd ed. (New York: Columbia University Press, 1990), 112.

14 The concept of a "middle landscape" is offered by Leo Marx, *The Machine in the Garden: Technology and the Pastoral Ideal in America* (New York: Oxford University Press, 1964). An illuminating review of the concept is found in Howard P. Segal, "Review: Leo Marx's 'Middle Landscape': A Critique, a Revision, and an Appreciation," *Reviews in American History* 5, 1 (March 1977): 137-50.

15 *Chinook Camera Club Bulletin,* November 1965, 1-2.

16 *Chinook Camera Club Bulletin,* 14 December 1973.

17 On notions of "old stock" in this area, see Lorelei L. Hanson, "The Disappearance of the Open West: Individualism in the Midst of Agricultural Restructuring," in *Writing off the Rural West: Globalization, Governments, and the Transformation of Rural Communities,* ed. Roger Epp and Dave Whitson (Edmonton: University of Alberta Press, 2001).

18 Freeman Patterson's career was launched by his participation in *Canada – A Year of the Land* (Ottawa: National Film Board of Canada, 1967), which is discussed in Carol Payne's forthcoming work on the Still Photography Division of the National Film Board. I am grateful to her for sharing early drafts of this chapter with me.

19 Although human subjects were not entirely absent from the club's interests, competitive amateurs found it difficult to meet the standards of professional portrait photographers, who used medium-format cameras and professional studio lights. In contrast, there was a much smaller technological gap between "professionals" and "amateurs" in nature or landscape photography since both typically employed 35 mm cameras and the same slide-film varieties.

20 William Cronon, "The Trouble with Wilderness," in *Uncommon Ground: Rethinking the Human Place in Nature*, ed. William Cronon (New York: W.W. Norton, 1996), 80.

21 Maryjane Hooper Tonn, ed., *God So Loved the World: Reflections on the Beauty of God's Creation* (Milwaukee: Ideals, 1973); CCC Minutes, 6 January 1974, Claresholm Public Library.

22 See Finis Dunaway, *Natural Visions: The Power of Images in American Environmental Reform* (Chicago: University of Chicago Press, 2005), ch. 6.

23 The club did produce one show that veered from nature as the dominant theme. Entitled *Through the Eyes of a Child*, it offered a visual experience very different from that of previous and later shows but remained an exception to the rule.

24 Cronon, "Trouble with Wilderness," 80. Similarly, in discussing environmentalism's attitudes toward those who "work" in and on the land, Richard White makes the point that "our work – all our work – inevitably embeds us in nature, including what we consider wild and pristine places"; see his "'Are You an Environmentalist or Do You Work for a Living?': Work and Nature," in *Uncommon Ground: Rethinking the Human Place in Nature*, ed. William Cronon (New York: W.W. Norton, 1996), 185. My thanks to Finis Dunaway for reminding me of White's essay.

25 Tuan, *Topophilia*, 92-93.

26 Geoffrey Simmins, "Prairie Grain Elevators: An Old Purpose in Search of a New Form," in *Challenging Frontiers: The Canadian West*, ed. Beverly Rasporich and Lorry W. Felske (Calgary: University of Calgary Press, 2004), 206.

27 Patricia Vervoort, "'Towers of Silence': The Rise and Fall of the Grain Elevator as a Canadian Symbol," *Histoire sociale/Social History* 39, 77 (2006): 181-204.

28 *Claresholm Local Press*, 26 June 1980, 1, and 3 July 1980, 7.

29 Simmins, "Prairie Grain Elevators," 220.

30 Roger Epp and Dave Whitson, eds., *Writing Off the Rural West: Globalization, Governments, and the Transformation of Rural Communities* (Edmonton: University of Alberta Press, 2001); in this volume, see especially Geoffrey Lawrence et al., "Globalization, Neo-liberalism, and Rural Decline: Australia and Canada," 89-105.

31 Lucy R. Lippard, *The Lure of the Local: Sense of Place in a Multicentered Society* (New York: New Press, 1997), 20.

32 The complicated saga of the Oldman River Dam is detailed in Jack Glenn, *Once upon an Oldman: Special Interest Politics and the Oldman River Dam* (Vancouver: UBC Press, 1999).

33 Brian Reeves, "The Oldman River Dam and Alberta's Heritage: Conservation or Desecration?" in *Economic, Environmental, and Social Aspects of the Oldman River Dam*

Project, ed. Stewart B. Rood and Frank J. Jankunis (Lethbridge, AB: University of Lethbridge, 1988), 81-99.

34 Most, although not all, of the slides already included an approximate date since this information was often stamped on the cardboard edges as slides were processed.

35 On the long-standing question of Aboriginal presence and erasure in landscape representations, see Jonathan Bordo, "Jack Pine – Wilderness Sublime or the Erasure of the Aboriginal Presence from the Landscape," *Journal of Canadian Studies* 27, 4 (Winter 1992-93): 98-128.

36 Assessing the timing of and relative damage from vandalism and graffiti is difficult, but certainly the increased accessibility created by the park brought on a significant amount of damage to the rock art closest to the public facilities. Concern over this state of affairs led to the creation of an archaeological preserve in 1977 that covers much of the park's rock art. Restricting public access to interpretive guided tours has drastically reduced vandalism within the preserve, although it remains a problem in other parts of the park; see Michael A. Klassen, "Áísínai'pi (Writing-on-Stone) in Traditional, Anthropological, and Popular Thought," in *Discovering North American Rock Art* (Tucson: University of Arizona Press, 2005), 32, 40. See also Patricia Tomasic, "The (De)Construction of 'Indianness' at Writing-on-Stone Provincial Park" (MA thesis, Department of Art History, Concordia University, 2000); and Michael A. Klassen, "Icons of Power, Narratives of Glory: Ethnic Continuity and Cultural Change in the Contact Period Rock Art of Writing-on-Stone" (MA thesis, Department of Anthropology, Trent University, 1995).

37 Hugh A. Dempsey was one of the few to give serious consideration to the oral traditions of the Niitsitapi in his 1973 unpublished report, "A History of Writing-on-Stone," M4442, Glenbow Archives, Calgary. Dempsey relates an oral account of a "pilgrimage" to Áísínai'pi in 1924 (45), but for the most part he focuses on the site's connection to Niitsitapi life in the nineteenth century.

38 *Writing-on-Stone Provincial Park Management Plan* (Edmonton: Alberta Department of Environmental Protection, 1997).

39 CCC Minutes, 22 October 1982, Claresholm Public Library.

40 Michael A. Klassen, "Spirit Images, Medicine Rocks: The Rock Art of Alberta," in *Archaeology in Alberta: A View from the New Millennium,* ed. Jack W. Brink and John F. Dormaar (Medicine Hat, AB: Archaeological Society of Alberta, 2003), 178.

41 Joan M. Vastokas, quoted in Klassen, "Spirit Images," 181.

42 Klassen, "Spirit Images," 181.

43 The origin of the bullet holes is unknown, although these particular marks appear in 1897 photographs, so they clearly date from the nineteenth century. In the 1930s there were reports of "deliberate vandalism" of the pictograph sites by "target shooters who with .22 rifles have riddled these carved pictures with holes." See *Calgary Herald,* 14 November 1935, quoted in Dempsey, "History of Writing-on-Stone," 127.

44 Lippard, *Lure of the Local,* 180.

Part 3

AFTERWORD

Figure 11.1   Marlene Creates, *Marker No. 2 (Beach Boulevard)* from the series *HIDDEN HISTORIES AND INVISIBLE STORIES*, the City of Hamilton and the Royal Botanical Gardens, 2000 © CARCC 2010.

One of 5 steel markers, each 34 inches high × 28 inches wide (86cm high × 71cm wide), mounted on a steel pole, 8 feet high × 4 inches diameter (2.4m high × 10cm diameter), plus paint, steel base plate, and concrete footing.

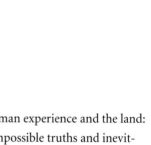

Complicating the Picture
Place and Memory between Representation and Reflection

JOAN M. SCHWARTZ

> I am interested in the relationship between human experience and the land:
> the intersection of geography with memory, impossible truths and inevit-
> able ambiguities. I am fascinated by the different layers – "natural" and
> human – that can occur in the same place. The land is important to me, but
> even more important is the idea that it becomes a "place" because someone
> has been there.
>
> – Marlene Creates

In this "Artist Statement" for her installation *HIDDEN HISTORIES AND INVIS-
IBLE STORIES, the City of Hamilton and the Royal Botanical Gardens, 2000,*
Canadian visual artist Marlene Creates addresses the relationship at the heart
of this collection.[1] Commissioned by the Art Gallery of Hamilton for the Millennium exhibition *Zone 6B: Art in the Environment,* Creates's site-specific
work consisted of five heavy, painted steel markers, each thirty-four inches
high by twenty-eight inches wide by three-sixteenths of an inch thick, each
cut in such a way that, looking through them, the words "Hidden Histories
and Invisible Stories" stood out against the sky.[2] Mounted on steel base poles,

each eight feet high and four inches in diameter, and set in concrete footings four feet deep, the markers were installed in public locations on the grounds of the Royal Botanical Gardens and on City of Hamilton property. "Drawn to the extraordinary fact that all places – parks, factories, streets, homes – hide invisible dimensions other than what we can see," Creates hoped her markers would "provide a reason to stop and wonder for a moment about the unknowable dimensions embedded, saturated, in these places."[3] Who has been there, and when? What did they do or experience? What was the significance of this place, and, perhaps more important here, why do we care?

Creates was inspired by the notion that two geographical features – the lake and the escarpment – played pivotal roles in Hamilton's development and that "this setting has affected much of what happens here – even, perhaps, the reason for the city's foundation."[4] This statement had particular resonance for me. I remember that in Grade 9 geography we were taught that there are six factors that determine the location of industry; I can recall only five with certainty: power, raw materials, labour, transportation, and market (perhaps climate was the sixth). Hamilton was the city used as a case study. To a curious ninth grader, this explanation seemed overly simplistic (and I like to think it was then and there that my interest in historical geography began). It might have accounted for Hamilton as a place of human settlement and industry in 1964, but why did the city start off there in the first place? How did Hamilton's fortunes change with the passage of time? And more generally, what happened in the place that we now think of as southern Ontario, in the distant and recent past, that helped towns and villages to take root, then grow or decline? The site of a waterfall, a rapids, a spring, a portage, or a natural harbour gave rise to many places; later, the coming of the railway or the establishment of a post office favoured some and bypassed others. So how does place in the present relate to place in the past, and how does history or memory help us to understand "place" in time?

Clearly location is not as simple to explain as my Grade 9 geography teacher would have had me believe. Indeed, "place" is a slippery concept, and the relationship between place and memory is even more difficult to pin down. The chapters in this book go a long way to enriching our understanding of this relationship. Just as James Opp and John Walsh employ Marlene Creates's *Places of Presence* as a springboard to launch the introduction to this book, this chapter draws on her more recent work to explore perspectives on place and memory between representation and reflection, between private meaning and public display, that resonate with and push beyond these chapters, thus complicating the picture even further.

HAMILTON, ONTARIO, JUNE 2000: *HIDDEN HISTORIES AND INVISIBLE STORIES*

In placing her steel markers at various sites around Hamilton, Creates did not make known the hidden histories nor make visible the invisible stories; rather, she asked viewers to reflect on the past beneath their feet. She did not list the usual events that are part of the grand narratives of Hamilton and vicinity history – the arrival of Étienne Brulé in 1616, the coming of the Loyalists in 1784, the Battle of Stoney Creek in 1813, the railway disaster at the Desjardins Canal in 1857. Rather, Creates encouraged viewers to imagine quotidian happenings and unremarkable goings-on. For example, on side panels at Marker #3 on the Valley Inn Road beside Sunfish Pond in the Royal Botanical Gardens, Creates drew attention to what one might have witnessed on the site over time:

- glacial melt water to a depth of thirty-five metres (115 feet) above the present water level
- a crossroads of Aboriginal footpaths, wagons, stagecoaches, railways, and highways
- a two-storey hotel, a horse barn, and a tollhouse
- a berm of 140,000 discarded Christmas trees from four municipalities, for estuary restoration
- three people in kayaks
- people feeding birds
- a conversation between Creates and a man fishing.

Elsewhere, Creates noted the conjunction of political jurisdictions – the Royal Botanical Gardens, CN property, the municipalities of Hamilton, Burlington, Dundas, and Flamborough – governing interactions between people and place: a bylaw forbidding the feeding of pigeons, pre-registration fees required for wedding photography, a national design competition to beautify the northwest entrance to the city. Like the chapters in this book, her markers also make us ponder the powerful influences that have shaped place and how it is remembered: the forces of nature eroding the escarpment, military authority maintaining British rule, Church of England power establishing land patterns through clergy reserves, market forces building social hierarchies.

In her essay "The Topography of Hidden Experience" in the *Zone 6B* exhibition catalogue, the Art Gallery of Hamilton's chief curator, Shirley Madill, suggests, "Like the strata on the escarpment rock, Creates' work represents deposits in a continuous succession of human layering of experience."[5] In effect, Creates leaves the exploration of those layers to the viewer's imagination. Her markers, while site-specific, are not intended to recall officially sanctioned heroic events or architectural gems associated with place, although they do share certain mnemonic aims and physical properties with the commemorative plaques of Canada's Historic Sites and Monuments Board. Yet, more generally in her art practice, Creates explores issues of place and memory, urging viewers to grapple with the meanings of land, landscape, and place, what is valued and how it is experienced and remembered, whether individually and privately or officially and collectively.

A similar layering of experience is examined in literary terms in Phil Jenkins' *An Acre of Time*.[6] Subtitled *The Enduring Value of Place,* it is a work of creative non-fiction, specifically history. In a statement that resonates with Marlene Creates's central concern in *HIDDEN HISTORIES AND INVISIBLE STORIES,* Jenkins' website points out, "*An Acre of Time* is about the way land becomes territory, territory becomes property, and property becomes real estate."[7] In the book, Jenkins reflects on the "process by which man inexorably alters the place he inhabits," on how a patch of land on LeBreton Flats in Ottawa, upstream along the river from Parliament Hill, has both changed and changed hands over time.[8] He declares:

> I've come here ... to unearth a story, a rolling tale of lava and glaciers, of tropical seas and waterfalls, of whales and white-tailed deer, of Indians and pioneers, millionaires and paupers, firestorms and bulldozers, railways and lumber mills, facts and gossip. It's the story, the biography, of the field beneath my feet. Every story has its borders; the borders of this story are the four sides of the acre I'm standing on, a single page from the book of land.[9]

Whereas Jenkins narrates and, by extension, defines for readers the successive layering on his acre, Creates's markers are neither descriptive nor prescriptive

Afterword

but rather serve only to pique curiosity and inspire contemplation of one's situation in time and space, or as Madill proposes, "in relation to people and the environment around us."[10]

Both Creates and Jenkins toil at the intersection of place and memory. Creates is a visual artist interested in landscape; Jenkins says of himself, "I'm a landscape artist, but I write word pictures on the page, not paint on canvas."[11] *An Acre of Time* describes; *HIDDEN HISTORIES AND INVISIBLE STORIES* evokes. *An Acre of Time* draws on historical sources and literary devices to present the chronological unfolding of a site-specific story about the local, reinforcing a linear sense of time in place; *HIDDEN HISTORIES AND INVISIBLE STORIES* uses site-specific artwork to draw broader lessons about the experience of the local, producing a diffuse sense of place through time. *An Acre of Time* recounts and makes publicly accessible and collectively known one version of a biography of place; *HIDDEN HISTORIES AND INVISIBLE STORIES* generates a privately experienced process of wonder and elicits an imaginative exercise in reflecting on the unknowable dimensions embedded in place. And finally, whereas the chapters in this book resonate more with Jenkins in his focus on memory in the public and collective sense, Creates opens up opportunities for further study of the tensions between public and personal expressions of place and memory. Comparison with a project of local distinctiveness, recently introduced into Canada, further exposes these tensions.

ST. ANDREWS, NEW BRUNSWICK, AUGUST 2009: PARISH MAPS AND LOCAL DISTINCTIVENESS

> Although the ancient custom of "beating the bounds" of village parishes has largely died out, the Millennium has been a stimulus to the recognition and remembrance of parish boundaries in the form of new parish maps made by the residents.[12]

On a warm August evening in 2009, a small group of St. Andrews, New Brunswick, residents gathered in the café of Kingsbrae Gardens for a workshop entitled "PARISH MAPS: England to America. Building a Sense of Place through the Work of Common Ground." Sue Clifford, co-founder of the British arts and environment group Common Ground,[13] discussed the history of Parish Mapping in the United Kingdom and explained the various ways in which communities in Britain have gone about creating community-based maps that express subjective responses to place and highlight local distinctiveness. First launched in England in 1987, Parish Mapping was presented as a community-building project designed to involve people in what they value in their locality. Brought to the Passamaquoddy Bay area by the Tides Institute and Museum of Art, Eastport, Maine, for a five-day residency, Clifford presented her workshop in five small communities and participated in a panel discussion on "Public Art and Sense of Place." The events marked the first presentation of the Parish Maps Project in North America; St. Andrews was the only Canadian venue.[14]

Quick to point out that the map does not have to be about a "parish" in the religious meaning of the word or need to be cartographically correct, the leaflet distributed to participants explained that "a Parish Map is a demonstrative, value-laden statement made by and for a community, exploring and showing what it cares about in its locality." The finished map, which is ultimately intended to be a very public, democratically fashioned, and politically empowering expression of place, can take a variety of forms: "sewn, woven, knitted, printed, drawn, painted, filmed, animated, performed and written." Examples brought to mind nineteenth-century county atlases and bird's-eye views; some resembled a cross between *mappae mundi* and folk art. Discussion centred on the aesthetics of mapping, largely ignoring the problematic nature of maps as representations. "The Parish Map," the leaflet advised, "should be hung in a public place – the village hall, library, community centre, museum, church or pub – to act as a continuing stimulus to discussion, inspiring us to look again at our surroundings and to discover new ways of encouraging responsibility for ordinary but well loved places."[15] Central to the creation of a Parish Map is the relationship of place and memory. Also implied are the "impossible truths and inevitable ambiguities" that Creates acknowledges to be part of her fascination with the relationship between human experience and the land.

Billed as "Canada's first seaside resort town," St. Andrews, with its strong and visible Loyalist roots and its long-standing reputation as a tourist destination with "no hay fever and a railway,"[16] seemed ideally suited to the Parish Map Project's focus on locally distinctive activities and "the everyday things that make a place significant and different from the next." In addition to

Afterword

"picturesque charm and natural beauty,"[17] St. Andrews boasts a National Historic District, as well as fine old churches, distinctive architecture, celebrated gardens, the world's highest tides, excellent whale-watching, and a world-class golf course. Nearby attractions include St. Croix Island, Ministers Island, and Campobello Island, all with storied pasts. But beyond official expressions of local history, the Parish Maps Project also emphasizes the importance of seemingly ordinary things and events, thus recognizing that it may be trees, hedgerows, orchards, ponds, wild life, work, recreational activities, landmarks, buildings, people, and festivals that are valued and preserved, remembered and to be remembered.

Clifford assured the audience that "the most successful maps reflect the jumble of overlapping interests and the jostle of varied values – some offer criticisms, most have a strong feeling for geography, history and nature" – and that, in the process of creating a parish or community map, there would be "crucial debates on what to put in and what to leave out."[18] With a year-round population of only about 1,800, which swells to some 2,500 with the coming of the "summer people" (not including tourists), St. Andrews would likely generate "crucial debates" between segments of the population with complementary, competing, and conflicting notions of local distinctiveness. St. Andrews, as elsewhere, is a place where very different subjective experiences and memories of place must be reconciled, or as David Crouch and David Matless claim, "a contested site of representation where different spatialities and temporalities conjoin."[19] Although situated in the present, the Parish Maps Project is very much an exercise in memory, the object of which is the creation of maps of things of value remembered and of things to value and remember. In keeping with Creates's notion that "land ... becomes a 'place' because someone has been there" and that, as a consequence, places carry invisible dimensions and change over time, Parish Maps seek to give visual or verbal or physical expression to personal, subjective, otherwise invisible dimensions.

In confronting the "questions around the social role of mapping and the production of local knowledge," Crouch and Matless also examine the relationship between "non-academic" investigations of place and debates within academic geography.[20] In so doing, they open up for serious scholarly scrutiny the work of Creates, Jenkins, and others whose work exposes the interdependence of place and memory for popular consideration. Such artistic or creative responses represent parallel explorations of the intellectual "turns" fuelling recent scholarly endeavour. They are historical geographies and geographical histories expressed in aesthetic and literary form.[21]

PLACING AND REMEMBERING: COMPETING AND COMPLEMENTARY PERSPECTIVES

Marlene Creates's *HIDDEN HISTORIES AND INVISIBLE STORIES* and Common Ground's Parish Maps Project share certain basic assumptions and agendas. Just as Opp and Walsh remind us in their introduction to this volume that "places and memories are always in a state of becoming," Creates acknowledges that the places where she installed her markers "will continue to change,"[22] and Common Ground promotes Parish Maps as a way to recognize and maintain local distinctiveness in the face of change. And like the stories teased out of Sturgeon Falls' mill history binder or out of the photographs from Japanese internment camps or like those read across the landscape of Jasper Avenue or Lake Minnewanka, Creates's markers and Parish Mapping both bring together memory and place through storytelling; however, they do so in different ways, address different audiences, and generate different acts of remembering. Creates's markers encourage viewers in the present to "look back" to the past beneath their feet; Parish Maps suggest how to view and value place in the present. Janus-like in their orientation to past, present, and future, they also offer competing and complementary perspectives on the nature, locus, and crisis of memory: individual and communal in origin, private and public in meaning, interior and exterior in manifestation. Can we then go beyond treating the work of Marlene Creates and Common Ground as a subject of research to think "with" them in an effort to further the discussion of "shared authority"?

Parish Maps, while democratically produced, have a prescriptive element to them: they not only record what individuals value but also preserve and make known what *should* be remembered collectively by the communities by and for whom they are created. Creates's markers remind us that there is a difference between history and memory and that we can "remember" only what we already know or have experienced. Creates urges viewers to ponder past place in imprecise terms and in ways that blur the edges of both time and space; Parish Maps codify and express local distinctiveness in concrete and readily understood ways.

Whereas Parish Mapping uses private memories to produce a communal expression of place for public display, *HIDDEN HISTORIES AND INVISIBLE STORIES* employs publicly displayed markers to prompt private contemplation of public places in personal terms. Whereas Common Ground attempts to invigorate a community's sense of place through the external, usually visual, representation of locally valued sites or memories attached to objects, Creates seeks to awaken the individual's sense of place through a return to internal, mental reflection on the community's site-specific collective past.

By example, by extension, and by extrapolation, this discussion of memory and place in the work of Marlene Creates and the Parish Maps Project dances across the chapters in this collection, inviting speculation on commonalities and incongruities in technologies of memory and on constructions of place. It has parallels in Russell Johnston and Michael Ripmeester's examination of monuments as a communicative mode of memory, in which they point out the differences between what monuments do (and don't) convey and how people develop a historical consciousness within a wider media environment. It resonates with Opp's analysis of the ways in which technologies of memory influence the "practice" of place, the "view-finding" process itself being an integral part of how landscapes are both seen and experienced by photographers. Kirsten McAllister's chapter invites consideration of the mutability of photographic meaning and the mobility of the photographic archive as a "place" of community and a site of individual and collective trauma. Running through the Parish Maps Project are concerns for local acts narrating community identity, which form a major theme of this book, from Steven High's mill history binder and Walsh's Old Boys' Reunions to the tensions of community inclusion and exclusion evident in the contributions of Frances Swyripa and Cecilia Morgan. As an episode of "hidden histories," Patrizia Gentile's work unveils sites of memory that sit in the shadow of Parliament Hill yet are unrecognizable to most of the tourists who walk past. Matthew Evenden's contribution shows how landscaping has purposely hidden other histories but remains open to reclamation in the use of Lake Minnewanka by recreational divers.

All of these chapters draw on archival materials and employ images, either as sources or as illustrations. While offering broader contexts for ruminating on the placement and message of Creates's markers and on the compilation and display of Parish Maps, they also invite close consideration of the authors' use of archives, especially visual images as primary sources, and of the mediating influence of the keepers of public and private collections. Archives are not "passive storehouses of old stuff,"; rather, they are "active sites where social power is negotiated, contested, confirmed." Through archives, "the past is controlled. Certain stories are privileged and others marginalized."[23] By extension then, "memory is not something found or collected in archives, but something that is made, and continually re-made."[24] This raises the issue of the power of the archive as a mediating influence. As Terry Cook and I have argued, archivists exercise "enormous power over memory and identity, over the fundamental ways in which society seeks evidence of what its core values are and have been, where it has come from, and where it is going."[25] Like the artists and community activists who explore and remind us of the relationship between place and memory, archivists then, no less than academics, are "an integral part of this story-telling,"[26] and scholars looking to the past must be cognizant of the mediating power of archivists, archival institutions, and archival practices to shape recorded memory, determining which documents and which images are preserved and made accessible.[27]

Here, McAllister's observation – that the meaning, authority, and use of photographs are shaped by their context of preservation – opens for discussion the ways in which archival materials, not just photographs, are framed, described, understood, and made accessible differently in a community-run archive than in a government-run repository. At the same time, her classic characterization of the archive as a "dimly lit" space of "deathly stillness ... where time accumulates and condenses in stacks of worn documents, pencil-drawn sketches and maps, fading photographs and film reels, ink-stained diaries, and carefully composed letters," is itself a construction, one that is quickly being superseded as search rooms and storage vaults are retrofitted to accommodate the technology and media of the digital archive of electronic communication and imaging. No longer will archives be what McAllister calls the "repository for the material of memory" in the literal sense of materiality, as documents, sketches, maps, photographs, diaries, and letters in physical form are recast as "legacy collections" and the electronic realm changes in profound ways how information is created, communicated, and preserved. In this digital world, creators of archives exercise enormous and immediate control over what the future will know of its past since digital images can be quickly erased or easily altered and e-mails and attachments can be readily deleted. The fragile nature of electronically recorded information complicates, indeed often thwarts, the relationship between "creators" and "keepers" of archives. Transposed to the digital world, the chapters in this volume raise questions about "the future of the past" and offer directions for further study.

COMPLICATING THE PICTURE: PLACE AND MEMORY IN THE DIGITAL AGE

Let me now complicate the picture even further. The already complex relationship between memory and place explored in this volume is made all the more complex when we consider the opportunities for and threats to processes of placing memory and remembering place in the digital age. For example, as the year 2000 approached, digital technology presented itself as both promise and threat. Simultaneously, as computer specialists in government offices struggled to prepare for and avert the predicted cataclysmic Y2K meltdown of electronic memory, community groups embraced the CD-ROM as the storage medium of choice for preserving local notions of place in time capsules that carried great appeal for their promise of longevity. Therein lies the irony. The prospect of massive failure of systems of documentation and data storage did not seem to dampen the enthusiasm of technologically savvy, historically minded individuals with faith in the longevity of digital memory devices. Thus, as the Y2K threat loomed large, CD-ROMs were placed in time capsules. The Y2K disaster never materialized, although it is not clear whether the anticipated problem was initially overstated or whether it was eventually averted with the expenditure of money and effort. But when the Millennium time capsules are opened, what will be the fate of those CD-ROMs created – using software and operating systems that in 2010 are already outdated – to show what places looked like and what people valued?

Time capsules, of course, are not associated only with celebrations of the Millennium, nor are they unique in their purpose to ensure that what is valued as distinctive about a place in the present will be known individually and collectively in the future through conscious placement and preservation of records and objects at designated sites of memory – cornerstones or cairns, for example. Nor, for that matter, are the problems of volume, instability, and obsolescence entirely new. Librarians have already been forced to cope with the "slow fires" of early papers made from acidic wood pulp, and archivists have struggled with the long-term preservation of super-8 family movies, 8-track cartridges, beta-format video recordings, and enormous holdings of nitrate negatives. At issue here is the nature, legibility, and longevity of mnemonic devices – the forms that the exteriorization of memory can take and the changing role of recording technologies in the relationship between place and memory – a theme that threads its way through the contributions to this volume.

CD-ROMs in time capsules embody tensions between form and function in the inherent contradiction between the creator's desire to preserve information and the projected audience's potential inability to recover that information in readable form. Their creation is an inherently vulnerable exercise in placing memory and remembering place, predicated on a faith in technology and a desire to ensure that the future knows something of its past. But the CD-ROM in the time capsule represents the tip of a technological iceberg that poses a much larger threat to the relationship between place and memory in a rapidly changing universe of electronic communication where there are no guarantees that the hardware, the software, and the expertise necessary to read them will be available in one hundred, two hundred, or five hundred – even fifty – years. In everyday communication, as blogs replace diaries, electronic records replace paper files, and digital images replace photograph albums, will the information society of the twenty-first century suffer serious amnesia at the individual and collective level?[28]

These threats, presented by digital technologies and our headlong rush to embrace them, are balanced by new opportunities for placing memory and remembering place. Beyond the panoply of obvious applications for word processing, text messaging, web browsing, and data storage, two developments in particular – one backward-looking, the other forward-looking – merit mention in the context of this collection. Both chart new terrain in the relationship between memory and place; both have implications for the nature of historical consciousness.[29]

Credited with revealing the past in new ways, Historical Geographic Information Systems (GIS) technology uses "digital renditions of historical maps to study historical landscapes, the maps themselves, and how places changed over time. GIS is breathing new life into historical maps by freeing them from the static confines of their original print form."[30] It enables comparison with historical maps, the reconstruction of past boundaries, and the geo-referencing of parish or census records or other spatial data, including descriptions of place. For example, the web-based Historical GIS Project *A Vision of Britain through Time* offers "a vision of Britain between 1801 and 2001" through maps, statistical trends, and travel writing.[31] Visitors to the website can explore cartographic, literary, and statistical sources and in the travel-writing section see what writers have said about their town or village. Place-names within the text are hyperlinked, and dots on a map of Britain, like Creates's markers, invite exploration of past places. But unlike Creates, who points to quotidian happenings, and unlike Parish Maps, which present vernacular perspectives, *A Vision of Britain* offers official narratives and published accounts. Such Historical GIS projects, offering unprecedented access to a complex web of carefully selected and digitized sources, are heavily mediated, on the one hand, and technologically fragile, on the other, dependent on unseen forces, both intellectual and financial, to sustain them.

Whereas Historical GIS opens up access to the past, the future of the process of placing memory and remembering place takes on a whole new dimension in the geo-tagging device launched by Sony in 2006. "Organize Photos by 'Where' Not 'When' with Global Positioning System [GPS] for Sony Digital Cameras," the press release declared.[32] Promotional copy explained that, by linking time and location recordings from Sony's GPS device to the time stamp from a Sony digital camera or camcorder, users could plot their digital images to a map and pinpoint foreign cities visited, routes followed, wilderness paths explored, and even new restaurants visited.[33] "Adding a geographic context to your digital images helps organize and make use of your photos in entirely new ways," claims David Johns, product manager for digital camera accessories at Sony Electronics.[34] In the process, the experience of place is personalized and preserved; private experiences and memories are overlain onto existing cartographic expressions of place. As in the Parish Maps Project, official representations of space – ordnance or topographic survey maps, for example – are used as the basis of individual encounters with the local; however, unlike the publicly displayed Parish Map intended to shape a community's sense of its local distinctiveness, Sony's GPS mnemonic technology encourages the appropriation of publicly available maps into private spaces of remembrance.

Both memory and place are subjects that, as Opp and Walsh point out in their introduction to this volume, have launched scholarly inquiry and generated a vast literature across a range of disciplines. The act of remembering place is, in itself, part of the much larger and more complex issue of how we remember. Addressed, sometimes directly, sometimes obliquely, in the burgeoning literature on memory, it raises questions about the nature and locus of memory, whose memory, devices of memory, and commemorative practices. Statues, monuments, and other commemorative markers – the memory theatres dating back to Classical antiquity and extending into the Renaissance, the cabinets of curiosities popular from the sixteenth to the eighteenth centuries, and the modern museum, which emerged in the nineteenth century – all represent the intersection of place and memory. Placing memory necessarily involves changes in the organization and meaning of space over time and demands consideration of the ways in which *space* on the ground is transformed into *place* in the mind,[35] as well as attention to the role of representations in the cognitive and imaginative processes involved in that transformation. But what about Internet sites? Are they "places" in cyberspace? And is digital storage a reliable memory medium? The very tendency to cite websites with the date accessed is an overt acknowledgment of the ephemeral nature of electronic memory.

However, the loss of recorded information is not simply about unstable storage media. It is also about attitudes to recorded information, its purpose and place in society. In *About Looking*, John Berger writes:

> What served in the place of the photograph before the camera's invention? The expected answer is the engraving, the drawing, the painting. The more revealing answer might be: memory. What photographs do out there in space was previously done within reflection.[36]

More than 150 years ago, there was an "iconic revolution" in the "exteriorization" of memory when the invention of photography changed both the way that people related to place and the way that they remembered. Today, born-digital images are taken, viewed, e-mailed, and erased. Hard drives crash. Hardware becomes obsolete. Software becomes obsolete. Information becomes unreadable. Data is not always migrated. No doubt, CDs and DVDs, too, will go the way of 12-inch, 8-inch, 5.25-inch, and 3.5-inch floppy diskettes. What remains to be seen is how new digital mnemonic technologies will influence the relationship between place and memory. If daguerreotypes outlast digital

Afterword

images, will we know more about the last century than the next century will know about ours?

Returning to Creates's "Artist Statement," we can ask: What is the future of the past? Of memory? Is the current "crisis of memory" a direct consequence of the digital age? Does it represent conscious and unconscious anxiety over the fragile and ephemeral nature of electronic records? And might it, in fact, herald an even larger crisis, a sea change in the nature and locus of memory and its relationship to place, a profound shift in attitudes to the value of the past in the present, and a decline in history as popular pursuit and academic discipline? In fact, will the rising historicism of the nineteenth century give way to a new presentist paradigm in the age of electronic communication, imaging, and recorded information? Perhaps, for the very reason that external mnemonic aids may not survive, we shall come to appreciate Berger's observation and witness a return to the core process linking place and memory in the pre-photographic era: internal reflection.

In their introduction, Opp and Walsh launch this collection with the central premise of Marlene Creates's *Places of Presence*, that "the land is not an abstract physical location but a *place*, charged with personal significance, shaping the images we have of ourselves."[37] This chapter carries forward their emphasis on place as a site made meaningful by memory and commemorative practices to frame the tensions between the personal and public expressions of memory and between official histories and vernacular stories. It also flags the mediating influence of archives and suggests the problematic nature of memory and place in the digital age. Whereas Parish Maps resonate closely with the themes of this book, *HIDDEN HISTORIES AND INVISIBLE STORIES* opens them up for discussion. Bringing the notion, introduced by Opp and Walsh, that "it is the acts of inhabiting, returning, or moving through specific locations that produce or confirm memories of place" to bear on Marlene Creates's *HIDDEN HISTORIES AND INVISIBLE STORIES*, I conclude with a personal response to her art installation exploring place and memory.

MEMORIES IN PLACE: BEACH BOULEVARD, SUMMER 1957

The poetic art of Marlene Creates, her interest in exploring how the natural and human elements of the landscape interact [,] will continue and be embedded in our future landscape as will our own journeys guided by our family histories, by individuals and places that we will come in contact with, thereby contributing to the creation of a new awareness of our sense of place.[38]

At each of the five sites in *HIDDEN HISTORIES AND INVISIBLE STORIES*, Creates placed a list of natural history and human events associated with the location; she also invited passers-by to send her their own stories. Creates's markers "are meant to evoke the particularities of individual experience that either contrast or correspond with the larger social and cultural context that penetrates life and shifts over time."[39] The changes and events listed at Marker No. 2 located at the intersection of Beach Boulevard and Eastport Drive prompted viewers to imagine a prehistoric fishing camp, ice-cutting on Burlington Bay, road paving for the war effort, and the amusement park, with its ferris wheel, merry-go-round, and bathhouse, which closed in 1978 after seventy-five years in operation. *Marker No. 2 (Beach Boulevard)* took me back to my childhood, to a landscape that is no more, and to a sense of place shaped by family history. What follows is my hidden history of individual experience and an invisible story about placing memory and remembering place.

I remember the curving line of the beach along Burlington Bay, the amusement park, and especially the ferris wheel and the merry-go-round, so exciting to a small child. We passed it on Beach Boulevard leading to the old lift bridge at the entrance to Burlington Bay whenever the family – my uncle, my mother, my grandmother, and me – set out from Toronto on a Saturday outing, sometimes to visit Niagara Falls, other times to have lunch in Buffalo and do a little cross-border shopping at a time when the exchange rate favoured the Canadian dollar. Often the bridge was up, and a line of cars, motors shut off, snaked back along the boulevard under the rising piers of the new Burlington Bay Skyway. There, we waited for the lift bridge's barriers to open and allow traffic to pass. It was a welcome stop in what always seemed an interminably long drive in our old blue 1951 Pontiac, with its Indian-head hood ornament and multi-coloured, plastic-weave seats that stuck to your bare legs in hot weather. Beach Boulevard was a place where my uncle whiled away the time telling stories about the family excursions of his childhood. In those days, before the fruit belt was paved over to widen the highway, before barns gave way to warehouses, and before orchards were turned into vineyards, there were roadside stands selling freshly picked fruit and vegetables. More than once, he told the story of how my mother plucked a ripe tomato from the newly purchased basket and hurled it out the back window at a tailgating motorist. I always liked this tale of vigilante justice. Her spunk still brings a wry smile, for this story, told in the shadow of the new bridge, is part of the way I came to know and remember the mother I lost to cancer when I was just nine.

The Burlington Bay Skyway carrying the Queen Elizabeth Way across the shipping channel that links Lake Ontario and Burlington Bay opened in 1958; my mother died two years later. Our last excursion along Beach Boulevard and across the old lift bridge would have been in the summer of 1957. Except during an occasional drive across the new Burlington Bay Skyway, high over the old road that ran beside the now long-gone amusement park, I have rarely thought of that place or the stories associated with it. Marlene Creates's *Marker No. 2 (Beach Boulevard)* suddenly and unexpectedly triggered thoughts of those family excursions to Buffalo and Niagara Falls, the Pontiac, the amusement park, the bridge, and my mother's defiant act – memories of place and memories attached to and triggered by place: that old two-lane highway beside the beach, the lift bridge over the entrance to the Bay, the orchards in the lee of the Escarpment, the fruit stands at Jordan and Grimsby – place and time, place in time. For me, *Marker No. 2 (Beach Boulevard)*, like the larger work of which it is a part, encapsulates and extends the theme of this book: placing memory and remembering place.

ACKNOWLEDGMENTS

The ideas explored in this chapter owe a great deal to Brian Osborne and Terry Cook, who have nurtured my interest in, and expanded my outlook on, place, memory, and the relationship between them. I am grateful to Jim Opp and John Walsh for their encouragement and editorial suggestions and offer special thanks to Marlene Creates, whose work has long intrigued and inspired me, for permission to reproduce the photograph of *Marker No. 2 (Beach Boulevard)*.

NOTES

1 Marlene Creates, "Artist Statement," for Site 11 *HIDDEN HISTORIES AND INVISIBLE STORIES*, in *Zone 6B: Art in the Environment*, Catalogue of a collaborative project between Hamilton Artists Inc., the Art Gallery of Hamilton, Burlington Art Centre, McMaster Museum of Art, 21 June-4 September 2000 (Hamilton: Hamilton Artists Inc.,

April 2003), 32. This "Artist Statement" also appears on the webpage for *HIDDEN HISTORIES AND INVISIBLE STORIES, the City of Hamilton and the Royal Botanical Gardens, 2000* at http://www.marlenecreates.ca/works/2000histories.html.

2   The title of the exhibition *Zone 6B: Art in the Environment* refers to the climatic zone in the lee of the Niagara Escarpment.

3   Ibid.

4   Ibid.

5   Shirley Madill, "The Topography of Hidden Experience," in *Zone 6B: Art in the Environment,* 10.

6   Phil Jenkins, *An Acre of Time: The Enduring Value of Place* (Toronto: McFarlane, Walter and Ross, 1996), 3.

7   See http://www.philjenkins.ca/acres.htm.

8   Ibid.

9   Jenkins, *Acre of Time,* 3-4.

10 Madill, "The Topography of Hidden Experience," 10.

11 See http://www.philjenkins.ca/acres.htm.

12 Octavia Pollock, *Country Life,* 10 May 2007, 119.

13 According to its website, Common Ground "is internationally recognised for playing a unique role in the arts and environmental fields, distinguished by the linking of nature with culture, focussing on the positive investment people can make in their own localities, championing popular democratic involvement, and by inspiring celebration as a starting point for action to improve the quality of our everyday places"; see http://www.commonground.org.uk. See also Susan Clifford, "Common Ground: Promoting the Value of Local Places," *Landscape Research* 12, 1 (1987): 2-4.

14 The American workshops were held in four Maine villages – Lubec, Dennysville, Pembroke, and Calais – and the panel discussion was held in Eastport. Other panel participants were noted writer, art critic, and activist Lucy Lippard; internationally known British walking artist Hamish Fulton; and Canadian artist and arts educator Ron Shuebrook. http://www.tidesinstitute.org/parishmaps.html.

15 All quotes from the leaflet *Parish Maps: Common Ground* (Shaftesbury, Dorset, 1996), n.p.

16 See Willa Walker, *No Hay Fever & a Railway: Summers in St. Andrews, Canada's First Seaside Resort* (Fredericton, NB: Goose Lane Editions, 1989).

17 http://www.standrewsbythesea.ca/.

18 *Parish Maps: Common Ground,* n.p.

19 David Crouch and David Matless, "Refiguring Geography: Parish Maps of Common Ground," *Transactions of the Institute of British Geographers,* n.s., 21, 1 (1996): 238.

20 Ibid., 236.

21 In response to H.B. George's contention that "history is not intelligible without geography," Alan Baker has argued "the complementary premise that geography is not intelligible without history"; see Alan Baker, *Geography and History: Bridging the Divide* (Cambridge, UK: Cambridge University Press, 2003), xi. In this comprehensive

exploration of the nature of historical geography, Baker examines in detail the "bridge" between history and geography and celebrates the different perspectives and practices of the two disciplines.

22 Creates, "Artist Statement."

23 Joan M. Schwartz and Terry Cook, "Archives, Records, and Power: The Making of Modern Memory," *Archival Science* 2, 1-2 (2002): 1.

24 Terry Cook and Joan M. Schwartz, "Archives, Records, and Power: From (Postmodern) Theory to (Archival) Practice," *Archival Science* 2, 3-4 (2002).

25 Schwartz and Cook, "Archives, Records, and Power: The Making of Modern Memory," 1.

26 Ibid.

27 See also Tom Nesmith, "Seeing Archives: Postmodernism and the Changing Intellectual Place of Archives," *American Archivist* 65 (Spring/Summer 2002): 24-41; Eric Ketelaar, "Tacit Narratives: The Meanings of Archives," *Archival Science* 1, 2 (2001): 131-41; and Carolyn Hamilton et al., eds., *Refiguring the Archive* (Dordrecht, NL: Kluwer Academic Publishers, 2002).

28 The threat to collective memory is exacerbated in institutions where cash-strapped collection managers embrace digitization on a widespread basis as the permanent preservation solution to growing storage problems arising from fragile materials, voluminous holdings, and space shortages. Parallel lessons can be drawn from the panic, in the world of archives and libraries, over the appearance of red spots, or "redox blemishes," and concerns over silver-image stability that followed the widespread adoption in the 1960s of microfilming as a copying technology for the preservation of rare, fragile, or deteriorating books, newspapers, and paper documents.

29 See Peter Seixas, ed., *Theorizing Historical Consciousness* (Toronto: University of Toronto Press, 2006); and Sam Wineburg, *Historical Thinking and Other Unnatural Acts: Charting the Future of Teaching the Past* (Philadelphia: Temple University Press, 2001).

30 David Rumsey and Meredith Williams, "Historical Maps in GIS," in *Past Time, Past Place: GIS for History,* ed. Anne Kelly Knowles (Redlands, CA: ESRI Press, 2002), 2. See also Anne Kelly Knowles, *Placing History: How Maps, Spatial Data, and GIS Are Changing Historical Scholarship* (Redlands, CA: ESRI Press, 2008).

31 See http://www.visionofbritain.org.uk/.

32 Press release, 1 August 2006 http://news.sel.sony.com/en/press_room/consumer/digital_imaging/release/23993.html.

33 For product information on Sony's GPS image tracker, go to http://www.sonystyle.ca and click on Digital Cameras-Camera Accessories-Other Camera Accessories. The SonyStyle GPS-CS3KA, a GPS unit, is an image tracker for use with most digital cameras and Sony handycam camcorders. The original CS1 was a twelve-channel GPS unit that was three and one-half inches long and weighed a mere two ounces (fifty-six grams). The newest model, weighing only slightly more at seventy grams, boasts twenty channels and innovative features that let users harness the capabilities of GPS to "Map Your Memories."

34 http://news.sel.sony.com/en/press_room/consumer/digital_imaging/release/23993.html.

35 For an extended exploration of this theme, see Joan M. Schwartz and James R. Ryan, eds., *Picturing Place: Photography and the Geographical Imagination* (London: I.B. Tauris, 2003).

36 John Berger, "Uses of Photography," in *About Looking* (New York: Vintage, 1991), 54.

37 Marlene Creates, *Places of Presence: Newfoundland kin and ancestral land, Newfoundland 1989-1991* (St. John's, NL: Killick Press, 1997), 6.

38 Madill, "Topography of Hidden Experience," 10.

39 Ibid., 9.

Afterword

Contributors

Matthew Evenden is Associate Professor of Geography at the University of British Columbia and most recently co-author of *The River Returns: An Environmental History of the Bow* (2009) with Christopher Armstrong and H.V. Nelles.

Patrizia Gentile teaches in the Pauline Jewett Institute of Women's and Gender Studies at Carleton University. She is co-author of *The Canadian War on Queers: National Security as Sexual Regulation* (2010) with Gary Kinsman.

Alan Gordon teaches history at the University of Guelph and writes about history and memory. His second book, *The Hero and the Historians: Historiography and the Uses of Jacques Cartier*, was recently published by UBC Press.

Steven High is Canada Research Chair in Public History at Concordia University. He is the author of *Industrial Sunset: The Making of North America's Rust Belt* (2003) and *Corporate Wasteland: The Landscape and Memory of Deindustrialization* (2007).

Russell Johnston teaches in the Department of Communication, Popular Culture and Film at Brock University. His research explores the history of cultural industries in Canada and includes *Selling Themselves: The Emergence of Canadian Advertising* (2001).

Kirsten Emiko McAllister is in the School of Communication at Simon Fraser University. She is co-author of *Locating Memory: Photographic Acts* (2006) and author of *Terrain of Memory: A Japanese Canadian Memorial* (2010) as well as other articles on photography and cultural memory.

Cecilia Morgan is a professor in History of Education, OISE/UT. Her most recent major publication is *"A Happy Holiday": English-Canadians and Transatlantic Tourism, 1870-1930* (2008).

James **Opp** is Associate Professor in the Department of History, Carleton University. He is the author of *The Lord for the Body: Religion, Medicine, and Protestant Faith Healing in Canada, 1880-1930* (2005) and has published articles on photography, memory, and archives.

Michael Ripmeester is in the Department of Geography at Brock University. He has published articles on landscapes of memory, the lawn, and First Nation historical geographies.

Joan M. Schwartz is Associate Professor in Art History and Geography at Queen's University. Formerly a photography specialist at the National Archives of Canada, she is the editor, with James R. Ryan, of *Picturing Place: Photography and the Geographical Imagination* (2003).

Frances Swyripa is Professor of History in the Department of History and Classics at the University of Alberta. She examines issues of place and memory in her forthcoming *Storied Landscapes: Ethno-Religious Identity and the Canadian Prairies* (University of Manitoba Press).

John C. Walsh is Assistant Professor in the Department of History, Carleton University as well as a research associate of the Carleton Centre for Public History. Most recently, he co-edited *Home, Work, and Play: Situating Canadian Social History* (2006, 2010).

Index

audiences: of historical pageants, 39; and memorial spaces, 9; for memorials, 135; for memory entrepreneurs, 135-36; of storytelling, 300

Autumn Leaves (Opp, D.), 277-78, 279

Ayukawa, Midge, 224

Bal, Mieke, 33

Baldwin, Stanley, 54n39

Banff (AB), 251, 252

Banff National Park, 254

Bankhead coalmine (AB), 252, 253

Barthes, Roland, 217

Basu, Paul, 124

Bay, The. *See* Hudson's Bay Company, store

Beach House Hotel (Lake Minnewanka), 251, 252

Belchem, John, 124

Bell, David, *Mapping Desire,* 190

Berger, John, *About Looking,* 306

Berlant, Lauren, 232, 239

Bhabha, Homi, 50

Big White Owl, 69

Billig, Michael, 134

Bird Commission, 218

Bodnar, John, 19n23, 135-36

Bothwell, Mary, 81

Boyle, David, 60

Boym, Svetlana, 33

Brant Historical Society (BHS), 39, 60, 63-64, 69-70

Brant-Sero, John Ojijatekha, 61

Brenner, Neil, 19-20n29

British Empire Exhibition, Glasgow, 115-16, 118

Brock, Sir Isaac, 136-37

Brock's Monument, Queenstown Heights (ON), 142, 153

built town, 49; and forest, 40-44

Burlington Bay (ON), 308-9

Calgary Power, 252-53, 254-55, 256, 257, 259, 264

Canadian National Parks Association, 253, 255

Canadian Shield, 109-10

The Canadian War on Queers, 190-91

Cape Breton Island: Cabot Trail, 116, 122; clachan (shieling) in, 116; Hector's Point, 117, 118, 123; Highlands National Park, 116; industries, 117-18; landscape, 123; Scottish settlers on, 107-8; settlement on, 112-13; St. Ann's Gaelic College, 115. *See also* Highland Village Museum (Cape Breton)

capitalism: and displacement, 181, 185n62; print-, 109

Carleton Place (ON): Old Boys' Reunion in, 27, 31, 32; Old Home Week in, 27, 40-43, 44

Casey, Edward, 7-8

Casey, Frank, 175

Castells, Manuel, 134-35

CD-ROMs, 303-4

Certeau, Michel de. *See* de Certeau, Michel

Champlain, Samuel de. *See* de Champlain, Samuel

Charles, Prince of Wales, 100

Chauncey, George, 212n17; *Gay New York,* 190

Chinook Camera Club (CCC), 271-72, 273, 274-75, 276, 277, 278, 284, 285, 286

Churchill, David, 188, 208

civic architecture. *See* built town

civil service. *See* federal government, public service

Claresholm (AB), 272, 273, 274, 281

class: and attachment to place, 165-66; and narratives of disappearance, 49; and "out of place," 196

Clifford, Sue, 297-98

Cold War, 188, 191, 208

historical narratives: "before" and "after," 45-48; and boundaries of local community, 34-35; civic architecture and, 43; forest in, 44-45; gender in, 45, 49; Japanese Canadians and, 223; and race, 36, 37; Six Nations and, 58-59, 76; in St. Catharines, 138-39

historical pageants: in Ottawa Valley, 34-39; Six Nations and, 64, 70

"The Historical Position of the Six Nations" (Hill), 61-63

histories: hidden, 301 (*see also HIDDEN HISTORIES AND INVISIBLE STORIES* [Creates]); official, 307

Hobsbawm, Eric, 14

Hodgkin, Katharine, 10

Hogg, Thomas, 259

homecomings, 10, 26-27, 30-39, 48-49; archives of, 29; hosts of, 29; in newspapers, 32-33; to Perth, 26-27, 29. *See also* expatriates; Old Boys' Reunions; Old Home Weeks

homosexuals/homosexuality. *See* gays/ lesbians

Honey Coulee (Opp, F.), 275, 277

Hoskins, Gareth, 11

Howe, C.D., 255

Hudson's Bay Company, 86; anniversary parade, 96; fort, 85, 88; store, 85, 87-88, 98-100; University of Alberta and, 99-100

Hunter, Dave, 168

Huyssen, Andreas, 5

identity/-ies, archives and, 302; community, 301; creation from available resources, 134-35; ethnic, 108-9, 110; group photographs and, 240; imagined landscape and, 8; internment camps and, 242; of Japanese Canadian youth, 233-35; of Japanese Canadians, 218, 239, 240, 242; landscape and, 5,

135; material commemorations and, 152-53. *See also* collective identity/-ies

imagined communities, 8; and Aboriginal peoples, 37; ethnic identity and, 108-9; Highland Scots of Nova Scotia and, 124; local as, 123; and national identities, 109; in scholarly thinking, 108-9; territoriality of, 109

immigration. *See* migration

Indian Act, 65, 66-67, 73, 75

industry/-ies: on Cape Breton Island, 117-18; construction of nature vs, 264-65; landscapes of, 45-48; locations of, 294; within Rocky Mountains Park, 252. *See also* mills

inscriptions, 9; photography and, 273

Insider, 173, 176, 179

Internet sites, 306

internment camps: communal life of, 220; description of purpose, 220; establishment of, 215-16; in ghost towns, 228; institutional life of, 224, 230-31, 240; and Japanese-Canadian identity, 240, 242; living conditions, 229; in memoryscapes, 220; as mythic sites, 220; photographs of, 216-17, 219, 224, 230-31, 240; professional photographers in, 224-25; records saved from, 217; reunions, 241, 243n25; self-support, 244n41, 245n45; silence regarding, 218; as sites of racial eradication, 220; witnessing to, 218

In Wildness Is the Preservation of the World, 278

Iraq War, 96, 102

Ironside, C., 263

Iroquois people, 59, 62, 132

James I and VI, King, 112

Japanese Canadian National Museum (JCNM), 215, 217, 222-23

Japanese Canadians, 240-41; after war, 218; in BC social/cultural landscape, 217, 222-23, 227-28, 240; compensation for, 218; and education, 233, 235; group photographs, 224, 225-26, 227-29, 240; identity/-ies, 218, 226, 229, 239, 240; internment of, 215-16; labour of, 229; and landscape, 228; male, 244n38; photographs of, 216-17; and place of residence, 218; and places associated with, 222; and popular culture, 232, 235-37; postwar relocation of, 229-30, 237; postwar segregation of, 246n59; professional photographers, 224-25; reunions, 232-33; as skilled workforce, 245n54; youth, 221-22, 232-39

Jasper Avenue (Edmonton), 8; 3rd Battalion, Princess Patricia's Canadian Light Infantry and, 101-2; 49th Battalion and, 93-94, 101, 102; 101 Street intersection, 90; 109 Street intersection, 92; 110 Street overpass and, 87; changes in ritualistic role, 97-98, 100; entertainment and, 96-97; First World War and, 90, 92-93; future of, 102-3; parades/processions down, 90-96, 102, 103; photographs, 85-86, 86(f), 89(f), 99(f); prominence within Edmonton, 90; protests and, 95-96; royalty and, 91-92, 100-1; Second World War and, 90; social order and, 97; sports teams and, 97; triumphal arches on, 89. See also Hudson's Bay Company

Jenkins, Phil, An Acre of Time, 296, 297
Jennings, P.J., 258
Jessop, Bob, 19-20n29
John Paul II, Pope, 106n37
Johns, David, 305
Johnson, Nuala, 132
Johnson, Pauline, 64, 78n21
Johnson, William, 70

Johnston, Russell, 9, 10, 15, 301
Jones, Martin, 19-20n29
Jones, Peter, 69

Kaslo (BC) camp, 237, 243n25
Katsuno, Marie, 224, 232, 243n25
Kent, Tom, 118
King, William Lyon Mackenzie, 215-16, 239, 255
Klassen, Michael, 284
Klein, Kerwin Lee, 20n33
Kogawa, Joy, 219
Kuhn, Annette, 221, 225, 235, 239

Lacroix, Mike, 165, 166
Lake Minnewanka. See Minnewanka, Lake (AB)
Lanark (ON), Old Boys' Reunion in, 27, 30, 31-32
land, alteration of, 296; as archive, 6-7; debasement of, 282; human experience and, 293, 298; as place, 3, 16, 299, 307; relationship to vs response to wilderness, 278-79
landscape(s): of Cape Breton, 123; colonized, 167; commoditization of, 148; as contested, 285; historicization of, 282; ideal vs depictions of local, 273; and identity, 5, 8, 135; industries, 45-48; Japanese Canadian internees and, 228; as medium of exchange, 287n7; and memory, 5; mnemonic, 9; national, 109-10; past in, 27, 29; photographs/photography, 15, 228, 273, 285, 301; scenic, 277-78; Scottish, 110, 114, 123; and sense of place, 110; significance and meaning of, 132; as theatre/stage, 132, 150
Landscapes of Devils (Gordillo), 5
landscaping: of Lake Minnewanka, 259-64, 301; of nature, 48
Langenback, Randolph, 162

Langford, Martha, 179-80; *Suspended Conversations,* 169

Latour, Peaches, 197-98, 202

Laurier, Sir Wilfrid, 88

LeBelle, Wayne, *Sturgeon Falls, 1895-1995,* 171

Lefebvre, Henri, 7, 183n13

Lemon Creek (BC), 237; high school, 232-39; Japanese United Church, 216(f)

lesbians, bars and, 203-4, 205; invisibility of, 203, 206; social-sexual networks, 204-5; social-sexual space, 203-6. *See also* gays/lesbians

Lesbians of Ottawa Now (LOON), 205, 207

Lessnoff, Michael, 109

Lethbridge Northern Irrigation District (LNID), 282

lieux de mémoire, 4, 5, 133

Lippard, Lucy, 285; *The Lure of the Local,* 281

local: as centre of meaning, 6; commemorations and, 8; disruptions and, 15; expatriates and, 33; and geographies of vulnerability, 188; globalization and, 6, 111, 162; ideal landscape vs, 273; landscape photographs and, 15, 285; memory and, 6-7; and monuments, 15; place as site of mediation and, 50; queer communities and, 190, 192; and sense of place, 274; stretching of boundaries of, 33, 34. *See also* Parish Mapping

local history: historical pageants and, 34-38; knowledge of, 146-47, 150; mass media and, 150; material commemorations and, 146-47; Six Nations and, 65

locale, meaning of, 110

location(s): as geographical co-ordinates, 110; of industry, 294; photographs and, 217-18, 226, 285; of places of memory, 250-51; places vs, 250

Loft, Bernice, 65-66

longhouse peoples, 73-74

Loo, Tina, 18n17

Lortie, Ray, 180

Louter, David, 265

Low, Setha M., 183n12

Loyalists, 59, 61, 132

The Lure of the Local (Lippard), 281

Macdonald, Angus L., 112, 115-16, 117

MacKenzie, A.W.R., 115

Mackenzie, Hugh, 123

Mackenzie, William Lyon, 133

MacLeod, C.I.N., 116-17

MacLeod, Cameron, 119, 123

MacMillan Bloedel, 167, 174, 176

MacNeil, James, 115

MacNeil, Michael Eoin, 107, 124

MacNeil, Neil, *Highland Heart of Nova Scotia, The,* 107-8, 109, 113-14, 117

Madill, Shirley, 296, 297

Mah Yuen, 81, 87

Malpas, Jeff, 111

Mapping Desire (Bell; Valentine), 190

maps/mapping, aesthetics of, 298; community-based, 298; digital technology and, 304-5; geo-tagging and, 305; of homosexual activity/spaces, 187-88, 190, 191; Parish Mapping, 297-301, 302, 307; place/memory relationship and, 298; social role of, 299

Marcoux, Raymond, 180

Margaret, Princess, 106n37

Martin, Milton, 79n32

"The Masque of Nations," 35-36

Massey, Doreen, 13-14, 111, 182; "Places and Their Pasts," 162

material commemorations: attitudes toward, 147-48, 151-52; geographical dispersal, 139; governments and, 140-42, 150; and identity, 152-53; interpretation and, 135-36; and knowledge

Mires, Charlene, 135, 136

Mississauga people, 59, 75-76

Mitchell, Clare, 148

Mitchell, W.J.T., 287n7

mnemonic narratives: intertextual, 151; material commemorations vs, 150; and memory, 136; memory entrepreneurs and, 150-51; national vs local, 137, 140, 146, 152; place and, 132; plaques and, 137, 151; Salem Chapel and, 131; St. Catharines and, 133; tourism and, 148, 150, 151

modernity: and Aboriginal peoples, 64-65; archives and, 12; "folk" and, 50; reunions and, 30, 49-50

Montour, Nelles, 60

Monture, Ethel Brant, 58, 65-66

monuments: Brock's Monument, Queenstown Heights, 142, 153; as communicative mode of memory, 301; and human landscape, 133; local and, 15; local citizens and, 9; as media, 133; Osborne and, 5; queer sites as, 208; and tourism, 9. *See also* material commemorations

Morgan, Cecilia, 8-9, 39, 301

Moses, Arnold, 64-65

Moses, Elliott, 63, 66-75, 76

Moses, Nelson, 66, 72

Mosher, Scott, 178

museums, government support for, 121, 124; and memory, 111; pioneer-village, 113, 120. *See also* Highland Village Museum (Cape Breton); Japanese Canadian National Museum (JCNM)

Muzaini, Hamzah, 134

Nakoda people, 250, 251, 258-59, 265

narratives: of community, 11-12; of disappearance, 49; foundation, 136-73, 140; memory, 135, 136; oral, 166-67. *See*

also historical narratives; mnemonic narratives

national identities: imagined communities and, 109; landscape and, 109-10; and natural landscape features, 109-10; Osborne and, 6; Scottish, 114

National Parks Act, 253-54, 255

national security: and gays/lesbians, 191, 192-93, 207; heterosexual hegemony and, 193; and Japanese Canadians, 215-16; and memories, 202; and queer place, 187; and social relations, 193; spaces of, 188; state, 187, 188, 192-93, 207, 208

Native peoples. *See* Aboriginal peoples

nature, industrialism vs construction of, 264-65; landscaping of, 48; photography, 273, 277-78, 286; relationship to land and, 278-79; southern Alberta and, 275

New Credit reserve, 59-60

New Denver (BC) internment camp, 232, 242n4

Niagara region: and Canada's national character, 143-44; mnemonic landscape of, 9; signifiers of, 136-37; tourism of, 144-45, 148, 150

Niitsitapi people, 283-84

Noël, Françoise, 29, 52n8

non-cooperation: and community-building, 194; by gays/lesbians, 188, 207; queer communities and, 192

Nora, Pierre, 4, 12, 133; *Realms of Memory*, 4, 80n55

North-West Mounted Police, 91

nostalgia, home and, 10; homesickness and, 33; and landscape photography, 273; and reunions, 33-34; Scottish identity and, 112; structuring effect of, 40-43

Nova Scotia, Gaelic language in, 114-15; Highland identity in, 115; Highland

Village in, 116-17; history of, 112-13; Museum, 124; as New Scotland, 112, 113; origin of name, 112; Scottish identity, 14, 108, 109, 112, 120, 124-25; Scottish settlement in, 113, 120; tourism in, 108, 115, 117, 118, 121-22. *See also* Cape Breton Island

Now Voyager, 239

Nye, David, 48

O'Hare, Kristen, 180

Old Boys' Reunions, 10, 48-50; in Arnprior, 27, 30, 31(f); in Carleton Place, 27, 31, 32; in Lanark, 27, 30, 31-32; in Pembroke, 27, 32; in Perth, 27, 31, 34, 40; in Renfrew, 27; in Smiths Falls, 27, 32

Old Home Weeks, 10, 48-50; in Almonte, 27, 32; in Carleton Place, 27, 40-43, 44; in Eganville, 27, 43; in Pembroke, 27, 45-48; in Perth, 27, 29, 44-45; in Renfrew, 27

Old Strathcona. *See* Edmonton (AB), Old Strathcona

Oldman River Dam, 282

Olwig, Kenneth R., 287n5

Ontario Historical Society (OHS), 60, 61

Ontario Publicity Bureau, 36

Opp, Don, 271-72; *Autumn Leaves,* 277-78, 279; *Corner Post,* 276-77, 279; and petroglyphs of Writing-on-Stone Provincial Park, 284-85; *Rainbow's End,* 279-81

Opp, Frankie, 271-72; *Harvest Time,* 274-75; *Honey Coulee,* 275, 277; *Road to the Mountains,* 274, 281-83, 284

Opp, James, 10, 11, 12, 62, 300, 301

Osborne, Brian, 5-6, 91

Ottawa (ON): Byward Market, 195, 199; Champagne Public Baths, 199; Chateau Laurier, 195-96, 199; Chez Henri, 198-99, 200(f), 201; Coral Reef, 205-6; Honeydew, 199, 201; lack of gay village, 208; Laurentian Terrace, 203, 204; lesbian space in, 203-6; Lord Elgin Hotel, 195, 196-97, 201; Mackenzie Street, 195, 199; Major's Hill Park, 195, 199, 200, 201(f); Nepean Point, 199; police, 194, 197-98; queer cartography of, 191; queer spaces in, 13, 195-203; Remic Rapids Lookout, 200-1; sites of homosexual social-sexual activity, 208-9; Townhouse Motel, 205; YMCA, 196

Ottawa Valley (ON): migration from, 25-26. *See also* Old Boys' Reunions; Old Home Weeks; *and names of individual localities*

parades: and Jasper Avenue, 8, 90-96, 102, 103; military, 93-94, 101-2; for Ottawa Valley homecomings, 30; and Whyte Avenue, 102

Parish Mapping, 297-301, 302, 307

Park Structures and Facilities (Good), 264

parks: in Ottawa, 195, 200-2; policy, 253-54; recreational use, 253. *See also* Rocky Mountains Park

Parr, Joy, 18n17, 182n6

past: in landscape, 27, 29; multiplicity of readings of, 162. *See also* historical narratives; historical pageants

Patterson, Freeman, 277

Pembroke (ON), Aboriginal peoples of, 36-38, 39; Historical Pageant, 34-39, 44; "The Masque of Nations" in, 35-36; Old Boys' Reunion in, 27, 32; Old Home Week in, 27, 45-48

Perth (ON), homecomings to, 26-27, 29; Old Boys' Reunion in, 27, 31, 34, 40; Old Home Week in, 27, 29, 44-45

petroglyphs, 271, 283, 285

photograph albums, 169, 179-80; internment camps in, 219; Japanese Canadian families and, 219; removed for

archives, 239; of suspected homosexuals, 201-2

photographs, 10, 11; and collective identities, 226; content of, 225, 227-28; context of preservation, 302; contexts of
use, and meaning, 217; donated to
archives, 217, 224-25; in family albums
vs archives, 239; and family memory,
225; group, 221-22, 224, 225-26, 227-
29, 240; and hope, 235; of internment
camps, 216-17, 219, 220, 230-31; of
Japanese Canadian families, 222-23; in
JCNM, 222-23; of Lake Minnewanka,
249; landscape of internment camps
in, 228; and locations, 226; and memory, 281; as memory objects, 220-21;
mobility of, 301; mutability of meaning, 301; as personal records, 220;
popular culture in, 232, 235-37; of
postwar relocation, 229-30; of prairies,
274-75; prewar vs camp, 227-28, 231;
produced for camp internees, 225-26;
and social relations, 226; in Sturgeon
Falls mill history binder, 174, 175

photography: digital, 286; GPS technology
and, 305; and inscriptions, 273; invention of, 306; landscape, 15, 273, 301;
nature, 273, 277-78, 286; relationship
to land and, 279; scene composition
in, 276; single-lens-reflex (SLR)
cameras, 275-76; as social practice,
225-26; time and, 273. *See also* colour
slide photography

pictographs, 271, 283

Piikáni Nation, 282

pioneers: and Aboriginal peoples, 37; and
forests, 43; museums and, 120

place attachment: of blue-collar workers,
181; capitalism and, 185n62; class and,
165-66; displacement and, 163; to industrial worksites, 162, 179; landscape

commoditization and, 148; re-creations
of, 163; retrospective activation of,
169-70; social relations and, 162; and
workplace bonding, 164

place identity. *See* place attachment

place/memory relationship, 4; commemorative markers and, 306; Creates's
markers and, 296-97; digital age and,
303-7; division between place and
memory, 7; geo-tagging and, 305; and
maps, 298; Nova Scotian Scottish
identity and, 124-25; photographic
excursions and, 272-73; and resistance,
15; and transformation of space into
place, 306

place(s), abstractions of, 277; authenticity
and, 14; authority and resistance in
making of, 13; change and, 181; commemorative practices and, 4, 307;
composition vs, 277; creation of
meaning and, 152; and exclusion, 14;
as existing in time and space, 182;
globalization and, 6, 111; and imagination, 125; influences shaping, 295-96;
Japanese Canadian families and, 222;
Japanese Canadians and, 218; land as,
3, 16, 299, 307; linking global and local,
111; locations vs, 250; Massey and, 111;
as meaningful location, 110; mnemonic narratives and, 132; openness and,
132; "out of," 188, 196, 197, 205; politics
of, 13-14, 284-85; as purposeful/
accidental, 272-73; remembrance of,
295-96; sense of (*see* sense of place);
as social/spatial process, 181; space
and, 110, 306; as staging/event, 132,
134-35, 150; struggle and, 13-14; time
and, 111, 296; unmaking/demolition
of, 162-63

Places of Presence (Creates), 2(f), 3-4, 294,
307

"Places and Their Pasts" (Massey), 162

plaques: and foundation stories, 136; inventory of, 137-38; at Lake Minnewanka, 247, 249, 265; memory entrepreneurs and, 139-40, 142; mnemonic narratives and, 137, 151; in Salem Chapel, 130-31; in St. Catharines, 139

Porter, Eliot, 278

power relationships: archive(s) and, 12, 302; commemoration and, 133; homecomings and, 29; knowledge and, 12; place and, 14; and public memory, 8-9; tradition and, 14

Pretty, Lawrence, 180

Pultney (AB), 279, 280-81

queer communities/networks: in federal public service, 194; and local, 190, 192; non-cooperation by, 192; resistance by, 192; social-sexual space, 188; surveillance of, 187, 190

queer place(s): as contested, 209; establishment of, 195; and memories, 190; plotting of, 187; and spaces of security state, 188

queer space(s), 13; as contested, 188, 190, 197; as limited, 194; mapping of, 190, 191; as monuments, 208; as sanctuaries, 188, 193, 208; surveillance of, 187

queers. See gays/lesbians

race, historical pageants and, 35-38; and Six Nations, 63-64

Radstone, Susannah, 10

Rainbow's End (Opp, D.), 279-81

Ranger, Terence, 14

Realms of Memory (Nora), 4, 80n55

reification, 191

religion, Highland Village and, 121; Six Nations and, 74

resistance, archiving and, 15; and boundaries of queer space, 188; decriminalization and, 207; by gays/lesbians, 15; Japanese Canadians and, 15; from mill workers, 15; and queer communities, 190, 191, 192, 194; surveillance and, 197

Restoule, Randy, 164, 177

reunions: internment camp, 241, 243n25; of Japanese Canadian internees, 232-33. *See* Old Boys' Reunions; Old Home Weeks

Ripmeester, Michael, 9, 10, 15, 301

Road to the Mountains (Opp, F.), 274, 281-83, 285

Robertson, Marie, 207

rock art, 283, 284. *See also* petroglyphs; pictographs

Rocky Mountains Park, 251, 252-53, 254

Rose, Ethel, 74-75

Rosebery (BC) internment camp, 232, 237

Rosenzweig, Roy, 135, 136

Ross, Becki, 203, 204

Royal Botanical Gardens (Hamilton, ON), 294

Royal Canadian Mounted Police (RCMP), exposure threats by, 195; and gays/lesbians, 207-8; and homosexual activity, 187; and Japanese Canadians, 244n38; and Jasper Avenue parades, 95; and names of gays/lesbians, 192-93; and queer spaces, 13; Security Panel and, 192; and Six Nations, 63; surveillance of gays/lesbians, 194, 196-97, 206, 207; use of informants, 201-2

Royal North-West Mounted Police, 92

Sakamoto, Kerri, 219

Salem Chapel (ON), 130-31, 151, 153

Sandon (BC) internment camp, 232, 243n25

Schama, Simon, 110

Schwartz, Joan M., 4, 10-11, 15

Scotland, Canadian population originating from, 113; emigrants on Cape Breton, 107-8; emigrants in Nova Scotia, 113, 120; Highland culture as national imagery for, 114; landscape of, 110, 114, 123. *See also* Highland Scotland

Scott, Sir Walter, 114

Scottish identity/ethnicity: and exclusion, 14; Highland Village Museum and, 108, 111; local vs global, 108, 125; of Nova Scotia, 14, 108, 109, 112, 120, 124-25

Second World War: and displaced workers, 160; and Edmonton, 101; and electricity supply, 254; and Japanese Canadian photographs, 217; and Jasper Avenue, 90; and Lake Minnewanka, 249-50, 254; and Minnewanka dam, 247, 249. *See also* internment camps; war memorials

Secord, Laura, 133, 136-37, 139

security. *See* national security

Security Panel, 192, 193, 202

Sekula, Allan, 223

sense of place, 110-11; abstractions of place and, 277; community, 301; landscape and, 110; local and, 274; memory and, 111, 181; mill closures and, 164

A Sense of Wonder, 278

Shoshone people, 283-84

Six Nations, 8-9; agriculture of, 73; assimilation of, 64; and Brant Historical Society, 63-64; and Britain, 61, 62; and Canadian nation-state, 66; commemorative activities, 58-59; Confederacy, 59; Euro-Canadian relations with, 58, 63-64; and First World War, 62-63, 72; and gender, 70-73, 74; government, 68; hereditary council, 63, 70-72; historic places of, 75; and historical knowledge, 65-66; and historical narratives, 58-59, 76; and historical pageants, 64, 70; Indian Act and, 66-67; and legal equality, 61; and local history, 65; and national status, 61; and Ontario Historical Society, 60-63; and other Canadian Indians, 61; and religion, 74; reserve, 39, 59-60; sovereignty, 63

Slocan (BC) internment camp, 228(f), 232, 237, 243n25

Smiths Falls (ON), Aboriginal peoples of, 39; historical pageant in, 39; Old Boys' Reunion in, 27, 32

social relations: and locale, 110; national security and, 193; photographs and, 226; and place identity, 162; and queer networks/sites, 187, 190; resistance and, 191; surveillance and, 191

Somers, Bruce, 197

souvenirs, 10, 11, 29

space(s): lesbian, 203; place and, 110, 182, 306; of security state, 188. *See also* queer space(s)

Spanish River Pulp and Paper Company, 167

Spence, Jo, 225

Spray River (AB), 252, 253, 254

St. Andrews (NB), 298-99

St. Catharines (ON): history, 132-33; location, 133; plaques in, 139; survey conducted in, 138-39; war memorials, 134

Stevens, Gerry, 166

storytelling, place/memory relationship and, 300, 302; and reunions, 30, 34, 49

Strathcona. *See* Edmonton (AB), Old Strathcona

Sturgeon Falls, 1895-1995, 171

Sturgeon Falls (ON), 12-13; town, 161, 164, 165, 166-67

Sturgeon Falls (ON) paper mill, 160(f), 164-65, 175(f); archive of, 173; closure,

Whyte Avenue. *See* Edmonton (AB),
    Whyte Avenue
wilderness: depictions in colour slides,
    278-79; Lake Minnewanka and, 250,
    265; relationship to land vs response
    to, 278-79; spiritual language and, 278;
    western orientation and, 275; wind-
    shield, 265
Wilford, Lisa, 30
Williams, David, 60

With Our Own Eyes (Truly), 241
Woods, Michael, 29
World Trade Center, 133-34
Writing-on-Stone Provincial Part (AB),
    271, 272, 273, 283-85

Yeoh, Brenda, 134

Zerubavel, Eviatar, 136; *Time Maps,* 11

Printed and bound in Canada by Friesens

Set in Machine, Meta, and Minion by Artegraphica Design Co. Ltd.

Copy editor: Robert Lewis

Proofreader: Stephanie VanderMeulen

Indexer: Noeline Bridge

Cartographer: Eric Leinberger